ROBERT A. PHILLIPS, JR.

ROBERT A. PHILLIPS, J

The Treatment of Sexual Disorders

CONTRIBUTORS

Gerd Arentewicz

Roswitha Bulla-Küchler

Ulrich Clement

Martina Gaschae

Margret Hauch

Friedemann Pfäfflin

Gunter Schmidt

Gerhard Thiessen-Liedtke

Ingelore Wickert

THE TREATMENT OF SEXUAL DISORDERS

Concepts and Techniques of Couple Therapy

EDITED BY

Gerd Arentewicz and Gunter Schmidt

Translated by Tom Todd

Basic Books, Inc., Publishers   New York

Library of Congress Cataloging in Publication Data

Sexuell gestörte Beziehungen. English.
   The treatment of sexual disorders.

   Translation of: Sexuell gestörte Beziehungen.
   Bibliography: p. 329
   Includes indexes.
   1. Sexual disorders. 2. Sex therapy. 3. Marital
psychotherapy. I. Arentewicz, Gerd. II. Schmidt,
Gunter. III. Bulla-Küchler, Roswitha. IV. Title.
[DNLM: 1. Marital therapy. 2. Sex disorders—Therapy.
WM 611 S514]
R0556.S49613   1983   616.85′83   82-71214
ISBN 0-465-08748-5

Contents

Foreword by Anke A. Ehrhardt   *vii*

Preface   *xi*

Introduction: *Sexuality and Relationships*   3

PART I
Causes and Treatment

Chapter 1: *Symptoms*   *11*

Chapter 2: *Etiology*   *34*

Chapter 3: *Psychotherapy*   *59*

PART II
Couple Therapy: Research and Results

Chapter 4: *Short-Term Results*   *77*

Chapter 5: *Long-Term Results and Limitations of Outcome*   *123*

Chapter 6: *Therapy Settings*   *147*

Chapter 7: *Difficult Patients, Undesired Side-Effects*   *160*

Chapter 8: *Dropping Out and Separations*   *178*

Chapter 9: *Couple Therapy in Groups*   *202*

Chapter 10: *Advanced Training*   *211*

PART III

Manual of Couple Therapy for Sexual Dysfunctions

Overview   225

Therapeutic Procedure   231

Additional Interventions   311

Bibliography   329

Name Index   341

Subject Index   343

Foreword

This is an exciting and unique book. American sex therapists will find new and useful information here.

Nowadays, specialized treatment for sexual dysfunctions is available in most parts of the United States—by clinicians in private practice, at community mental health clinics, or as part of university hospitals. The most commonly used therapeutic approach is based on the principles and guidelines that were described by William Masters and Virginia Johnson in 1970. However, surprisingly few studies have put these principles to a rigorous test, assessing which aspects of the original sex therapy are necessary prerequisites for clinical success and which are permissible and interchangeable modifications. The authors of *The Treatment of Sexual Disorders* have tested the main components of the widely used therapeutic approach to sex dysfunctions. They report on a study of more than 250 couples with sexual problems who were treated with a variety of modalities, which were then compared as to their effectiveness.

The project was conducted at the Division of Sex Research in the Department of Psychiatry at the University of Hamburg in West Germany. This division has a tradition of conducting pioneering empirical studies that have gained international acclaim in the field of sex research. To cite only two examples—in 1968, Hans Giese and Gunter Schmidt published their large survey on the sexual behavior of German university students;* and in 1970, Gunter Schmidt and Volkmar Sigusch published a study on women's and men's responses to pornography† that was included in the American report of the Commission on Obscenity and Pornography. §

---

* H. Giese and G. Schmidt, *Studenten-Sexualität. Verhalten und Einstellung* (Reinbek: Rowohlt, 1968).

† G. Schmidt, and V. Sigusch, "Women's Sexual Arousal," *Contemporary Sexual Behavior: Critical Issues in the 1970s* (Baltimore: The Johns Hopkins University Press, 1973).

§ *Technical Reports of the Commission on Obscenity and Pornography*, vol. 8 (Washington, D.C.: U.S. Government Printing Office, 1970).

This book describes the results of the authors' research, and at the same time includes a training program for clinicians who want to add to their repertoire of psychotherapeutic skills for the treatment of sexual problems. In contrast to other books on sex therapy, which usually focus very specifically on sexual problems only, the authors have broadened the scope of their program by including couples who have more complex conflicts affecting many facets of the couple relationship in addition to their sexuality. Clinicians who are often frustrated by the general rule of accepting only those couples for treatment who do not exhibit other than sexual problems will find the descriptions of how to combine communication training, sex therapy, and marital counseling of great use. It will enable them to treat the large percentage of couples with multiple problems.

In addition to the classical sexual dysfunctions among men and women, the authors include a discussion on "lack of desire," a sexual problem that has recently become of clinical concern and the subject of new investigations. At this point, "lack of desire" is the focus of some controversy about whether it is a separate sexual disorder or part of all sexual dysfunctions with no distinguishing features. Whatever the final decision might be, we already know that it is particularly important to see "lack of desire" in the context of other aspects of the couple's relationship and to treat it as such. This book gives valuable examples on how to approach such couples.

The Treatment of Sexual Disorders contains a wealth of new data on therapy outcome in short- and long-term follow-up. Most important, it demonstrates that clinicians can safely modify, without losing effectiveness, some of the essential components of the sexual dysfunction therapy originally described by Masters and Johnson. For instance, treatment success can be achieved by one experienced clinician just as well as by a therapy team consisting of a female and a male clinician working with one couple, although cotherapy is very useful for training. Treatment is equally effective done intensely on a daily basis or stretched out with weekly visits over several months. Couple therapy works for patients with lower socioeconomic backgrounds as well as for those who are highly educated. The sections on undesired side-effects of treatment, on how to deal with particularly difficult patients, and on group therapy for sexual problems will be particularly useful to any clinician.

One-third of the book consists of a manual for couple therapy and includes verbatim transcripts of therapy sessions. The authors emphasize that although this is not meant to be a self-help guide or a training manual for inexperienced counselors, it will be immensely valuable to experienced therapists who deal with complicated problems and for those who conduct training courses and workshops in sex therapy. It is likely to become a widely used text for supervision and teaching.

The Treatment of Sexual Disorders is a welcome and provocative addition to the current literature on treating couples with sexual dysfunctions.

Anke A. Ehrhardt, Ph.D.
Professor of Clinical Psychology
Department of Psychiatry
College of Physicians and Surgeons
Columbia University, New York

Preface

This book is the result of a research project conducted between 1972 and 1979 by the Division of Sex Research in the Department of Psychiatry at the University of Hamburg and funded by the Deutsche Forschungsgemeinschaft (German Research Society). The objective of the project was to design and evaluate an economic form of psychotherapy for sexual dysfunctions which would be accessible to all social classes on an outpatient basis.

Our therapy concept is a modification and extension of the couple therapy developed by Masters and Johnson (1970), which proved highly effective in treating sexual dysfunctions. The modifications relate to the structure of therapy: Masters and Johnson suggest one-couple therapy with a therapist team (male and female therapist) in a quasi-inpatient setting lasting between fourteen days and three weeks with daily sessions. In our program couples are also treated in outpatient settings (two sessions a week), sometimes by only one therapist and even in groups of couples.

The extensions relate to technique: our program allows for more treatment of individual psychodynamic problems and of conflicts arising from the dynamics of the couple relationship.

Two hundred and sixty-two couples with sexual dysfunctions were treated within the framework of the Hamburg couple therapy project. The project was divided into three parts:

1. From January 1972 until October 1973 we treated twenty-three couples in a pilot study. Therapy was always conducted by a therapist team in two sessions per week. The study served as a preliminary investigation to test whether the Masters and Johnson concept was applicable in West Germany, to gather therapeutic experience, and to design the therapy manual and so systematize therapeutic procedure in the main investigation. In the light of our experiences in the main investigation we then completely revised the manual, which is to be found in part III of this book. The results of the pilot study have been published elsewhere (Arentewicz et al. 1975).

2. In the main investigation 202 couples were treated for sexual dysfunctions between October 1973 and December 1977. Treatment was carried out in different settings (one therapist or a therapist team; two sessions a week for twenty to thirty weeks or daily sessions for three weeks) and was evaluated in an extensive research program. The investigation had the following aims: to test and improve the therapeutic program; to control the changes induced by therapy on various levels (sexuality, relationship in general, psychological stability); to compare the effectiveness of the different therapy settings; and to investigate the long-term stability of changes induced by therapy in several follow-ups (up to four and a half years after completion of therapy). The results are presented in chapters 4 through 8.

3. In a supplementary investigation we analyzed the viability of couple therapy in groups. Between 1976 and 1979 we treated thirty-seven couples in nine groups. The aim was to test whether couple therapy in groups is possible and with what results, and to determine to what extent the advantages of group therapy could be used in treating couples for sexual dysfunctions. The preliminary results of this study are presented in chapter 9.

In this book we offer a comprehensive presentation of the problems in sexually disturbed relationships on the basis of the results and experiences of the project. We discuss symptomatology, etiology, therapeutic principles and techniques, as well as evaluation of results, complications, and the limits of couple therapy. This book is meant to offer trained and active colleagues in psychotherapy not only a theoretical overview but also practical advice in adapting the concept and technique of couple therapy for sexual dysfunctions. The aim of the book—like that of the entire project—is to contribute to an improvement in therapeutic care for men and women whose relationships are sexually disturbed and who consequently feel that their lives in general are handicapped.

After some hesitation we decided to further this aim practically by publishing the therapy manual as part of this book. We are aware that this decision involves some risks: psychologists or physicians lacking adequate psychotherapeutic training might be tempted to misuse the manual for recipe-book therapy; the manual could even tempt distressed couples to make a completely senseless, if not dangerous, attempt at self-help. For this reason we stress emphatically that the manual is only to be used by psychotherapeutically trained colleagues who have grasped the theoretical principles of couple therapy for sexual dysfunctions (chapters 1 to 3), have studied our didactic concept for advanced training (chapter 10), and have, finally, arranged for ongoing supervision. We decided to publish the manual in spite of our misgivings, since our experiences have shown this manual to be a helpful guide for colleagues conducting couple therapy for sexual dysfunctions, provided they have met the requirements mentioned above.

All contributing authors also acted as therapists in the project. For time reasons, or because they left the team prematurely, not all the therapists could contribute to this book. We would, therefore, like to thank the following colleagues for conducting therapy and helping in team discussions to develop, modify, or extend the therapeutic concept: Dr. Sigfried Braun, Christa Breiholz (Dipl. Psychl.), Dr. Charlotte Köttgen, Dr. Karin Morisse, Dr. Wilhelm Schoof, Dr. Karin Schoof-Tams, Prof. Dr. Eberhard Schorsch, and Eva-Maria Schorsch (Dipl. Psych.). Our appreciation goes, as always, to Marianne Tode for her support and to Lutz Roland for the electronic data processing. For this American edition we are greatly indebted to Tom Todd for his interminable patience and unfailing precision in translating this book, with all its obsession for scientific detail. The authors who prepared and wrote the text are named at the head of each chapter. However, all chapters were discussed by the entire team, which carries the overall responsibility. Chapters 1 to 3 are the extended and revised version of a paper that was published in the *Handbuch der Psychologie*, vol. 8 (Schmidt and Arentewicz 1977).

Psychotherapists of varying backgrounds participated in our project: physicians and psychologists in psychoanalytic training, psychiatrists and psychologists trained in client-centered or behavior therapy. They worked together for five years, frequently as cotherapists in a team, learned from one another, and discovered again and again that it is possible to correlate or mutually complement theoretical concepts from different psychotherapeutic schools of thought. We have all learned that a supervision group (Balint group) led by a psychoanalyst can offer practical assistance and can help widen the approach of couple therapy, which is, after all, based essentially on behavior therapy principles. Our hope is that this book brings these experiences to light and illustrates not only the need for an integrative approach in psychotherapy but also the harm done by orthodox psychotherapists, of all schools, erecting barriers between one camp and the other.

Gerd Arentewicz
Gunter Schmidt

Hamburg, November 1982

The Treatment of
Sexual Disorders

Introduction

SEXUALITY AND RELATIONSHIPS

Gunter Schmidt

There can be no doubt as to the necessity for helping people with sexual problems; the development of adequate forms of therapy has been long overdue. Sexual problems often harbor an emotional misery that goes far beyond the sense of missing pleasure and satisfaction: a fear of not being loved, of being abandoned, and of loneliness; a deep-rooted insecurity in one's sense of self-esteem; feelings of humiliated and mistreated masculinity or femininity.

Although sexual disturbances presumably do not occur more or less often than they used to, relationships are now more vulnerable to sexual problems; they seem to be more dependent on sexuality and its related affects. One could see this as a sign of enlightenment, of progress reflecting the fact that people are more aware of the importance of their sexuality and refuse to passively endure sexual problems and sexual dreariness any longer. And this is without doubt one aspect of the problem. Nonetheless, by confining attention exclusively to this single aspect, as many "sex therapists" tend to do, one loses sight of the general trend that is shaping the societal function of sexuality and relationships, and one mistakes as a conscious act what is in part merely a blind reaction to changed conditions. We shall therefore outline the societal background to our psychotherapeutic work.

Couple relationships once formed the basis for jointly mastering life and rearing children. Couples experienced the ineluctable reality of having to spend their lifetimes together in the common struggle against everyday hardships and demands. Marriage and family were the means of coping with the exacting demands of the world. Nowadays, at least in the middle class, a couple relationship is no longer essential for the material and existential tasks of survival, if not quite superfluous. Satisfying primary needs (food, warmth, health) and accomplishing common tasks (child-rearing, care of relatives of all ages, joint economic obligations) have become possible without or outside such a relationship by making use of the consumer services provided by society. Whenever this possibility is denied, traditional lifestyles are artificially kept alive: couples then cling to the old division of roles and believe that it is still best to organize their children's upbringing, the household, and economic support as if domestic technology had not been invented or as if at least some opportunities for collective upbringing styles and a more equitable division of labor and domestic responsibility did not exist. In secret they have realized the senselessness of the way they organize their life, and this shines through the façade of a happiness they carry before them.

While couple relationships are being relieved of the pressure for joint survival, they are becoming more and more dependent on other, less reliable sources of gratification, that is, emotional and narcissistic sources. Emotional satisfaction—warmth, protection, love, sexuality, and intimacy—is vulnerable to interference and in any case is far more at risk than are material sources of satisfaction. But the dependence on narcissistic gratification seems particularly problematic. This need, too, has always played an important role: relationships and sexuality provide assurance that one is worthy of being loved and confirmation of one's masculinity or femininity. But this narcissistic function of relationships and sexuality has grown out of all proportion and threatens to burst its seams. We can only hint here at the roots of this development: one can observe that people are being deprived more and more of opportunities to feel they are worth something to others, to experience what they are doing as something of significance, and to know they are indispensable to the lives of their families or at least a few friends.[1] The experience of powerlessness, dependency, inner emptiness, and one's own meaninglessness becomes radical and merciless; the vacuum left behind sucks in any experiences which make one at least temporarily aware of one's own importance. Religious sects and drugs are important in this context, as is the psychotherapy boom, which offers a plethora of ways of replenishing emotions, from group dynamics and encounter groups to the psychoanalytic cure for people who do not really need it. A particularly important mode of compensation for narcissistic deprivation is the couple relationship or, more precisely, the emotions that it can mobilize, such as falling in love and sexual desire, and satisfaction.

Narcissistic and emotional demands overburden couple relationships in general and sexuality in particular. They lead to illusory hopes and end in the disappointment and hopelessness that we continually came across in couple relationships. The symptoms of this process are expressed in various forms.

First, there is the unspoken illusion that the intense sexuality experienced by couples when they fall in love is compatible with a long-term relationship. This is impossible because the closeness that comes from living together—sleeping, eating, and spending leisure time together and perhaps even bringing up children together—cannot endure sexual symbiosis. The most such closeness will allow is a sexuality that still conveys some tenderness and satisfaction. These are the bearable limits unless some kind of separation intensifies sexual experience and briefly reactivates the feeling of being in love again: a long geographical separation, a quarrel, or even using aggressive tension as an aphrodisiac, as Stoller (1975) observed in perversions. In steady relationships intense sexual experiences are possible only if they create a distance or resolve a recently created distance. The reduced intensity in the everyday sexuality of permanent relationships, its trivialization, is not just a blunting effect or boredom, but actually a necessary and meaningful way of protecting one's autonomy, and is thus an important safety valve in the balance between closeness and distance. Besides, it makes room for nonprivate activities.

An "intact" sexuality of this kind, somewhat boring compared to earlier ebullience, induces far more uneasiness and fear than it used to in previous generations; it sets a series of manipulations in motion that are ideologically glossed over by the slogan "free sexuality." For example, sophistication and technical skill are supposed to rejuvenate the old emotional uniqueness. Alex Comfort's best-seller *The Joy of Sex*, with its promise of acrobatic pleasure, is as much an example of this as are the professional "marital enrichment" and "sexual enhancement" programs, all refresher courses for pepping up the everyday routine of life together. Jumping from one love affair to the next is another widespread, nowadays conventional source of euphoric experiences. Extramarital relationships—which "of course," should not endanger the steady relationship and which "of course" are necessary because, after all, "one partner alone cannot satisfy all needs"—become the crowning glory of the pallid romantic ideal.

Another replenishment mechanism works by turning attention away from events outside the relationship to its inner world, by mirroring the relationship in continual conversations about wishes, problems, conflicts, and so forth, as if life reached no further than this inner world. Communication is certainly a desirable aim, but when it is made an end in itself it creates a hypochondriacal attitude toward the relationship and breeds precisely the illness it fears. Talking about problems is a way of evoking an apparent intimacy that the partners would otherwise be incapable of establishing. The relationship becomes its own topic, and idle talk stands proxy for the relationship itself; one feels what one says one feels. The notion that relationships and sexuality must compensate for everything that is experienced as meaningless, disappointing, or boring testifies to the desperate confusion that rules many relationships.

If adaptive mechanisms fail to resolve problems in a relationship then the illusions are merely transferred to another relationship. The failure is felt to have personal rather than structural reasons. That reading is painful because the failure is seen as one's own fault—or one's partner's. But it keeps alive hope for another attempt. The new middle-class ideology of emotionally and sexually intense relationships that never get over the stage of being passionately in love, of "limerence" (a fashionable term is quickly found), is the expression of a narcissistic deprivation that tempts one merely to reel from one love affair to another. Sexuality holds the potential for rapturous experiences, but if one expects these moments of happiness to last forever, one is doomed to search forever. Narcissistic degradation makes people incapable of standing up to the disillusionment that sets in when the feeling of being in love wears off. They compensate for this inability by changing relationships with an alarmingly compulsive repetitiveness, not so much for hedonistic greed but rather in a desperate search to find out what they are worth. Sexuality and infatuation provide some of the few remaining opportunities to feel, at least for a short while, that one is important to someone else. As soon as the futility of this hope emerges, depression and boredom set in at the point where infatuation could turn into a love of a deeper and more lasting kind. This narcissistic exploitation of sexual relations propels itself ad absurdum. The multiplicity of relationships demonstrates that the partners do not really feel for each other, they do not see each other as individuals; what counts is the emotional state of being in love which each partner attains by using the other. The illusion of a completely new emotionality and sexuality is, however, fascinating enough to delude a person as to his or her error—for a time at least.

Eventually the futility of this illusion leads to an aggressive and self-destructive renunciation of relationships, a fact recently snatched up by a euphorically proclaimed ideology—the so-called singles movement. Individuality, "lonesome cowboy" sentimentality, and the masochistic pleasure taken in solitude all impart a new, short-lived feeling of one's own grandeur. The ultimate, dismal form this syndrome takes has been outlined in a recently published analysis of contemporary literature in West Germany (Raddatz 1978), that commented on developments also existent in other Western societies. Eroticism and sexuality amount merely to being alone, solitude, irrelation, and estrangement; fellow beings have nothing to do with one another and so fall back into themselves; autoeroticism is the sign of the complete collapse of emotional attachment; sexual intercourse is an awkward variation on masturbation. Raddatz concludes this analysis with a quotation from Ingomar von Kieseritzky's book *Trägheit oder Szenen aus der Vita activa* (sloth, or scenes from the vita activa):

She lay in the gentle pose of one surprised by death; the aureoles of her breasts were deep red. She licked her lips several times and looked at me with a half-open eye. I joined in the slurping with no particular resolve. She exhaled the soft fragrance of caramel bonbons. Her teeth glittered . . . and it happened without our doing much, without our wanting it either, as of itself; and I let out a teaspoonful of feeble semen virile, not more than the amount indicated by Spariel in 'incisum,' together with a little twitch in my calf.

An interpretation of coldness is all too easily reached by believing that sexual liberation has not brought people together but led them away from one another. Liberation is actually an attempt (in vain) to overcome this coldness, which is after all why "sexual freedom" is no longer sanctioned by society. All that separates a person repeatedly infatuated with new love affairs from the figures in Kieseritzky's novel is that the former still believes in the replenishing effect of relationships, whereas the latter no longer do so. Sexuality and relationships collapse under the overburdening demands.

By comparison with the epidemic flood of problems in relationships, dysfunctional sexuality is a rare and, one might be tempted to say, comparatively harmless phenomenon, were it not that "harmless" sounds cynical in view of the emotional distress experienced. It would be too easy to invent recipes: understanding that love can only start to grow once the promise of happiness imparted by infatuation has been dispelled; reconciliation with disappointments and inevitable forbearance; refusal to mistake the inner world for the outer and to waste more and more energy rummaging around in the private sphere. But what instead? Good advice is useless. These problems are far from being solvable individually, for example, in psychotherapy—not just because they are too numerous, but because they are anchored in the structures of society itself. However, the consciousness that there can be no psychotherapeutic solution is dwindling.

NOTE

[1] We deliberately refer to this as deprivation and not as a growth in narcissistic tendencies. To claim the latter is true, as Christopher Lasch does, is as misleading as the belief that the inhabitants of the Sahara are starving because their hunger has grown.

PART I

Causes and Treatment

Chapter 1

SYMPTOMS

Gunter Schmidt and Gerd Arentewicz

In this chapter we have confined our discussion of sexual dysfunctions to a consideration of how these dysfunctions are manifested as symptoms. We have intentionally restricted our perspective by taking symptoms out of their context, in other words, without taking into account a person's life history, his or her relationship and current overall situation. We describe forms of behavior without analyzing their causes and meaning and without asking how the person experiences the behavior. Our reason for doing this is that analyzing symptoms in terms of behavior is of great value in designing a therapy plan and thus should be an essential part of history taking. Moreover, our description of the symptoms is intended to clarify what sexual dysfunctions actually are. For example, when can an orgasmic or erectile problem or rapid ejaculation be considered an orgasmic, erectile, or ejaculatory *dysfunction*?

We begin by briefly describing the symptoms of twelve couples to demonstrate vividly the heterogeneity of sexual dysfunctions. The examples were selected to cover a wide range of sexual dysfunctions.[1]

COUPLE 1: A thirty-two-year-old housewife and a painter three years older than she have been married for ten years. They have an eight-year-old daughter. Sexual difficulties have existed since the relationship began fourteen years ago. The wife has never had an orgasm and has never felt sexually aroused during caressing, petting, or sexual intercourse. She has never tried masturbation. She can do without sexuality and any kind of tenderness, which she feels is merely a nuisance. All she likes is cuddling with her daughter. She experiences no sexual desire at all; she maintains sexual relations with her husband only to be a "good wife to him." She and her husband have agreed on a strict schedule: they have intercourse twice a week on specific days for as short a time as possible. The wife endures it in the hope that "it will soon be over." Neither partner has had sexual relations with other partners before or during their marriage.

COUPLE 2: A thirty-one-year-old saleswoman married for nine years to a carpenter her age has lost all interest in sex since the birth of her only child eight years ago. She does not care for sexual intercourse and tries to avoid or dodge sexual contact. She rarely has to endure intercourse (once every other month) and is then indifferent, detached, and afterward irritable and aggressive. After the child's birth, her interest in sexual relations vanished almost "like a shot." Initially she "put on an act" for her husband, but it became unbearable. In the two years preceding the birth the couple had intercourse two to three times a week, during which she usually reached orgasm. She has never tried masturbation, and neither partner has had sexual relations with other partners before or during their marriage.

COUPLE 3: A twenty-three-year-old saleswoman has been married for three years to a telecommunications engineer three years older than she. Since sexual relations began five years ago she has felt a strong aversion to sexual contact, and she tries to avoid sexual intercourse or to keep it to a minimum by making excuses or openly refusing. She can only put up with tenderness of an explicitly nonsexual nature, which makes her feel protected. A man's genitals and her own disgust her. When she agrees to intercourse she occasionally becomes aroused and sometimes reaches orgasm. She is, however, unable to enjoy her sexual reactions and endures them almost against her will. She can masturbate to orgasm but rarely does so because she finds this kind of orgasm also unacceptable. She responded in exactly the same way with another partner before the marriage.

COUPLE 4: A thirty-year-old linguist and a graphic artist ten years older than she had an intimate relationship for two years. In the preceding ten years she has had sexual relationships with five or six men. She has only had a coital orgasm twice, "the same feeling I have by masturbating." She seldom reaches orgasm during petting, no matter who the partner is. She is aroused by foreplay and can find intercourse pleasant, without behaving defensively or feeling sexual aversion. Sexual intercourse takes place three or four times a week. She used to put herself "under enormous pressure to achieve a real [coital] orgasm." She can climax when masturbating in front of her partner although it takes longer than it does with solitary masturbation.

COUPLE 5: A twenty-four-year-old nurse has been lovers for three years with a civil engineer two years older than she. She has never experienced coital orgasm, either in this or in earlier relationships. Her sexual desire is strong, and she insists on frequent sexual contact. She becomes extremely aroused but only reaches orgasm if she and her partner stimulate each other orally and if her partner addresses her obscenely or narrates obscene episodes. She does not find intercourse itself unpleasant; she is merely disappointed because it never suffices to bring her to climax. She has never masturbated.

COUPLE 6:   A twenty-seven-year-old clerk has been married for three years to a machine builder two years older than she. They have known each other for five years. The wife has only once had an orgasm during intercourse with her husband. She never becomes fully aroused by foreplay and does not care for intercourse. She feels that sexual contact with her husband is like an impending danger, and she does all she can to avoid it. Intercourse takes place less than once a month. Since the relationship began her husband has been a premature ejaculator; he has also had erectile problems for a year and a half. In previous relationships these disturbances were nonexistent. The wife has no problem in regularly achieving orgasm by masturbating. Before marrying she was involved with a man twenty years her senior. In that relationship she easily reached orgasm, was readily aroused, felt strong desire, and initiated sexual activity. This man "showed me what it can be like."

COUPLE 7:   A twenty-eight-year-old kindergarten teacher has been married for five years to a physician somewhat older than herself. Neither partner had had a premarital relationship with other partners nor had they been involved sexually with each other before their marriage. Despite many attempts during their five-year marriage, intercourse was never possible. On attempting intercourse the wife is cramped and has a tense, unpleasant feeling in her entire body. She is afraid of pain, and attempts at penile insertion hurt her. She can insert a finger without feeling any pain, but she is "somehow glad when the finger is out again." She is readily aroused by petting and regularly reaches orgasm with caressing or during femoral intercourse. She is very fond of this kind of sexual activity and often takes the initiative. She has no difficulty in achieving orgasm by masturbating.

COUPLE 8:   A twenty-five-year-old saleswoman has been married for six years to a salesman of the same age. Five years ago she had a particularly difficult birth (perineal rupture). Ever since she has been terrified of sexual intercourse and of pain, and coital attempts have been unsuccessful. The penis cannot be inserted, and when intercourse is attempted she has spasmodic feelings in her vagina which spread over her entire body. Initially this feeling overcame her at any gesture of tenderness. Later, half a year after the child's birth, she came to an agreement with her husband not to try coitus any more. Since then the couple has engaged in petting regularly and she nearly always reaches orgasm. They occasionally perform anal intercourse without difficulty and reach orgasm. Before the birth the couple had intercourse regularly, and the wife almost always reached orgasm. Neither partner has had extramarital relationships, and she has never masturbated.

COUPLE 9:   A thirty-seven-year-old tradesman has been married for sixteen years to a woman of the same age. They have two children. The wife is not employed but assumes the household duties. Since first having intercourse the husband has ejaculated prematurely. After inserting his penis he ejaculates rapidly, at the latest after twenty cautious movements but usually earlier. In the early years of their marriage he often ejaculated prior to intromission. He feels he is quite incapable of controlling ejaculation, and he experiences coitus as a defeat. He thus reduced frequency of intercourse in the last two years to once or twice monthly; he would prefer to avoid the problem. The same difficulties arose in an extramarital relationship. When he masturbates, which is seldom because he dismisses it as being "immature," he can retard ejaculation for as long as he likes. His wife has no sexual problems; she becomes aroused and reaches orgasm. Her interest in intercourse has, however, declined because of her husband's difficulties and his concern about them.

COUPLE 10: A thirty-six-year-old art historian has been married to a thirty-two-year-old nurse for four years. Neither of them has had a premarital relationship, and they only attempted intercourse after they were married. These attempts are made regularly and in vain. The husband fails to erect fully; during foreplay his penis stiffens briefly to an erection and then subsides immediately. He has morning erections almost every day. He has a full erection on masturbating and ejaculates every time. Remarkably enough, he does not masturbate by rubbing his glans through the foreskin. He is afraid of revealing the glans under the foreskin; his glans is highly sensitive and pulling back the foreskin irritates him.

COUPLE 11: A male and a female student, both twenty-six years old, have been steady friends for a year. Coitus is always impossible because his penis never stiffens fully or simply becomes flaccid "at a stroke" as soon as penetration is attempted. His erection is maintained and ejaculation is achieved during masturbation and petting so long as sexual intercourse is explicitly excluded. Over the last ten years he has had sexual intercourse with fifteen partners. Erectile problems have always troubled him but not as markedly as in the present relationship. His partner has had coital relations with other men and has no orgasmic difficulties.

COUPLE 12: A forty-year-old plumbing contractor, married for eighteen years to a saleswoman, (they have two children) had no sexual problems in the first thirteen years of marriage. Five years ago erectile difficulties arose after an infection of the testicles. When he attempts intercourse, usually once every two weeks, he does not achieve a full erection. As soon as he is able to penetrate he ejaculates immediately. Occasionally ejaculation occurs simply when his penis is touched. He becomes extremely nervous during foreplay and coital attempts, and he is quickly gripped by the panicky fear that again it will not work. His heart palpitates and he sweats profusely. He occasionally has morning erections. He has not had extramarital relationships, and since marrying he has given up masturbating. His wife participates unenthusiastically in coital attempts and has not had an orgasm since the problems arose; this she attributes to his difficulties.

The variety of sexual dysfunction exemplified by these brief vignettes has led some observers to try ordering and classifying them into a staggering number of groups and subgroups, which, no matter how differentiated, are grossly oversimplified and hence provide no adequate description of individual cases. We have resisted the temptation to add to existing classifications since every classification creates the misleading impression that a sexual dysfunction can be clearly distinguished and closely defined as a homogeneous clinical "entity." Rather we have replaced the classifications with a set of descriptive characteristics that provide a precise description of sexual disturbances and their symptoms. This kind of descriptive system puts an end to the futile dispute about the most appropriate classificatory system and at the same time offers detailed specifications for history-taking of dysfunctional couples, at least as far as symptoms are concerned.

Our case histories illustrate two main aspects from which we can derive descriptive characteristics of sexual dysfunctions:

1. Which sexual functions are affected? Sexual disturbances can be distinguished by the phase of sexual interaction they affect. Some of the patients in our case histories feel no desire for sexuality whatsoever and circumvent it. Others are incapable of experiencing sexual arousal; some are unable to perform intercourse; and others have difficulty experiencing orgasm or reach it too rapidly. Many have all or several of these problems.

2. When and how does the disturbance appear? Sexual disturbances can be distinguished formally by their circumstances and conditions as well as their duration, incidence, and severity. In the case histories a few patients have had a disturbance since their first sexual relations while others were first affected after a trouble-free period. Some encounter difficulties with all, others only with some partners or forms of sexual activity. Some experience the disturbance every time, others only occasionally. In one case the disturbance may be chronic, in another it may have only recently set in.

All existing classifications of sexual dysfunctions compound characteristics from both aspects in varying combinations. Our descriptive characteristics are, thus, by no means new. We simply apply them in a different way than do most authors: not to construct taxonomies of dubious value, but to describe individual cases in therapy-related terms. A similar procedure was suggested by Fordney-Settlage (1975).

Which Sexual Functions Are Affected?

Sexual interaction between two partners can be very roughly subdivided into five phases: sexual approach (initiation of sexual activity and response to the initiative); sexual stimulation (caresses, bodily contact, genital stimulation during foreplay); penile intromission and coitus (in heterosexual encounters that go beyond petting); orgasm; the period immediately after orgasm (see table 1.1).

LACK OF SEXUAL DESIRE, SEXUAL AVERSION

Lack of desire and aversion to sexuality are the most important problems in the phase of sexual approach. In rare cases lack of desire

TABLE 1.1
Sexual Problems in the Different Phases of Sexual Interaction

Phase	Male dysfunctions	Female dysfunctions
Sexual approach	*Lack of sexual desire, sexual aversion:* desire never or only seldom felt; indifference to sexuality; passive resistance; feels molested, reluctant, disgusted; fear of "failure"; avoidance behavior.	
Sexual stimulation	*Erectile dysfunctions:* Duration and strength of erection insufficient for intromission	*Arousal dysfunction:* Duration and strength of arousal insufficient
Insertion of penis, coitus		*Vaginismus:* Insertion of penis impossible or painful owing to spasmodic constriction of vaginal orifice
	Painful intercourse (dyspareunia): burning, stabbing, and/or itching in the genital area	
Orgasm	*Premature ejaculation:* ejaculation before insertion of penis into vagina, on insertion, or immediately afterward *Ejaculatory incompetence:* no ejaculation despite full erection and intensive stimulation	*Orgasmic difficulties:* orgasm never or only seldom reached
	Ejaculation without satisfaction: ejaculation without feeling pleasure or sense of orgasm	*Orgasm without satisfaction:* "physiological" orgasm without feeling pleasure and sense of orgasm
Postorgasmic response	*Postorgasmic dysphoria:* irritability, inner uneasiness, disturbed sleep, weeping fits, irritation in the genital area.	

can affect sexuality totally: such people have never experienced sexual desire for any other person and for any form of sexuality (see couple 1). However, more often sexual desire tends to subside or dry up. Lack of desire affects only particular partners (see couple 6), for example, a marital partner but not a lover, or only specific forms of sexual activity, such as coitus but not masturbation. These forms of lack of desire are more frequent in women than in men.

A few authors (for example, Matussek 1971; Eicher 1975) apply the concept of "loss of libido" to the various forms of lack of desire. This term does not seem to us particularly helpful because it implies that the "sexual instinct" is missing or has scarcely developed and thus denies there is any connection between sexual desire and the social-emotional environment. It disguises the fact that lack of sexual desire frequently arises only with partners who evoke inhibitions or are no longer attractive or seductive, or never were. Nor do we find it helpful to subsume the manifold forms of lack of desire under the label "inhibited sexual desire" and so declare it a clinical entity, as Kaplan (1979) does, even going so far as to create a special kind of therapy ("psychosexual therapy," see also p. 71). In our view, lack of desire is just one descriptive characteristic of sexual problems and not a diagnostic category or a syndrome.

Lack of desire is almost always accompanied by sexual aversion, particularly if the other partner desires and demands sexuality. Aversion might be expressed by passive resistance, annoyance at being molested, antipathy, or disgust (see couples 1, 2, 3, and 6). These reactions appear far more frequently in women than men. Another form of sexual aversion is fear of failure (see couples 9 and 12), which is more frequent in men. In any case, aversion is accompanied by avoidance behavior, by attempts to circumnavigate sexuality. A partner's sexual wishes are met by aggressive refusal, resigned patience, or the impulse to escape.

Lack of desire and aversion are not sexual dysfunctions. Their occurrence and strength are, however, important descriptive characteristics of men and women with sexual problems. As a rule, lack of desire and aversion arise from the same anxieties or conflicts that cause dysfunctions, or are in a few cases the consequence of a dysfunction.

In rare cases lack of desire and aversive reactions appear in men and women without dysfunctions. If these men or women indulge in sexual activity in spite of antipathy and lack of desire, they become aroused and reach orgasm. However, they experience these orgasms as ungratifying and mechanical and at the same time block their emotions toward their partner or keep an emotional distance (see couple 3). Aside from these exceptions, lack of desire and aversion turn up in combination with dysfunctions; on the other hand, dysfunctions can exist even when sexual desire is felt and there is little evidence of aversion.

ERECTILE AND AROUSAL DYSFUNCTIONS

If adequate sexual stimulation does not evoke sexual arousal then the man's erection or the woman's lubrication-swelling reaction fail (Kaplan 1974a). In men we call this erectile dysfunction and in women arousal dysfunction.

Erectile dysfunctions: duration and strength of penile erection are insufficient for intercourse (see couples 10, 11, and 12).[2] The penis remains completely flaccid or only partially stiffens or erection recedes before ejaculation, either on attempting insertion or shortly after penetration. Most patients' erectile capacity malfunctions only on attempting coitus but not during masturbation or petting. In the rare case when erectile ability is completely nonexistent (no erection in all sexual activity, no "spontaneous erections" at night or on waking in the morning), physical examination is always necessary. Lack of erection is often combined with a failure to ejaculate. Some men do, however, ejaculate with a flaccid penis. These orgasms are often experienced as weak and barely gratifying.

Arousal dysfunctions in women: arousal strength and duration are insufficient for pleasure to be felt and enjoyed during petting or coitus. Genital hyperemia (pooling of blood), which is triggered by effective sexual stimulation in women not troubled by arousal disturbances (see Masters and Johnson 1966), is minimal or completely absent. The woman experiences no, or only slight, vaginal lubrication-swelling of the major and minor labia and clitoris and no balloonlike expansion of the inner two thirds of the vagina (tenting effect). This impairment of the lubrication-swelling reaction (Kaplan 1974a) is paralleled by a subjective lack of arousal and pleasure: genital stimulation is often felt only as touching. In a few cases women report adequate lubrication-swelling reactions but do not feel aroused.

In contrast to men with erectile problems, women with arousal disturbances can perform sexual intercourse. This sometimes involves pain and discomfort as a result of insufficient lubrication. The majority of women with arousal disturbances show distinctly aversive sexual reactions (see couples 1 and 2). However a few are able to enjoy petting and coitus, which they experience as tenderness and physical closeness. As Kaplan observed (1974b), some women with arousal dysfunctions have sudden, short, and weak orgasms. These exceptions are rare: almost all women with arousal disturbances also have orgasmic disturbances.

Arousal dysfunctions are either restricted to sexual intercourse and foreplay (see couple 6) or affect all other forms of stimulation as well (masturbation, fantasies, erotic books and films, and so forth; see couples 1 and 2). These two forms of arousal dysfunction are almost equally frequent. If a woman has never been sexually aroused Kaplan speaks of "general sexual unresponsiveness" (1974b; see couple 1). If the term should be used at all, one could speak of "frigidity" here in the sense that it continues to be applied by many authors (for example, Frick 1973; Schnabl 1974; Eicher 1975).[3]

VAGINISMUS AND PAINFUL SEXUAL INTERCOURSE

Vaginismus and pain during coitus are problems that are manifested on inserting the penis into the vagina or during coitus itself. (Erectile and arousal disturbances that sometimes become manifest in this phase of sexual interaction have already been mentioned above and do not require further discussion.)

Vaginismus: the constriction of the vaginal orifice due to involuntary spasms of the pelvic musculature and the outer third of the vagina in response to a real or imagined attempt at vaginal penetration (see couples 7 and 8). Walthard, who provided a description of this dysfunction in 1909 that is still valid today, considered vaginismus a reflexlike defensive movement.

Vaginismus appears in varying degrees of severity. In most serious cases a physician can only examine the vagina by giving a general anesthetic. Serious cases make it impossible to insert a finger or use a tampon. In less serious cases a finger or tampon can be inserted but not a penis; finally, in the milder cases coitus is occasionally possible but still involves pain. The majority of vaginistic women are capable of orgasm during petting. Some of them are even decidedly responsive and take the initiative if they are certain that coitus will not be attempted.

One should distinguish vaginismus from coital phobias without vaginal cramp. In the latter, fear of intercourse is so great that a woman cannot even allow an attempt to be made. She refuses the attempt or responds with a panicky impulse to escape. Because therapy for coital phobias does not differ from that for vaginismus, we will not discuss it separately.

Vaginismus is a psychogenic defense response. However, physical traumas affecting the genitalia (complicated childbirth, genital surgery, diseases such as endometriosis) can trigger fear of pain during coitus and thus enhance the development of vaginismus (see couple 8).

Painful sexual intercourse. Masters and Johnson (1970) believe that inadequate lubrication is the most common reason for women experiencing painful intercourse (dyspareunia or algopareunia). If poor lubrication is not organically caused, as for example, in a postmenopausal woman with an atrophied vaginal wall, pain during coitus is a parallel symptom of arousal disturbance. In cases of vaginismus, coitus, if at all possible, is also painful.

Some cases of dyspareunia have full or partial organic causes (Masters and Johnson 1970; Eicher 1975). Pain can take a number of forms: burning, stinging, or itching on penile insertion; a dull pain inside the vagina; spasms on orgasm similar to labor pains or diffuse abdominal pains. Dyspareunia requires gynecological examination. There are "cases with a severe psychical component" (Eicher 1975, p. 128), in which pain continues even after the organic causes have been removed. There are also reports of psychogenic dyspareunias, which appear as phobic anticipation of pain or misinterpretation of genital sensations as pain and are termed "cognitive sexual pains" by Sharpe and Meyer (1973). In general, long-term organic dyspareunias may in the long run result in impairment of general sexual functioning: women then develop arousal and orgasmic disturbances and sexual aversions.

Pain during coitus is also experienced by men, but far less often than by women. Men express nonorganic dyspareunic complaints as a fear of pain when the glans is touched after pulling back the foreskin (see couple 10). A (noncircumcised) subject with pain anticipation is irritated by his glans being touched. This "cognitive sexual pain" makes coitus or attempts at it an unpleasant, painful, "castrating" event, and erectile difficulties or avoidance of coitus often develop in response.

We will not discuss dyspareunic complaints further. Dyspareunic complaints that are psychogenic rarely occur independently of other dysfunctions. They can usually be removed by systematic desensitization of fear of pain in couple therapy.

EJACULATORY AND ORGASMIC DYSFUNCTIONS

Disturbances that arise in the orgasm phase are premature or retarded ejaculation or ejaculatory incompetence in the male, and difficulty in achieving orgasm in the female.

Premature ejaculation: ejaculation is very rapid and occurs either before penile insertion ("ante portas"), on intromission, or immediately after penetration (see couples 6, 9, and 12). Ejaculation prior to intromission is rare and can be easily diagnosed. In extreme cases the man ejaculates as soon as he is touched or embraced, even when both partners are still dressed. Other men ejaculate during foreplay, on body contact or genital touching, or when the penis and vagina first touch in coital attempts.

Cases in which ejaculation occurs immediately after intromission are far more frequent. It is extremely difficult to define what "immediately after" means. Some authors choose time as a criterion and label ejaculation premature when it takes place within thirty to sixty seconds after insertion. Others take the number of coital movements as a basis; an ejaculation is considered premature if it occurs after ten to twenty pelvic movements. These mechanical definitions are rejected by other authors. Masters and Johnson (1970) suggest incorporating the woman's reactions into the definition and speak of premature ejaculation when the man is unable to control ejaculation for long enough to satisfy his partner in at least 50 percent of their coital connections. Hastings (1971) suggests considering the man's subjective judgment and defines as premature any ejaculation that the man does "not yet" want.

In our opinion, these definitions go too far in broadening the concept of premature ejaculation. In Masters and Johnson's view, for example, a man would complain of premature ejaculation if his partner seldom reached orgasm during prolonged intercourse even though she experienced orgasm before or after intercourse with manual or oral stimulation. In Hastings's case, a man would even ejaculate "prematurely" during prolonged intercourse if he advocated a potency norm that only recognized coitus lasting half an hour. Kinsey et al. (1948) were the first to warn against overextending the concept of premature ejaculation and viewing rapid ejaculation fundamentally as dysfunctional or pathological. Any man can learn to retard ejaculation, "but it is only a portion of the male population that would consider the acquirement of such an ability as a desirable substitute for direct and rapidly effected intercourse" (p. 581).

Men who prefer a rapid orgasm presumably have a fundamentally different conception of sexuality from that of those who find prolonged coitus more satisfying. The former experience sexual intercourse as a rapid increase and explosive discharge of physical tension; the latter take more pleasure in playing with arousal. Partner problems caused by rapid ejaculation in the first group can be solved in other ways than by restructuring their sexuality, for example, by suggesting that the male stimulate his partner manually or orally before or after coitus or with repeated coitus. We consider it necessary to distinguish between rapid ejaculation and premature ejaculation, which requires treatment, and therefore consider the narrow and mechanical definitions mentioned above to be the most appropriate.

Shapiro (1943) distinguishes two forms of premature ejaculation. The more common type is experienced particularly by young men: they are readily aroused and erect rapidly to full strength. The second, rarer form is found particularly in older men and is usually secondary, that is, it follows a long period free of problems. Parallel symptoms are erectile difficulties and low sexual arousability. These men ejaculate with little arousal.

Most premature ejaculators can prolong ejaculation for far longer while masturbating than during sexual intercourse. Several have no problem in controlling ejaculation during intensive petting.

Ejaculatory incompetence. Men with this problem fail to ejaculate even when the fully erect penis is intensively and continuously stimulated. Retarded ejaculation, that is, ejaculation only after lengthy stimulation, should be interpreted as a milder form of ejaculatory incompetence and so does not require detailed discussion. Men who suffer from ejaculatory incompetence often report coitus with ferocious movements lasting half an hour or more, sometimes until both partners are exhausted. Despite strong arousal and a passionate desire for orgasmic release, they are unable to ejaculate. The disturbance is often limited to intravaginal ejaculaton; such men never attain orgasm during coitus but have no difficulty while petting or masturbating. Other men do not reach orgasm during petting either, but only while masturbating. In the most severe cases, which are rare, ejaculation is never voluntary; that is, it is never attained by intentional stimulation during coitus, petting, or masturbation, but only as nocturnal emission. If nocturnal emission does not occur, then one can as a rule diagnose an organic disturbance that requires physical examination and treatment.

A distinction should be made between ejaculatory incompetence and retrograde ejaculation (Sigusch and Maack 1976), when the semen is discharged not outward via the urethra but into the bladder, no matter what form sexual contact takes. In contrast to ejaculatory incompetence, the man does experience orgasm and sexual release. Retrograde ejaculation is easily diagnosed by examining the urine. The causes are practically always organic, and physical examination and treatment are required.

Ejaculation and orgasm without satisfaction. There are extremely rare cases of men who ejaculate without any feeling of orgasmic pleasure. What usually underlies this symptom is a denial of or defense against intense emotional responses to sexuality. This disturbance must be clearly distinguished from the dissatisfaction that some men show with the intensity of their orgasm. According to Kinsey et al. (1948) at least a fifth of all men have orgasms of low intensity. They show "little or no evidence of body tension; orgasm [is] reached suddenly with little or no build-up; penis becomes more rigid and may be involved in mild throbs, or throbs may be limited to urethra alone; semen . . . seeps from urethra without forcible ejaculation; climax passes with minor after-effects" (p. 160). These men are often unable to accommodate their orgasmic experiences to their concept of sexual pleasure and consequently seek help. Orgasms of low intensity ought not in any case be interpreted as more than a physiological variation of the normal. Reich (1927) mentions cases of diminished orgasmic potency despite normal ejaculatory and erectile potency and points out the psychodynamic roots of this characteristic. Nonetheless, counseling for men with this problem will as a rule have to be confined to the therapeutic possibilities for reconciling high expectations with reality. In very rare instances women also report having physiological orgasms without any orgasmic sensation or satisfaction, that is, they sense only the contractions of the vaginal musculature. Moreover, it is far more frequent that women are dissatisfied with orgasmic intensity. These phenomena should be assessed in exactly the same manner as they are for men.

Orgasmic problems in women. Some women never or rarely reach orgasm in sexual encounters (see couples 1 to 6). We will discuss the problems involved in this "rarely" later. The physiology of the female orgasm can be described and defined just as precisely as that of the male orgasm (Masters and Johnson 1966, 1970; Sigusch 1970, 1973).

Orgasmic difficulties may be accompanied by arousal problems (see couples 1 and 2) or may appear separately as a specific inhibition of orgasm despite intact arousability (see couple 4). The women in the latter group often take the sexual initiative, are readily aroused, enjoy petting and coitus but come to a "standstill" on a specific level of sexual arousal. Some authors (Frick 1973; Kaplan 1974a, 1974b; Schnabl 1974; Eicher 1975) refer to this orgasmic problem as anorgasmia or orgasmic disturbance; orgasmic problems combined with arousal dysfunctions are termed "frigidity" or "general sexual unresponsiveness." Women with combined arousal and orgasmic disturbances form a large percentage of those who seek sexual counseling or treatment.

Female orgasmic problems can also be described by observing frequency and regularity of occurrence. By comparison with men who, when not affected by such adverse conditions as illness, tiredness, or old age, always or almost always reach orgasm, frequency of female orgasm during coitus is on average considerably lower and has a wider range of individual variations. By reference to data from more extensive investigations on the frequency of *coital* orgasm (Kinsey et al. 1953; Gebhard 1966; Giese and Schmidt 1968; Schmidt and Sigusch 1971; Schnabl 1972; Fisher 1973), one can estimate that in a population of younger, sexually experienced women (under forty years of age, having had regular intercourse for at least a year) 5 to 10 percent never have an orgasm during coitus, 20 to 25 percent do so occasionally (between 1 and 3 times in 10 coital connections), 20 to 30 percent do so often (between 4 and 7 times in 10), 40 to 50 percent do so almost always or always (8 or more times in 10). The orgasm rate for masturbation, lesbian contacts, and petting is much higher.

Women in the last group ("almost always or always") doubtlessly have no orgasmic difficulties, whereas the first group ("never") has problems, during coitus at least. It is more difficult to estimate partial orgasmic failure during coitus in women who "occasionally" or "often" reach orgasm. They seldom approach a counseling center and most of them do not subjectively feel that they have sexual problems. Orgasmic failure only becomes a problem for such a woman if her partner's offended narcissism causes him to complain and he puts her under pressure, or if she herself sets unrealistic orgasmic standards. Most women do not mind occasional failure of coital orgasm if they climax while petting before or after intercourse or experience nonorgasmic coitus as a pleasant and satisfying feeling of closeness, tenderness, and security. Therefore women with irregular coital orgasm should not be stamped as "patients."

In discussing the frequency of coital orgasm we touch on another problem needing closer examination: how are orgasmic disturbances related to forms of sexual activity? Orgasmic problems are either limited to coitus or to several forms of sexual activity (for example, coitus and petting), or they extend to all forms of sexual activity (including masturbation and sexual fantasies). Orgasmic difficulties that are related to technique (see couples 4, 5, and 6) and those that are "total" (see couples 1 and 2) are almost equally frequent. Coital orgasmic difficulties or, to be precise, the question as to the significance of where and how orgasm is triggered, has been discussed for decades (see the surveys in Kinsey et al. 1953; Moore 1961; Kaplan 1974a). The debate was kindled by Freud (1905, 1916) and has continued since under the rubric "clitoral versus vaginal" orgasm. Freud postulated that in the course of psychosexual maturation erogenous arousability is transferred from the clitoris to the vaginal orifice. Orthodox analysts, particularly Hitschmann and Bergler (1936), inferred that any woman who does not achieve vaginal orgasm is frigid. In their opinion, failure of vaginal orgasm is the only criterion of frigidity. Psychoanalysts are themselves divided on this thesis. While many male analysts endorse this view (for example, Fenichel 1945; Moore 1961; Matussek 1971) it has been fiercely disputed, mainly by female analysts (for example Benedek, quoted in Moore 1961; Deutsch 1965; Sherfey 1966; Fleck 1969).

The clitoral/vaginal orgasm hypothesis postulates two types of female orgasm and defines the clitoral orgasm, which is triggered by stimulation of the clitoral region in petting or masturbation, as being inferior, more infantile, immature, and neurotic than vaginal orgasm in coitus. This hypothesis is no longer tenable for two reasons in particular:

1. No matter what kind of sexual stimulation or technique is involved, the complex physiological reactions in female orgasm are always the same; there are not two physiologically distinct types of female orgasm. For example the vaginal contractions (contraction of the orgasmic platform) that occur during orgasm are triggered by both masturbation and coitus. Women often experience coital orgasm differently from orgasm stimulated by petting or masturbation, but this is primarily due to psychological factors, such as a feeling of greater intimacy, of opening, of penetration and receiving of symbiosis. These emotions can also augment sensual arousal and so facilitate orgasmic release. Shainess (1975) claims that the experiential quality of vaginal arousal and coital orgasm is influenced additionally by physical sensations: "nerve-endings responding to deep pressure predominate in the vagina . . . stretch on ligaments and other organs, and pressure . . . when the vagina is expanded by the penis" (p. 149). Presumably these sensations do not trigger orgasm, or only rarely, but they can modify sexual experience.

2. Irrespective of the kind of sexual stimulation or technique, stimulation of the clitoris is almost always the decisive stimulus effecting orgasm. (Exceptions are orgasms triggered by fantasies or extragenital fondling or those that occur under severe situations of stress.) Vaginal stimulation by the penis may well be experienced as arousing and pleasant, but obviously does little to bring about orgasm (Kaplan 1974a). In coitus the clitoris is indirectly stimulated by the rhythmic penile thrusts and the ensuing distention of the minor labia; it is directly stimulated by the partners rhythmically pressing their bodies against each other. This clitoral stimulation is primarily responsible for effecting "vaginal" orgasm. For Deutsch (1965) the female genitals consists "of two parts with a definite division of labor: the clitoris is the sexual organ, the vagina primarily the organ of reproduction. . . . This central role of the clitoris is not merely the result of masturbation, but is a biological destiny" (p. 360). This is subjectively registered by women. According to Fisher (1973) two thirds of the women he interviewed claim that clitoral stimulation contributes more to an orgasm than vaginal stimulation, while a sixth of the women attribute more orgasmic effectiveness to vaginal stimulation. The remainder do not differentiate. Schnabl (1974) reported similar results.

Orgasm is therefore primarily triggered by clitoral stimulation and gives rise to vaginal contractions. In this context one should remember the fact that 50 to 60 percent of all women do not regularly reach orgasm through coitus alone but often need additional clitoral stimulation, and that some women never reach orgasm at all during coitus. Although the clitoral area is stimulated during coitus, this is not the most effective means of clitoral stimulation. Coitus provides by far the more optimal sexual stimulation for men (penile friction) than it does for women. Many women sometimes or always need direct manual or oral stimulation of their clitoral region. In isolated cases, particularly if coitus is experienced negatively, this may be due to psychodynamically derived fears of and defense reactions to intercourse. Kaplan (1974a) discusses the question of varying orgasmic thresholds in women and states that, for women with a low threshold, coitus and, in extreme cases, sexual fantasies without any kind of physical stimulation suffice for orgasm. Women with a higher threshold are dependent on direct clitoral stimulation and in special cases on highly intense stimulation with a vibrator. We agree with Kaplan that coitally "anorgasmic" women generally represent a normal variation of female sexuality. These women often resort to psychological or medical treatment merely on the insistence of their partner, or because they themselves have mistaken ideas about "natural" sexuality and only fully recognize coital orgasm. These women do not suffer from sexual dysfunction. In such cases we advise both partners to accept the need for direct clitoral stimulation as a normal variation and to stimulate the clitoris before, during, or after intercourse.

POSTORGASMIC DYSPHORIA

Postorgasmic difficulties resemble the aversive reactions described earlier in that they are not, strictly speaking, dysfunctions but are an equally important descriptive characteristic of sexual experience. These "emotional disturbances accompanying full sexual functioning" (Matussek 1971, p. 793) manifest themselves physically or psychically. For example, some men and women report feeling genital irritation, unpleasant twinging or itching, after coital orgasm or orgasm from masturbation. Some feel tired, battered, and worn out the next morning or the whole following day and cannot get into the swing of things. Still others complain of pains in the small of the back immediately after orgasm or a day later. We assume that all these symptoms are due to problems in coping psychologically with sexuality. These physical reactions are far less frequent than postorgasmic ill-temper, which takes a variety of forms including inner uneasiness, irritability, insomnia, depression, and sadness with outbursts of weeping, a sense of inner emptiness, disgust, dysphoric-aggressive moods, the desire to be alone, or a cool detachment from one's partner. This dysphoria can be either short-lived or still persist the next day. It can result in downright fear of orgasm. Regular postorgasmic irritation or ill-temper is extremely rare when functions are intact. It should be distinguished from postcoital reactions of anger, disappointment, sadness, feelings of failure or of being used, and so forth, in men and women with dysfunctions.

When and How Does a Dysfunction Appear?

We will now briefly outline the most important formal descriptive criteria that have repeatedly been attributed diagnostic and therapeutic relevance in the literature. These criteria are applicable to all sexual dysfunctions in men and women. Some of the criteria overlap, others are mutually exclusive.

We apply the term *primary* to sexual dysfunctions that have existed from the start of sexual relations (see couples 1, 7, 9, and 10) and *secondary* to those that appear after a period free of symptoms (see couples 2, 8, and 12).[4]

Initial dysfunctions coincide with the first sexual experiences. A man who achieves no erection or only a partial or a short-lived erection at his first coital attempt has, for example, initial erectile difficulties. These initial sexual problems, which should be clearly distinguished from chronic primary dysfunctions, either recede of their own accord with growing sexual experience or can be easily remedied in counseling.

Technique-related dysfunctions arise only in particular forms of sexual activity, for example, during coitus or coitus and petting, but not in others, for example, masturbation, sexual dreams, homosexual activity (see couples 4, 5, 6, 10, and 11). Disturbances *not related to technique* occur with all sexual techniques in which the man or woman concerned is experienced (see couples 1 and 2).

Partner-related dysfunctions are those that appear only with one particular partner (see couple 6). A woman who is always extremely aroused by her lover but never by her husband has a partner-related arousal problem. We refer to disturbances as being unrelated to the partner if they arise with all partners (see couples 4 and 9). In the case of a patient who has only had sexual relations with one partner since the problems arose it is impossible to determine partner-relatedness.

Situational[5] dysfunctions occur only under certain circumstances. For example, erectile disturbances may occur only in permanent relationships and not with temporary partners, or vice versa. A dysfunction can disappear suddenly during a vacation or appear at times of severe stress at work or during a period of virulent conflict between partners. In isolated cases sexual functioning is influenced by unusual external conditions (see couple 5).

The *severity* of a dysfunction can at first be described in terms of frequency and permanence. For example, an erectile disturbance is either partial (coitus is at least possible on occasion) or total (coitus is never possible). Aside from this general criterion of severity there are special indicators for each disturbance: for example, the strength and duration of erection in erectile disturbances; the moment of ejaculation in premature ejaculation (before, during, or after penetration); the intensity of vaginal spasms in vaginismus (insertion of a finger is possible or impossible).

Finally, another important descriptive characteristic is the *duration of disturbance*. As a rule patients have lived with their disturbances for quite some time before they begin suitable treatment or find an appropriate opportunity for treatment. Most of the patients we treated had been suffering from their symptoms for more than five years (see table 4.1).

This broad discussion of the descriptive characteristics of sexual dysfunctions is not intended to create new abstract verbiage for symptom classification (for example, secondary, technique- and partner-related, partial arousal and orgasm disturbance with sexual aversion and post-orgasmic dysphoria). On the contrary, we wish to specify criteria that enable us to explore individual cases precisely and describe the symptoms of sexual dysfunctions accurately. It is important to emphasize here that "functioning" constitutes only a small component in the sphere of experience called sexuality. "Intact" sexual functioning is little or no indication of the intensity and depth of experience, of pleasure and satisfaction (see Reich 1927; Shainess 1975).

Incidence

TOTAL POPULATION

There are practically no data available on the incidence of sexual dysfunctions in the total population or in specific subpopulations. At best, rough estimates can be derived from empirical investigations on sexual behavior.

Estimates on erectile dysfunctions are the simplest to make. Kinsey et al. (1948) state the following percentages for men with "permanent" erectile disturbances: less than 1 percent of men under thirty, less than 2 percent of forty year-olds, and less than 3 percent of fifty-five year-olds. Percentages then increase to 7 percent of fifty-five year-olds and even 25 percent of sixty-five year-olds. These data were recorded thirty to forty years ago and dealt only with the population of the United States, but they are nevertheless still the best available estimates. Kinsey explicitly emphasizes that an increase in erectile disturbances in old age cannot be attributed to physical aging alone, that "much of the impotence which is seen in older age is psychologic in its origin"

(p. 323). One of the causes is that older people fail to cope psychologically with their declining sexual arousability (see Masters and Johnson 1966). Kinsey's data refer to permanent erectile disturbances. Episodic erectile difficulties are, of course, far more common. Kaplan (1974a) estimates that roughly 50 percent of all men have experienced occasional failures in erectile functioning. In Schnabl's investigation in the German Democratic Republic (1972) a third of the men report having erectile problems on at least one or two occasions. These transient erectile difficulties have little or no clinical significance.

Gebhard's special analysis (1966) of Kinsey's data has thrown some light on the incidence of premature ejaculation. It seems that 4 percent of all married men ejaculate within one minute of vaginal penetration. Schnabl (1972) reports similar statistics: 4 percent of women and 6 percent of men estimate that coitus lasts on average less than one minute. These figures are maximum estimates for the incidence of clinically significant cases of premature ejaculation; they include men who deliberately ejaculate rapidly, who have no control problems, or who are not distressed by the rapidity of their orgasm. To the best of our knowledge there exist absolutely no data on the incidence of failure to ejaculate. It is, however, generally agreed that this dysfunction is far more rare than erectile disturbances or premature ejaculation and comprises only a tiny fraction of all male dysfunctions (see p. 32).

It is even more difficult to estimate the incidence of female dysfunctions. We have already mentioned data on the frequency of coital orgasms (p. 24) and pointed out how difficult it is to subject them to clinical evaluation. However, one can assume that the number of adult women aged between twenty and forty who are completely anorgasmic—that is, who have never had an orgasm during masturbation, petting, coitus, homosexual relations, or through fantasies—lies at present between 5 and 10 percent. Kaplan's assumptions are comparable (1974a). Probably many more women are unable to develop adequate and uninhibited sexual responsiveness owing to partner conflicts, to psychodynamic factors, to their sexually destructive socialization, and to male-dominated sexuality in the relationship. However, it is impossible to state exact figures here or for the incidence of arousal dysfunctions and vaginismus. We only know that vaginismus, like ejaculatory incompetence, is one of the relatively rare sexual dysfunctions.

CLINICAL GROUPS

Epidemiological investigations of clinical groups provide information on the relative frequency of different sexual dysfunctions and on social data of patients who seek counseling and treatment for dysfunctions. Our analysis on the needs for medical and psychotherapeutic care of patients with sexual problems (Schorsch et al. 1977) demonstrates how often physicians in private practice are confronted with sexual disturbances. This investigation showed that in one week at least 1,100 patients with sexual problems consult a physician in Hamburg (a general practitioner, urologist, gynecologist, internist, dermatologist, or neurologist). More than one thousand of these patients, over 90 percent, are sexually dysfunctional. The most common dysfunctions are female arousal and orgasmic dysfunctions, followed by erectile dysfunctions, premature ejaculation, and then, least frequent of all, vaginismus. All in all, more women than men consult a doctor about a sexual problem. A realistic estimate of the annual total number of patients cannot be made simply by multiplying the figure by fifty-two. As a rule, patients either visit several physicians a year with their problems or are treated for some length of time by one physician. It is, however, safe to assume that in a city like Hamburg, with just under two million inhabitants, the number of men and women who seek medical or psychotherapeutic advice on their problems amounts to tens of thousands a year. This clearly shows how widespread sexual disturbances are, even if one takes into account that many of these patients can be helped by information or brief counseling, that many sexual problems are transient and need no professional treatment, and that only a minority have problems serious enough to warrant a special type of psychotherapy.

Only a small fraction of the patients who have complaints are ultimately admitted to outpatient sex counseling services. In these services the patients are selectively screened: men in the lower age range (up to thirty-five years) and patients with higher education are over-represented (Raboch 1970; documentation of the Division of Sex Research, University of Hamburg, in Schoof 1975 and Brand 1979). About 55 percent of all patients requesting treatment or counseling for a dysfunction at the counseling center of the University of Hamburg Division of Sex Research are men, even though these disturbances are more common in women. In recent years, however, women have become much more willing to remedy sexual problems (see Brand 1979). We expect that in the near future more young women than men will make use of sexual counseling.[6] Half the men and 90 percent of the women who seek counseling are under thirty-five. Only 25 percent of our male patients are blue-collar workers; 25 percent are academics or students; about half the patients have attended "Hauptschule" (nine years of school) and almost a third have "Abitur" (at least thirteen years of school). These figures are remarkable because sexual disturbances are particularly widespread in the lower social strata, especially female disturbances (Kinsey et al. 1953; Rainwater 1965, 1966). Such women very often remain untreated. This is determined in part by lack of familiarity with the psychological and medical services that are oriented to the middle class, acceptance of sexual problems and burdens as woman's fate, and the priority of social and economic problems over sexuality.

Most of the men (56 percent of N = 416) who consulted us from 1975 to 1977 about a dysfunction complained of erectile disturbances (see Brand 1979); 23 percent complained of premature ejaculation, 10 percent of erectile problems and premature ejaculation, 6 percent of ejaculatory incompetence. Raboch's documentation (1970) of male patients in the sexological outpatient department in Prague shows a similar distribution of diagnoses. This contradicts the assumption of Kaplan (1974a) and Schnabl (1972) who claim that the most common male dysfunction is premature ejaculation. However, the relative distribution of disturbances in a clinical population may not correspond with that in the total population because different disturbances can create varying degrees of suffering and, thus, varying needs for counseling.

Of the women who consulted our division about a dysfunction from 1975 to 1977 (N = 353), 12 percent complained of vaginismus and almost 90 percent had orgasmic or arousal disturbances. A third of the latter group had never experienced an orgasm or felt sexual arousal and so suffered from general sexual unresponsiveness, as Kaplan terms it. Roughly a third had orgasmic and arousal disturbances affecting only petting and coitus but not masturbation; the remaining third complained only of orgasmic dysfunctions without arousal problems.

Kinsey et al. (1948) and Masters and Johnson (1970) have already observed that premature ejaculation is far more frequent in the higher social classes. Our results also show that the relative frequency of erectile and ejaculatory disturbances differed according to the patient's class: 34 percent of the academics, but only 18 percent of the workers, consulted us about premature ejaculation. We can also confirm Rainwater's observation (1965, 1966) that women from the lower social strata suffer more often from extremely severe sexual disturbances. We found that women with little school education (nine years or less) who seek advice suffer from general sexual unresponsiveness more often than do women qualified for college (59 percent versus 29 percent); they often feel strong aversion to sexuality and often react with

disgust (77 percent versus 48 percent); their orgasmic problem is frequently independent of technique (64 percent versus 36 percent), for
example, a relatively large number have not even experienced an orgasm yet during petting or masturbation. There is a similarity here
with the findings of Fordney-Settlage (1975); she demonstrates that
women from lower income brackets especially complain of dyspareunic pains in addition to orgasmic disturbances. Women from the
lower social strata thus have particularly serious sexual problems, and
if they turn to a counseling center at all it is only when the problems
have escalated to such a degree as to be unbearable.

NOTES

1. In the interest of patient anonymity all personal data in the case histories have
been changed.

2. "Potency disturbance" and "impotence" are still used as synonyms for erectile dysfunction (by Bancroft 1970; Masters and Johnson 1970; Hastings 1971; Matussek 1971;
Schnabl 1974). We avoid these terms for two reasons: first, they are not applied consistently (for example, they are used as terms for ejaculatory dysfunctions as well); second,
they are judgmental and discriminatory. We avoid the term "frigidity" for the same
reasons.

3. See chapter 1, note 2.

4. Masters and Johnson (1970) distinguish between primary and secondary orgasmic
dysfunction in a different sense: a woman is primarily anorgasmic only if she has never
reached orgasm in any kind of sexual activity.

5. Masters and Johnson (1970) and Kaplan (1974a) apply this term only to orgasmic
dysfunctions, thus describing difficulties as "situational" which in our terminology are
either partner-related, technique-related, or situational.

6. This is now already true of our patients undergoing couple therapy: although only
about 46 percent of our outpatients (counseling service sample) with sexual dysfunctions were female, in 56 percent of couples treated (therapy sample, see chapter 4) the
woman was dysfunctional, in 33 percent the man, and in 10 percent both partners. A
disproportionate number of women were, therefore, indicated for couple therapy. This
can only be partly explained by the fact that more men than women without partners
registered for counseling (22 percent versus 7 percent). In addition, women are more
easily motivated for couple therapy than are men because they are less reluctant to
accept psychological problems and partner conflicts as causes of their sexual disturbance. Men tend to cling to a somatic explanation; they often have difficulty in facing
up to their own sexual problems for the length of time demanded by therapy. This is
frequently the case with men of little education (nine years of school), who, in contrast
to women with the same education, are underrepresented in the therapy sample as compared to the counseling service sample.

Chapter 2

ETIOLOGY

Gunter Schmidt and Gerd Arentewicz

Organic Causes

There are a great number of organic conditions that can cause, or at least contribute to sexual dysfunctions. Nevertheless, there is agreement in the clinical literature that organic causes play only a subordinate role in the etiology of sexual dysfunctions. In view of their insignificance relative to psychosocial factors, we shall confine ourselves to a few basic remarks on organic causes and refer to the available reviews and surveys (Masters and Johnson 1970; Ellison 1972; Kaplan 1974a; Kolodny 1972; Kolodny et al. 1974; Cole 1975; Eicher 1975; Geboes, Steeno, and DeMoor 1975; Raboch, Mellan, and Kohlicek 1976; Sigusch and Maack 1976; Sigusch 1980a; Wagner and Green 1982; on the side-effects of medication see Story 1974; Sandler and Gessa 1975; Segraves 1977; Kaplan 1979).

The estimates on the percentage of male dysfunction that is fully or partially caused by organic disturbances ranges from 5 percent (Mirowitz 1966; Shusterman 1973; Masters and Johnson 1970 for secondary erectile disturbances) to 26 percent (Geboes, Steeno, and DeMoor 1975). The high rate quoted by Geboes was derived from patients in an andrological clinic and, because of the criteria for screening patients, can scarcely be considered representative of the general population of males with sexual dysfunctions. The causes of erectile disturbances most often cited are genital deformities and traumas, sequels to surgery, inflammatory diseases in the urogenital area (for example, urethritis, prostatitis), blood-supply disorders in the pelvic and genital areas, spinal cord traumas and diseases, gonadal and pituitary dysfunctions, diabetes mellitus, and side-effects of medication (for example, neuroleptics). Sigusch and Maack (1976) believe that ejaculatory dysfunctions are organically caused even less often than are erectile dysfunctions. In premature ejaculation inflammatory processes in the genitourinary area may have an effect. Ejaculatory incompetence may be caused by spinal cord lesions, sequels to surgery on the abdominal area, or the side-effects of medication (for example, neuroleptics and antidepressants).

Information in clinical literature on the organic causes of female arousal and orgasmic dysfunctions is very imprecise. In all probability, organic factors are of still less significance than in erectile disturbances. Those given particular mention are: diseases of the genitourinary area, side-effects of some psycho-active drugs, diabetes mellitus, and endocrinal factors associated with hormonal contraceptives or an adrenalectomy. In addition, physically caused dyspareunic complaints may have such secondary effects as arousal and orgasmic disturbances. Vaginismus is a psychogenic response. In contrast, dyspareunic complaints in women are considered for the most part to be organically caused insofar as the pains are not the result of vaginismus or of insufficient lubrication due to arousal disturbances. The most important causes are: organic peculiarities or changes in the genitals (for example, resistant hymen, scars from a perineal rupture, concrescence of the minor labia); bacterial, trichomonal, or fungal infections of the vagina (colpitis, vaginitis); allergic or hypersensitive reactions to intravaginal contraceptives (foam, suppositories, condoms, diaphragms); hormonally induced atrophy of the vaginal mucous membrane (after menopause or oophorectomy); injury to or deformation of the uterine support ligaments, oviducts, or ovaries; endometriosis; tumors and cysts in the genital tract; diseases of the bladder or intestines (for further details see Masters and Johnson 1970; Eicher 1975).

The following have been mentioned as causes of the rare dyspareunic complaints in men: irritation of the glans owing to smegma, bacterial, trichomonal, or fungal infection; allergic reactions of the glans to the natural pH levels of the vagina or to intravaginal contraceptives; strictures of the penile urethra (for example, following gonorrhea); infections or tumors of the prostate (Masters and Johnson 1970).

Physical factors often have a serious effect on sexual functioning only if they coincide with particular psychological conditions. Lidberg (1970) believes that a phimosis (too narrow a foreskin) increases the chances of erectile disturbance. He found a phimosis in the life histories of 22 percent of his patients with erectile disturbances, compared with 3 to 5 percent of the overall male population. A phimosis does not impair erectile capacity directly but does cause pain during erection, masturbation, and, if surgical action is taken too late, during coitus. This leads to conditioned fears of pain and mobilizes fears of injury to the penis or even castration anxieties. An erectile disturbance resulting from these fears can persist after surgery, when sexual arousal and activity are no longer painful. A further example of the interaction between physical and psychological factors can be seen in diabetes mellitus. The decrease in erectile capacity organically caused by this illness can be such a shock for a man, unleashing hidden potency fears and jeopardizing his male identity, that any chance left of responding sexually is choked by panic (see Renshaw 1975). Finally, fear of sexual failure and the self-reinforcing mechanism in sexual disturbances, which we shall discuss later, can induce an organically caused sexual dysfunction to persist although the organic cause has long been removed. Thus, counseling and psychotherapy can effectively complement medical treatment required for dysfunctions due entirely or partly to physical factors. On the other hand, it is absolutely imperative to check for organic causes and contributory causes before psychotherapeutic treatment.

In the notions patients have about the causes of their sexual disturbances, sex hormones play what can almost be called a magical role. The fact that physicians frequently prescribe hormone medication for dysfunctional patients (Schorsch et al. 1977) demonstrates that they too believe that sex hormones can play a causal role in sexual dysfunction. For a comprehensive review of this topic see Bancroft 1983.

Ovarian hormones, estrogen and progesterone, appear to have little direct effect on sexual functioning. Reduction in the level of these hormones during menopause or following an oophorectomy has only a mild effect on female sexuality. Estrogen deficiency can give rise to anatomical and physiological changes which may secondarily impair female sexual experience (Lauritzen and Müller 1977). In postmenopausal women estrogen deficiency leads to a number of changes: the skin of the vulva loses elasticity and becomes thinner; the vagina shrinks, and the vaginal orifice gapes open due to loss of elasticity; the vaginal epithelium deteriorates and is easily bruised; the capacity to lubricate declines. Accordingly, these women often complain of dryness, soreness, burning, and pains during or after coitus, sometimes even of difficulty with penile insertion. Estrogen therapy induces an improvement of these genital symptoms; it has no direct influence on arousability but removes the disturbing factors. In contrast, androgens, the "male" sex hormones, may influence female arousability directly. In women androgens are secreted by the adrenal cortex. Should the adrenal gland have to be surgically removed, a reduction or loss of arousability and sexual activity often occurs within a few months as it does when the pituitary gland is surgically extracted, unless the adrenal androgens are medicinally substituted.

Existing studies on men which investigate the consequences of castration, the effects of hypogonadism (subnormal functioning of the gonads), of hypogonadotropism (subnormal functioning of the pituitary gland involving the gonad-stimulating hormone), and of treatment with antiandrogens (substances that inhibit the effectiveness of androgens) show that the absence of androgens impedes male sexual response. The capacity to erect, to maintain an erection, and to ejaculate is dependent on androgens. Androgen deficiencies, however, have varying effects from one individual to another. For example, some castrated adult men experience loss of function very rapidly, others only months later; in exceptional cases castrated men have retained potency for years and are able to have regular sexual intercourse with "dry" orgasm. Androgen deficiencies due to castration or to other factors can be compensated for within a short period by substituting artificial androgens.

Sexual dysfunctions can be expected in both sexes if a pathological androgen deficiency arises after a serious illness, but such deficiency is rare. In contrast, variations in hormonal levels have no effect on sexual functioning as long as they remain within the physiological tolerance limits. Sexual functioning is sustained by a specific androgen level and cannot be further enhanced by administering additional hormones. Normal androgen secretion in males exceeds this critical level by a factor of three or four.

Psychosocial Causes

As in other areas of clinical psychology, assumptions about the psychosocial origins of sexual dysfunctions seem to be formulated in total disregard of one another. The following statements on premature ejaculation—the first by a clinical psychologist, the second by a psychoanalyst—illustrate how contradictory these assumptions can be:

Our premature ejaculation clients typically have directly been trained, or have trained themselves, to ejaculate as quickly as possible and with as minimal an amount of stimulation as possible. This may have occurred during adolescent masturbation, when the boy feared being caught by his parents . . . ; or during premarital intercourse, again for fear of being caught or the girl changing her mind. One of our clients taught himself to ejaculate with no direct genital stimulation, during necking sessions, so he could obtain orgasmic release from pain caused by pelvic vasocongestion. Another was "trained" in the context of having intercourse in a car during a snowstorm with his adolescent friends shivering outside, urging him to hurry up. [LoPiccolo and Lobitz 1973, p. 346]

Premature ejaculators are men who are afflicted by strong . . . resistances to specifically male, active performance. . . . [This], however, is a reactive phenomenon . . . [which] has replaced the all too brutal, sadistically violent impulses. [P. 49] In [their] phantasies the penis is sadism's weapon. . . . Premature detumescence and ejaculation eliminates the danger. [P. 50]

The patients feel distinct fear of the female genitals. Psychoanalysis regularly reassures us that the woman's lack of a penis is what originally evoked castration anxiety. Everytime patients physically approach the female they are again gripped by this terror. . . . This anxiety is closely related to a second: that of losing the penis by performing the act of intercourse. [P. 52] The patient is motivated unconsciously to get out of harm's way at the last moment. [P. 53]

The libido of our patients remains for the greater part fixed in the narcissistic phase. Just as the small boy wets his mother with urine he is not yet able to hold back, the neurotic wets a woman by ejaculating prematurely, and in her we recognize with clarity the mother substitute. [P. 55] Ejaculatio praecox thus contains an exhibitionistic tendency. [P. 56] [This] exhibiting . . . [has] an ambivalent character. It is not merely proof of love with the tendency of wanting to be . . . admired, but at the same time a sign that he rejects the woman. . . . Ejaculatio praecox, and particularly ejaculation occurring ante portas, is a defilement of the woman with a substance representing urine. [P. 57] [Abraham 1917, pagination of the 1969 edition]

Both of these statements were made by experts in the field. Although Abraham's essay was first published in 1917, it is still considered an important psychoanalytic contribution (see Becker 1975). LoPiccolo and Lobitz are recognized as proponents of empirical clinical sex research based on learning theory. Similar theoretical discrepancies can be found in hypotheses on the etiology of erectile and orgasmic dysfunctions. In the case of premature ejaculation, however, the discrepancies are particularly remarkable considering that the symptomology is relatively uniform.

In the following section, we present a survey of the multiplicity of etiological hypotheses mentioned in the literature; we examine only those hypotheses that were helpful in our therapeutic work. The etiological causes of sexual dysfunctions can be ordered according to their psychological meaning, that is, the function they serve in the individual's emotional life and in couple dynamics. One can distinguish five kinds of meaning or function of sexual dysfunctions. They may be a defense against sexual anxieties, an expression of nonsexual motives, a manifestation of or expression of partner conflicts, an indication of deficiencies in experience and skills, or, finally, the consequence of anticipation anxieties. In most cases dysfunctions combine all these aspects, although the emphasis varies: they involve multiple determinants. Sexual disturbances arise from a chain of varied experiences at different stages of life. There is no such thing as one single pathogenic experience, no matter how traumatic.

This section, like the description of symptoms, is intended to sharpen therapists' awareness in history-taking and therapy. It is meant to help therapists formulate the questions they should ask about causes, to describe what they should look for, and how to obtain etiological hypotheses on dysfunctions. Nonetheless, we believe that a full understanding of the complex etiology is not possible and not necessary in treatment. We were often bewildered at discovering how little we knew about the deeper causes of a couple's problems after therapy had been progressing positively for thirty or forty sessions, and we concluded that therapy success is often possible without fully understanding the etiology of the dysfunctions. This might well be the reason why couple therapists as a rule discuss etiological problems only superficially. Masters and Johnson (1970) confine their discussion almost exclusively to sexual taboos, derived from religion which play a decidedly subordinate role in our patients' difficulties. The comprehensive *Handbook of Sex Therapy* by LoPiccolo and LoPiccolo (1978) makes practically no mention of etiological problems. This points to an attitude we cannot accept because we believe that couple therapy is appropriate for patients with strongly developed neurotic and partner conflicts (see chapter 7) and that these patients should not be ruled out as rigorously as Anglo-American therapists tend, or tended, to do. In our view, the therapist must gain a basic understanding during history-taking of the causes of the couple's disturbance, deepen this understanding in the course of therapy or adapt it to new information, and, above all, be in a position to develop etiological hypotheses in difficult therapy situations or when therapy stagnates. These hypotheses can then help determine therapeutic intervention for resolving the crisis. This chapter is intended as a pragmatic aid to formulating such hypotheses.

A description of the etiology of specific dysfunctions becomes useless because no specific etiology exists. Dysfunctions are the expression of sexual inhibition, whether they manifest themselves as lack of desire, erectile, ejaculatory, arousal, or orgasmic disturbances or as vaginismus.

DEFENSE AGAINST ANXIETY

Psychoanalysts in particular (for example, Fenichel 1945), but behavior therapists, too, (Lazarus 1963) conceive of sexual dysfunctions as protective mechanisms against irrational anxieties associated with sexuality. Sexual activity, arousal, and orgasm are experienced, usually unconsciously, as dangerous, or a sexual partner is seen as a threat. Fear of these dangers is warded off by "dispensing with functioning" (Freud 1926; 1948 edition, p. 114) and renouncing pleasure. These sexual dysfunctions are "clinical manifestations and bulwarks of defence itself" (Fenichel 1945, p. 170). The symptom has a stabilizing function because it allows a "neurotic equilibrium relatively free of anxiety" to be established (Becker 1975, p. 7). Attempts to remove the symptom threaten this equilibrium, actuate anxieties, and mobilize resistance to such attempts.

The anxieties that are warded off by sexual inhibitions can be divided into anxieties over instinctual demands, attachment anxieties, anxieties over gender identity, and moral anxieties. They originate in the conditions of early childhood socialization. A child can become disposed to later sexual disturbances at any or all stages of his or her development (Moore 1961). We will not be able to describe in detail the numerous ramifications worked out by psychoanalysis but shall only describe anxieties by means of examples and refer to the stages of childhood socialization that represent a particular risk to sexual development. It is important that the therapist recognize anxieties in the form they take in the present. Inference of anxieties from early childhood experiences, as attempted in broad outline below, is usually impossible and unnecessary for couple therapy.

Instinct anxieties. In the confrontation between early sensual needs and the environment, patterns of experience and anxieties develop that are sometimes later expressed in adult sexuality. For example, frustration of a baby's oral needs for immediate satisfaction of hunger, for sucking, skin contact, and warmth may engender a basic feeling of missing out and the fear of always being left unsatisfied and disappointed. In such a case, sexual desires activate fear of "inevitable" disappointments, and sexual disorders protect the person against such "inevitable" frustration. In the anal stage a child has the wish to draw as much pleasure as possible from his or her excretory functions by exercising autonomy in surrendering and withholding the excretions. If this desire collides with the parents' sanitary demands, the balance between the two extremes of "bodily control" and "letting oneself go" swings in favor of control. This can lead to an inhibition of the ability to enjoy sexual pleasure and of orgasmic ability since these forms of experience presuppose "letting oneself be overpowered by involuntary biopsychological changes" (Meyer 1971, p. 989). The fear of losing control over one's body and emotions blocks sexual functioning. Physical needs may be generally associated with dirt and disgust at this stage of development; this is often how *sexual disgust and mysophobias* (fears of dirt) originate. If a child learns to use his or her physical needs aggressively against the environment in the first anal-stage conflicts with authority, or senses that the environment perceives these needs as being hostile, the child may well later experience sexuality as an aggressive act. In this case inhibition of sexual functioning is caused by the fear of violence that fantasy associates with sexuality. In the phallic stage, previously induced fears of activities involving physical pleasure are transferred to genital desires in particular and are reinforced by new confrontations with the environment. The child may again experience physical pleasure as something that plunges him or her into conflicts with the environment, that is a transgression, that is considered undesirable and evil, and that leads to withdrawal of love or immediate punishment. Real or imagined punishments for sexual activity or curiosity invest sexual experience with fear. From a psychoanalytic viewpoint, castration anxieties instilled by early threats or the anticipation of punishment play a major role in the etiology of male dysfunctions.

Attachment anxieties. Early relations to father and mother figures determine whether a person is later able to enter relationships without irrational fear of being abandoned, of self-disintegration, or dependency. In recent years psychoanalysts have emphasized how relevant early pre-oedipal mother-child relationships are to sexual dysfunctions (Benedek, Bychowski, both quoted in Moore 1961; Fleck 1969; Becker 1975). If the early symbiotic relationship with the mother is ineffectively resolved due to, for example, early loss of the mother or the mother's possessive behavior, the desire arises to reestablish the old symbiotic relationship. The ego experiences these strong regressive desires for fusion, which are transferred to the partner, as highly threatening: anxieties of complete absorption, total helplessness, and dependency result. The sexual inhibition allows avoidance of the dangerous temporary ego regression that is a prerequisite for experiencing orgasm.

Other anxieties arise in the later stages of the parent-child relationship. In empirical investigations an explicit fear of partner loss was often observed in men and women with sexual dysfunctions (O'Connor and Stern 1972; Fisher 1973). They came from families in which one parent was actually or "psychologically" absent or had taken a hostile or negative attitude toward the child. Furthermore, they had frequently been separated from their families in childhood by unavoidable hospitalization (Sarrel and Sarrel 1978). For women the paternal relationship has far more significance than the maternal; similar findings for men do not exist (Fisher 1973). If the paternal relationship is traumatic, the ensuing insecurity in affectional relations makes it difficult for a woman or a man to give and take intimacy and closeness, to dare losing a grip on herself/himself in her/his partner's presence. Moreover, every relationship of some intimacy mobilizes the fear of being abandoned again, of repeating the old disappointing experiences. Anticipation of the childhood traumas chokes every kind of sexual response to a partner. Object-loss in childhood has taught such a woman or man not to believe in permanency. Fisher (1973) believes that another reason why a woman with object-loss anxieties experiences sexuality as so great a danger is that restricted consciousness on orgasm causes the partner to "fade away" and thus mobilizes her basic anxieties.

On the other hand, too strong an attachment to the parents, particularly to the contrasexual parent, has time and again been emphasized as a cause of sexual dysfunction (Freud 1905; Bergler 1937, 1944; Moore 1961; Fenichel 1945; Becker 1975). Ineffective resolution of the oedipal situation was considered, at least in early contributions on psychoanalysis, one of the most fundamental causes of sexual dysfunctions. If the son's oedipal mother fixation persists, all his later partners or potential partners will be unconsciously identified with his mother, thus arousing the old fears of incestuous desires; sexual disturbances then result. Furthermore, all real partners seem to be merely second-class, "actual" objects, diminished by comparison with the mother. A similar pattern results from an unresolved father fixation in women.

Anxieties in gender identity. We concur with Money and Ehrhardt (1972, p. 4) that "gender identity is the sameness, unity, and persistence of one's individuality as male or female, or ambivalent in greater or lesser degree." For the most part, sexual identity is established in the first few years of life. An untroubled development of sexual identity in childhood presupposes a number of factors: a same-sex parent (or some other key figure) to whom the child has a close emotional attachment and with whom he or she can identify; a contrasexual parent who accepts the child's gender and enables the child to gather confirmatory experience of gender identity in dealings with the opposite sex; a positive resolution of the early, close attachment to the mother.

To avoid misunderstanding, let it be said that intact gender identity does not imply acceptance of traditional sex-role norms; it is rather a measure of how closely a boy or girl identifies with, respectively, masculinity or femininity. A girl who rejects her traditional sex role may well possess a fully developed gender identity; she merely stands for another type of femininity.

The relevance of gender identity to sexual disturbances has been discussed by psychoanalysis in terms of "penis envy" and "castration anxiety." We find the concept of gender identity a more useful term for three reasons. First, penis envy and castration anxiety may be an expression of disturbed gender identity but are not causes of this disturbance. Second, disturbed gender identity is not necessarily or essentially manifested in dissatisfaction with or fear for one's own genitals. Third, the concept of penis envy reduces socially determined inequality of the sexes to biological differences and refuses to recognize that the subjective feeling of genital inferiority sometimes engendered in women is the consequence of such inequality.

Men and women with unstable gender identity are also insecure in their sexuality. They are deeply afraid of not being a real man or woman, and feel they are not very lovable or desirable, are sexually incompetent, and will be sexual failures. A man reacts by avoiding tenderness, devotion, and surrender, which he considers signs of weakness, passivity, and femininity; or he overcompensates for his shaken male identity with genital-centered, explosive sexuality (premature ejaculation) or with an untiring potency (ejaculatory incompetence). If this insecurity is combined with fear for genital integrity, the man is then unconsciously afraid of injuring himself during coitus or vigorous masturbation. A woman may feel her sexual organ is a wound, a revoltingly damp hollow, and try to eliminate genitals from her body image; she would thus find it difficult to experience arousal and orgasm. The relevance of gender identity to sexual experience is obvious from the frequency of secondary dysfunctions at times when gender identity is threatened or shaken, for example in old age, after a debilitating illness, when physical attractiveness fades, or after setbacks in a career.

Insecure gender identity should be distinguished from rejection of or an ambivalent attitude toward one's own sex, which is more frequent in women than in men, because of the existing sociocultural definition of sex roles. Such women compete with men and feel their own gender assigns them a socially disadvantaged position. They often feel their genitals are the target of male aggression and the place of their own subjugation, and thus they regard their genitals with ambivalence. Coitus and orgasm are interpreted as positive recognition of male dominance and so are to be denied. This deep-rooted and often unconscious rivalry ensuing from a rejection of gender identity must be distinguished from protests directed overtly against claims to dominance and from the refusal to engage in sexuality when fighting these claims.

Moral anxieties. Many conditions combine to subject sexual development to a clandestine, subversive environment of taboos. Some of these are: punishment a child experiences in conjunction with early instinctual needs; the "conspiracy of silence" pervading sexuality (Meyer 1971, p. 990); repudiation of a child's sexual interests; and the impression parents give of being without needs for sexuality and tenderness. A child then starts to think about sexuality in archaic terms of propriety, of good or evil. These ideas are then likely to be reinforced by socialization in prepuberty, puberty, and adolescence. All schools of thought pursuing the study of sexual dysfunctions have emphasized the etiological significance of sexual taboos in the inhibition of sexual development. Freud's most detailed discussion of sexual dysfunctions (1908) is not concerned with the psychodynamic aspects but with the sociological determinants of sexual socialization. He explains how sexually disturbed women are literally bred by education, by the high rewards for innocence. The detrimental effects of taboos have been emphasized repeatedly ever since. Fenichel (1945) also identifies an upbringing that associates sexuality with danger as the most common cause of female dysfunctions. The simplistic concept of religious orthodoxy in Masters and Johnson (1970) is the most important aspect of their etiological ideas. However, nowadays the taboos of childhood are not brought to bear on adolescence with the same continuity as they were a decade ago (Schoof-Tams, Schlaegel, and Walczak 1976); "childhood morality" is often superseded in adolescence by liberal concepts. In Becker's view (1975) this can lead to a collision between the sexually negating superego of the child and the sexually affirmative ego ideal, a collision that mobilizes fears against which sexual disturbances act as a defense.

Warded-off anxieties and sexual symptoms. Initial indication that anxieties have been warded-off by sexual dysfunctions can be deduced from a patient's sexual behavior and particular symptoms: from sexual fantasies, favored forms of sexual activity, and particularly from the specific situation in which the sexual disturbance arises.

Sexual fantasies express a patient's sexual conflicts, his or her wishes and fears, and how the patient deals with them. A woman suffering from vaginismus, who imagined while masturbating that she was being raped, expressed in fantasies her fear of being sexually overwhelmed, of sexual violence. Her arousal and orgasm were facilitated by these fantasies with which she took the fear into her own hands; by forming her own picture of what she feared she had it in her control. She could dismiss the fantasies the moment they became too great a threat and could always reassure herself that the feared incident was not real (see Stoller 1975). Another woman, who could never reach orgasm with her partner but who had orgasms through masturbation, imagined she was surprised masturbating by men who "shouldn't know that I do," men who were usually father figures, for example, an uncle or an old teacher. Her feelings at this point in the fantasy were of profound humiliation and, simultaneously, extreme stimulation. As in the previous example, she took control of the fear-producing situation, in this case the fear of being detested for her passionate nature and her wantonness; her management of this fear enabled her to experience orgasm. A man who had never been able to have intercourse with his wife owing to a primary erectile dysfunction, expressed his fear of women in fantasies during successful masturbation: he would show tenderness to chained women who found him irresistible after initial rejection; he would be in a dark, locked room with a woman and would try to "catch" her and put a chain around her neck. He did not fantasy any other acts of violence with these women, but they always approached him in a submissive posture before he had intercourse with them. The theme throughout these fantasies, which disappeared once the erectile dysfunction had been remedied, is easily recognized: the women are at his mercy, they cannot injure him, they are harmless.

An analysis of favored sexual techniques is similarly informative. For example, some women's preference for thigh pressure in masturbation may show that they are able to accept sexuality only as an outlet for tension but not as enjoyment of pleasure. It is probably a sign of anxiety for the vulnerability and integrity of their genitals when some men adopt overly cautious masturbatory techniques. A strong emphasis on coitus and orgasm together with an avoidance of tender foreplay and caressing may signal the attempt to circumvent the almost unbearable intimacy and closeness by escaping to the high stages of arousal. The sexual clumsiness and lack of understanding of some men may be motivated by the fear of a sexually responsive and "potent" woman.

Situational dysfunctions offer further important examples. One patient, who had no erectile problems during petting but whose erection vanished in coital attempts, imagined that the vagina was as murky and threatening as "a coal pit where the penis has to slave away in damp and stifling surroundings and can only 'take a breath' once it's out." Sexual involvement with a woman was a cramping, castrating, and decimating experience. Another patient, who had erectile problems with his wife and in all his previous steady relationships, felt sexually attracted to what he described as "socially inferior, easy girls, who take me down a few pegs on the social ladder." He had no erectile problems with these women; his fears of intimacy allowed him to make sexual contact only when all other aspects of a relationship were precluded.

Defense against anxieties is most clearly evident in partner-related dysfunctions. For example, a woman with a strict and sexually hostile superego was indifferent to sex with undominating men of the same age but was orgasmic and passionate with partners who were older, dominating, and paternalistic. These men invalidated her parental prohibitions and relieved her of the responsibility for sexuality and thus her fear of it. On the other hand, a woman who was afraid of being subjugated and oppressed by men could react only with aggression and hostility to paternalistic and dominating men. She could develop her sexual responsiveness only with a gentle, submissive, and uncompetitive man who could put up with a woman who took the initiative and had "phallic" intercourse with him. In the company of a sexually active, "potent" woman, a man with an insecure gender identity developed an erectile disturbance or premature ejaculation for fear of his unmanliness. He could respond without sexual inhibition only to sexually reserved women who made him feel he was the more potent of the two. Stekel (1921, p. 84) believes that "the ultimate orgasm ... is only triggered if the individual achieves his secret sexual purpose." These examples show that the strength of erotic attraction that one person exercises on another is decisively determined by the degree to which he or she makes it possible to overcome the partner's secret sexual fears.

RELEASE OF REPRESSED IMPULSES

According to psychoanalytic theory sexual dysfunctions, like neurotic symptoms, may on occasion provide disguised release for certain instinctual demands, for example, masochistic or aggressive impulses (Fenichel 1945). For example, premature ejaculation can be partially induced by pleasure in defiling a woman or the aggressive gratification had in disappointing her (Abraham 1917; Salzman 1954). Ejaculatory incompetence may be caused by the anal pleasure of retention (Bergler 1937). Vaginismus may be an expression of the aggressive wish to turn the penis into a ridiculously ineffective organ (Fenichel 1945). This instinctual aspect of sexual dysfunctions is, however, mainly secondary and is far less significant than the defense aspect discussed earlier.

PARTNER PROBLEMS

A couple's relationship and their feelings for each other determine how frequently and intensely sexuality is desired and how it is experienced—as symbiotic union or isolation, loving or aggressive, passionate or cold-hearted, with or against each other, and so forth. Consequently, sexual dysfunctions are a manifestation of and vehicle for partner conflicts. The banality of this interaction probably explains why the causal relevance of partner dynamics has so seldom been analyzed in detail. Many authors merely mention in passing that anything from a lack of attraction to physical disgust, from implied rejection of a partner to open contempt, from differences of opinion to profound disappointment and mistrust—in short, the disappearance of affection and mutuality—impedes sexual responsiveness and experience. If such severe conflicts lead to sexual problems, one can refer to them, as Kaplan does (1974a), as "adequate" sexual disturbances.

In this section we shall illustrate a few of the processes in partner dynamics that can stabilize or cause sexual disturbances. We are not interested in establishing a typology of partner conflicts that impair sexuality. Rather, our inquiry is directed at the meaning and function of a sexual disturbance within a relationship. We shall discuss four mechanisms a therapist needs to recognize in order to establish the connections between a relationship and a sexual disturbance—that is, mechanisms that are of diagnostic and therapeutic relevance: delegation, arrangement, symptom use against partner, and ambivalence management.

Delegation. The "functional" partner may have an interest in his or her partner's dysfunction. It could be that the functional partner needs the disturbance to mask his or her own problems. For example, a woman whose husband has erectile problems may find a plausible explanation and an alibi for her own orgasmic problems; she hands over her disturbance, as it were, to her husband and spares herself the disquieting insight into her own sexual fears. We have found that hidden female problems are particularly common in couples who sought treatment for the man's premature ejaculation. A man whose partner is sexually reticent and inhibited may find comfort in the fact that she will never make demands he "cannot" fulfill; her sexual problem serves to soothe his potency fears.

A man or woman might also find pleasure in his or her dysfunctional partner's weakness, feel superior, and then act out hostility and revenge by treating the partner with condescension and contempt. There is nothing to stop her "unmasking" this "sissy" as often as she likes; he can slander his anorgastic wife as being "frigid", inhibited, and unfeminine. One partner sometimes finds the other's problem reassuring because the problem is the occasion for tolerant understanding that seems to stabilize the relationship.

The following case history illustrates a woman's investment in her husband's symptoms: symptoms help her deny her own problems; she wards off fears of attachment and uses the symptoms as a tool of aggression against him. The example also demonstrates that delegation is just one link in the chain of causes and that the symptomatic partner is particularly susceptible to sexual problems.

COUPLE 13:   The man, a carpenter, is in his late twenties and suffers from premature ejaculation and erectile dysfunctions. His wife, a secretary, is eight years older than he and has been married twice before. She herself has no sexual problems, but she is "fed up" with his difficulties and, because of them, feels no desire for him. The couple got to know each other four years ago and married a few months later. Previous experience has made both of them vulnerable in relationships. She is an illegitimate child and grew up with her mother and stepfather. Her mother was continually ill and suffered under her brutal stepfather, who repeatedly had affairs with other women. Her mother divorced this man when she was fourteen. She had never felt real affection for her stepfather and accepted the divorce with indifference. She met her first boyfriend at seventeen, and she says she left him when he insisted on sexual intercourse. She met her first husband when she was eighteen. She was prepared to have coitus then because she wanted a child and she wanted to get away from home. The couple divorced a year later. She married a second time, again for no longer than a year. She says she had no sexual problems in these relationships.

The husband also had a difficult family life: he was fourteen when his father died. He had never gotten along with his father. He describes his mother as a hard and unfeeling woman who could never show affection. Before marrying he had had sexual intercourse with ten to fifteen women. All these relationships were short-lived; he slept several times with each woman but never developed a lasting friendship with any of them. He tended to ejaculate prematurely but hardly ever had erectile problems.

The present sexual difficulties arose a few months after the husband and wife met, just after the marriage. The wife aggressively places the responsibility for the problems on his head alone; she says it is his fault that she is sexually dissatisfied and no longer feels she is a woman. She abruptly rejects any attempt to discuss her part in the matter. She derides and insults him for being a failure and even comments on his attempts at sexual approach by remarking how "stupid he acts." If they fail to "get it off," she calls him a "weakling" or a "dumb pansy." He complains that she always "wants to get down to it" immediately and refuses manual or oral stimulation (although she did not do so in earlier relationships); he reacts with dismay and retreats. At therapy onset she refuses to be drawn into caressing exercises and remarks: "I need a man, none of this rubbish." She later rejects caresses because she is disgusted by him touching her. She keeps on doing all she can to stick to her "fault-finding" version. After a few sessions the couple no longer appears for therapy.

The way in which sexual disturbances are induced or reinforced by one partner in another can be seen as a reversal of the procedures employed in treating sexual dysfunctions: exerting performance pressure; maintaining a cool distance or even demonstrating hostility to intercourse or coital attempts; receiving stimulation with a bored, reluctant attitude; initiating sexual approaches when the partner is unwilling; deliberately rebuffing specific sexual wishes, for example, intense manual stimulation. This sabotaging of sexuality usually occurs involuntarily (Kaplan 1974a). Resistance to therapeutic reversal of symptoms, including dropping out of therapy or the wish to separate, more often stems from the "functional" partner in these cases. Masters and Johnson (1970) describe the case of a woman whose only motivation for therapy was her wish that the therapists convince her "impotent" husband that there was no hope of improvement; she wanted to prove the problem was incurable and so destroy his masculinity. Therapy can succeed only if the functional partner relinquishes his or her investment in the other's dysfunction and can be made to accept the other's functioning fully. If the sexual symptom is removed without the functional partner's acceptance, then that partner, as yet seemingly untroubled, can develop symptoms. We have often observed such a shift of symptom; in particularly severe cases the functional partner's psychological equilibrium, which was previously balanced by the patient's dysfunction, may break down. Kaplan and Kohl (1972) described these undesirable effects of therapy as "adverse reactions": in one case, immediately after successful resolution of a premature ejaculation problem that had lasted for twenty years, the woman became depressive and reacted with a suicide attempt; she was admitted to inpatient treatment, where she developed paranoid and obsessive ideas that were soon remedied by psychiatric treatment. In successfully treating an erectile disturbance we once observed how a woman reverted to a claustrophobia she had suffered from years before. It is, however, extremely rare (Kaplan and Kohl 1972) for the previously functional partner to react in such a seriously adverse manner. We will return later to a more detailed discussion of the undesired side-effects of couple therapy (see chapter 7).

Arrangement. A sexual dysfunction can take the form of tacit, unconscious arrangement between the partners that benefits them and their relationship. It has been repeatedly observed that the husbands of women who suffer from vaginismus are often especially peaceable and gentle, passive, sensitive, shy, and sometimes excessively considerate (Mayer 1932; Mears 1958; Ellison 1968, 1972; Friedman 1962). Moreover, they are often as sexually inexperienced as their wives, act as if they have few sexual impulses, and are sexually unaggressive. Women with vaginismus and their husbands often choose each other unconsciously because the choice enables them to ward off their sexual fears, particularly their fears of the aggressive aspects of sexuality. By relieving each other of sexual anxiety, both partners feel they have placed their problems in good hands; a long-term status quo is thus often formed that stabilizes the partnership and is frequently the basis for a harmonious relationship lasting for years. In some cases it is impossible to say whether vaginismus, erectile problems, or both are the reason why coitus is not performed. Avoidance of sexual intercourse becomes a downright conspiracy: at the beginning, coital attempts are delayed as long as possible by moral rationalizations; the partners then soon abstain after the first failures. Treatment is not attempted, or only half-heartedly, or is broken off after set-backs. Therapy is often given serious consideration only years later when, for example, the wish to have children can no longer be ignored. Such tacit arrangements can be motivated by other reasons than the joint defense against sexual anxiety. Arentewicz, Schorsch, and Schorsch (1976) have pointed out how sexual disturbance can be used to cover up other deep-rooted partner conflicts. These conflicts sometimes assume such proportions as to incur massive fears of separation and dissolution of the relationship. By focussing their energies on sexual disharmony, the real conflict is covered up, and the anxiety it evokes is warded off by the incantation, "if sex worked, we wouldn't have any problems and would have a happy marriage."

Symptom use against partner. In some cases the sexual dysfunction is used against the partner to express underlying hostility or to act out power conflicts. Men and women tend to use sexuality differently in the expression of hostility: a man expresses his hatred and claims to power through potency, that is, by making sexual demands stripped of all tenderness; the primary aim is assertion and subjugation. A woman, on the other hand, uses sexual disturbances to express hatred, to exercise power, or just to withstand claims to power. She is left with two possibilities: either she induces and consolidates a dysfunction in the man—as described in the section on delegation—or she herself reacts with a disturbance.

Because power is unevenly distributed between the sexes, becoming sexually dysfunctional is frequently one of the few ways a woman can stand up to her male partner. Either male claims to dominance choke her ability to develop sexually or she revolts, "rises" against these claims armed with a disturbance. Full sexual functioning would augment her feelings of weakness and would amount to renouncing the last vestiges of autonomy. The woman's reticence provokes the man's desire for sexuality, affection, and assertion. More and more, he slips into a sexually offensive role, makes demands, takes the initiative, uses pressure and sometimes violence. The woman's reactions are increasingly defensive; she resorts to refusal and escape. The power struggle slowly swallows up sexuality. The situation ends with an all-out offensive and defensive that mutually reinforce and propel each other. The consequences are female "loss of libido" and disgust, male anger and helplessness. The appeal made to women by certain feminist factions to refuse sex is merely the demand to make conscious what many women have silently accomplished long ago without quite knowing why.

COUPLE 14: The couple has been married for fifteen years. Both are in their early forties, and they have two children. He is a post office employee, she is a housewife. The wife has not felt the slightest desire for sexual intercourse for years because she finds it painful rather than arousing; she has allowed a minimum of sexual activity "for his sake." She describes how unloving her parents were; her relationship with her father was always estranged. Her memories of early sexual experience are coupled with negative feelings. At seven she was caught playing doctor with a young boy and was punished for it. Because her family lived in cramped conditions, she often knew when her parents were having intercourse and responded with a mixture of fear and shame; her mother never made a secret of her opinion that sexuality was a tiresome burden. Although the patient masturbated between the ages of fourteen and twenty without feeling any conflicts, mainly to calm her fears and general inner uneasiness, she abruptly gave it up at twenty-one after a physician told her that this was the cause of her depressive states. She was shy with boys and avoided all contact. She found her husband in the personal columns and married with little enthusiasm: she says she has never really liked her husband, but she felt he was a suitable mate and that she could at last get away from home.

The husband is small in height and slimmer than she; one has the impression that he constantly rationalizes his problems, thus ignoring the difficulties. He is absolutely incapable of listening, talks in "capital letters," and emphasizes every little detail. He wishes to make the impression of a successful, strong-willed, and loved man who is not involved in conflicts he cannot himself handle. He describes his history in terms that would support such an impression: life at home was "superb," he was successful at school, became an apprentice mechanic and then a civil servant. That this façade conceals a high degree of insecurity is demonstrated by a previous suicide attempt, which was followed by a short stay in a psychiatric clinic. In puberty he took little notice of women because he was more interested in his accomplishments. He says that he was always successful with women, if he so wished, and has "had" too many rather than too few. In contrast, one notices that he got to know his wife through a newspaper advertisement his father had placed for him. He stresses, too, that he felt no particular liking for his wife when they met.

It is striking that he never lets his wife finish a sentence or, when possible, never lets her speak. He is, so to speak, continuously on the prowl, controlling her behavior and taking charge where necessary. In this way he overcompensates his own insecurity; by speaking for her he avoids having to listen to her criticism or her offensive remarks. She complains that their entire life together is characterized by this patronizing and intervening attitude; it pervades discussion about the children's education, household work, and joint activities. She feels quite defenseless because any attempt she makes to get her own way is throttled by his interminable, compulsive monologues, which she can only stop by keeping quiet. Her reaction is one of profound resignation mixed with anger. Sexuality is the only area in which he does not have the say.

In contrast to this case history, sexual problems can be used against the partner with explicit offensiveness and aggression: "the joys of triumph" (Stekel 1921, p. 239) are then the bonus for dispensing with sexuality: for sexual dysfunctions can be a withholding of pleasure, an expression of not loving or not wanting to be loved, a denial of the partner's sexual self-esteem, or a blow to his or her gender identity. The dysfunction becomes a tool of aggression: "It is used as an active instrument to push, force and coerce, although the users often appear to be passive individuals" (Salzman 1954, pagination of the 1963 reprint, p. 318).

Ambivalence management. Every relationship mobilizes a person's conflicts from earlier relationships (see Willi 1975). How much closeness can a person take without feeling afraid of being too vulnerable, of being less and less himself or herself, of being swallowed up? How great a distance can a person endure without feeling abandoned and lonely or threatened by separation? How weak can he allow himself to be without having to fear being destroyed, powerless, and unprotected? How much power can he exert without undermining the other's equal standing? How much dependence can a person allow himself or herself without losing autonomy, feeling helpless, tied down, and trapped? How much autonomy can be permitted while still maintaining the intimacy of a couple attached to each other? In all these relationship conflicts sexuality plays an important regulative role in reconciling conflicting demands. We will illustrate this function of sexuality by describing how the closeness-distance problem affects the genesis of sexual dysfunctions.

First of all, sexuality can evoke closeness and appease the threat felt when drifting apart. It is an everyday occurrence that a couple makes love after a heated argument, thereby reassuring themselves that the rift can be bridged and that they wanted it bridged. On occasion sudden changes in the closeness-distance equilibrium may even relieve chronic sexual dysfunctions, at least temporarily (see couple 15). When sexuality assumes the function of restoring disrupted closeness, it is often an extremely intense experience.

Of more interest to this discussion is the reverse process, when sexual dysfunction and lack of desire act as a distancing, an escape from threatening closeness. Men and women who are strongly ambivalent about closeness—those who have a deep desire for closeness but whose desire is at the same time cathected with anxiety—are particularly susceptible to sexual problems. We have already indicated the conditions from which such ambivalence may originate (p. 41). Of course, different partners mobilize fear of closeness to varying degrees. One partner may feel the other clings too much, thus overstepping that partner's limits, even if he or she has a high level of tolerance for closeness. Willi (1975) has shown that closeness-distance conflicts are often handled "collusively" by partners: the ambivalence each partner carries in himself or herself is acted out by distributing roles, so to speak: one partner takes up a distance and the other closes in. This kind of collusion prevents the partners from seeing their mutual involvement.

There are many situations that affect the closeness-distance equilibrium and in which sexual dysfunctions originate or become evident: after the partners have moved in together; after marrying or deciding to marry; after a woman has given birth and then feels even more bound to the male partner and dependent on him; or when a woman retires from professional life to devote herself to the family household, confines her social and emotional contacts to home life, and is left the sole option of withdrawing sexually. The following case illustrates the significance of closeness-distance ambivalence in sexual disturbances.

COUPLE 15: Both partners are in their late twenties; he is a self-employed businessman, and she is a trained secretary who is now a housewife. They have been married for seven years and have two daughters. When the relationship began she had no sexual problems: she liked sleeping with him and occasionally reached orgasm; she found nonorgasmic intercourse satisfying, too. After half a year together she became pregnant, and they married. During the pregnancy sexual relations worsened. Since then she has been averse to sexual intercourse; everything in her struggles against it. She prefers to get over with intercourse as quickly as possible "like brushing my teeth." She says she sometimes wants to cry afterwards, and she feels she has been used as an object. In one extramarital relationship, she found sexuality satisfying. She reacted to the two births with psychosomatic problems. After the first child she lost a lot of weight, and after the second she was tormented by obsessive ideas that she would somehow harm her children. During this period she also had psychogenic heart attacks, which sometimes required medical treatment; she still has unpleasant physical sensations: she feels a lump in her throat, has tremors, jittery feelings in her stomach.

Her husband had sexual relations with three women before the marriage but could never ejaculate. This disturbance rapidly disappeared in the beginning of the relationship with his wife-to-be. At the time he frequently tried to make love with her to prove to himself "that it can work."

The couple sees therapy as the final attempt to save the marriage, but they refuse to cooperate with the therapists. Instead, the acute partner conflicts, the arguments, and unproductive accusations are aggravated right from the start of therapy. After just a few sessions, they take separate vacations. The husband then meets another woman, comes home, and tells his wife he has decided to leave her. Although she had often wished for separation, she reacts despairingly and tries to make him change his mind. For the first time in years she feels a strong sexual desire for her husband; they make love nearly every night for about two weeks, and she is almost always active and reaches orgasm. These are the most sexually active and uncomplicated moments in their relationship. But she cannot convince him to stay, and when they finally separate, she continues to despair.

In the follow-up three months later, it seems she has come to terms with the separation more effectively than he. She plans to live with the lover she had an affair with during the marriage. Her husband then tries to change her mind, but she is as adamant as he was then. She appears to be confident and content with the decision to separate. He is despondent and full of dismal accusations about the unreliability of women.

LEARNING DEFICITS

In their empirical investigation, Pocs and Godow (1976) found that students of both sexes underrate the frequency of parental coitus by more than half. Children do not see their parents as sexual beings, and parents give their children the impression of being less sexual than they really are. Many people can only abstractly imagine their parents having a sex life. Fathers tend to be thought of as having more sexual interests than mothers, who are felt to be victims of male desire—a perception that often corresponds with reality. Since important model figures appear to be removed from sexuality, sexuality is assigned a distinctly special status. Children learn very early on that a "normal" adult pursues a career, gets married, brings up children, has hobbies, and so on. Erotic and sexual relations are veiled from sight, and sexual experience remains completely void of expectations, behavioral patterns, or "scripts" (Gagnon and Simon 1973). In the educative process, the social context built up around sexuality is either vague and negative or simply nonexistent; the former leads to anxiety and guilt feelings and the latter to uncertainty and confusion. The first sexual experiences in puberty and adolescence become risky enterprises; they frequently lead to initial failures that are all too often consolidated by a self-reinforcement mechanism and so cause permanent sexual dysfunctions.

In the opinion of Gagnon and Simon (1973) and Gagnon (1974), denial of learning opportunities has particularly decisive influence on the sexual socialization of girls. This is evident in the different meaning that masturbation has for boys and girls. Even now, of all the forms of sexual behavior masturbation shows the greatest intersexual differences (Sigusch and Schmidt 1973): far fewer women than men masturbate in youth or adolescence, and they do so far less frequently. About half of the women who masturbate at all start doing so only after their first experiences with a partner, whereas men almost always have their first orgasm by masturbating. Although these differences between the sexes nowadays are far less marked than they were ten or twenty years ago, they are still quite distinct.

The causes of these differences are plain to see: masturbation, more than any other sexual activity requires a person to take the initiative, to be active, to experience sexuality outside the context of a love relationship, and not to wait for a partner to "awaken" sexuality. Consequently, girls find it much more difficult to accommodate masturbation in their acquired image of "female sexuality" than boys in their image of "male sexuality." Denying girls the opportunity to learn from masturbation has a decisive influence on their sexual development. By masturbating men gain a competence over their sexual functions and develop a familiarity with their physical and sexual reactions which girls seldom have at the beginning of sexual relations. Because of women's inhibitions in discovering specific areas of their bodies, they experience their genital regions as a "blank space," even as something uncanny which they dislike looking at, touching, or being touched. On the first experience of petting or coitus men have, as a rule, already had an orgasm several times by masturbating; women have to learn this ability gradually—only a few have had an orgasm by masturbating before their first sexual relations with a partner.

Furthermore, by masturbating, men become aware of sexuality as something one can also experience autonomously for one's own satisfaction. This is far more difficult for women, who usually first encounter sexuality in a relationship with a man. This is also the reason why a woman tends to concentrate more on her partner's sexual needs and wishes than on her own; she is led to "collaborate without participating" (Shainess 1968, p. 70), to comprehend sexuality as something she does mainly to please a man but not herself. She may thus easily come to experience sexuality as a foreign or even hostile activity of which she is the target. In contrast to men, women fail to become acquainted with sexuality as an activity one can at least occasionally detach from an emotional and social context. In their sexuality they are far more dependent on the feeling of closeness and intimacy than is a man and react far more sensitively to acute and chronic partner conflicts. In boys masturbation activity plays an important role in sexual socialization and defining the limits of their sexual experience. The standard masturbatory practice of young men is centered on the genitals and organs but rarely involves a sensuous approach to the entire body. In their fantasies the genital images overpower the affectionate. They thus develop a sexuality that aims at release of tension, is focused on orgasm and genital stimulation rather than tenderness, and thus paves the way for conflicts with a future partner.

The absence of learning opportunities in childhood and adolescence is of particular significance in view of contemporary sexual liberalization. The new liberal, but not always sexually positive, norms that boys and girls adopt stand in contradiction to this learning deficit. Women and men are pressured to adapt to this new norm which propagates sexual competence the moment sexual relations begin. We observe more and more frequently that women are immediately coerced into having orgasms, by their partners or their own expectations, when beginning coital relations, and this delays the indispensable learning process between the two partners or even chokes it. In Deutsch's opinion (1965), sexual ambition leads to "expectations of great performances. . . . The watchfulness and fearful observation and desperate expectation of . . . orgasm take the place of orgastic oblivion" (p. 362).

THE SELF-REINFORCEMENT MECHANISM

Ever since sexual dysfunctions were first investigated and treated, it has repeatedly been recognized how efficiently anticipation and failure anxieties generate and sustain sexual dysfunctions. Stekel (1920), for example, sees a fear of failure underlying many dysfunctions, the "fear of fear, the autosuggestiveness of fear" (p. 267). According to Benedek (1974), anorgastic women watch their reactions during intercourse with "anxious impatience; interfere with what they are seemingly eager to achieve" (p. 580). Frankl (1975) sees the demanding character that coitus has for patients with sexual problems as an important cause of the disturbance, for "pleasure is one of the things that will always be an effect and cannot be achieved voluntarily" (p. 119). In the opinion of Watzlawick, Weakland, and Fisch (1974), erectile and orgasmic disturbances are one of the "be-spontaneous paradoxes." However, the real credit for having systematically elaborated this mechanism, up to then only mentioned in passing, goes to Masters and Johnson (1970), who impressively described several case histories, and drew the essential therapeutic conclusions and so improved the chances of treatment for patients with sexual dysfunctions to an unprecedented degree.

The line of thought is quite simple: the first, perhaps coincidental occurrence of dysfunction leads to performance demands and fear of failure, which then impedes full functioning, which in turn augments fears and demands. This self-reinforcement mechanism, or "self-maintaining vicious cycle" (Lobitz et al. 1974), in sexual dysfunctions is combined with and accelerated by anxious self-monitoring ("spectator role"), feelings of inferiority, and possibly by the partner's increasingly demanding and hostile attitude. Every time sexual activity is avoided and desire is suppressed, the situation generating anxiety and the anticipation of failure are circumvented and accordingly reinforced.

This self-reinforcement mechanism plays an important role in the etiology of all sexual dysfunctions. No matter what the deeper causes of a sexual disturbance might be (early childhood conflicts and anxieties, partner conflicts, learning deficits), they are all consolidated by the self-reinforcement mechanism. It allows the dysfunction to dissociate itself completely from the original causes and to function autonomously. As Masters and Johnson have demonstrated (1970), the resolution of the self-reinforcement mechanism thus forms a central aim in therapy for sexual dysfunction.

How rapidly this mechanism establishes itself in men and women or how traumatic the effect of occasional sexual failure is depends, of course, on factors we have discussed in the various sections of this chapter. For example, a man in an overwrought and inebriated state who fails for the first time to have an erection can accept it as an explicable, "normal" event. But he could, perhaps because he always secretly had potency fears, also react with despair and the fear that he is now once and for all afflicted by impotence as if by an illness. In his case the self-reinforcement mechanism takes immediate effect and confirms his worst suspicions. The partner's reactions will influence this reinforcing tendency, too. A man who sees a woman's orgasm as essential confirmation of his own sexual identity will respond to his partner's orgasmic difficulties with panic, and, in so doing, probably drive her into a chronic dysfunction. In this sense, a woman's sexual dysfunctions are often a reflection of a man's potency fears, and vice versa.

Chapter 3

PSYCHOTHERAPY

Gerd Arentewicz and Gunter Schmidt

In the few cases when somatic factors play a part in sexual dysfunctions, (see p. 34), it is necessary to treat the basic illness. However, as a rule psychotherapy or counseling are the forms of treatment indicated. Senseless and ineffective attempts to treat unequivocally psychogenic dysfunctions are still a common occurrence in day-to-day medical practise: physicians administer sex hormones as well as so-called aphrodisiacs and psychoactive drugs. Contemporary technological developments increasingly result in radical and mutilating surgical intervention: surgical implantation of penile prostheses (see Rieber 1979); surgical relocation of the clitoris closer to the vaginal orifice so as to facilitate direct stimulation of the clitoris during sexual intercourse (Burt 1977); vaginal incision or vaginal dilation under narcosis in cases of vaginismus (although this is now more rare in contrast to the surgical interventions mentioned above). We are not merely referring to isolated medical blunders: Rieber states that in 1976, for example, 373 cases of penile prostheses implantation were reported; Burt reports 100 cases of clitoral displacement operations. Such operations should be classified as careless and irresponsible. One can except only the extremely rare cases of penile implantation in patients with somatically caused and otherwise irreversible erectile dysfunctions where preparatory and postoperative couple counseling is ensured. For the remainder, we do not believe they serve any meaningful purpose.

Of course, not all sexual dysfunctions are severe enough to require psychotherapy. A good many problems can be alleviated or resolved by counseling with one or both partners in a few sessions. This is often the case with initial dysfunctions, with acute disturbances following traumatic failure, or with problems that can be attributed to unrealistic attitudes or informational deficits (for example, when orgasm is triggered both by coitus and manual stimulation and the woman considers this insufficient or abnormal). A general theory of sexual counseling does not now exist, let alone scientifically developed or proved methods. We thus consider it sufficient to state that the techniques applied are basically the same as those in psychotherapy for sexual dysfunctions and that these techniques take the form of extremely short-term, concentrated psychotherapeutic intervention.

Before proceeding we would like to make one final remark. There is no such thing as "sex therapy," that is, a special kind of psychotherapy applicable only to sexual dysfunctions (see Sigusch 1980). In psychotherapeutic treatment of sexual dysfunctions, the general principles of psychotherapy are applied and specifically adapted to each symptom. The remaining chapters in this book are concerned with couple therapy for sexually dysfunctional partners. In this chapter we shall discuss the precursors of our concept of couple therapy and its special features.

Masters and Johnson: Their Program and Its Modifications

The most significant contribution to a symptom-centered treatment of sexual dysfunctions is that of Masters and Johnson (1970). Between 1959 and 1969 they treated 510 couples in a therapy program for male and female sexual dysfunctions; in 1970 they published the results of their long-term research and treatment program.

Masters and Johnson did not develop their concept from theoretical principles of psychology. Rather, their therapy pragmatically combines procedures that had until then been employed either separately or unsystematically. Furthermore, their approach is based on physiological studies on human sexual response (Masters and Johnson 1966). The couple therapy proposed by Masters and Johnson, and its numerous variations, is the most widespread and probably the most promising form of psychotherapy presently available for sexual dysfunctions (O'Connor 1976). All more recent approaches take the concept of Masters and Johnson as their premise and have developed it further without producing any fundamental innovations (see in particular Lobitz and LoPiccolo 1972; LoPiccolo and Lobitz 1972; Kaplan 1974a; Caird and Wincze 1977).

Masters and Johnson's concept is built on the framework of the couple, the team, and intensive therapy. When possible, that is, if partners wish to continue their relationship and the nondysfunctional partner is willing to cooperate, Masters and Johnson treat the couple as a unit: "there is no such thing as an uninvolved partner in any marriage in which there is some form of sexual inadequacy" (Masters and Johnson 1970, p. 2). Because sexual problems arise between two people, the solution depends on both partners changing and thus contributing to an improvement in their relationship. Treatment is conducted with a dual-sex therapist team so that both partners will have "a friend in court as well as an interpreter" (p. 4) who can use his or her own basic experiences to understand them. In addition, a therapist team can absorb far more information than can a single therapist, and they provide reciprocal control and correction. Finally, transference and countertransference can be prevented from impeding therapy or at least held within limits by the therapists' "relationship." Intensive therapy in Masters and Johnson's program is conducted under semi-inpatient conditions: the daily sessions last from two to three weeks, during which the patients stop working and live away from their home environment so they can concentrate entirely on therapy. This means that the couple has no way of evading confrontation with difficulties by hiding behind daily distractions, duties, and worries. Feedback from therapists on the couple's new experiences is immediate; problems arising during therapy can be dealt with at once. Finally, the intensive therapy setting supposedly reduces the risk of transference and countertransference, which cannot be dealt with by this method. According to Masters and Johnson, the actual therapeutic agent consists of a sequence of behavioral instructions or "exercises" that a couple performs between therapeutic sessions. Experiences gathered in these exercises are discussed and evaluated in the next therapy sessions. The "difficulty" of the exercises is increased in the course of therapy: they range from touching each other's entire bodies in turn, except the genitals ("sensate focus") and six or seven intermediate steps (for example, explorative genital touching, stimulative touching and playful arousal, petting to orgasm, intromission of the penis without movements, coitus with exploratory movements) to sexual activity that is individually desired by the partners without the restriction of behavioral instructions.[1] During therapy, sexual activity is confined to the exercises. We shall return later to the psychotherapeutic effects of step-by-step exercises.

Masters and Johnson complement this basic schedule with special instructions for treating premature ejaculation and vaginismus. For premature ejaculation they suggest the "squeeze technique" (which has since become more uncommon): the woman repeatedly stimulates the penis with her hand until ejaculation is imminent; at this point she stops stimulation and squeezes firmly on the frenulum. For vaginismus the woman inserts dilators of graduated size (up to the size of a penis) into her vagina on her own and then together with her partner. The purpose of dilators is not the mechanical dilatation of the vagina; through this exercise a woman can dissipate her fear of being hurt by penile insertion or of not being able to tolerate a foreign body in her vagina.

For each dysfunction Masters and Johnson thus prescribe a framework of behavioral tasks for therapeutic use. Of course, these standardized instructions have to be adapted specifically to each couple and to accommodate any special problems. This process of adaptation is elucidated in the treatment reports of Lobitz et al. (1974), who came to the following conclusion: "While the overall treatment strategy is uncomplicated (perhaps even simplistic), and seemingly could be implemented by anyone who has read the available literature, in reality the therapy process is quite complex and involves a good deal of clinical and interpersonal skills" (p. 3).

As we remarked, the special value of Masters and Johnson's program is that they have compounded various approaches and strategies in a systematic program for treatment. Graduated behavioral instructions for relieving sexual anxieties and dysfunctions had already been applied more or less systematically by, for example, Cooper (1963, 1968, 1969b, 1969c), Johnson (1965), and Garfield, McBreaty, and Dichter (1968). Until that time therapists had simply let patients follow through graduated "exercises" in their imagination along the lines of systematic desensitization, either by the use of progressive muscle relaxation (Wolpe 1958; Lazarus 1963, 1965; Haslam, 1965), of relaxation induced through medication (Brady 1966; Kraft and Al-Issa 1968; Friedmann 1968) or of hypnosis (Mirowitz 1966; Kraft and Al-Issa 1967; Salzman 1968).[2] These approaches are based on the paradigm of reciprocal inhibition according to which sexual arousal and anxiety are antagonistic to each other. Should anxiety be successfully resolved, sexual responses can then evolve in sexually motivating situations.

Anxiety is meant to be reduced by systematic desensitization. The anxiety hierarchies applied correspond to the Masters and Johnson exercises, which represent a standardized hierarchy of items for in vivo desensitization.

Psychotherapeutic use of dilators in treating vaginismus, again on the principle of systematic desensitization, had already been recommended in 1909 by Walthard to convince patients of the "fallacy of their phobia" (p. 1999). Since then the insertion of dilators to gradually reduce the anxiety reflexes of vaginismus has been repeatedly used (Mayer 1932; Malleson 1942; Johnstone 1944; Frank 1948; Mears 1958; Friedman 1962; Haslam 1965; Ellison 1968; Cooper 1969a). The "squeeze technique" for treating premature ejaculation originates in Semans (1956). Frank had already reported on the relieving effect of coital prohibition and its psychotherapeutic advantages in 1948. Participation by the non-dysfunctional partner was suggested before Masters and Johnson (Gutheil 1959; Reding and Ennis 1964; Dicks 1967; Madsen and Ullmann 1967), as was treatment by a therapist team (Reding and Ennis 1964; Dicks 1967).

Since 1970 many modifications of the Masters and Johnson program have been suggested. The most important conceptual alteration is the attempt to emphasize and integrate psychodynamic and partner-dynamic aspects in couple therapy for sexual dysfunctions (Kaplan 1974a; see also our concept of couple therapy, p. 66). The numerous technical modifications and supplements, for example, the creation of new exercises, are less important, but they do facilitate therapy. Most of these amendments can be grouped under the heading "arousal reconditioning" (Lobitz and LoPiccolo 1972) and are explicitly aimed at enhancing sexual responsiveness and arousability. The implicit model in Masters and Johnson of "buried instincts," the idea that "natural" sexual function only has to be freed of inhibitions and blocks to evolve of its own accord, is too simple; a lack of anxiety is certainly a necessary but by no means a sufficient prerequisite for sexual fulfillment (see Gagnon 1975). Some of the numerous suggestions for "arousal reconditioning" techniques are: bodily self-awareness and systematic learning of masturbation for women who have never had an orgasm (LoPiccolo and Lobitz 1972; Kohlenberg 1974); the use of intensive mechanical stimulation (vibrators) for orgasmic dysfunctions (LoPiccolo and Lobitz 1972) and for ejaculatory incompetence (Vogt 1974); introducing bizarre or deviant masturbatory fantasies into therapy (Marquis 1970); acquisition and elaboration of sexual fantasies (Flowers and Booraem 1975; Wish 1975); the use of disinhibiting role games, for example, feigning an exaggerated orgasm (Lobitz and Lo-Piccolo 1972). These modifications have been compiled in reviews by Lobitz and LoPiccolo (1972), LoPiccolo and Lobitz (1973), Kaplan (1974a), and LoPiccolo and LoPiccolo (1978).

Other modifications involve organizational aspects of therapy. Couple therapy was conducted with one therapist instead of two; with a long-term approach (one or two sessions a week with a total of fifteen to forty sessions) instead of the intensive, short-term approach (see Lobitz and LoPiccolo 1972; McCarthy 1973; Kaplan 1974a); and even as two-and-a-half day "marathons" (Blakeney et al. 1976). In his review of the literature Hogan (1978) comes to the conclusion that these therapy settings cannot be shown to differ in their efficiency. Our results corroborate this view; intensive treatment compared with long-term treatment and therapy with one therapist compared with a therapist team are equally effective (see chapter 6).

Furthermore, attempts have been made to apply therapeutic principles developed by Masters and Johnson to groups of couples. Kaplan et al. (1974), McGovern, Kirkpatrick, and LoPiccolo (1976), and Golden et al. (1978) treated groups of three to four couples in which the men complained of premature ejaculation with the same success as in single-couple therapy. Leiblum, Rosen, and Pierce (1976) report on group work with couples with differing symptoms. The empirical findings are, however, still highly fragmentary and cannot be conclusively evaluated (compare our experiences, chapter 9).[3]

Couple therapy for sexual dysfunctions has finally been applied to homosexual male couples (McWhirter and Mattison 1978; Masters and Johnson 1979) and to lesbian couples (Masters and Johnson 1979). Their results coincide roughly with those for heterosexual couples.[4]

The prerequisite for couple therapy of sexual dysfunctions is a steady relationship; this precludes the many single men and women with dysfunctions. It cannot, for example, help men who are so discouraged by their erectile and ejaculatory dysfunctions that they are unwilling to associate at all with women. Masters and Johnson did attempt therapy with these men by working with "surrogate partners," that is, with women who were paid to assume the role of partner in therapy. For legal and ethical reasons Masters and Johnson discontinued this form of therapy. Since then the method has rarely been employed by reputable couple therapists, presumably because of the incalculable psychological risks involved for the man (strong attachment to partner) and the therapeutic shortcomings of this approach (social inhibition, although often the main difficulty, is not dealt with). The procedure preferred nowadays for individual or group therapy for this relatively large male population of patients is as follows: variations of assertive training to improve the ability to approach women and establish friendships; counseling on the gradual development of affectionate and sexual contact in a new relationship; systematic desensitization of anticipation and failure anxieties; imagination training for undisturbed sexual contacts in masturbatory fantasies so the imagination can prepare for real sexual relations free of anxiety (see Obler 1973, 1975; Kockott, Dittmar, and Nusselt 1973; Zilbergeld 1975; Auerbach and Kilmann 1977; Arentewicz, Höflich, and Eck 1978; Zeiss, Christensen, and Levine 1978; Lobitz and Baker 1979; Price et al. 1981). This kind of procedure is often able to reduce sexual difficulties or may at least encourage the patient to start a relationship.

Counseling and treatment have been carried out with women who had never experienced an orgasm and were not prepared to make therapy dependent on cooperation with a partner. Individual therapy (LoPiccolo and Lobitz 1972) and particularly group therapy with female therapists (Barbach 1974; Wallace and Barbach 1974; Schneidman and McGuire 1976; Leiblum and Ersner-Hershfield 1977; Barbach and Flaherty 1980) produced good results. The aim was to extend self-confidence and develop a positive attitude toward their own bodies and to desensitize anxieties and elicit orgasm by means of masturbation. These women's groups are an alternative to couple therapy for primary orgasmic problems even if the woman is involved in a steady relationship. In our opinion this is not true of systematic desensitization for groups of women (Husted 1975; Sotile and Kilmann 1978). Use of dilators (by women themselves or by a female physician), combined with supporting psychotherapy for vaginistic women, can be successful even without partner participation (Friedman 1962).

In terms of therapy results the research by Masters and Johnson is again highly important, especially in view of the large number of patients treated and the long follow-up period of five years. They report a failure rate of 19 percent at the end of therapy, in other words, 81 percent of their patients reported improvement. The relapse rate after five years for 313 patients in follow-up reached a mere 5.1 percent. Unfortunately, Masters and Johnson fail to include detailed reports on the extent of improvement. They define lack of success on completing therapy in highly equivocal terms as the failure of "the two-week rapid-treatment phase . . . to initiate reversal of the basic symptomatology of sexual dysfunction" (1970, p. 352).[5] More exact methods of assessing results of therapy for sexual dysfunctions are described in particular by LoPiccolo and Steger (1974), Arentewicz et al. (1975), Kockott, Dittmar, and Nusselt (1975a, 1975b), and Mathews et al. (1975).

The majority of publications on the psychotherapy of sexual dysfunctions—no less than fifty since Masters and Johnson—contain serious methodological flaws: they are based on small samples; describe background data, symptomatology, and screening criteria inaccurately or inadequately; are based on generalized and vaguely defined criteria of success; and are restricted to the evaluation of therapy results by therapists or to the partner's self-ratings. Furthermore, they limit their concern to changes in sexual symptoms, disregarding other areas (quality of the relationship, psychological traits, sexual behaviour); dispense with control groups and even with waiting-list groups; have no systematic recording of pretherapeutic data; and limit follow-up to short periods.[6] For these reasons, and in view of their varying assessment methods these studies cannot be compared.

We shall, therefore, refrain from summarizing these research results, refer to more recent reviews (Reynolds 1977; Sotile and Kilmann 1977; Hogan 1978; Kilmann 1978; Kilmann and Auerbach 1979; Marks 1981), and conclude with a general summary. The majority of investigations state that couple therapy for sexual dysfunctions induces an alleviation of symptoms in 70 to 80 percent of all patients, both in single-couple treatment and in group treatment, in intensive and long-term therapy, with one therapist and with a therapist team. The improvement rate is slightly higher for vaginismus and premature ejaculation, but it is lower for secondary arousal and orgasmic dysfunctions. That our summary is so brief is a mark of the present state of research on this subject: systematic therapy research is still in its infancy. Our investigation is intended as a step forward in this direction.

Our Concept of Couple Therapy

Our discussion of etiology has made clear that psychotherapy for sexual dysfunctions should strive for the following objectives: first, resolution of the self-reinforcement mechanism; second, compensation of sexual learning deficits; third, understanding of the meaning a sexual dysfunction has in the partner relationship so that underlying partner conflicts may be resolved or uncoupled from sexuality; fourth, understanding the causative psychodynamic conflicts and anxieties, working them through or disengaging them from sexuality. These objectives vary in relevance according to each couple's specific problems, and couple therapy is an adequately flexible method for achieving them.

The first and central aim of therapy is to resolve the self-reinforcement mechanism because it consolidates every sexual dysfunction and allows it to function autonomously (see p. 57). Therapy is most effective if it includes behavioral instructions that involve both partners since the self-reinforcement mechanism is a component of a couple's interaction pattern. We have already pointed out that because of this mechanism sexual dysfunctions still persist even when the deep-rooted conflicts or partner problems have been (psychotherapeutically) handled and resolved. Therapy is able to remove the symptom by concentrating exclusively on the psychodynamic and partner-dynamic causes but only in the few cases in which the self-reinforcement mechanism has not started to work; for example, when treatment is rapidly initiated immediately after the first failure experiences. As a rule, however, therapy that treats primary conflicts without resolving the self-reinforcement mechanism fails to remove the sexual symptom, although it does bring about emotional stabilization in the patient or even a more intact relationship. This experience is reflected in Helene Deutsch's complaint: "I was . . . bitterly disappointed in the results of psychoanalytic treatment of frigidity. I have seen cases in which the most severe neurotic illness was helped by psychoanalysis without in the least influencing the same patient's frigidity" (1965, p. 358). The functional autonomy of sexual dysfunctions explains the disconcerting discovery of many psychoanalysts that although they "have long attempted to formulate the causes of these difficulties, their therapeutic results have not kept pace with their theoretic formulations" (Lorand 1939, pagination of the 1966 reprint, p. 244). We have seen patients whose sexual symptom has not changed at all after several years of psychoanalytic treatment. In such cases, a symptom-oriented therapy aimed at resolving anticipation fears can quickly help to completely eliminate the problem because psychoanalytic treatment has, so to speak, made the problem psychodynamically superfluous and it persists solely of its own accord.

Our etiological considerations have, however, made it clear that in order to relieve a dysfunction it does not suffice to resolve the self-reinforcement mechanism, or even to additionally elicit more liberal attitudes toward sexuality and more adequate forms of sexual behavior, all of which are objectives emphasized by Masters and Johnson. A limited approach of this kind requires strict screening of couples and can only succeed under two conditions.

First, this limited approach is sufficient only if deep-rooted psychodynamic and partner conflicts are minor factors contributing to the sexual dysfunction. Masters and Johnson (1970) suggest that a sexual dysfunction originates from an activating trauma (for example, a particularly painful failure on first coitus) and that predisposing factors determine that the trauma will give rise to vulnerability. The weaker the predisposing factors are, the more severe the trauma has to be to engender a sexual disturbance, and vice versa. Many people are spared a dysfunction only because they gain their first sexual experiences or encounter occasional sexual failures under favorable circumstances, whereas others only become dysfunctional because they meet with particularly destructive circumstances in their sexual experiences. Disturbances predominantly caused by traumatic factors are reversible simply by relieving fears of failure; this can often be effected merely by counseling—or by an understanding partner. In our experience such dysfunctions are rare or are at least seldom of clinical importance.

Second, the approach can only succeed if deep-rooted psychodynamic or partner conflicts no longer exist, but the dysfunction persists by virtue of its functional autonomy. The conflicts may have been overcome after a time through a personality development, resolved in a relationship or in psychotherapy. In these instances the dysfunction is, so to speak, a psychodynamic anachronism and is thus easily dissipated by methods aimed at resolving self-reinforcement.

It is far more common, however, that patients entering treatment for sexual dysfunctions are distressed by virulent psychodynamic or partner conflicts. The intensity of conflicts varies from couple to couple, but according to our observations it does not correspond as unequivocally to the type of problem or symptom as Kaplan (1979) believes it does. (In her opinion such conflicts are more severe in cases of lacking sexual desire than in female arousal disturbances or erectile dysfunctions, and the latter in turn are more severe than in orgasmic and ejaculatory dysfunctions.) Resolving conflicts and anxieties are by no means always necessary to relieve sexual symptoms and increase sexual fulfillment. Therapists are often unable to even identify and diagnose the deeper causes during couple therapy (see chapter 2). However, in such cases they might succeed in uncoupling the untreated conflicts and anxieties from sexuality and thereby reduce their destructive effects on sexuality. In this regard Kaplan (1974a) refers to "bypass mechanisms" that protect vulnerable sexual functioning from the destructive influence of neurosis or marital discord: defenses can be built up "against . . . anxiety in sexual situations, while diminishing the defenses . . . constructed against the erotic responses" (Kaplan 1974a, p. 484). Fleck (1969) describes one facet of bypassing in patients whose defense mechanisms work in such a way that the sexual sphere of experience apparently remains free of conflicts. A woman, for example, "with hostile impulses, which are activated again and again during intimacy with lovers by her unresolved ambivalence conflict, can exclude them from the sexual act by displacement . . . to the possible consequences she fantasies" (p. 64). She might then develop a strong fear of pregnancy or elaborate abortion fantasies. Bypass processes that do not involve symptom displacement, as in the example just mentioned, can be effected in couple therapy. Treatment of sexual dysfunctions is, thus, in principle and in a large number of cases possible without resolving the deeper conflicts.

In our experience, the most important bypass technique is to induce discrimination learning by means of which the underlying anxieties with regard to sexuality, or more specifically to coitus and orgasm, are extinguished or at least defused. To mention but one example: a man in his mid-thirties who had been married for three years consulted us because, as a result of erectile difficulties, he had never been able to perform coitus. Contributory causes were a strong mother bond and equally powerful and diffuse fears of being injured in intercourse. He had never touched his glans because his imagination depicted it as a festering wound and he believed it would be extremely painful. When masturbating he did not pull back the foreskin of his partially erect penis. Desensitization of this fear in couple therapy restored full erectile capacity, doubtlessly without relieving him of his deep-seated castration anxieties or working through his mother problems. Resolution of the dysfunction was possible because these anxieties and conflicts had been prevented from spreading to sexual functions, coitus, or penile stimulation. Another example: a woman in her late twenties who had been married for seven years had always been prevented from coitus by a severe vaginismus. This vaginismus was partly caused by strong masochistic wishes that triggered profound fears of being "destroyed" by intercourse. After her few visits to male and female gynecologists, she always burst out weeping, felt tormented, raped, wounded, and reacted with violent abdominal pains. In therapy she learned by desensitization procedures to insert dilators of increasing size into her vagina, and she found out that her anxieties were not realistic. She was then able to accept coitus; it had been fenced off from her maso-chistic conflicts although the masochism problem itself had not actually been treated. To quote a third, similar example, Friedman (1962) re-ports on a woman who was relieved of her vaginismus by dilator exer-cises. As soon as she was able to equate her husband's penis with the harmless instrument she herself had used, she was able to relinquish her fear of injury. The experience of being able to insert and retract the dilators at will also helped her to dispense with the fantasied idea that her vagina was an infathomable cavern devouring everything. Further examples of the delimitation or bypassing of anxieties that had originally been warded off by the sexual symptom are easily found. Discrimination learning restrains an exaggerated acting-out of such anxieties, enables them to be tested against reality, and thus opens awareness to their irrationality.

Another way of bypassing underlying conflicts is to alter a person's or a couple's sexual situation or to modify it in such a way that it is not affected by the conflict. Fenichel (1945) showed that many people in-voluntarily develop "subjective conditions of love, that is, conditions instrumental in soothing inconscious anxieties which oppose the sexu-al pleasure" (p. 171). Stekel (1920) took advantage of this fact in thera-py and attempted to adjust the situation of some patients to their se-cret sexual anxieties and worries, that is, to alter the situation but not necessarily the anxieties and conflicts. Friedman (1962) reports on a dominating woman who suffered from vaginismus because she was afraid of being subjugated in intercourse. In therapy she was success-fully shown that a woman can "take charge" in intercourse, can be active and enterprising, and is strong enough to accept a man's poten-cy. Partner conflicts can similarly be fenced off from sexuality: a cou-ple that uses sexuality for its power conflicts and so is caught up in an escalation of sexual demands and denials can be brought to see through these mechanisms. Sexuality can then be partially purged of rivalry, which can be fought out in areas less harmful to the relation-ship. If a person's sexuality is being choked by a closeness-distance conflict, therapy can explore other ways for the couple to maintain some distance: for example, spending some leisure time separately; taking up part-time work or further education. Such planned distance can make a greater closeness in sexuality endurable.

In cases where the various possibilities of bypassing do not suffice or are impracticable, success of treatment for sexual dysfunctions inev-itably depends on the deeper and more remote conflicts being at least partially worked through in couple therapy. In such cases Kaplan

(1979) applies the term "psychosexual therapy" instead of "sex therapy." We find this dichotomy artificial because couple therapy, as we understand it, always involves psychodynamic analysis from which a strategy is derived. We have encountered fewer and fewer patients for whom "prescription" of and discussion of behavioral instructions alone suffice.

Psychotherapeutic changes are induced by *corrective emotional experiences* (Alexander and French 1946), that is, by experiences that help remedy the traumatic input of earlier experiences or help compensate for experiences missed. The various forms of psychotherapy—psychoanalysis, behavior therapy, client-centered psychotherapy, gestalt therapy, and so forth—are different techniques for facilitating corrective emotional experiences. In this respect the behavioral instructions in couple therapy are an important method; the new experiences they provoke correct sexual behavior and emotions in the following manner.

First, fears of failure and avoidance behavior are dissipated and the self-reinforcement mechanism is thus resolved. The exercises can be seen as a standardized anxiety hierarchy for graduated in vivo desensitization that can reduce anxieties step by step. By prohibiting all other sexual contacts than those prescribed by the exercise (for example, coitus), further negative reinforcement of the dysfunction by failure is prevented. By setting the patients tasks the therapists make it easier for them to relinquish avoidance behavior and to discontinue further reinforcement of avoidance by reducing anxiety. The emphasis placed on the importance of nondemanding and nongenital sexuality and (at onset of therapy) on the priority of relaxation over arousal eases the patients' fixations on sexual functioning, orgasm, and performance. By linking sexual experiences to physical relaxation the former lose their aversive quality. In addition, a detailed discussion of the new experiences in therapy sessions can function as unsystematic symbolic desensitization in reducing anxieties. The exercises give the couple the opportunity to unlearn failure, anxieties, performance demands, and avoidance, and to experience little by little, perhaps for the first time, tenderness and sexuality without fear, with pleasure and desire, and, finally, without dysfunction.

Second, therapy can serve to remedy learning deficits and to initiate relearning. Being experts, therapists can be particularly effective in providing educational information and correcting misunderstandings about the physiology or psychology of sexuality. Inhibitory attitudes can be modified, for example, nakedness taboos, negative attitudes toward masturbation and manual or oral sexual stimulation, sex-role clichés. However, more important is that by continually discussing their sexual exercises in detail the patients learn to express their sexual feelings and wishes freely, to recognize when the partner's wishes diverge from their own, and to find solutions to these situations—in other words, to improve their sexual communication. Finally, they can experiment with new forms of sexual behavior and so work their way out of rigid patterns. Relaxation and arousal act as reinforcers in this operant conditioning process.

Third, psychodynamic and partner conflicts become visible, are made transparent, and can be handled therapeutically. The behavioral instructions encourage the partners to enter situations that evoke anxiety. The exercises thus produce a wealth of psychodynamic and partner-dynamic material that can be used in therapy (just as other therapies employ free association, dreams, or psychodramatic reconstruction of early experiences). These anxieties and conflicts are often dealt with simply by repeating the exercise, by "habituation," so to speak. The role that specific behavioral instruction plays in psychodynamics and partner dynamics depends on the particular problems involved, and it must be clarified for each individual case. Here are a few examples in the wide range of possibilities. Prolonged, nondemanding touching (see part 3) of the whole body with no opportunity for escape into activity or arousal confronts the couple with their limited tolerance of physical closeness and creates the opportunity to gradually widen the limits. Attitudes of rivalry and competition during exercises reveal power conflicts or how sexuality is used to punish or reward the partner. The strict division of activity provokes gender identity fears—in men of being sexual passive, in women of being sexual active. Prohibition of petting and coitus provides relief from genital performance and enables regression to pregenital sexuality, revives partial instinct fears of voyeurism, of exhibiting and touching oneself. Exercises for bodily self-awareness and detailed exploration of one's own body in the mirror confront the individual with, and reconcile him to, the injured, narcissistic feelings toward his physical imperfection; showing one's body in full partner view creates the feeling of being accepted along with one's physical flaws. Fears of dirt are aroused and appeased by spreading vaginal fluid during exploratory caressing and moistening genitals with saliva and lubricants. Mutual exploration of the genitals and consciously manipulating them manually resolves fear of imagined genital injury or vulnerability. Therapist encouragement to enjoy sexuality even without an erection diminishes fear of impotence and soothes castration anxieties. Insertion of the penis without thrusting movements makes the couple aware of the regressive, protective qualities of coital experience by combining pregenital and genital elements. The basic rule of being "selfish" in sexuality, of concentrating on *one's own* feelings forms the experience of being able to remain autonomous and oneself in situations of giving when fears of fusion may become too great. When a woman with vaginismus inserts dilators into her vagina she herself refutes her own fear of bursting or of being stabbed. The "magical" effect of the therapist's role as expert can help to overcome archaic anxieties from previous sexual prohibitions and to modify the infantile superego.

The exercises enable the partners to sound out their limits and to test the reality of irrational anxieties step by step under the protection of therapy. Anxieties that do not affect sexual function alone, but involve sexuality, can be bypassed by the exercises without being fully resolved. The exercises are of considerable psychodynamic significance, whether the therapist is aware of it or not. However, recognizing this significance means that the therapeutic potential of behavioral instructions and the experiences gathered through them can be brought to bear with far greater "corrective" effect.

NOTES

1. For an exact description of the behaviour instructions see the therapy manual in part 3.

2. We have dispensed with a detailed review of the literature on systematic desensitization for sexual dysfunctions and refer to the surveys by Reynolds (1977) and Sotile and Kilmann (1977).

3. Group therapy with couples not suffering from sexual dysfunctions was carried out by LoPiccolo and Miller (1975a, 1975b), Kaufman and Krupka (1975), and Kilmann, Julian, and Moreault (1978) among others, with the aim of making "normal" sexuality more satisfying and "richer" (so called "sexual enhancement" or "marital enrichment").

4. In their new book Masters and Johnson (1979) also report on attempts to treat bisexual (Kinsey rating 2, 3, and 4; N = 55) and homosexual (Kinsey rating 5 and 6; N = 12) men and women in couple therapy with a partner of the opposite sex (usually the husband or wife). The explicit aim of this therapy is reversal or conversion to heterosexuality. We reject any such approach. Every attempt to change the orientation from homosexuality to heterosexuality means nothing more than shifting the prejudice against homosexuality from the moral onto the medical or psychotherapeutic plane, where it remains discriminatory.

5. We were surprised that the criticisms published by Zilbergeld and Evans (1980) on the research results of Masters and Johnson met with considerable interest from the general public even ten years after their results were published: the criticisms, which we believe are justified, have long been known. The limitations in Zilbergeld and Evans's methodological concept is evident in their demand for replicability of the Masters

and Johnson study. This work cannot be replicated, but not because of methodological shortcomings; rather because it is firmly rooted in the social environment of the American Midwest in the 1950s. Zilbergeld and Evans are deluded by the belief that an optimally elaborated method of measurement could solve all the problems in psychotherapy research. By contrast, developments in the last ten to fifteen years (that is, also following Masters and Johnson) have shown that further elaboration and specification, which always proceeds from the experience and efforts of previous research, can in the final analysis only provide approximate solutions and, in so doing, repeatedly give rise to new questions (see p. 131). In a rejoinder to Zilbergeld and Evans, Kolodny (1981) presents a post hoc definition of outcome criteria used by Masters and Johnson and new outcome statistics from their institute which are in accordance with those presented in 1970.

6. According to the criteria: inclusion of a pretest and follow-up covering several areas, and use of control groups and/or systematic control of at least one therapeutic variable; the following investigations are of particular methodological interest: Obler 1973; Husted 1975; Kockott, Dittmar, and Nusselt 1975a, 1975b; Mathews et al. 1975; McGovern, McMullen, and LoPiccolo 1975; Everaerd 1977.

PART II

Couple Therapy:
Research and Results

Chapter 4

SHORT-TERM RESULTS

Ulrich Clement and Gunter Schmidt

This and the following two chapters document the results of our therapy research project. We shall describe, in particular, how couple therapy modified symptoms, sexual behavior, relationships, and general psychological status. Furthermore, we shall examine the stability of therapy results and the effectiveness of different settings in treatment.[1]

The Study

THE COUPLES

All couples were referred by physicians or psychotherapists to the outpatient clinic of the Department of Sex Research. The appropriateness of couple therapy was assessed by a physician or psychologist (first consultant) in the outpatient clinic. Recommendation was given only for couples who, first, had sexual disturbances so serious or chronic that they could not be helped by counseling or information; second, couples who fulfilled certain specific conditions (existence of a steady relationship that both partners basically wished to continue; enough time available for therapy, and so forth; see p. 228); third, couples who were not acutely psychotic or addicted to drugs or alcohol. We did not assess contraindication on the basis of neurotic characteristics or partner dynamics, that is, even couples with pronounced neurotic problems or serious partner conflicts were accepted, as long as sexual symptoms predominated or the couple thought they did. Our definition of the limits of recommendation is thus far broader than that of many couple therapists in the United States who rejected as many as 50 percent of the couples seeking help for psychological problems or partner conflicts (LoPiccolo and Lobitz 1973). Masters and Johnson have changed their screening policy nowadays in a way that is comparable to ours (Kolodny 1981).

All couples who were selected and who agreed to the suggested treatment were placed on a waiting list. The patients had to wait a minimum of three months and a maximum of twelve, in most cases five to ten months, before therapy began. A total of 275 couples were indicated for therapy. Seventy-three couples (27 percent) did not start therapy (so-called waiting list drop-outs): they did not complete the questionnaires we had given them after the initial interview and were therefore no longer included, as we had agreed with them. Others failed to appear at the scheduled therapy appointment or gave up the idea of therapy as they saw little hope of improvement or because their problems had changed in the meantime.[2]

Two hundred and two couples actually started the treatment program. In twenty-one couples both partners suffered from a sexual dysfunction so that there were 223 dysfunctions that were spread over the four diagnostic groups as follows: 108 (48 percent) cases of female arousal and/or orgasmic dysfunction (including lack of desire, hereinafter termed orgasmic dysfunction for simplicity's sake), 27 (12 percent) cases of vaginismus, 57 (25 percent) cases of erectile dysfunction, 31 (14 percent) cases of premature ejaculation.

The couples' ages and family and social situations are shown in tables 4.1 and 4.2. The "average" patient was about thirty years old and married (almost three quarters of the couples); the marriage or steady relationship had lasted about eight years. Almost half of the couples had children. In comparison to the total population, more than an average number of patients were from the middle classes, had obtained above average school education, and seldom had a working-class background. This social bias in the sample of patients seeking help for sexual problems has been described and discussed above (p. 31).

There were only minor variations in the overall picture of the average patient as regards diagnoses. Women with vaginismus were particularly young (on average, twenty-six) compared with other diagnostic groups; men with erectile disturbances formed the oldest group (on average, thirty-four). The comparatively low average age of women with vaginismus can be explained by the fact that this symptom is so incisive as to be immediately recognized as a problem by women (although recognition does not necessarily lead to immediate treatment). By comparison, orgasmic disturbances and premature ejaculation were apparently often not acknowledged as problems for some time or were played down in the hope that they would improve on their own. The reason why men with erectile problems were well above the average age is that the symptom quite frequently emerged as a secondary disturbance when they were over thirty-five. All disturbances have the common feature of being chronic. Only a tenth of our patients started therapy less than two years after symptom onset. Men with erectile dysfunctions tended to seek treatment sooner than all other patients; this symptom is obviously felt to be especially threatening. In contrast, men who ejaculated prematurely waited quite a long time.

Our patients' sexual dysfunctions had become chronic primarily because they had difficulty in finding suitable therapeutic help (see Schorsch et al. 1977); however, this was also due to their resistance in facing up to the problem. Some patients even incorporated experts' helplessness into their systems of defense: after consulting their physicians in vain, they felt they had made an effort and could then go on living with their symptoms, reassured by this confrontation with the physicians' helplessness. Such cases were, of course, exceptions. The majority of patients we treated had been keenly interested in assistance for years.

Evaluation of the data on sexual behavior (see table 4.3) was difficult because there were no figures for a control group of undisturbed men and women. By comparison with data from larger empirical investigations on sexual behavior—which were, however, conducted with different age groups, generations, social classes, and in other countries (Kinsey et al. 1948, 1953; Giese and Schmidt 1968; Schmidt and Sigusch 1971; Hunt 1974)—we can cautiously conclude the following:

1. Men with sexual dysfunctions masturbated more often than the population of same-aged men in steady relationships (in terms of the active incidence of masturbation, that is, the percentage of those who masturbated at least occasionally). The same applies for men whose partners were sexually dysfunctional. As sexuality with their partners was unsatisfying, masturbation apparently continued to play a relatively important role for the men we examined. Incidentally, this confirms clinical findings that show that male sexual dysfunctions are rarely accompanied by a general loss of appetence.

2. Women whose partners had a sexual problem were probably more active and experienced in masturbation than the population of same-aged women in steady relationships. They, too, had more fre-

quent recourse to masturbation as a result of disappointing partner sexuality. Women who were themselves dysfunctional were presumably not less active or experienced in masturbation than women without sexual problems. This is further evidence that dysfunctions in women, as in men, frequently only affect sexual relations with a partner.

3. Sexual intercourse was less frequent in comparison with the same-age population of couples in steady relationships, particularly in cases of dysfunctions that directly impaired performance of coitus (erectile disturbances, vaginismus).

Tables 4.4 and 4.5 show how couples treated deviated from the population as regards personality traits in tests with the Freiburg Personality Inventory (FPI) and the Giessen Test (GT). (These tests are the most widely accepted personality inventories in West Germany.) The trends can be summarized as follows (see also Clement and Pfäfflin 1980):

1. Dysfunctional men and women showed deviations from the population in three or four of our diagnostic groups on the FPI scales 6, 7, and M and on the GT scales 1, 2, and 4.[3] In all of these scales (except FPI M) patients with psychogenic disturbances, psychosomatic patients, and patients in psychotherapy all showed deviations in the same direction. In female dysfunctions additional deviations appear on the FPI scales 8 and N, as well as on the GT scale 5, again in the same direction as psychoneurotic or psychosomatic patients. Men and particularly women with sexual dysfunctions present a picture of themselves in these questionnaires similar to that of other patient groups with psychogenic symptoms.

2. These deviations in the personality tests can be described thus: many men and women with sexual dysfunctions did not like themselves much and found themselves scarcely lovable; they possessed little self-confidence, were self-doubting, and picked at themselves a great deal (FPI 6, M; GT 1, 4). They found it hard to believe that they had anything to offer other people, and they felt unattractive and unloved; they attached little importance to their appearance, which they had difficulty in accepting (GT 1). They described themselves as labile, easily irritated and disappointed, and quick to be impatient with other people (FPI 6; GT 2), as low-spirited, anxious, despondent, not very robust or lively (FPI 6, M; GT 4). They tended to be less active in coping with difficulties, not so good at tackling problems with their environment assertively, (FPI 7) and were more inclined to swallow

their anger (GT 4). Furthermore, sexually dysfunctional women tended to be reserved and afraid of being open, of daring to drop their façades; in relationships, they felt vulnerable and were afraid of soon being exploited once they got involved (GT 5). This characterization is, of course, an average personality profile of men and women with sexual dysfunctions; it goes without saying that individual cases may deviate appreciably.

3. Significant deviations from the normal population can also be seen in the partners of dysfunctional men and women. They tended in the same direction as the patients themselves. Partner deviations were not as strong as in dysfunctional females and about as strong as in dysfunctional males.

Personality questionnaire results for sexually dysfunctional men and women and their partners deviated in a way similar to psychoneurotic and psychosomatic patients. These findings are particularly pronounced in women with orgasmic dysfunctions and vaginismus, and evaluating them is difficult: we are unable to say whether diminished self-confidence, emotional lability, low spirits, and so forth, were reactions to sexual difficulties or whether the sexual difficulties were the expression of general neurotic tendencies.

Evaluating the findings for partners is even more difficult. Neurotic tendencies may have been a reaction to sexual difficulties or may indicate that people with neurotic behavior patterns tend to choose partners with sexual problems because they are less likely to mobilize anxieties; or, finally, they may mean that a partner with neurotic behavior patterns increases the probability of a sexual disturbance emerging. Our findings show that our patients' and their partners' deviations receded after therapy and suggest that these characteristics were at least partly a reaction to the sexual problem.

To conclude, the brief description below of the sexual symptoms in the four diagnostic groups should give an impression of the severity of the dysfunctions.

Orgasmic dysfunctions. Two thirds of the women in this group had never experienced an orgasm during petting or intercourse. In the year before therapy 83 percent were anorgastic in coitus, 78 percent in petting; 3 percent (coitus) and 11 percent (petting) regularly reached orgasm (that is, at least once out of three occasions). Sexual aversion was the main complaint here. Nearly half the women (46 percent) had no orgasmic problems in masturbation. More than half (52 percent) had arousal as well as orgasmic dysfunctions, that is, they were very seldom or never aroused by petting, foreplay, or coitus. Pronounced avoidance behavior and various degrees of lack of desire were noticeable in the large majority of women (about 80 percent).

Vaginismus. In our classification 55 percent of the women in this group suffered from fairly severe vaginismus—coitus was impossible, but they could still insert a finger into the vagina; 45 percent complained of severe vaginismus which made insertion of even a finger impossible. The majority (75 percent) regularly reached orgasm in petting. Almost half masturbated at least occasionally and without orgasmic problems.

Erectile dysfunctions. A fourth of erectile dysfunctions were primary, that is, the men had never been able to perform sexual intercourse. Just under 40 percent of all men had never had an erection in foreplay or coital attempts; the others complained of not having an erection often enough, of not having a full erection, or of the erection subsiding before ejaculation. In 60 percent of the cases erectile capacity in masturbation was intact or considerably better than in coitus; only about 20 percent had erectile disturbances during masturbation. (The remaining men did not masturbate.)

Premature ejaculation. Of premature ejaculators, 90 percent always ejaculated on intromission or immediately afterward; the remaining 10 percent ejaculated prematurely in at least half of their coital attempts. Of the men in this diagnostic group, 10 percent showed signs of having erectile problems.

DESIGN OF THE STUDY

In the scientific study of therapy results and effectiveness, we analyzed three areas: sexuality, relationships, and general psychological status. Data were recorded on six different occasions (two pretests, four follow-up tests) and by four observers (therapists, first consultants, and both partners).

The six investigations controlling therapy were carried out at the following times:

Pretest 1 (P1): after the initial interview and recommendation for couple therapy in the Division of Sex Research, at least three months and at the most twelve months before therapy.

Pretest 2 (P2): immediately before onset of therapy (after an introductory session with the therapists).

Short-Term Results

Follow-up 1 (F1):   immediately upon completion of therapy.

Follow-up 2 (F2):   three months after completing therapy.

Follow-up 3 (F3):   one year after completing therapy.

Follow-up 4 (F4):   two and a half to four and a half years after completion of therapy.

The assessment procedures aimed at eliciting information on: (1) sexual symptoms, function, and behavior (frequency of coitus, petting, masturbation; sexual wishes and desires; sexual techniques; satisfaction with sexuality; attitudes toward sexuality) and modifications in these areas; (2) the relationship in general between the partners (understanding, affection, openness, ability to communicate, joint activities) and modifications in this area; (3) general psychological status (psychovegetative symptoms, depressivity, emotional lability, self-acceptance, and so forth) and modifications in this area.

In all three areas data were collected by several observers using different methods (rating scales, questionnaires, psychological tests):

Therapists. The therapists assessed sexual function and the relationship between the partners on the basis of interviews and two rating scales; the first scale recorded details of the patients' sexual functioning (R1), and the second contained a general classification of therapy outcome (R2). In addition the therapists wrote a detailed case history, including an account of developments in therapy, after completion of therapy which they later completed at follow-up.

First consultants. The physician or psychologist who recommended therapy in our division rated patients' sexual functioning (R1) after an initial interview. We refer to these observers as "independent" because they did not take part in therapy itself.

The two partners. The patient and his or her nondysfunctional partner[4] kept a multiple-choice diary describing their sexual behavior for a week (Q1) without consulting each other. They filled out questionnaires on: sexual behavior covering the three months immediately preceding the questionnaire (Q2); on their attitudes toward sexuality (Q3); and after therapy on how they assessed changes in sexuality and the relationship (Q4). They then underwent three psychological tests: the Freiburg Personality Inventory (FPI), the Giessen Test (GT, self-description, description of partner) and the Emotionality Inventory (EMI, Ullrich, de Muynck, and Ullrich 1977; a German mood List).

83

The questionnaires R1 and Q1 to Q4 were designed by us and have been published in Arentewicz et al. (1975). The three rating scales in questionnaire R2 are shown in the appendix to the tables for this chapter (pp. 120–121).

The complete follow-up program, as outlined in table 4.6 was carried out only with couples who completed therapy. Where therapy was discontinued therapists restricted F1, F3, and F4 to an interview; all questionnaires and F2 were dropped. We could not expect patients who had dropped out of therapy to participate in the full follow-up program and so confined ourselves to interviews with them.

Table 4.7 shows that follow-up could not be conducted with all couples. This was partly due to objective reasons beyond the scope of psychological interpretation: (1) a follow-up examination was not yet possible because on completion of the project or at the last follow-up (F4) therapy had only been completed less than one or, respectively, two and a half years previously; (2) couples could no longer be contacted because they had moved; (3) couples who lived far away from Hamburg requested exemption from follow-up for economic reasons; (4) the first consultants gave rise to another problem in follow-up. Coordinating follow-up appointments with the therapists often proved difficult; moreover, one of the first consultants had left the department during the second half of the project.

What affected the evaluation of our follow-up results more was that some patients did not appear for follow-ups although they had been notified by mail (about 20 percent in F3 and F4). Other couples came and were interviewed but did not return questionnaires, despite two reminders (about 20 to 30 percent of couples who had been given questionnaires for F1 to F4). Many of these couples probably had some resistance to further confrontation with previously distressing problems in follow-up sessions or questionnaires after therapy. This refusal seems to imply various things: disappointment with the limitations of therapy success; ambivalence, hostility, or anger toward therapists who were often unable to fulfill the couples' unrealistic hopes and to whom they had revealed their problems and weaknesses; assertion of independence from therapists after long periods of partial dependence in therapy. A lack of motivation and indolence were probably further reasons for not completing the lengthy questionnaires—the diary was particularly problematic because completion required ten to fifteen minutes every morning for a whole week.

The missing couples (refusal or out of reach) raise questions on how biased follow-up data are; after all, one cannot exclude the possibility that couples missing in follow-up form an atypical subgroup in the total sample in terms of therapy results; whether their status changed after therapy, that is, whether symptoms recurred more frequently or more rarely; or whether separation was more frequent or rare, and so forth. This problem raises a series of specific questions which we will now briefly examine in the light of our data.

1. Were couples who did not attend follow-up sessions 3 and 4 atypical in terms of therapy outcome? A comparison of couples completing therapy, whether present or not at F3, shows that in the evaluation of therapy outcome by therapists immediately after termination of treatment[5] there was a slight, but not statistically significant, tendency for couples completing therapy successfully not to attend F3. The results for F4 show the same trend (p = .10). The findings for F3 and F4 are thus presumably applicable to the entire sample since the differences are so minimal. The reason we are uncertain about this is that our data only show that on completion of therapy couples present and couples missing at follow-up did not differ. It is possible that the two groups developed differently after therapy. Our data do not allow any definitive statement on this question.

2. Were couples who refused to complete questionnaires more or less successful than other couples? Couples who returned the first follow-up questionnaires (F1) were rated at therapy termination as being "distinctly improved" or "cured" more often (p = .05) than those who did not (68 percent versus 52 percent). A similar trend was not observed in F2 or F3. All in all, refusals seem to have biased questionnaire results only to a minor degree; it is, however, probable that positive results were slightly overestimated by the questionnaires at F1.

3. Did therapists unwittingly favor couples successfully treated when arranging follow-up sessions with first consultants? There was a trend (p = .10) for couples assessed by therapists as "cured" to be interviewed more often by first consultants at F1. A similar trend was not observed at F3 one year after therapy. Couple selection probably biased the first consultants' results only slightly; a slight exaggeration of positive results in the first follow-up cannot, however, be discounted.

THE THERAPY SETTINGS

We carried out couple therapy in three different settings and assessed differences in effectiveness.[6] We wanted to find out whether the only setting for couple therapy applied and recommended by Masters and Johnson (1970)—two therapists, daily sessions—might not be replaceable at least under certain circumstances by settings that were more economical (one therapist) and less inconvenient to patients (two sessions a week instead of daily sessions). We defined the three settings thus:

1. *Two therapists, intensive.* Dual-sex therapy team; daily sessions for three weeks (six a week); a total of eighteen sessions (two of which were devoted to history-taking by each therapist with each partner). Sixty-seven couples and seventy-seven dysfunctions were treated in this setting.

2. *Two therapists, long-term.* Dual-sex therapy team; two sessions per week; therapy was planned for five to six months with a total of approximately thirty-five sessions (including individual history-taking by each therapist with each partner). Eighty-two couples and eighty-seven dysfunctions were treated in this setting.

3. *One therapist, long-term.* Male or female therapist; frequency and number of sessions the same as in setting 2; fifty-three couples and fifty-nine dysfunctions were treated in this setting, twenty-nine by a male therapist, twenty-four by a female therapist.

The three therapy settings were not distributed evenly over the different diagnostic groups (see table 4.8). Intensive therapy was conducted very frequently with patients who had erectile dysfunctions and vaginismus because many of them lived far away, and long-term treatment was therefore impossible. Long-term therapy with one therapist was especially rare in cases of vaginismus. Because we expected very few patients with this symptom, we had planned only two settings for them (long-term, two therapists; intensive); for technical reasons (no therapy teams were available) single-therapist treatment was necessary on a few occasions. The fact that premature ejaculators were frequently treated by one therapist is an unintentional effect that was probably due to these patients being labeled initially as relatively easy cases for treatment, and to therapist teams involuntarily being assigned to dysfunctions judged more complicated. We will take account of the varying distribution of diagnoses in our comparative analysis of therapy settings in chapter 6.

Disregarding patients who dropped out, long-term therapy comprised a minimum of fifteen sessions and a maximum of sixty, on average thirty-eight sessions see (table 4.9). Three fifths of all long-term therapies were completed within twenty-five to forty-five sessions. On average, long-term therapy lasted eight months. The average number of sessions thus confirms the expectations and experiences in our pilot study; more time than expected was involved. The prolonged duration was due in part to sessions being canceled, but particularly to couples or therapists taking vacation. The number of sessions varied with the diagnosis (see table 4.9): for female dysfunctions we needed on average forty sessions, for male dysfunctions about thirty-four.

In intensive therapy two booster sessions were usually necessary in addition to the sixteen scheduled sessions, thus requiring roughly half as many sessions as in long-term therapy. This was the result of partners concentrating closely on their problems during these three weeks, the lack of distractions and of opportunities to avoid confronting themselves and their problems. It was clear that we needed more sessions for both long-term and intensive therapy than did most of our American colleagues, whose programs are generally restricted to two weeks for intensive therapy and twelve to twenty sessions for long-term therapy (LoPiccolo and LoPiccolo 1978). This we attribute to our less selective criteria for admission to therapy (p. 77) and to the more intense work on partner-dynamic and psychodynamic problems that resulted form these criteria.

The length of therapy sessions was not fixed; it was meant to be adaptable but not to exceed one hour. In actual practice sessions in long-term therapy lasted on average thirty minutes and in intensive therapy about forty minutes, not counting the time spent on preparation and evaluation (see table 4.9). In view of the more condensed procedure in intensive therapy more time had to be spent in therapy sessions working through the exercises. The length of sessions quoted is only an average; it varied widely from session to session.

THE THERAPISTS

The core group of therapists consisted of eight women and eight men who treated at least ten, at the most fifty-four, and on average twenty-one couples. These therapists performed 85 percent of all treatments; the remaining 15 percent were conducted by seven female and six male therapists from other therapeutic institutions, who led therapy with an experienced therapist to gain experience in couple therapy. If a therapist can be called "experienced" after conducting therapy with four couples, then only 2 percent of all couples were treated exclusively by inexperienced therapists (see table 4.10). Long-term team therapy and intensive therapy were conducted in about a half and about a third of cases, respectively, by one experienced and one inexperienced therapist. Single-therapist therapy was rarely carried out by an inexperienced therapist.

Of the core of sixteen therapists, five were physicians (psychiatrists or psychiatric residents) and eleven were psychologists. The physicians were taking part in psychoanalytic training; the psychologists had been trained in client-centered therapy and/or behavior therapy. We did not consider it necessary to pair psychologists and doctors in team therapy, as some authors suggest doing. Four percent of team therapies were carried out by two physicians, 58 percent by two psychologists, and 37 percent by a psychologist and a physician. In single-therapist treatment, 69 percent of therapists were psychologists and 31 percent were physicians.

The sixteen therapists were aged between twenty-four and forty-two. Five were employed full-time by the Division of Sex Research; eleven were employed part-time on a fee basis and were payed from research funds. Therapy was always free of charge for the couples.

Between 1973 and 1975 therapists supervised their own work in weekly group conferences. From 1976 on supervision took place once a week in a Balint group led by a female psychoanalyst.

Short-Term Results

We will begin by outlining the changes that had been induced by the end of therapy and continue in the next chapter by describing the stability of these changes in the follow-up period. For the sake of clarity we have made a selection from the data collected. The selection had already been made in part before evaluation, but always with a view to relevance rather than the elimination of variables that produced statistically insignificant scores. This selection compensates for a mistake in our planning: the accumulation of a mass of redundant, incomprehensible data which would have required reams of tables and text to explain and would not have provided any more pertinent information than will now be presented.[7]

OVERALL THERAPY OUTCOME

According to therapist evaluation (see table 4.11), therapeutic intervention proved a success: the sexual dysfunctions of 75 percent of all couples had "improved"; 78 percent found sexuality more satisfying than before therapy; 58 percent had improved their relationships by communicating more openly, cooperatively, and with less hostility. The symptoms, sexual experiences, and relationships of the majority of couples were thus modified to the intended effect. As we shall demonstrate, this result was in principle confirmed by the evaluation of independent experts (first consultants) and by the self-assessments and self-ratings of both partners.

Nonetheless, 17 percent of couples broke off therapy prematurely, some (4 percent) because they dissolved their relationships (see table 4.11). The problems involved in dropping out and separation will be described in full detail in chapter 8. Another 7 percent showed no improvement or only minimal positive changes in symptoms on completion of therapy. Thirty-five percent of the patients were "cured", that is, sexual function was intact after therapy. Seventeen percent were "distinctly improved", that is, their dysfunctions had disappeared for the most part but still recurred on occasion. Finally, 23 percent were classified as "improved"; their dysfunctions were evident less often or only in a milder form (for example, sexual aversion and arousal dysfunction had been reversed but not orgasmic dysfunction). As a rule, these couples were far more able to tolerate their reduced sexual problems than before therapy; the problems were less distressing and caused less suffering. To summarize, full reversal of sexual symptoms was achieved only with a small, but nevertheless significant, minority (35 percent). For about as many patients (40 percent) we achieved an improvement in symptoms and a greater ease in the way they dealt with the now less frequent or diminished dysfunction.

The four diagnostic groups varied considerably from the overall picture. Of patients with erectile dysfunctions, premature ejaculation, and vaginismus, 63 to 76 percent were "distinctly improved" or "cured," but only 36 percent of women with orgasmic dysfunctions showed similar results. The orgasmic dysfunction group had the most dropouts (24 percent) and the fewest full reversals (19 percent). In contrast to the other groups, those with orgasmic dysfunction showed the highest number in the "improved" category. After therapy, these women found sexual intercourse pleasurable, their aversion to sexuality and their avoidance behavior had been reversed, but they still did not reach orgasm during petting or coitus.

Changes in the partners' relationship vary only slightly between diagnostic groups (see table 4.11). Three fifths of the couples with orgasmic dysfunctions, erectile dysfunctions, and premature ejaculation were able to improve their relationships in the sense that they were more open and less hostile; this figure is lower for vaginismus, which is due to the large number of relationships that were rated as "intact" before therapy onset. Differences in sexual satisfaction (see table 4.11) were also negligible between groups. Greater satisfaction in sexuality than existed before therapy was achieved by 90 percent of couples who entered treatment for vaginismus, compared with 71 to 83 percent in the other three groups.

The relative lack of success in treating orgasmic dysfunctions was thus particularly evident in orgasmic ability but not so much in positive changes in the relationship and in sexual experience. We shall discuss and analyze this outcome in closer detail (see p. 99), but we would point out that in terms of the "sexual function" criterion, orgasmic dysfunctions are the most difficult to treat.

SEXUAL FUNCTION

After depicting overall therapy outcome, we will continue with a detailed description of the modifications induced by therapy. We have only included units completing therapy (83 percent of the sample) because no statistical data were recorded in follow-up for other patients.[8] We will begin with changes in sexual function induced by therapy as evaluated by therapists, by first consultants not involved in therapy (so-called independent experts), and in couple self-rating.

Orgasmic dysfunctions. On completion of therapy, the interviews by therapists and independent experts with women treated for orgasmic dysfunction showed there was a significant increase in ability to lubricate, in sexual arousability, and frequency of orgasm during coitus and petting (see table 4.12). In terms of orgasmic capacity the changes were, again, limited to a minority (see table 4.13): about three fifths, that is, the majority, were still anorgastic during sexual intercourse. The women's self-ratings and ratings made by their partners produced highly similar findings (see table 4.18). The behavioral data from the diary (Q1) and the questionnaire on sexuality in the last three months immediately preceding the questionnaire (Q2) also confirmed that anorgasmia had only been reversed in a minority and that regular coital orgasm was an exception. In the diary they kept for a week after therapy, only 42 percent of all women recorded coital orgasm during at least one occasion; in the three months after therapy only 25 percent of the women reached orgasm during coitus at least 50 percent of the time. In the population of younger, coitally more experienced women the figure is about 60 to 80 percent (see p. 24). Both figures are, however, significantly higher than before therapy.

Vaginismus. Therapists and first consultants observed reversal of vaginismus in almost all the women in this group (see table 4.14). This is reflected in their changed sexual behavior: in the three months after therapy about 90 percent had sexual intercourse at least occasionally (Q2); about as many said they had coitus at least once in the week they kept the diary (Q1). The corresponding pretherapy figures were under 10 percent. Orgasm frequency during coitus after therapy was, moreover, significantly higher (p = .05) for formerly vaginistic women than for women we treated for orgasmic problems. It is therefore by no means the case that vaginismus was replaced by arousal or orgasmic problems.

Erectile dysfunctions. In the evaluation by therapists and first consultants, therapy induced a significant increase in erectile ability in coitus or coital attempts (see table 4.15). After therapy about 80 percent of the patients always or almost always achieved an erection when they desired intercourse with their partners (see table 4.16). Before therapy this was true of only a quarter, at the most a third. Nine tenths of the distressed men themselves claimed an improvement in erectile ability; this was confirmed by their partners (see table 4.18). The data on sexual behavior (Q1, Q2) reflect reconstituted functioning by showing a significant increase in coital frequency. The average frequency of coitus in the three months after therapy was, for example, five times a month, in the three months before therapy less than once a month.

Premature ejaculation. Therapists and first consultants assessed that therapy had significantly enhanced ejaculatory control (see tables 4.15 and 4.17). Four fifths of the patients had normal ejaculation, and only a fifth still ejaculated prematurely on at least 50 percent of coital occasions. There was a particularly distinct reduction in the number of men who always ejaculated prematurely—from over 80 percent before therapy to less than 10 percent after therapy. The affected men themselves and their partners recorded highly similar changes: four fifths confirmed an improvement (see table 4.18).

SEXUAL BEHAVIOR AND ATTITUDES TOWARD SEXUALITY

We have already mentioned that in vaginismus and in erectile dysfunctions the frequency of coitus increased after therapy. Similar, though somewhat less distinct, trends were visible in orgasmic dysfunctions and premature ejaculation. Figures 4.1 and 4.2 show the changes in sexual behavior for all diagnostic groups combined to provide an overall view. Both the data on the "three months preceding questionnaire" (Q2)[9] and the diary (Q1) show that frequency of coitus was higher in the immediate posttherapy period; this is confirmed by the data of the patient and his or her partner. For example, coital fre-

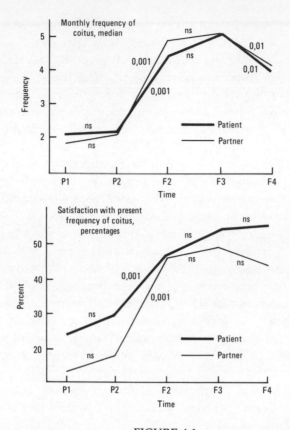

FIGURE 4.1

Data on Sexual Behavior "in the Last Three Months Preceding Questionnaire,"
Before and After Therapy.

Note: Data from the questionnaire on sexual behavior in the last three months preceding questionnaire (Q2), all four symptom groups combined. Only couples completing therapy were included. The
number of cases at the five different times of collecting data varied between N=166 and N=82.
Statistical significance according to sign-test.

quency per month rose from an average of twice before therapy to an
average of four to five times immediately after completion of therapy.
This increase was accompanied by modified emotional experience of
sexual intercourse, again both in the patient and the partner: both the
absolute frequency of coitus experienced as satisfying and the percentage of sexual encounters experienced as satisfying increased. Finally,
the percentage of partners who were satisfied with the frequency of
coitus rose from just under 30 percent (symptomatic partners) or 20
percent (functional partner) before therapy to about 50 percent immediately after therapy.

Masturbation changed significantly only for women with orgasmic

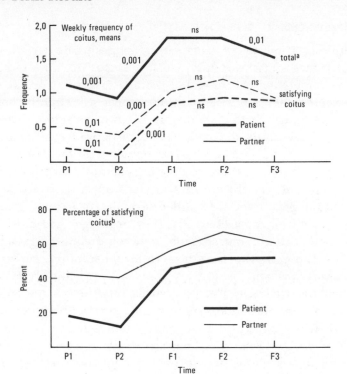

FIGURE 4.2
Data on Sexual Behavior in One Week, Before and After Therapy.

Note: Data from diary on sexual behavior (Q1), all four symptom groups combined. Only couples completing therapy were included. Statistical significance according to sign-test.[a] The curve for partners is identical (± 0.1 units).[b] Calculation of statistical significance not possible.

dysfunctions. Ten of these women (almost all of them went through the therapeutic program for bodily self-awareness, see p. 311) learned to masturbate during therapy, others allowed themselves to masturbate more freely and without feeling guilt. The frequency of masturbation after therapy by women with orgasmic dysfunctions averaged twice a month in contrast to once a month before therapy ($p = .05$).

Attitudes toward sexuality also changed in the course of therapy (see table 4.19): men and women with sexual dysfunctions and, in general, their partners as well took a more liberal attitude after therapy and conformed less to sex-role stereotypes. This meant that they rejected double standards and saw fewer differences between "male" and "female" sexuality. Finally, they were not as "romantic" as before, that is, they tended less to describe sexuality as a mere expansion of love and harmony. Therapy thus managed to convey to the patients the ideology of sex embodied in the concept of treatment.

The couples' self-ratings of therapeutic changes particularly involve sexual experience and the couples' relationships. For nine tenths of the couples completing the program, therapy dissipated sexual problems (see table 4.20); a quarter classified them as "slightly better," three fifths as "much better"; but only a tenth considered that the difficulties had been fully removed. The latter figure is well below the percentage of men and women whose dysfunctions were "objectively" reversed (almost a half of those completing therapy). This is evidence of the fact that the real change in symptoms often remained several steps behind the great hopes of fulfilled sexuality; or it demonstrated a hesitancy to admit to themselves that they no longer had any sexual problems at all. The differences found between diagnostic groups are the same as those in the therapists' and consultants' evaluation; "cured" vaginismus and "slightly improved" orgasmic dysfunction were particularly frequent. The differences between groups with orgasmic dysfunctions and other symptom groups were, however, not so pronounced, which indicated that many couples found their sexual problems had distinctly improved despite unchanged orgasmic ability. Furthermore, it is striking how closely patient and partner ratings coincided.

The self-ratings show as clearly as the data on sexual behavior that the sexual experience of many couples had changed (see table 4.21; table 5.1, column F1): immediately after therapy both partners were able to enjoy sexual relations more (80 percent), looked forward more to sex with each other (80 percent), and found more satisfaction in sexuality (60 to 70 percent). Fear of failure and of disappointments had also decreased (about 80 percent). Sixty percent reported augmented sexual desire. These changes were just as pronounced for both partners (dysfunctional, nondysfunctional), with minor variations.

There are minor differences between the four diagnostic groups (see table 4.21). Only the scores for the category "sexual desire" are worth mentioning here: 80 percent of the men who had previously had erectile dysfunctions felt greater desire, but only 32 percent of the men who had formerly suffered from premature ejaculation did. However, more important is the fact that orgasmic dysfunctions differed only slightly from other groups as regards changes in sexual experience.

In general terms, four fifths of all couples (both partners) consider their relationship was better after therapy; half even thought it was "much better" (see table 4.20). The therapists' impression that the relationship often developed positively in therapy was thus confirmed.

Changes in the symptomatic partner were evaluated independently of the diagnosis. In terms of the nondysfunctional partners, a great many of the men with formerly vaginistic partners considered their relationship was distinctly improved, while very few of the women whose partners had been premature ejaculators thought this was so. Table 4.22 shows the various meanings of "improvement" in a relationship (see also table 5.1, column F1): there was a greater sense of affection, communication was more effective, and hostility had been dissipated. Many couples, 60 to 70 percent, were capable of being more affectionate and found it easier to talk about sexual wishes and problems; 40 to 50 percent felt more affection for each other, spent more time with each other, found more constructive solutions to nonsexual conflicts, and were less aggressive toward each other. Both partners assessed these changes almost identically. There were no appreciable differences between diagnostic groups, and orgasmic dysfunctions did not form a special category in this regard either.

CHILDREN

An important aspect of dysfunctional sexuality is reproduction, at least for primary erectile dysfunctions and primary vaginismus, that is, men and women who are and were incapable of sexual intercourse. Treatment of thirty-four couples with dysfunctions of this kind was successful. At least nine of them had a child by the time the project had been concluded. The number of couples for whom reversal of their sexual dysfunctions had similar consequences was probably higher, but not all were available for follow-up.

THE INFLUENCE OF SOCIAL CLASS

In terms of selection and prognosis, many forms of psychotherapy are oriented specifically to particular social strata, namely, the middle and upper classes. In our sample, too, couples from the upper social classes or with higher education were overrepresented (see p. 78), although there is no evidence for sexual dysfunctions being especially common in these groups. The reasons for this imbalance are as follows: first, couples from the lower classes are even more perplexed by the jungle of psychosocial welfare than are the upper classes; they are less well informed about available facilities; they are worlds apart from special psychotherapeutic units in a university clinic. Second, these men and women distinctly tend to believe that sexual dysfunctions are physically caused and have difficulty in imagining that there is any sense or hope in psychotherapeutic intervention, or they are at least sceptical. Finally, they often have to resign themselves passively to their sexual disturbances because they simply have more urgent problems to solve.

The question is whether men and women from the lower classes would have less of a chance for success in couple therapy if they decided to enter it. Also in question is the influence of intelligence, which we consider to be a variable linked to social class, on therapy outcome. Table 4.23 shows the most important findings from therapist ratings of overall outcome immediately after completion of treatment. These findings demonstrate that there was no relation between school education and therapy outcome. Working-class couples (defined by the male partner's job) made as much progress as academic couples; but couples in which the man was a low-ranking or middle-ranking civil servant or an employee with a comparable position, that is, a member of the lower middle class, had significantly less success. This applies to both male and female dysfunctions. From the perspective of the female partner's occupation, the results were striking only for the housewife group: regardless of educational level and previous occupation, women who only took care of the family had significantly lower chances of achieving a decisive improvement in their sexual disturbances in couple therapy. This should be viewed in the light of the fact that the sexuality of housewives is often severely impeded, particularly by arousal and orgasmic dysfunctions combined with virulently aversive reactions to sexuality. Their sexuality has been stifled: they have been sucked dry by the family's various emotional demands, are confined to the narrow household environment, dependent on their husbands, and exhausted by the monotony of daily life. The disturbance is an escape from these burdens and the emotional demands made on her by the family; it is the only opportunity she has left to counteract closeness and dependency with distance and autonomy. Therapy often could do little to change this situation, although we concentrated attempts on relieving these women's situation by encouraging them to work part-time and to spend some of their leisure time on their own outside the family circle.

There were no signs whatsoever of a connection between therapy outcome and intelligence (see table 4.23) insofar as this was tested by the "Berufseignungstest" (German adaptation of the "General Aptitude Test Battery"; Schmale and Schmidtke 1966/1967). This result was particularly important in terms of verbal intelligence: low language proficiency apparently did not affect therapy outcome negatively.

Our aim to develop a form of therapy equally accessible to all social classes could only be partly achieved because access for men and women from the lower classes to psychotherapeutic institutions, particularly if they are not an integral part of the community health care, is impeded by inner and outer barriers. Our couple therapy was, however, independent of class insofar as the prognosis for workers and men and women with only nine years of schooling or with low scores in intelligence tests was in no way prejudiced.

EVALUATION OF RESULTS

Our data show that couple therapy induced a positive modification in sexual function, sexual experience, and relationships. Some of the fundamental problems involved in defining therapy success will be discussed in chapter 5; in the following we will consider methodological and therapeutic problems.

The problem of validity. Because the therapists assessed their own work, our data are based on subjective judgments, regardless of the attempts to operationalize their ratings as far as possible. The "independent" first consultants did not themselves conduct the treatments they assessed but were involved in the project as a whole, that is, they treated other couples and were committed to helping develop an effective therapy program. The couples assessed themselves, that is, their own efforts, and their tendency to deny partial failures may have biased their ratings positively, just as may have their desire to make a friendly goodbye gesture to the therapists. Our reasons for believing we are able to sketch an adequately objective and valid picture of reality, despite these sources of error, are fourfold:

1. The assessments made by therapists and first consultants resulted for the most part in a comparable distribution of variables (see tables 4.12 to 4.17).[10] The trend was for therapists to be stricter in their assessments than were the first consultants. This can presumably be explained by the effect of selection: the consultants did not assess all couples, and they tended to include a disproportionately high percentage of "successful" patients in follow-ups.

2. The distribution of patients' and partners' self-ratings generally coincided, insofar as the same topics were assessed (see tables 4.18 and 4.20; figures 4.1 and 4.2).[11]

3. Although patients and therapists used different rating procedures, their descriptions coincided in content to a large extent, for example, in terms of changes in sexual problems and relationships (see table 4.17 and table 4.20) and as regards sexual function (see tables 4.13, 4.14, 4.16, 4.17, and 4.18).[12]

4. The different questionnaire procedures for the couples (diary, Q1; questionnaire on sexual behavior in the three months preceding the

questionnaire, Q2; self-assessment questionnaire, Q4) produced roughly similar answers, for example, as regards incidence and frequency of coitus and masturbation.

Because our findings determined by the four observers and the different procedures concurred, we deduce that our data are valid; they enable us at least to characterize therapeutic changes in rough terms.

Comparison with Masters and Johnson. To what extent do our results concur with those of other research teams working on couple therapy for sexual dysfunctions? This question is difficult to answer for two reasons: First, there is no way of telling whether samples of patients treated are in any way comparable. This is even true of relatively simple questions, such as severity of dysfunctions and duration of symptoms; above all, it is quite impossible to estimate to what extent the sexual problem was accompanied by neurotic and partner conflicts in the various samples because the criteria for selection varied (p. 77). Second, the criteria for describing therapy outcome varied considerably and were, moreover, by no means precisely defined. Thus, a comparison of our results with those of other research teams is impossible. We shall, however, attempt a comparison with the data Masters and Johnson published because our treatment program is based on the methods they developed and our investigation is, at least in terms of sample size, most comparable with theirs.

Masters and Johnson chose the "initial failure rate" as a criterion for therapy outcome. Initial failure is defined "as indication that the two-week rapid-treatment phase has failed to initiate reversal of the basic symptomatology" (Masters and Johnson 1970, p. 352). They do not, however, define the degree of symptom improvement that therapy should achieve before a reversal can be said to have been "initiated." If we assume that a "reversal of the basic symptomatology has been initiated" in all our "improved patients,"[13] we then arrive at the following comparable figures:

Failure Rates on Completion of Therapy

	Masters and Johnson		Hamburg Team	
Orgasmic dysfunction	19%[a]	(N = 342)	31%	(N = 108)
Vaginismus	0%	(N = 29)	22%	(N = 27)
Erectile dysfunction	28%[b]	(N = 245)	21%	(N = 57)
Premature ejaculation	2%	(N = 186)	16%	(N = 31)
Total	17%	(N = 802)	25%	(N = 223)

[a] *Primary, secondary, and situational orgasmic dysfunctions combined.*
[b] *Primary and secondary erectile dysfunctions combined.*

Excepting erectile dysfunctions, with which we had slightly more success, Masters and Johnson report considerably less failure for orgasmic dysfunctions, vaginismus, and premature ejaculation. The differences in therapy settings (Masters and Johnson conducted only intensive therapy) can hardly be responsible for this, as we shall demonstrate later on. One certainly cannot exclude the possibility that the Masters and Johnson team were more successful in therapy. It is probably more realistic—and a relief to us, as well—to assume that the differences in results were caused by variations in patient screening: Masters and Johnson presumably treated prudish, sexually restricted Midwestern couples in the 1960s; we mainly treated sexually well-informed and on the whole sexually liberal urban couples in the 1970s, who had little need for the educational part of our therapy program,[14] something Masters and Johnson placed great emphasis on. They selected their couples with a view to a minimum of partner conflicts and of psychopathology, whereas we did not eliminate patients on the grounds of neurotic symptomatology or partner dynamics. Finally, we noticed that their percentage of so-called bilateral dysfunctions (both partners dysfunctional) is extremely high (44 percent compared to our 10 percent). They presumably equated minor disturbances that emerged in the wake of a partner's severe problem with dysfunctions, and so they possibly included a whole series of problems in their outcome statistics which we would not consider dysfunctions.

Difficulties in treating orgasmic dysfunctions. It is clear from our earlier analysis of results that, of the four diagnostic groups, orgasmic dysfunctions assume a special status: in terms of sexual function, failures (no improvement in symptoms) were particularly frequent and success in the sense of symptom reversal particularly rare. On the other hand, in terms of changes in relationships and in sexual experience induced by therapy, there were far fewer differences between the diagnostic groups. One can infer two things from this fact: first, it is more difficult to reverse orgasmic dysfunctions than other disturbances.[15] In contrast to Masters and Johnson, all the more recent investigations come unanimously to the same conclusion (for example, Faulk 1971; Lobitz and LoPiccolo 1972; Meyer et al. 1975; McGovern, McMullen, and LoPiccolo 1975; Mathews at al. 1975; Snyder, LoPiccolo, and LoPiccolo 1975). Second, in the case of many couples reversal of orgasmic dysfunction is obviously not necessarily required for them to feel considerably relieved and disburdened in sexuality and their relationship after therapy.

The women who were "improved" after therapy without their orgasmic ability having changed (33 percent of women with orgasmic dysfunctions; see Table 4.11) felt a relative, subjective satisfaction with their sexual lives. Almost all judged that their sexual difficulties were at least partly improved after therapy, and more than half even said they were greatly improved; four fifths considered their relationships were distinctly improved, and as many were able to enjoy sexuality more, were more pleased at the thought of intercourse, and more satisfied afterward. (The changes in women whose orgasmic ability was enhanced by therapy were, however, significantly more pronounced, except for changes in relationships.) The discrepancy between unchanged orgasmic ability and these judgments can be explained if one considers the initial situation of these women. Most of them had not only orgasmic problems but arousal dysfunctions as well and, more important, frequently a strong aversion to sex in general which made them feel every approach was a nuisance or a torment. They fled from sexuality or endured it unwillingly, which often led to serious tensions and conflicts in the relationship.

Therapists described, in case histories of the "improved" group, how the patient, her partner, and their relationship was decisively relieved of distress and how avoidance behavior, repugnance to sex, and physical irritation on sexual intercourse were reversed. Sexuality and tenderness were no longer invested with anxiety, no longer something one had to escape; tenderness could be enjoyed because it was no longer a warning signal of threatening sexuality. Sexual intercourse was experienced as pleasurable; it no longer represented fulfillment of a tiresome duty or subjugation to the partner's wishes, but was experienced as a moment of tenderness, warmth, and affection. Both partners were able to communicate their sexual wishes more openly, found it easier to say "no," and to accept the partner's "no"; and they realized that sexual intercourse is not always necessary and that touching, body contact, or "petting" can suffice. Women often learned to accept their own bodies more; almost a third started masturbating or masturbated more freely. As women they felt more "normal" and self-assured. The performance pressure they felt or exerted on their partners, and their partners' feelings of failure, were less strong. Women in whom we found these changes were by no means always satisfied with the therapy outcome; they still desired orgasm in petting and intercourse "sometime in the future." But the problem was no longer so distressing, and both they and their partners were more relaxed in coping with it.

The pretherapy state of despair of many women with orgasmic dysfunctions was definitely one of the reasons for the relative lack of success compared to the other diagnostic groups. However, sexual symptoms were not the only causes of this difficult initial situation. In women with orgasmic dysfunctions, we very often observed strong neurotic and partner conflicts, which made treatment more difficult. That these women had more serious psychological difficulties than other dysfunctional partners is demonstrated by the psychological tests. These patients described themselves as being particularly depressive, emotionally labile, and unsure of themselves.

Another reason for the difficulty in treating orgasmic dysfunctions is the therapeutic procedure itself. In its original form, the therapeutic concept of Masters and Johnson places far too much emphasis on removing sexual fears, fears of failure, and performance pressure. It is far too dependent on the concept of "buried instincts," which assumes that sexual desire and functioning develop of their own accord, so to speak, once inhibitions have been removed. Orgasmic dysfunctions are, however, often not merely symptoms of inhibition. It does not suffice to remove anxieties unless the patient builds up an acceptance of her body and opens up to the experience of sexual arousal and orgasm. Our data suggest that therapeutic interventions that aim to enhance bodily self-awareness and self-stimulation can result in an improvement of therapy outcome for orgasmic ability. Such intervention was frequently employed in treating orgasmic dysfunctions in 1976 and 1977, and the number of women rated as "distinctly improved" and "cured" was significantly higher than it was in treatment between 1973 and 1975 (48 percent versus 29 percent, p = .05). However, the difference might not be due only to the new elements in treatment but also to an increase in therapist experience.

Finally, motivation for therapy in women with orgasmic dysfunctions was very often more problematic than in other diagnostic groups. It was often the male partner who suffered from his partner's dysfunction: he felt unsatisfied and sexually deprived; it offended him that his wife frequently rebuffed him and that she did not feel he was the lover he would like to be. Women with primary arousal and orgasmic dysfunctions were quite unable to sense that "something was missing." At the start of therapy many of them claimed they could actually dispense with sexuality. The primary reason they wanted therapy was to be more capable of satisfying their partner's wishes or because they were afraid the sexual problem could seriously undermine the relationship in the long run. Under these circumstances women with orgasmic dysfunctions found it particularly difficult to develop an intrinsic motivation; in any case, motivation often originated from an external source and was vested with interests foreign to them. It is as important as it is difficult for therapists to give a woman the opportunity to find out her own wishes and to locate her own needs in therapy. Their task is to help her understand that therapy is not possible unless she expects some personal gain and unless she wants to find out whether sexuality holds any new experiences in store. Women often find therapy in female groups easier and more convincing in this respect than couple therapy. (A motivation problem is exemplified in the case history couple 39 on p. 249.)

List of Abbreviations Used in the Tables

OD   orgasmic dysfunction
VA   vaginismus
ED   erectile dysfunction
PE   premature ejaculation
P1   pretest 1 (three to twelve months before therapy)
P2   pretest 2 (immediately before therapy)
F1   follow-up 1 (immediately after therapy)
F2   follow-up 2 (three months after therapy)
F3   follow-up 3 (one year after therapy)
F4   follow-up 4 (two and a half to four and a half years after therapy)
N   number of individual cases
Nc   number of couples
ns   statistically not significant
m   mean
s   standard deviation

TABLE 4.1
Background Data of Couples Treated

		OD (N=108)	VA (N=27)	ED (N=57)	PE (N=31)	Total (N=223)
Age (years)	range	20–41	20–36	20–51	23–45	20–51
	mean	28.2	26.3	34.1	32.9	30.1
Age of partner (years)	range	22–48	23–52	18–46	21–44	18–52
	mean	30.8	29.4	31.5	29.0	30.6
Marital status	married	73%	82%	72%	71%	74%
	single	27%	18%	28%	29%	26%
Children	0	52%	93%	63%	48%	59%
	1	26%	7%[a]	19%	23%	21%
	2 or more	22%	0%	18%	29%	19%
Duration of relationship (years)	range	1–20	3–16	1–27	1–20	1–20
	mean	8.0	7.1	8.9	8.2	8.1
Duration of dysfunction						
	up to 2 years	10%	7%	18%	3%	11%
	3 to 5 years	30%	33%	29%	19%	29%
	6 years or more	60%	59%	54%	77%	61%

[a] Two women had secondary vaginismus.

TABLE 4.2

Occupation and School Education of Couples Treated

	Patient				Partner			
	OD (N=108)	VA (N=27)	ED (N=57)	PE (N=31)	OD (N=108)	VA (N=27)	ED (N=57)	PE (N=31)
Occupation								
skilled or unskilled workers	3%	11%	21%	26%	26%	26%	9%	3%
employees, civil servants	31%	63%	30%	19%	31%	30%	37%	35%
higher ranking employees, civil servants	0%	4%	7%	6%	6%	4%	4%	0%
self-employed	0%	0%	7%	6%	2%	7%	4%	0%
academics	9%	15%	26%	19%	16%	26%	5%	7%
housewives[a]	37%	0%	–	–	–	–	32%	35%
student/apprentice	20%	7%	9%	23%	18%	7%	11%	19%
Employment								
none	31%	0%	0%	0%	2%	4%	26%	35%
part-time	17%	19%	4%	0%	3%	0%	25%	19%
full-time	32%	74%	88%	77%	78%	89%	39%	26%
(student/apprentice)	(20%)	(7%)	(9%)	(23%)	(18%)	(7%)	(11%)	(19%)
School education								
9 years (Hauptschule)	36%	52%	44%	36%	40%	30%	40%	36%
10 years (Mittlere Reife)	32%	30%	19%	19%	25%	41%	40%	32%
13 years or more (Abitur)	31%	18%	37%	45%	35%	29%	30%	32%

a Including women employed by the hour. Women who fulfill household duties but are also employed part-time do not count as housewives in these statistics.

TABLE 4.3
Sexual Behavior of Couples Treated

	Patient				Partner			
	OD (N=108)	VA (N=27)	ED (N=57)	PE (N=31)	OD (N=108)	VA (N=27)	ED (N=57)	PE (N=31)
Masturbation								
incidence, total[a]	62%	56%	97%	94%	86%	89%	72%	84%
mean age at first experience (years)[b]	16.5	16.2	13.8	13.1	13.6	15.2	17.0	17.6
incidence, active[c]	46%	51%	84%	74%	81%	85%	58%	56%
incidence with orgasm, active[c]	39%	48%	—	—	—	—	44%	56%
Coitus								
mean age at first experience (years)[b]	18.6	—	19.6	20.2	18.6	20.2	18.4	18.8
frequency, active[c]								
never	12%	96%	44%	11%	12%	100%	43%	15%
up to 5 a month	49%	4%	48%	48%	52%	0%	48%	44%
6 or more a month	38%	0%	8%	41%	36%	0%	9%	41%
orgasm in women, never[c]	81%	—	—	—	—	—	34%	79%

a At least once prior to therapy.
b Only patients with experience in masturbation or coitus.
c In the three months prior to therapy (pretest 1).

TABLE 4.4

Personality Traits of Couples Treated: Freiburger Persönlichkeits Inventar (FPI) Scales[a]

	Patient				Partner			
Scale	OD (N=103) vs. norm	VA (N=27) vs. norm	ED (N=51) vs. norm	PE (N=29) vs. norm	OD (N=103) vs. norm	VA (N=27) vs. norm	ED (N=51) vs. norm	PE (N=29) vs. norm
1. Nervousness	—	—	(+).10	—	—	—	—	—
2. Aggressiveness	(+).10	(−).10	—	—	—	—	—	—
3. Depression	—	—	—	—	—	—	—	—
4. Arousability	—	—	—	—	(−).10	—	—	—
5. Sociability	—	—	—	—	—	—	—	(+).05
6. Calmness, relaxation	(−).001	(−).001	—	(−).10	(−).05	—	(−).05	—
7. Dominance	(−).01	(−).01	(−).01	(−).05	(−).001	(−).05	(−).01	(−).001
8. Social inhibition	(+).05	(+).05	—	—	—	—	—	—
9. Openness	—	—	—	—	—	—	—	—
E. Extraversion	—	—	(−).10	—	—	—	—	—
N. Emotional lability	(+).05	—	—	—	—	—	—	—
M. Masculinity	(−).05	(−).01	(−).01	(−).10	(−).001	(−).05	—	—

[a] Comparisons with norm scores for adult women/men (Fahrenberg, Selg, and Hampel 1973). Statistical significance of mean differences according to t-test. + = significantly higher mean than norm; − = significantly lower mean than norm.

TABLE 4.5

Personality Traits of Couples Treated: Giessen-Test (GT) Scales[a]

Scale	Patient				Partner			
	OD (N=101) vs. norm	VA (N=25) vs. norm	ED (N=51) vs. norm	PE (N=29) vs. norm	OD (N=101) vs. norm	VA (N=25) vs. norm	ED (N=51) vs. norm	PE (N=29) vs. norm
1. Social resonance (negative-positive socially resonant)	(−).001	(−).001	(−).001	(−).01	(−).01	(−).05	(−).01	(−).05
2. Dominance (dominant-accommodating)	(−).001	(−).05	—	(−).05	—	—	(−).05	(−).10
3. Control (undercontrolled-overcontrolled)	—	(−).05	—	—	—	—	—	(−).10
4. Basic mood (hypomanic-depressive)	(+).001	(+).001	(+).001	(+).01	(+).01	(+).05	(+).001	(+).001
5. Permeability (open-retentive)	(+).01	(−).05	—	—	—	(+).10	—	—
6. Social potency (socially potent-socially impotent)	—	(+).10	—	—	—	—	—	—

[a] Comparison with norm scores for adult women and men (Beckmann and Richter 1972). Statistical significance of mean differences according to t-test. + = significantly higher mean than norm; − = significantly lower mean than norm.

TABLE 4.6

Design of Assessment Methods

Rater	Method[a]	Time
First consultant[b]	Interview	P1, F1, F3
	Rating of sexual functioning (R1)	P1, F1, F3
Therapist(s)	Interview	P2, F1, F3, F4
	Rating of sexual functioning (R1)	P2, F1, F3
	Rating of therapy outcome (R2)	F1, F3, F4
	Case history	F1, F3, F4
Patient	Diary (1 week) on sexual behavior (Q1)	P1, P2, F1, F2, F3
	Questionnaire on sexual behavior in the last 3 months (Q2)	P1, P2, F2, F3, F4
	Questionnaire on attitudes toward sexuality (Q3)	P2, F1, F3
	Self-rating of changes in sexual relations (Q4)	F1, F2, F3, F4
	Psychological tests:	
	Freiburg Personality Inventory (FPI)	P2, F3
	Giessen Test[c] (GT)	P2, F1, F2, F3
	Emotionality Inventory (EMI)	P2, F1, F2, F3
Partner	(see patient)	

[a] Our questionnaires (R1, Q1–Q4) are published in Arentewicz et al. 1975; R2 is to be found in the appendix to the tables on p. 120–121.

[b] Psychiatrist or psychologist in the outpatient service of the Department for Sex Research who selected the couple for therapy.

[c] Self-rating (GT-S) and rating on partner (GT-Fm, GT-Fw).

TABLE 4.7

Sample Size (Number of Couples [Nc]) in Follow-ups

	Therapy completed (Nc = 164)			Therapy drop-outs (Nc = 38)	Total (Nc = 202)
	Ratings, therapists	Ratings, first consultants[a]	Question-naires, couples	Interview therapists	Rating, interview therapists
F1 (immediately after therapy)	164(100%)	119(73%)	133(81%)	38(100%)	202(100%)
F2 (3 months after therapy)	—	—	108(66%)	—	—
F3 (1 year after therapy)[b]	116(71%)	62(38%)	87(53%)	25(66%)	141(70%)
F4 (2½–4½ years after therapy)[c]	99(60%)	—	76(46%)	18(47%)	117(58%)

[a] The high rate of missing data is due to the difficulty in coordinating the follow-up appointments between first consultant and therapists and to the fact that one of the four first consultants left our department.

[b] At the end of the research project, therapy completion or drop-out by 11 couples dated back to less than one year (9 completers, 2 drop-outs); 14 couples (11 and 3) had moved to an unknown address. 36 (28 and 8) did not appear for follow-up.

[c] In the last follow-up (spring 1981) therapy completion and drop-out by 7 couples (5 and 2) dated back to less than 2½ years previously. 38 (31 and 7) couples had moved to unknown addresses. 40 (29 and 11) couples did not come to follow-up.

TABLE 4.8

Sample Size (Number of Patients) in the Different Therapy Settings

	OD (N=108)	VA (N=27)	ED (N=57)	PE (N=31)	Total (N=223)
2 therapists, long-term	52	14	15	6	87
1 therapist, long-term	31	3	12	13	59
2 therapists, intensive	25	10	30	12	77

TABLE 4.9

Duration of Therapy, Number and Length of Therapy Sessions[a]

	Mean duration of therapy in weeks	Mean number of sessions	Mean length of sessions in minutes
Long-term therapies			
total (N=111)	32	38	31
2 therapists (N=63)	32	39	30
1 therapist (N=48)	31	36	33
OD (N=57)	32	39	32
VA (N=16)	34	42	31
ED (N=22)	27	33	29
PE (N=16)	33	35	30
Intensive therapies			
total (N=67)	3[b]	16[b]	39

[a] Couples who dropped out of therapy are not included in this table. Dropout occurred on average after 19 sessions and 14 weeks.
[b] For intensive therapies 16 sessions in 3 weeks were planned. On average two additional booster sessions were arranged.

TABLE 4.10

Therapeutic Experience of Therapists[a]

	2 Therapists, long-term (N=87)	1 Therapist, long-term (N=59)	2 Therapists, intensive (N=77)	Total (N=223)
The therapist or both therapists inexperienced	1%	5%	1%	2%
One therapist inexperienced, one therapist experienced	48%	—	31%	29%
The therapist or both therapists experienced	51%	95%	68%	68%

[a] *"Experience" is defined as having conducted at least four couple therapies.*

TABLE 4.11

Overall Outcome of Therapy; Ratings by Therapists[a]

	OD (N=108)	VA (N=27)	ED (N=57)	PE (N=31)	Total (N=223)
1. Sexual functioning					
(1) drop-out, separation of couple	6%	4%	0%	7%	4%
(2) drop-out, unimproved	13%	7%	11%	3%	10%
(3) drop-out, slightly improved	5%	0%	2%	3%	3%
(4) therapy completed, unim- proved	2%	0%	4%	0%	2%
(5) therapy completed, slightly improved	4%	11%	4%	3%	5%
(6) therapy completed, improved	33%	0%	14%	20%	23%
(7) therapy completed, distinctly improved	17%	11%	16%	23%	17%
(8) therapy completed, cured	19%	67%	49%	40%	35%
2. Relationship in general					
(0) inapplicable, drop-out	24%	11%	13%	13%	17%
(1) disturbed as before	5%	7%	6%	3%	5%
(2) disturbed as before, but more aware of problems	8%	4%	10%	14%	9%
(3) positive state unchanged	5%	30%	12%	7%	10%
(4) deteriorated	1%	0%	0%	0%	0%
(5) improved	42%	44%	44%	45%	44%
(6) distinctly improved	16%	4%	14%	17%	14%
3. Sexual satisfaction					
(0) inapplicable, drop-out	24%	11%	13%	13%	17%
(1) less satisfying than before therapy	0%	0%	2%	0%	0%
(2) just as unsatisfying	5%	0%	6%	3%	4%
(3) somewhat more satisfying than before therapy	28%	43%	28%	24%	29%
(4) satisfying	43%	47%	50%	59%	49%

[a] *Ratings of overall outcome R2; for a definition of categories see p. 120.*

TABLE 4.12

Female Dysfunctions: Sexual Responses Before and After Therapy; Ratings by Therapists and First Consultants[a]

	OD		VA	
	P1-F1 (1st consultant) (N=56)	P2-F1 (therapist) (N=81)	P1-F1 (1st consultant) (N=16)	P2-F1 (therapist) (N=23)
Lubrication, frequency in coitus/petting	(+).001	(+).001	(+).05	(+).05
Lubrication, degree in coitus/petting	(+).01	(+).001	(+).10	(+).05
Arousal in coitus/petting	(+).001	(+).001	ns	ns
Frequency of orgasm in coitus	(+).001	(+).05	inapplicable	
Frequency of orgasm in petting	ns	(+).01	ns	ns
Frequency of orgasm in masturbation	ns	ns	ns	ns

[a] *Ratings of sexual responses R1. The data apply only to couples completing therapy. The table shows direction of changes (+ = greater, − = lower at follow-up) and the level of significance of these differences (according to sign-test).*

TABLE 4.13

Orgasmic Dysfunctions: Frequency of Coital Orgasm Before and After Therapy; Ratings by Therapists and First Consultants[a]

	1st Consultant		Therapist	
	P1 (N=56)	F1 (N=56)	P2 (N=81)	F1 (N=81)
Frequency of orgasm on coitus				
never	89%	58%	77%	63%
seldom (up to 25%)	5%	11%	19%	8%
sometimes (25–50%)	4%	4%	0%	6%
often (50–75%)	0%	12%	1%	4%
almost always (more than 75%)	2%	9%	2%	8%
always	0%	7%	0%	11%
	.001		.05	

[a] *Ratings of sexual responses R1. The data refer only to couples completing therapy. Statistical significance according to sign-test.*

TABLE 4.14

Vaginismus: Incidence Before and After Therapy;
Ratings by Therapists and First Consultants[a]

	1st Consultant		Therapist	
	P1 (N=16)	F1 (N=16)	P2 (N=23)	F1 (N=23)
No vaginismus	0%	94%	0%	78%
Mild vaginismus[b]	18%	6%	0%	9%
Fairly severe vaginismus	37%	0%	61%	13%
Severe vaginismus	44%	0%	39%	0%
	.01		.001	

[a] *Ratings of sexual responses R1. The data refer only to couples completing therapy. Statistical significance according to sign-test.*
[b] *"Mild"—coitus possible but painful; "fairly severe"—coitus impossible, insertion of finger possible; "severe"—coitus and insertion of finger impossible.*

TABLE 4.15

Male Dysfunctions: Sexual Responses Before and After Therapy;
Ratings by Therapists and First Consultants[a]

	ED		PE	
	P1-F1 (1st consultant) (N=35)	P2-F1 (therapist) (N=45)	P1-F1 (1st consultant) (N=19)	P2-F1 (therapist) (N=26)
Frequency of erection in coitus/coital attempts	(+).001	(+).01	ns	ns
Degree of erection in coitus/coital attempts	(+).001	(+).001	ns	ns
Frequency of erection in masturbation	ns	ns	ns	ns
Degree of erection in masturbation	ns	ns	ns	ns
Frequency of ejaculation in coitus	ns	ns	ns	ns
Frequency of premature ejaculation in coitus/coital attempts	ns	ns	(−).001	(−).001

[a] *Ratings of sexual responses R1. The data refer only to couples completing therapy. The table shows the direction of changes (+ = greater, − = lower at follow-up) and the level of significance of these differences (according to sign-test).*

TABLE 4.16

Erectile Dysfunctions: Erection in Coitus Before and After Therapy;
Ratings by Therapists and First Consultants[a]

	1st Consultant		Therapist	
	P1 (N=35)	F1 (N=35)	P2 (N=45)	F1 (N=45)
Frequency of erections in coitus/ coital attempts				
never	14%	0%	9%	0%
seldom (up to 25%)	38%	0%	29%	2%
sometimes (25–50%)	11%	0%	11%	2%
often (50–75%)	14%	6%	13%	12%
almost always (more than 75%)	11%	50%	11%	46%
always	11%	44%	27%	37%
		.001		.01
Degree of erections in coitus/ coital attempts				
totally flaccid	3%	0%	7%	0%
slightly stiff	38%	0%	18%	2%
half-stiff	35%	14%	47%	17%
totally stiff	24%	86%	29%	81%
		.001		.001

[a] *Ratings of sexual responses R1. The data refer only to couples completing therapy. Statistical significance according to sign-test.*

TABLE 4.17

Premature Ejaculation: Control of Ejaculation in Coitus Before and
After Therapy; Ratings by Therapists and First Consultants[a]

	1st Consultant		Therapist	
	P1 (N=19)	F1 (N=19)	P2 (N=26)	F1 (N=26)
Moment of ejaculation				
"ante portas"	0%	0%	0%	0%
premature	89%	21%	96%	19%
"normal"	11%	79%	4%	81%
		.001		.001
Frequency of premature ejaculation				
never	0%	39%	0%	38%
seldom (up to 25%)	11%	39%	0%	23%
sometimes (25–50%)	0%	6%	0%	15%
often (50–75%)	0%	6%	12%	8%
almost always (more than 75%)	5%	6%	8%	8%
always	84%	6%	81%	8%
		.001		.001

[a] *Ratings of sexual responses R1. The data refer only to couples completing therapy. Statistical significance according to sign-test.*

TABLE 4.18
Sexual Responses Before and After Therapy; Couple Self-Rating [a,b]

		Patient	Partner
Orgasmic dysfunction		(N=65)	(N=65)
Vaginal secretion on sexual intercourse is now . . .	fully sufficient	11%	13%
	increased	51%	44%
	unchanged	38%	43%
	decreased	0%	0%
I/my partner now have/has orgasm on sexual intercourse . . .	always, almost always	13%	14%
	more often	33%	30%
	unchanged	54%	55%
	less often	0%	2%
My orgasm/my partner's orgasm on sexual intercourse is now . . .	more intense	38%	45%
	unchanged	60%	55%
	less intense	2%	0%
Erectile dysfunctions		(N=40)	(N=39)
Erection on sexual intercourse is now . . .	fully sufficient	26%	31%
	better	62%	59%
	unchanged	13%	10%
	worse	0%	0%
Premature ejaculation		(N=22)	(N=22)
I/my partner now control(s) the moment of ejaculation . . .	better	86%	76%
	unchanged	14%	19%
	worse	0%	5%

[a] *Questionnaire Q4. The data refer to couples completing therapy.*
[b] *Questionnaire Q4 contains no special questions for vaginistic women.*
Statistical significances according to sign-test (negative vs. positive changes): patient: p=.001 for all items; partner: p=.001 for all items

TABLE 4.19

Changes in Attitudes Toward Sexuality on Completion of
Therapy and One Year Later[a]

	Patient		Partner	
Scale	Female dysfunction (N=50)	Male dysfunction (N=33)	Female dysfunction (N=52)	Male dysfunction (N=32)
Restrictiveness				
statistical significance[b]	.05	(.10)	(.10)	.01
trend[c]	decrease	(decrease)	(decrease)	decrease
Romanticism				
statistical significance[b]	.001	.05	ns	.05
trend[c]	decrease	decrease		decrease
Sex-role conformity				
statistical significance[b]	.001	.05	ns	.05
trend[c]	decrease	decrease		decrease

[a] *Questionnaire Q3. The data refer only to couples completing therapy who completed questionnaire Q3 at all three test times (P2, F1, F3).*

[b] *Analysis of variance, three times of measurement (P2, F1, F3), repeated measurement.*

[c] *Decrease = means for P2 statistically significantly higher than for F1 and F3; no statistically significant differences of means between F1 and F3; according to t-test for dependent samples. (Decrease) = t-tests not significant.*

TABLE 4.20

Overall Outcome of Therapy; Couple Self-Rating[a]

		OD		VA		ED		PE		Total	
		Patient (N=65)	Partner (N=65)	Patient (N=18)	Partner (N=18)	Patient (N=40)	Partner (N=39)	Patient (N=22)	Partner (N=22)	Patient (N=145)	Partner (N=144)
Our sexual problems are now...than before therapy	worse	2%	0%	0%	0%	0%	0%	0%	0%	0%	0%
	unchanged	3%	3%	0%	6%	2%	5%	4%	0%	3%	4%
	slightly better	29%	38%	11%	0%	13%	18%	36%	33%	23%	27%
	much better	64%	52%	61%	59%	73%	67%	55%	62%	65%	58%
	fully removed	2%	6%	28%	35%	13%	10%	5%	5%	8%	11%
Our relationship is now... than before therapy	worse	2%	2%	0%	0%	0%	3%	0%	10%	1%	8%
	unchanged	13%	13%	17%	12%	15%	13%	27%	14%	16%	13%
	slightly better	33%	38%	28%	24%	31%	24%	23%	38%	30%	32%
	much better	52%	48%	56%	65%	54%	61%	50%	38%	53%	52%

[a] Questionnaire Q4. The data refer only to couples completing therapy.

TABLE 4.21

Sexuality Before and After Therapy; Couple Self-Rating[a]

		OD		VA		ED		PE	
		Patient (N=65)	Partner (N=65)	Patient (N=18)	Partner (N=18)	Patient (N=40)	Partner (N=39)	Patient (N=22)	Partner (N=22)
1. Our sexual problems are not ... than before therapy	worse	2%	0%	0%	0%	0%	0%	0%	0%
	unchanged	3%	3%	0%	6%	2%	5%	4%	0%
	better	95%	97%	100%	94%	98%	95%	96%	100%
2. I now enjoy sexual contacts ... than before therapy	more	89%	82%	83%	94%	97%	85%	100%	86%
	unchanged	8%	15%	17%	6%	3%	15%	0%	14%
	less	3%	3%	0%	0%	0%	0%	0%	0%
3. I now look forward to sexual intercourse ... than before therapy	more	75%	68%	81%	94%	95%	76%	77%	77%
	unchanged	23%	23%	19%	6%	5%	24%	23%	18%
	less	2%	9%	0%	0%	0%	0%	0%	5%
4. My sexual desire is now ... than before therapy	stronger	59%	39%	44%	65%	80%	67%	32%	50%
	unchanged	39%	45%	56%	35%	20%	28%	59%	46%
	weaker	2%	17%	0%	0%	0%	3%	9%	4%
5. My sexual satisfaction after intercourse is now ... than before therapy	greater	83%	61%	—	—	86%	76%	82%	73%
	unchanged	16%	36%	—	—	9%	24%	18%	27%
	less	0%	3%	—	—	6%	0%	0%	0%
6. My fear of failing sexually is now ... than before therapy	less	83%	76%	89%	88%	97%	92%	77%	77%
	unchanged	16%	22%	11%	12%	3%	5%	18%	18%
	stronger	2%	2%	0%	0%	0%	3%	5%	5%
7. If things do not work out sexually my disappointment is now ... than before therapy	less	78%	84%	94%	100%	97%	97%	96%	96%
	unchanged	17%	13%	6%	0%	3%	3%	4%	4%
	greater	5%	3%	0%	0%	0%	0%	0%	0%
8. We now have intercourse ... than before therapy	more often	61%	58%	—	—	79%	82%	46%	68%
	unchanged	22%	31%	—	—	21%	18%	50%	23%
	less often	17%	11%	—	—	0%	0%	4%	9%

[a]Questionnaire Q4. The data refer only to couples completing therapy.
Statistical significance according to sign-test (negative vs. positive changes):
Orgasmic dysfunctions, Patient and partner: p=.001
for all other items
Vaginismus, patient: p=.05 for item 5, p=.01 for item 4, p=.001 for 1, 2, 3, 6, 7, 8

Vaginismus, partner: p=.01 for item 5, p=.001 for all other items
Erectile dysfunctions, patient and partner: p=.001 for all items
Premature ejaculation, patient: ns for item 4, p=.05 for 8, p=.001 for 1, 2, 3, 5, 6, 7
Premature ejaculation, partner: p=.01 for item 4, 8, p=.001 for items 1, 2, 3, 5, 6, 7.

TABLE 4.22

Relationship Before and After Therapy; Couple Self-Rating[a]

		OD Patient (N=65)	OD Partner (N=65)	VA Patient (N=18)	VA Partner (N=18)	ED Patient (N=40)	ED Partner (N=39)	PE Patient (N=22)	PE Partner (N=22)
1. Our relationship is now ... than before therapy	worse	2%	2%	0%	0%	3%	3%	0%	10%
	unchanged	13%	13%	17%	12%	15%	13%	27%	14%
	better	85%	85%	83%	88%	82%	84%	73%	76%
2. I like my partner now ... than before therapy	more	49%	42%	44%	47%	45%	51%	45%	50%
	unchanged	51%	57%	56%	47%	55%	49%	55%	45%
	less	0%	1%	0%	6%	0%	0%	0%	5%
3. Being affectionate to my partner is now ... than before therapy	more difficult	0%	5%	0%	6%	0%	0%	0%	0%
	unchanged	25%	17%	28%	18%	22%	31%	18%	36%
	easier	75%	78%	72%	76%	78%	69%	82%	64%
4. The time we spend with each other is ... than before therapy	more	57%	51%	44%	59%	67%	53%	50%	64%
	unchanged	40%	41%	56%	35%	28%	47%	50%	27%
	less	3%	8%	0%	6%	5%	0%	0%	9%
5. We can now find ... solutions to nonsexual problems than before therapy	more easily	66%	62%	56%	47%	55%	68%	50%	57%
	unchanged	34%	38%	44%	53%	45%	29%	50%	33%
	less easily	0%	0%	0%	0%	0%	3%	0%	10%
6. My aggression toward my partner is now ... than before therapy	more frequent	9%	8%	6%	12%	13%	8%	0%	9%
	unchanged	32%	39%	44%	35%	38%	31%	41%	41%
	less frequent	59%	53%	50%	53%	49%	61%	59%	50%
7. I now find it ... to talk about our sexual wishes and problems than before therapy	more difficult	0%	0%	6%	0%	0%	0%	0%	0%
	unchanged	18%	23%	11%	6%	23%	8%	9%	23%
	easier	82%	77%	83%	94%	77%	92%	91%	77%

[a]Questionnaire Q4. The data refer only to couples completing therapy.
Statistical significance according to sign-test (negative vs. positive changes):
Orgasmic dysfunctions, patient and partner: p=.001 for all items
Vaginismus, patient: p=.01 for items 2, 4, 5, 6, p=.001 for 1, 3, 7
Vaginismus, partner: p=.05 for items 2, 6, p=.01 for 3, 4, 5, p=.001 for 1, 7
Erectile dysfunctions, patient, partner: p=.01 for item 6, p=.001 for all other items
Premature ejaculation, patient: ns for item 6, p=.001 for 1, 3, 4, 5, 7
Premature ejaculation, partner: p=.01 for items 2, 4, 5, 6, p=.001 for 1, 3, 7

TABLE 4.23
Social Class and Overall Outcome; Ratings by Therapists[a]

Class characteristics		Female dysfunctions			Male dysfunctions		
		(1–5) drop-out, not/slightly improved	(6) improved	(7, 8) distinctly improved, cured	(1–5) drop-out, not/slightly improved	(6) improved	(7, 8) distinctly improved, cured
School education							
9 years (Hauptschule)	(N =52;N =36)	27%	23%	50%	25%	14%	61%
10 years (Mittlere Reife)	(N =41;N =17)	34%	20%	46%	24%	18%	59%
13 years or more (Abitur)	(N =38;N =32)	24%	42%	34%	9%	19%	72%
			ns			ns	
Occupation of male partner							
skilled/unskilled worker	(N =35;N =21)	20%	23%	57%	14%	10%	76%
employee/civil servant	(N =40;N =23)	38%	30%	33%	35%	22%	43%
academic	(N =27;N =21)	15%	26%	59%	10%	10%	81%
			(.10)			.05	
Occupation of female partner							
skilled/unskilled worker, employee[b]	(N=60)	20%	22%	58%			
academic[b]	(N=15)	0%	47%	53%			
housewife	(N=40)	40%	25%	35%			
			(.10)				
Intelligence as per BET[c]		m (s)			m (s)		
BET 2 (space)		15.2(4.9)	16.3(6.7)	15.1(5.0)	19.3(5.0)	8.5(5.0)	19.6(4.7)
			ns			ns	
BET 6 (number)		11.4(4.1)	12.4(7.9)	9.9(4.3)	13.7(4.5)	14.9(4.0)	11.9(3.4)
			ns			ns	
BET 7 (verbal)		25.4(6.2)	24.1(8.4)	22.2(9.6)	31.0(6.5)	28.6(9.0)	26.2(8.3)
			ns			ns	
	N	19	23	39	7	8	30

[a] Ratings of overall outcome R2 (sexual functioning) at follow-up 1; for definition of categories see p. 120–121.
[b] Women who are employed at least part-time.
[c] Berufs-Eignungs-Test (Schmale and Schmidtke 1966/67), a German adaptation of the General Aptitude Test Battery. Only these three scales were given. Statistical significance for school education and occupation calculated according to chi-square, for intelligence scales according to analysis of variance.

Appendix to the Tables: Therapist Ratings of Overall Therapy Outcome (R2)*

RATING OF SEXUAL DYSFUNCTION (CATEGORIES 3–8 COMPARED TO THERAPY ONSET)

1. Drop-out, separation of couple during therapy (at F3 and F4, separation after completing therapy).
2. Drop-out, unimproved.
3. Drop-out, slightly improved.
4. Therapy completed, unimproved (all steps completed, categories 5–8 invalid).
5. Therapy completed, slightly improved. (The dysfunction—erectile dysfunction, premature ejaculation, vaginismus, lack of sexual arousal and orgasm—is unchanged; the couple can, however, cope better with these difficulties.)
6. Therapy completed, improved. (The dysfunction is visibly improved, but still present. ED:+ intromission possible more often than before, but sometimes no erection and/or frequently no full erection. PE: less frequent than before, but still occurs sometimes. VA: intromission possible most of the time, but sometimes impossible and/or mostly unpleasant and painful. OD: intercourse experienced as pleasurable, however, orgasm never achieved in coitus; orgasm frequency during petting unchanged compared to pretherapy status.)
7. Therapy completed, distinctly improved. (The dysfunction has been largely removed. ED: intromission always or almost always possible, sometimes full erection. PE: never or hardly ever occurs; however, the patient still has to be careful, for example, must pause, or use cautious movements. VA: intromission always or nearly always possible, but sometimes still unpleasant or painful. OD: intercourse is pleasurable, orgasm still seldom achieved (every fifth intercourse at best) during intercourse or manual stimulation during intercourse; or no orgasm during intercourse but distinctly more frequent during foreplay and petting than was the case previously.)
8. Therapy completed, cured. (The dysfunction has been removed. ED: always or nearly always complete erection on intercourse until ejaculation. PE: never occurs, even without particular caution. VA: intromission always possible without discomfort. OD: orgasm in intercourse or with additional manual stimulation during intercourse fairly regular, at least once every fourth intercourse.)

RATING OF RELATIONSHIP IN GENERAL (COMPARED TO THERAPY ONSET)

0. Inapplicable (therapy not completed).
1. Disturbed as before (hostile, rejecting, inadequate communication, uncooperative).
2. Disturbed as before, but more aware of problems.

120

3. Positive state unchanged (acceptant, not hostile, cooperative, satisfying communication).

4. Deteriorated (more hostile, greater rejection, less satisfying communication, less cooperation).

5. Improved (less hostile, less rejecting, more satisfying communication, more cooperation).

6. Distinctly improved (acceptant, not hostile, cooperative, satisfying communication).

RATING OF SEXUAL SATISFACTION (COMPARED TO THERAPY ONSET)

0. Inapplicable (therapy not completed).
1. Sexual relations less satisfying than before therapy.
2. Sexual relations just as unsatisfying as before therapy.
3. Sexual relations somewhat more satisfying than before therapy.
4. Sexual relations satisfying (even if dysfunction not removed).

---

*The other tests for measuring therapy outcome (R1, Q1, Q3, Q4) are published in Arentewicz et al. 1975.

+ED, erectile dysfunction; PE, premature ejaculation; VA, vaginismus; OD, orgasmic dysfunction.

NOTES

1. In this chapter we refer exclusively to the 202 couples in the main investigation. Chapter 9 reports on the results for couple groups.

2. The number of waiting list drop-outs varies significantly according to diagnosis. It is particularly high for orgasmic dysfunctions and particularly low for vaginismus. This reflects the ambivalent motivation for therapy of many women with orgasmic dysfunctions (see p. 100).

3. The dominance scales of the two tests (FPI 7 and GT 8) produced apparently contradictory findings. In the GT our patients described their dominance as above average, in the FPI as below average. The reason is that the two scales define "dominance" differently and in any case only correlate slightly ($r = -.36$). On the FPI scale the reactive-aggressive element is emphasized, that is, the tendency to react offensively to frustration and to respond to one's social environment directly and brusquely. In contrast, the GT scale measures the tendency to be impatient and obstinate with other people, to act out inner conflicts impulsively, and to dominate covertly. Other patients with psychogenic disturbances also describe their dominance as above average in the GT and below average in the FPI.

4. We are aware of the dubious nature of the term "patient" (for the dysfunctional partner) as opposed to "partner" (for the nondysfunctional partner) since we regard the couple itself as the patient. These terms are used here in a purely descriptive sense to identify the partner who has or who does not have a manifest sexual dysfunction.

5. Evaluation based on therapist rating of overall outcome R2, item A (see p. 120).

6. In a further investigation we examined the effectiveness of a fourth setting: therapy for couples in groups (see Chapter 9).

7. Data selection principally affected questionnaires Q1, Q2, and Q4: from the diary (Q1) and the questionnaire on sexuality in the three months preceding the questionnaire (Q2) we evaluated only the basic data on sexual behavior; from the questionnaire on therapeutically induced changes (Q4) we deleted all the questions that asked the partners to evaluate what they assumed were their partner's reactions (for example, "I feel my partner's sexual satisfaction is greater/the same/less than before therapy").

8. We only have qualitative interview material available for follow-ups with couples who dropped out of therapy or separated during therapy (see chapter 8).

9. This questionnaire was not handed out at F1 because "the last three months" coincided with therapy. In this case we took the data from F2, which covered the three months following therapy.

10. Such equivalence or similarity in the distribution of variables is no measure of the inter-rater reliability for these variables. Inter-rater reliability (Pearson product-moment correlation between the ratings of therapists and "independent" first consultants) ranged between .69 and .72(P1) and .35 and .59 (F1) for male dysfunctions in the items erectile frequency on intercourse and frequency of premature ejaculation in intercourse. The reduction in inter-rater reliability at F1 is due to the shrinking variances for both variables after therapy and thus reflects therapy success, so to speak. For female dysfunctions the correlations for the items frequency of lubrication, frequency of desire in intercourse and foreplay, frequency of orgasm in intercourse, petting, and masturbation varied between .49 and .63 (P1) and .56 and .70 (F1).

11. The correlations between the partner's and the patient's ratings amount, for example, to .65 (male dysfunctions) and .67 (female dysfunctions) for the changes in sexual problems, and .82 (male dysfunctions) and .57 (female dysfunctions) for the changes in the relationship.

12. The correlations between the rating of sexual satisfaction by the therapists (R2, item C) and the rating of changes in sexual problems by the patient amount, for example, to .80 (male dysfunctions) and .81 (female dysfunctions). These self-ratings correlate with therapists' ratings of sexual functioning (R2, item A) only between .50 and .60; the couples thus based their rating of "sexual problems" more on their sexual experiences than on sexual functioning.

13. According to therapist rating of overall outcome R2, item A (see table 4.11).

14. It might be of interest here that the few very prudish and "inhibited" couples we treated often made particularly rapid and dramatic progress in couple therapy.

15. A comparison between women who were treated only for orgasmic dysfunctions (N = 50) and women who had an arousal and an orgasmic dysfunction (N = 55) showed a slight tendency for more positive results in the first group, which are, however, not statistically significant (Clement 1980). We are therefore unable to corroborate Kaplan's claim (1974a) that cases of "pure" orgasmic dysfunction are more successful in therapy.

Chapter 5

LONG-TERM RESULTS AND LIMITATIONS OF OUTCOME

Ulrich Clement and Gunter Schmidt

Stability of Therapy Outcome

So far we have described changes observed immediately after completion of therapy. These changes may be stable or may be transient effects of therapy. In addition, it is possible that changes induced by therapy become evident only some time after conclusion of therapy. Consequently long-term follow-ups are indispensable to evaluation of therapy outcome. We conducted three follow-ups of this kind: three months (F2), one year (F3), and two and a half to four and a half years (F4) after completion of therapy.

THREE MONTHS AFTER THERAPY

The period immediately after completion of therapy is especially critical: the partners leave the protective therapy environment and then have to cope with their relationship and sexuality on their own and master their fear of this situation. By carrying out the second follow-up as soon as three months after therapy completion, we were able to study how the partners coped with this difficult adaptive phase following "separation" from the therapists. We did not ask the patients to visit us at this point but simply sent them questionnaires. For

F2 we thus only have self-assessments (Q1, Q2, Q3). Moreover, the follow-up was restricted to patients completing therapy.

In most cases there was considerable delay in returning questionnaires: we had to send more than half the couples reminders four weeks later, and a third had still failed to return questionnaires after a second reminder. The motives for this refusal have already been described (p. 84). Data from F2 are available for 108 couples, that is, 66 percent of patients completing therapy (see table 4.7).[1] The reluctance to complete questionnaires also led to a prolongation of the follow-up period: instead of the three to four months planned, it took on average five months (mean) until the questionnaires had been completed. Our three-month follow-up thus lasted from three to six months. We have already pointed out (p. 108) that therapy outcome as assessed by therapists on termination of therapy did not differ for remitters and nonremitters. Remitters did not constitute a special group as regards initial therapy outcome. We can thus assume that our results for F2 are valid for the whole group of patients completing therapy.

Table 5.1 shows the results of self-assessment by patients and their partners. Data from all symptom groups have been combined because differences between diagnoses were minimal. In all fifteen items both patients and partners claimed that their status had significantly improved since onset of therapy. Almost 90 percent felt that their sexual problems were less distressing than before therapy; 60 to 80 percent enjoyed sexual contacts more, anticipated sexual intercourse with more pleasure, were more satisfied after intercourse, were less afraid of failing, and were less disappointed if "things didn't work out" once in a while. Half performed intercourse more often and felt their sexual desire was stronger (32 percent of partners in the latter case). Three quarters rated their relationship as generally improved compared to before therapy; couples found it easier to be affectionate to each other (62% of partners) and to talk about sexual wishes and problems. About 40 to 50 percent spent more time with each other, found better solutions to nonsexual problems, were less hostile to each other, and believed they loved one another more. These distinct changes observed by the patients themselves had already been recorded by us at F1.

There was once again a noticeably large degree of congruity between patient and partner self-perception, that is, in the changes they saw in sexual experience and their relationship. At F2, however, the changes were no longer so pronounced as immediately after therapy (see table 5.1). This decrease in positive changes is further highlighted by the breakdown of data in table 5.2: the number of patients who found their sexual problems were "much better" or "fully removed" sank from 77 percent (patient) and 74 percent (partner) at F1 to 62 percent at F2. The percentage of those who described their relationship as "much better" than before therapy sank from 57 percent (patient) and 55 percent (partner) at F1 to 42 percent and 39 percent at F2. Similar trends are evident in almost all items, regardless of whether they apply to sexual problems or the relationship.[2]

As regards symptom-linked variables, F2 shows distinct improvements compared to both pretests (see tables 5.3 and 5.4). Insofar as a comparison with F1 is at all possible—the number of cases is too small—there seem to be no consistent trends. As recorded in the "diary," there were no significant differences in coital behavior between F1 and F2 (see figure 4.2): frequency of coitus remained stable as did frequency of coitus experienced as satisfying. Thus, in terms of coital behavior there is no evidence of the trend observed in self-assessments. Coital frequency at F2 (and F1) was distinctly and significantly higher than in the pretests.

We can summarize thus: self-assessment shows that there were considerable improvements in sexual experience and relationships as well as in sexual functioning and coital behavior in the three to six months after therapy by comparison with the period before therapy. The self-assessments show a minimal, but statistically significant, reduction in improvements compared with status immediately after therapy. In general terms, therapy outcome remains satisfactorily stable in the difficult months of adaptation after treatment.

ONE YEAR AFTER THERAPY

During the twelve months following therapy, there probably emerged for every couple something resembling a "final" therapy outcome: developments propelled by therapy but still in process at therapy completion had then "matured" through the couples' self-help efforts. On the other hand, initially, apparently successful therapy results retrogressed. For this reason we conducted a third follow-up one year after therapy. The couples were interviewed by therapists and first consultants and filled out questionnaires (see table 4.6). Delays in questionnaire remittance prolonged the follow-up period from twelve to fifteen months. Again, only the results of those completing therapy are presented. Results of follow-up interviews for therapy drop-outs will be discussed in chapter 8.

Of the couples completing therapy,[3] 116 or 71 percent were interviewed again. Nine couples (5 percent) could not be included because they had completed therapy less than one year earlier. Eleven couples (7 percent) could no longer be reached by mail or requested exemption from the follow-up because they lived too far away. Twenty-eight couples (17 percent) refused follow-up for reasons unknown to us; they did not appear despite repeated pleas (see table 4.7). Of the 116 couples participating in F3, only 87 returned their questionnaires. We have already pointed out that there were no significant differences in results at the end of therapy between couples who did and couples who did not participate in F3, nor between responders and nonresponders (see p. 84). Our results for F3 can thus be considered valid for the entire group of patients completing therapy.

The findings with regard to couple self-assessment are fairly similar to those in the two previous follow-ups. Patients and their partners described considerable changes in sexual relations and their relationships in general (see table 5.1). These findings are somewhat more positive than those at F2, but the trend is statistically significant only in one of the fifteen items. In general, self-assessment in the three follow-ups clearly shows that the weak trend for initial success to regress in the three to six months after therapy comes to a halt and levels off at the rate established at F1. Table 5.2 shows two items as examples of this.

Therapists' ratings are compiled in table 5.5. Seven couples completing therapy had separated in the course of the year. Taking all couples completing therapy together, therapists evaluated sexual functioning one year therapy as "improved," "distinctly improved," or "cured" in 86 percent of the couples; on completion of therapy the percentage was slightly higher (91 percent). The results for sexual functioning, therefore, remained very stable one year after therapy. A breakdown by symptom groups shows a slight, almost statistically significant reversion of "cured" premature ejaculators to their earlier symptoms; in contrast, couples with orgasmic dysfunctions in this group increased, although insignificantly.

The similarity in ratings for sexual functioning at F1 and F3 (as shown in table 5.5) can be explained in two ways: either the individual couples did not change or the same number of couples improved as worsened. Tables 5.6 and 5.7 support the latter view. Only a half of all couples had the same ratings at F1 and F3, a fifth improved, and a fifth worsened. However, these changes were in general relatively minor, for example, from "cured" to "distinctly improved," or from "distinctly improved" to "improved," or vice versa; as a rule they do not exceed more than one point on the scale. Relapses were observed in 7 of 128 couples (5.5 percent). The percentage of "delayed remissions," that is, couples whose sexual functioning did not change during therapy but who were classified at least as "improved" a year later, is almost as high—6 of 128 (4.5 percent). Table 5.6 shows again that deterioration was relatively frequent for premature ejaculation in the year after therapy. Furthermore, table 5.7 illustrates that couples who were rated as "not improved," "slightly improved," or "improved" on completing therapy had an almost 40 percent chance of reaching the categories "distinctly improved" or "cured" in the year following therapy. Almost four fifths of the "distinctly improved" or "cured" couples remained in one of these two categories.

One year after treatment the therapists rated the relationships of 66 percent of the couples to be "distinctly improved" or "unchanged" (see table 5.5), a reduction from the 73 percent at F1 that is marginally significant. There were also minor negative changes in sexual satisfaction as assessed by therapists at F3, which are significant at the 10 percent level.

In terms of symptom-linked variables (see tables 5.6 and 5.2), there was an increase in orgasmic ability, arousability, and lubrication capacity in women with orgasmic dysfunctions one year after therapy as compared to pretherapy status. Almost all women with vaginismus were able to have sexual intercourse; men with erectile dysfunctions could control their erections, and premature ejaculators their ejaculations, much better. Insofar as comparisons with the two previous follow-ups are possible, there are no differences apart from a slight reversal of positive changes in premature ejaculators.

Coital frequency and satisfaction with coital activity are distinctly greater than they were before therapy (see figures 4.1 and 4.2). The diary (Q1) data at F3, show a slight but significant reduction compared with the results for F1 and F2. A similar reversal in sexual behavior in the "three months preceding questionnaire" (Q2) was not observed; there was even evidence of a contrary, but statistically insignificant, trend. Attitudes toward sexuality were also more liberal one year after therapy, less compliant with sex-roles, and less romantic than before therapy (see table 4.19).

In summary, results one year after therapy were stable, even though there were signs of slight deterioration compared to F1. This is of importance only in the case of premature ejaculation. The relative instability of results for this symptom group may be an indication that therapists all too readily considered premature ejaculation a purely technical problem and so were distracted from dealing with deeper-rooted problems between the partners or in the patient. Dramatic changes, in the sense of a relapse, were an exception in all symptom groups; moreover, they were scarcely more frequent than "late remissions." All in all, results one year after therapy are satisfactory: in this period the therapeutic improvements in sexual function, sexual experience, and partner relations were consolidated in almost all couples.

TWO AND A HALF TO FOUR AND A HALF YEARS AFTER THERAPY

To determine long-term effects we conducted a fourth follow-up (F4) at the end of the project (for couples treated by mid-1976) or two years after the project (for the remaining couples). Therapy had been completed at least two and a half years earlier. The couples were called in again and interviewed by their therapists; they were given a few questionnaires and were asked to send them back with answers (see table 4.6). We reduced the number of questionnaires because we thought it would be difficult to motivate couples to go through the whole comprehensive questionnaire program again so long after therapy completion. We preferred to have only a few data rather than to risk a high percentage of refusals to return questionnaires.

Ninety-nine of the couples completing therapy[4] (60 percent) were interviewed (see table 4.7). Five couples (3 percent) had terminated therapy less than two and a half years earlier and were disregarded. Thirty-one couples (19 percent) had moved to an unknown address; twenty-nine couples (18 percent) refused to participate either by not coming to the appointment suggested or by canceling. Follow-up with the ninty-nine couples was conducted between thirty months, at the earliest, and fifty-four months, at the latest, after therapy; on average thirty-nine months had passed since completion of therapy.

We have already explained (see p. 84) that there were only slight differences at F1 between couples who did and couples who did not come to F4. The results of our last follow-up can therefore be generalized for the entire sample. As in the previous follow-ups, about one fourth of couples refused to return the questionnaires.

Even two and a half to four and a half years after therapy the vast majority of couples considered that their sexual problems were better (four fifths), their relationship was better (three quarters), and their sexual satisfaction greater (three fifths) than before therapy (see table 5.8). These results were, however, consistently lower than in earlier follow-ups.

These findings were confirmed by therapist ratings (see table 5.9).

Apart from relationships that were rated as not changed relative to F1 and F3, the therapists gave a more negative rating for sexual function and sexual satisfaction at F4. (This result is only significant for sexual satisfaction.) All in all, fourteen couples relapsed to the old dysfunction (see table 5.10); eight of these couples were classified as "improved" at the end of therapy, six as "distinctly improved" or "cured." The relapses almost always occurred in later stages, that is, after the one-year follow-up.

Table 5.10 demonstrates further that in sexual functioning more couples worsened (25 percent) than improved (20 percent) and that almost half the couples obtained the same ratings at the end of therapy as they did two and a half to four and a half years later. However, there are notable differences (10 percent significance level) between the categories of orgasmic dysfunctions and vaginismus and the categories of erectile and ejaculatory dysfunctions: compared to F1, 24 percent of the female dysfunctions improved while 21 percent worsened; for males the figures are 14 percent and 32 percent. Long-term prognosis after therapy thus tends to be less positive for men than for women.

Frequency of sexual intercourse at the final follow-up was also significantly lower than at earlier follow-ups, but was still higher than it was before therapy (see figure 4.1). However, this reduction was not accompanied by a decrease in satisfaction with the frequency of coitus. In terms of orgasmic ability in women treated for orgasmic dysfunctions, there was no evidence of change: 51 percent never reached orgasm in intercourse in the previous three months (50 to 60 percent at F1 and F3); 41 percent climaxed on at least 50 percent of coital occasions—more than the 24 percent in the earlier follow-ups—but the difference is not statistically significant as the number of cases is so small. At all events, one can ascertain that there was no observable reversal of anorgasmia as a delayed effect of therapy: half of the women were still anorgasmic in coitus with their partners.

Two and a half to four and a half years after completion of therapy one can see a slight reversal in initial positive therapy results; for the majority, however, therapy results remained unchanged or improved. The long-term stability of therapy results can thus be considered satisfactory.

The data for follow-up 4 suffice to estimate the long-term outcome of therapy or, more precisely, to answer the question, What are the long-term prospects for a couple entering therapy?[5] Our findings two and a half to four and a half years after couples had completed or dropped out of therapy present the following picture: 15 percent of all couples had separated; 24 percent were unimproved but were still living together; 11 percent were improved; 16 percent were distinctly improved; 34 percent were cured.

These percentages are rough estimates because they are based only on subsamples. On this basis one can calculate the following probabilities for couples beginning therapy: three fifths would experience a permanent improvement in symptoms (at least for three to four years); one seventh would start another relationship in which they would as a rule have fewer or no sexual problems; one fourth would continue in the same relationship with the same problems. The last figure is the actual failure rate. We find it is too high: too many couples had to accommodate themselves to their sexual problems.

Psychological Stability

We will now briefly examine psychological stability as evaluated by our psychological tests. Because couples were only retested with FPI at the one-year follow-up (F3) and not on completion of therapy, we shall report only on long-term changes (see tables 5.11 and 5.12; Clement and Pfäfflin 1980).

In the personality questionnaires before therapy, men and women with sexual dysfunctions and their partners showed deviations typical of psychoneurotic and psychosomatic patients (p. 81). Although deviating couple scores in some scales did not significantly change following therapy, psychological stabilization in male and female patients and partners one year after therapy was distinctly noticeable. On average they were less depressive, dejected, and downhearted (FPI 3; GT 4); they were less labile, irascible, and tense (FPI N); they had fewer physical and psychovegetative complaints (FPI 1; EMI 3; complaint list); they tended less to react with anxiety (EMI 1, 3); and they were more self-confident and capable of asserting themselves (FPI 8; EMI 2). The GT, the EMI, and the complaint list in the diary produced quite similar findings immediately after therapy (F1). It is particularly striking that this psychological stabilization persisted: by solving sexual problems the partners were in the long run considerably relieved.

The Limitations of Therapy Success

In this chapter we have described the results of therapy in terms of statistics. Although this gives us an overall view and, in our opinion, an objective presentation of changes induced by therapy, each variable is viewed in isolation and a general perspective on the individual couple in its entirety is thus impossible. Our impression on reading what we have written above is that it corresponds only partially to our therapeutic experience with the couples. In this section and in chapters 7 and 8, which concentrate more on clinical case histories, we shall rely on intuition and experience in attempting a qualitative modification of statistics.

We begin by illustrating the limitations of therapy success and discussing the limitations of the measurements of therapeutic change that we used to describe the effects of therapy. Our impression is that our statistics tend to exaggerate the success of therapy. They tempted us to deny or repress disappointments with our therapeutic work until qualitative evaluation confronted us again with the case histories. All statistically evaluated success is probably positively biased because the general picture is taken apart, the individual aspects merely summed up, and the contradictions in individual cases thus eliminated. Even a more sophisticated statistical method, if at all applicable to clinical studies with their many missing data, would not be able to avoid this pitfall unless it was so elaborate, informative, and patient-centered that it again approximated a case history. This does not mean that we consider our statistics superfluous. On the contrary, they were indispensable in making a first approximation and in communicating it with economy.

The limitations of success were, curiously enough, best illustrated by therapies with the comparatively best results. These "optimal" cases, which were exceptional, illustrated how low the upper limits of therapy success were.

COUPLE 16: Both partners are in their early twenties; she is a saleswoman, and he is a tool mechanic. They have been married for a year and have no children. She has never had an orgasm in sexual intercourse, petting, or masturbating. She does, however, like caressing and body contact in general, which arouses her. Nonetheless, intercourse has become less and less pleasant recently because it causes her pain; she would prefer to avoid it. The therapists find that the couple is loving and understanding in their relationship. Therapy is completed after only fifteen sessions. They now make love frequently—about four to five times a week—and the woman always has an orgasm. Both play an active role. She speaks with relief, almost with ebullience, of the new scope of feelings she experiences; she frequently looks forward the whole day to her husband's company, to tenderness and making love. The couple gives the impression of enjoying a cheerful intimacy; they are curious to find out "what else we can do together." They take time for sexuality, and they are less fixated on sexual intercourse because caressing and body contact are very important to them.

Also seldom seen, although more often than couples whose sexuality was particularly satisfying, were couples whose reversed dysfunctions were followed by more openness and vitality in the relationship, by relief from psychosomatic disturbances or depression, or by greater self-confidence.

COUPLE 17: The married partners (an architect and a housewife) are both just over thirty, have been married for ten years, and have two children. The husband has been distressed by erectile dysfunctions for three years. They attempt intercourse about once a week, but insertion of his penis is only possible every other time. During intercourse he tries to ejaculate rapidly before the erection subsides. Orgasm is a lukewarm experience for him. Whenever his erection fails he is bathed in sweat. The difficulties appear especially when he is under stress at work.

He has psychosomatic gastrointestinal pains and complains of stomachaches and indigestion. He tends to see himself in a highly hypochondriacal manner and leads a strictly regulated, cautious life in order to minimize the complaints.

A year and a half before therapy, a severe crisis takes place in the relationship when his wife falls in love with another man who is everything her husband is not: unconventional, untidy, occasionally boorish, uninhibited, and with an eye to pleasure in his whole way of life. This aggravates the sexual problems still further. The couple is admitted to intensive therapy, to which the husband reacts with strong anxieties and is close to breaking it off after only a week. His psychosomatic pains and his complaints about them increase; during the day he can hardly think about anything else. The pains recede once he realizes that therapy strengthens his sexual self-esteem and that his erectile problems decrease. At the end of therapy he regularly gets an erection when they want to make love; through additional manual stimulation or petting afterward his wife climaxes. At the one-year follow-up the removal of sexual dysfunction has been consolidated. The couple has intercourse once a week, and he is always able to insert his penis. Additional caressing during coitus or petting always help her to reach orgasm. However, she complains that she feels sexuality is too routine and she would like to experiment more.

Both report how much he has changed: he has put on twenty-eight pounds and is back to normal weight for the first time in years. They say this is probably because he is not so fussy about food and anxious about his stomach. He now sees that his abdominal disorder is not physical, and that helps him to ignore his symptoms; he is much less of a hypochondriac. He is much more self-confident and acts more freely. He has resumed participation at professional conferences, loves to go on a holiday, and drinks alcohol again. He has learned, as they say, to do himself favors more often, which is of benefit to the relationship. At work, too, he has more confidence in his abilities and gets far more done; he is much more confident in dealing with his colleagues. The wife is pleased to find that the relationship is less regulated and that there are many more things they can do together. She is relieved that his moaning and groaning, which used to provoke a silent anger in her, has all but stopped. After a long interruption, they can again be "happy together."

We describe these couples' cases and the progress they made in therapy not to boast of success but, as we mentioned, to demonstrate the limits we came up against. These limits became even clearer when we saw that the relationships of couples whose sexual functioning had been restored by therapy were nonetheless just as cheerless as before and that their personalities had hardly been modified at all by therapy. Reconstitution of sexual functioning is an isolated event in these cases.

COUPLE 18: The wife, a beautician, is in her mid-thirties; the husband, a businessman, is in his late forties. They have been married for fifteen years. They have never been able to have sexual intercourse because of her severe vaginismus. During petting she reaches orgasm; she also occasionally masturbates to orgasm. The sexual difficulties did not bother her for years. However, she has become increasingly concerned in the last two to three years; she misses the sense of being a "full" woman and feels she is incomplete. She suffers from doubt about her femininity and now complains of psychosomatic circulation and heart disorders; when she went to the hospital several times, the organic findings were negative. Her husband clearly behaves as a father toward her, which she once felt was protective but now feels is increasingly confining. He pampers her and is extremely considerate of her, thereby belittling her and making a show of his importance for her; he is highly patronizing in his attitude toward her, something she resists more and more fiercely. He says everything is all right with him and that he only entered therapy for his wife's sake.

The vaginismus takes thirty-four long-term therapy sessions to reverse: the couple can now perform sexual intercourse. She sometimes still feels a slight burning sensation on intromission, but it recedes once the movements begin. However, she never finds pleasure in intercourse and does not climax. A year after completing therapy, intercourse is still technically free of problems; she feels much more like a "normal" woman, which she finds important. Moreover, she states that her heart troubles vanished into thin air six months ago; she ascribes this to acupuncture treatment, not to therapy. She also seems more willing to stand up to her husband. All the same, there has been no fundamental change in the relationship: her husband sticks to his patronizing

role and does not let problems come anywhere near him. One year after therapy he describes therapy as successful, against his better judgment, and their
relationship at present as extremely happy. Her lack of desire for intercourse
and difficulties in reaching orgasm during petting had increased. She would
prefer to withdraw from her husband sexually and senses a growing desire for
sexual contact with other men.

This case illustrates particularly clearly how problematic therapy for
vaginismus in complicated relationships is: on the one hand, the new
opportunity for intercourse adds to the woman's identity and self-esteem and in the long run perhaps even furnishes the possibility of
finding other relationships; on the other hand, she pays for this new
ability with pleasureless cooperation. The new competence remains a
joyless fulfillment of duties to her husband.

These couples, for whom full functioning amounted merely to indifferent sexuality and effected no fundamental change in partner problems, also formed a small group. Of the "functionally cured" couples,
those who reported satisfying sexual relations that were, however, not
especially exciting were the most common. As a rule, they experienced
removal of the dysfunction as relief from a burden but seldom as a
gain in new dimensions of pleasure or experience. When therapy succeeded in removing the symptom, these couples demonstrated what
therapy could at most achieve: reconstitution of the ordinary and
slightly trivial everyday sexuality of couples without dysfunctions, but
really nothing more.

COUPLE 19:   Both partners are in their late twenties and are employed in
commerce; they have been married for two years. They have never been capable of sexual intercourse: his penis always remains only partially erect, even
during petting; he cannot remember ever having had a full erection when
masturbating. Petting takes place once a week; without touching each other
with their hands, they furtively bring each other to orgasm by pressing their
bodies together. Before she got to know her husband, she "always wanted to
run away from seductive situations"; she was thus pleased with her relationship with her husband because he was sexually undemanding. She has avoided learning anything about sexuality and does not even know now what a
clitoris is. Both emphasize that the sexual problem is a burden to the relationship. He is often unmotivated and reticent. She complains that he is too taci-
turn and incapable of expressing feelings and that sometimes he has about as
much feeling for her as a block of ice. It should be mentioned that he had a
phimosis that was operated on two years earlier. He still has unpleasant sensations in his penis occasionally.

Long-term therapy is completed after twenty-seven sessions. The husband
now erects fully without problems, in petting and foreplay, and can ejaculate
every time they have intercourse. She almost always has an orgasm in inter-

course. After therapy both emphasize that a great load has been taken off their minds. A year later they both report that they are less annoyed and more free and easy with each other. They have intercourse once or twice a week. He would actually prefer it more often, but she feels no desire for more. Both still have difficulties in expressing their sexual wishes; they take little time for sexuality; that is, they usually have intercourse before falling asleep, and they try to reach climax quickly with as little foreplay as possible. They find it hard to share intimacy and tenderness.

By comparison with the high hopes many couples had of therapy for sexual problems, this kind of therapy outcome was disappointing to couples who were now "fully functional." They asked themselves whether that was the only benefit to sexual experience that removal of their dysfunctions could provide. In such cases it is the therapists' duty to revise ideas about sexuality in permanent relationships or correct dreams about the happiness sexuality can provide. Therapy can induce release from sexual anxieties, a gain in sexual knowledge and techniques, and a satisfactory measure of sexual functioning, but it cannot generate erotic attraction between partners. Therapy can only pave the way to desire for each other and for more intense sexual experiences; whether this actually happens depends on the quality of the relationship between two people, but it can in no way be instilled by therapy.

List of Abbreviations Used in the Tables

OD	orgasmic dysfunction
VA	vaginismus
ED	erectile dysfunction
PE	premature ejaculation
P1	pretest 1 (three to twelve months before therapy)
P2	pretest 2 (immediately before therapy)
F1	follow-up 1 (immediately after therapy)
F2	follow-up 2 (three months after therapy)
F3	follow-up 3 (one year after therapy)
F4	follow-up 4 (two and a half to four and a half years after therapy)
N	number of individual cases
Nc	number of couples
ns	statistically not significant
M	mean
S	standard deviation

TABLE 5.1

Stability of Therapy Results: Sexuality and Relationship on Completion of Therapy, Three Months and One Year Later; Couple Self-Rating[a]

	F1[b]		F2		F3	
	Patient (N=145)	Partner (N=144)	Patient (N=112)	Partner (N=112)	Patient (N=93)	Partner (N=93)
Our sexual problems are now better …	94%	95%	88%	88%	88%	90%
I now enjoy sexual contacts more …	80%	84%	79%	71%	83%	78%
I look forward to sexual intercourse more now …	79%	76%	71%	66%	71%	70%
My sexual desire is now stronger …	60%	51%	53%	32%	54%	34%
My sexual satisfaction after intercourse is now greater …	74%	63%	60%	57%	72%	54%
My fear of failing sexually is now less …	85%	80%	74%	65%	80%	75%
If things do not work out sexually my disappointment is now less …	81%	80%	76%	72%	77%	77%
We now have sexual intercourse more often …	63%	63%	49%	46%	60%	58%
Our relationship is now better …	80%	79%	74%	74%	76%	81%
I now like my partner better …	47%	46%	35%	42%	37%	46%
Being affectionate to my partner is now easier …	77%	73%	71%	62%	68%	60%
The time we spend together is now more …	57%	53%	42%	40%	37%	41%
We can now find solutions to nonsexual problems more easily …	59%	60%	57%	46%	54%	53%
My aggression toward my partner is now less frequent …	54%	54%	44%	48%	40%	51%
Talking about our sexual wishes and problems is now easier …	82%	83%	79%	78%	70%	69%
… than before therapy						

[a] Questionnaire Q4. The data refer only to couples completing therapy. Data are combined for all diagnostic groups. For simplicity's sake, only positive changes are shown in the table; none of the negative changes exceed 10%. Statistical significance of differences between positive and negative changes according to sign test: p=.001 for each item and all 6 groups.
[b] Data from tables 4.21 and 4.22.

TABLE 5.2

Stability of Therapy Results: Overall Outcome on Completion of Therapy, Three Months and One Year Later; Couple Self-Rating[a]

	F1-F2				F1-F3				F2-F3			
	Patient		Partner		Patient		Partner		Patient		Partner	
	F1	F2	F1	F2	F1	F3	F1	F3	F2	F3	F2	F3
Our sexual problems are now ...	(N=95)	(N=95)	(N=94)	(N=94)	(N=81)	(N=81)	(N=84)	(N=84)	(N=74)	(N=74)	(N=75)	(N=75)
worse	0	4	0	2	0	6	0	2	3	5	1	2
unchanged	1	6	2	7	1	3	4	6	3	4	6	7
slightly better	21	26	22	27	19	18	21	21	20	17	18	14
much better	65	52	62	51	55	44	51	41	43	38	44	41
fully removed	8	7	8	7	6	10	8	14	5	10	6	11
... than before therapy												
Statistical significance of changes between follow-ups[b]	.001		.01		ns		ns		ns		ns	
Our relationship is now ...	(N=95)	(N=95)	(N=93)	(N=93)	(N=82)	(N=82)	(N=82)	(N=82)	(N=75)	(N=75)	(N=76)	(N=76)
worse	1	3	3	3	1	4	2	1	4	4	3	1
unchanged	14	22	10	21	15	15	14	16	18	13	16	15
slightly better	26	30	29	33	26	23	25	21	21	23	25	19
much better	54	40	51	36	40	40	41	44	32	35	32	41
... than before therapy												
Statistical significance of changes between follow-ups[b]	.01		.01		ns		ns		ns		.05	

[a] Questionnaire Q4, selected items. The data refer only to couples completing therapy. In contrast to table 5.1 only those patients were included for whom data for both of the compared follow-ups were available.
[b] According to sign-test.

TABLE 5.3

Stability of Therapy Results, Male Dysfunctions: Sexual Responses Before and After Therapy; Ratings by Therapists and Couple Self-Rating [a]

	P1	P2	F1	F2	F3
Erectile dysfunctions	(—)	(N=46)	(N=45)	(—)	(N=28)
R1 erection almost always/					
always on coitus	—	39%	89%	—	82%
	(N=40)	(N=28)	(N=34)	(N=29)	(N=21)
Q1 coitus with full erection					
at least once in recent week	27%	12%	50%	79%	71%
	(—)	(—)	(N=39)	(N=28)	(N=24)
Q4 erection now better than					
before therapy	—	—	87%	79%	92%
Premature ejaculation	(—)	(N=26)	(N=27)	(—)	(N=21)
R1 premature ejaculation					
never/seldom/less often					
than every fourth coitus	—	0%	59%	—	48%
	(N=27)	(N=24)	(N=21)	(N=21)	(N=15)
Q1 coitus with controlled					
ejaculation at least once in					
the previous week	11%	13%	39%	48%	40%
	(—)	(—)	(N=22)	(N=19)	(N=16)
Q4 ejaculation control now					
better than before therapy	—	—	86%	68%	56%

[a] *Ratings of sexual responses R1, questionnaires Q1 and Q4; data refer only to couples completing therapy.*

TABLE 5.4

Stability of Therapy Results, Female Dysfunctions: Sexual Responses Before and After Therapy; Ratings by Therapists and Couple Self-Rating[a]

	P1	P2	F1	F2	F3
Orgasmic dysfunctions	(—)	(N=77)	(N=82)	(—)	(N=53)
R1 lubrication in coitus almost always/always	—	49%	70%	—	75%
R1 arousal in petting/coitus almost always/always	—	19%	62%	—	58%
R1 never orgasm in coitus	—	82%	62%	—	48%
R1 orgasm at least every second coitus	—	3%	23%	—	35%
	(N=78)	(N=78)	(—)	(N=51)	(N=42)
Q2 never orgasm in coitus in the last 3 months	81%	79%	—	49%	48%
Q2 orgasm in roughly every second coitus in the last 3 months	6%	10%	—	24%	24%
	(—)	(—)	(N=61)	(N=48)	(N=41)
Q4 lubrication is now better than before therapy	—	—	62%	49%	58%
Q4 orgasm is now more frequent than before therapy	—	—	46%	42%	46%
Vaginismus	(—)	(N=24)	(N=23)	(—)	(N=16)
R1 no vaginismus	—	0%	78%	—	88%
	(N=23)	(N=22)	(—)	(N=16)	(N= 9)
Q2 coitus in the last 3 months	4%	5%	—	93%	78%

[a] *Ratings of sexual responses R1, questionnaires Q2 and Q4; data refer only to couples completing therapy.*

TABLE 5.5

Stability of Therapy Results: Overall Outcome on Completion of Therapy and One Year Later; Ratings by Therapists[a]

	OD		VA		ED		PE		Total	
	F1	F3	F1	F3	F1	F3	F1	F3	F1	F3
Sexual functioning[b]	(N=56)	(N=56)	(N=17)	(N=17)	(N=33)	(N=33)	(N=22)	(N=22)	(N=128)	(N=128)
(1) Separation between F1 and F3	—	2	—	1	—	2	—	2	—	7
(4,5) not/slightly improved	5	5	2	1	3	4	1	1	11	11
(6) improved	27	21	0	0	7	1	5	8	39	30
(7) distinctly improved	13	10	2	3	6	7	6	9	27	29
(8) cured	11	18	13	12	17	19	10	2	51	51
statistical significance F1–F3[c]	ns		ns		ns		(.10)		ns	
Relationship in general[b]	(N=52)	(N=52)	(N=16)	(N=16)	(N=28)	(N=28)	(N=17)	(N=17)	(N=119)	(N=119)
(1) disturbed as before	2	1	2	0	1	0	1	0	6	1
(2) disturbed as before, but more aware of problems	5	7	1	1	4	4	2	2	12	14
(3) positive state unchanged	4	4	5	6	3	6	1	0	13	16
(4) deteriorated	0	2	0	2	0	0	0	3	0	7
(5,6) distinctly improved	41	38	8	7	20	18	13	12	82	75
statistical significance F1–F3[c]	ns		ns		ns		ns		.05	
Sexual satisfaction[b]	(N=52)	(N=52)	(N=16)	(N=16)	(N=27)	(N=27)	(N=17)	(N=17)	(N=112)	(N=112)
(1) less satisfying	0	0	0	1	1	0	0	0	0	1
(2) just as unsatisfying	2	6	0	1	1	3	0	0	3	10
(3) somewhat more satisfying	18	17	5	6	10	8	4	5	37	36
(4) satisfying	32	29	11	8	15	16	13	12	71	65
statistical significance F1–F3[c]	ns		ns		ns		ns		(.10)	

[a] The data only refer to couples completing therapy and couples who were interviewed at F1 and F3.
[b] Ratings of overall outcome R2. For a definition of the categories see p. 120.
[c] According to sign–test, excluding separating couples.

TABLE 5.6

Stability of Therapy Results; Differences in Sexual Functioning on Completion of Therapy and One Year Later; Ratings by Therapists[a]

Rating by therapists	OD (N=56)	VA (N=17)	ED (N=33)	PE (N=22)	Total (N=128)	
Same for F1 and F3	29	12	21	9	71	(55%)
Better at F3 than at F1	15	2	6	2	25	(20%)
No. of delayed "remissions"[b]	(2)	(2)	(1)	(1)	(6)	
Worse at F3 than at F1	10	2	4	9	25	(20%)
No. of "relapses"[c]	(3)	(1)	(2)	(1)	(7)	
Separations between F1-F3	2	1	2	2	7	(5%)

[a] *These data refer to couples completing therapy who were interviewed at F1 and F3. This table shows data on sexual functioning (R2) from table 5.5 in a different break-down. For statistical significances see table 5.5.*
[b] *Definition: ratings of 4 or 5 at F1 and of 6, 7, or 8 at F3.*
[c] *Definition: ratings of 6, 7, or 8 at F1 and of 4 or 5 at F3.*

TABLE 5.7

Stability of Therapy Results: Sexual Functioning on Completion of Therapy and One Year Later; Ratings by Therapists[a]

Follow-up 3	Follow-up 1		
	(4, 5) not/ slightly improved (N=11)	(6) improved (N=39)	(7, 8) distinctly improved/cured (N=78)
(1) separation between F1–F3	1 (9%)	2 (5%)	4 (5%)
(4, 5) not/slightly improved	4(36%)	5(13%)	2 (3%)
(6) improved	2(18%)	17(44%)	11(14%)
(7, 8) distinctly improved/cured	4(36%)	16(38%)	61(78%)

[a] *The data refer to couples completing therapy who were interviewed at F1 and F3. Data for all symptom groups were compounded. This table shows data on sexual functioning (R2) from table 5.5 in a different break-down.*

141

TABLE 5.8

Stability of Therapy Results: Overall Outcome Two and a Half to Four and a Half Years After Completion of Therapy; Couple Self-Rating[a]

| | F1-F4 | | | | F3-F4 | | | |
| | Patient | | Partner | | Patient | | Partner | |
	F1	F4	F1	F4	F3	F4	F3	F4
Our sexual problems are now . . .	(N=69)	(N=69)	(N=72)	(N=72)	(N=58)	(N=58)	(N=56)	(N=56)
worse	0	4	0	2	4	5	1	1
unchanged	0	10	1	8	2	5	2	5
slightly better	19	16	22	21	16	14	15	14
much better	41	24	39	29	24	21	28	26
fully removed	9	15	10	12	12	13	10	10
. . . than before therapy								
Statistical significances of changes between follow-ups[b]		(.10)		(.10)		ns		ns
Our relationship is now . . .	(N=69)	(N=69)	(N=72)	(N=72)	(N=59)	(N=59)	(N=59)	(N=59)
worse	1	5	2	2	2	6	2	2
unchanged	11	13	8	15	10	10	10	14
slightly better	18	17	23	23	17	16	15	16
much better	39	34	39	32	30	27	32	27
. . . than before therapy								
Statistical significances of changes between follow-ups[b]		(.10)		(.10)		ns		ns
My sexual satisfaction after intercourse is now . . .	(N=63)	(N=63)	(N=67)	(N=67)	(N=53)	(N=53)	(N=56)	(N=56)
much greater	16	14	14	15	13	14	11	12
greater	33	27	34	26	31	21	25	23
unchanged	14	18	19	22	8	15	18	19
less	0	4	0	4	1	3	2	2
. . . than before therapy								
Statistical significances of changes between the follow-ups[b]		ns		ns		(.10)		ns

[a] Questionnaire Q4, selected items. The data refer to couples completing therapy who were interviewed at F1 and F4 or F3 and F4. Couples who separated between F3 and F4 are excluded.
[b] According to sign-test.

TABLE 5.9

Stability of Therapy Results: Overall Outcome Two and a Half to Four and a Half Years After Completion of Therapy; Ratings by Therapists[a]

	Total		Total	
	F1	F4	F3	F4
Sexual functioning [b]	(N=111)	(N=111)	(N=94)	(N=94)
(1) Separation between F3–F4	—	13[c]	—	13[c]
(4, 5) not/slightly improved	14	19	8	15
(6) improved	27	14	25	13
(7) distinctly improved	19	21	21	14
(8) cured	51	44	40	39
statistical significance [d]	ns[e]		ns[e]	
Relationship in general [b]	(N=86)	(N=86)	(N=69)	(N=69)
(1) disturbed as before	4	5	2	5
(2) disturbed as before, but more aware of problems	7	6	7	5
(3) positive state unchanged	17	17	12	12
(4) deteriorated	0	2	2	1
(5, 6) distinctly improved	58	56	46	46
statistical significance [d]	ns		ns	
Sexual satisfaction [b]	(N=86)	(N=86)	(N=70)	(N=70)
(1) less satisfying	1	8	0	7
(2) just as satisfying	1	5	4	4
(3) somewhat more satisfying	35	22	21	14
(4) satisfying	49	51	45	45
statistical significance [d]	.05		.05	

[a] *The data refer only to couples completing therapy and to couples who were interviewed both at F1 and F4 or F3 and F4.*

[b] *Ratings of overall outcome R2; for definition of categories see p. 120.*

[c] *12 of 99 couples separated; in one couple both partners had a dysfunction; their data thus appear twice.*

[d] *According to sign-test, not including separating couples.*

[e] *Statistical significance of comparison "delayed remission" vs. "relapses" p=0.10 (F1–F4) and p=0.01 (F3–F4).*

TABLE 5.10

Stability of Therapy Results: Differences in Sexual Functioning on Completion of Therapy, One Year and Two and a Half to Four and a Half Years Later; Ratings by Therapists[a]

Ratings by therapists	OD	VA	ED	PE	Total	
	(N=51)	(N=16)	(N=29)	(N=15)	(N=111)	
Same for F1 and F4	20	9	14	5	48	(43%)
Better at F4 than at F1	13	3	4	2	22	(20%)
No. of delayed "remissions"[b]	(2)	(2)	(2)	(—)	(6)	
Worse at F4 than at F1	12	2	7	7	28	(25%)
No. of "relapses"[c]	(8)	(—)	(4)	(2)	(14)	
Separations between F3–F4	6	2	4	1	13	(12%)
Statistical significance ("better vs. worse")[d]	ns	ns	ns	ns	ns[e]	
	(N=44)	(N=14)	(N=23)	(N=13)	(N=94)	
Same for F3 and F4	22	9	11	2	44	(47%)
Better at F4 than at F3	8	1	2	6	17	(18%)
No. of delayed "remissions"[b]	(—)	(—)	(—)	(—)	(—)	
Worse at F4 than at F3	8	2	6	4	20	(21%)
No. of "relapses"[c]	(5)	(—)	(4)	(1)	(10)	
Separations between F3 and F4	6	2	4	1	13	(14%)
Statistical significance ("better vs. worse")	ns	ns	ns	ns	ns[e]	

[a] *The data refer only to couples completing therapy who were interviewed at F1 and F4 or F3 and F4. The table shows the data on sexual functioning (R2) from table 5.9 in a different break-down.*
[b] *Definition: ratings of 4 or 5 at F1/F3 and of 6, 7, or 8 at F4.*
[c] *Definition: ratings of 6, 7, or 8 at F1/F3 and of 4 or 5 at F4.*
[d] *According to sign-test, not including separating couples.*
[e] *Statistical significance of comparison "delayed remissions" vs. "relapses" p=0.10 (F1-F4) and p=0.01 (F3-F4).*

TABLE 5.11

Changes in FPI Scales, EMI Scales, and in Psychovegetative Complaints One Year After Therapy[a]

	Patient		Partner	
	female dysfunctions	**male dysfunctions**	**female dysfunctions**	**male dysfunctions**
FPI	(N=48)	(N=37)	(N=50)	(N=35)
1. nervousness	(−).05	−	(−).05	(−).10
2. aggression	−	−	−	−
3. depression	(−).001	(−).05	(−).001	(−).01
4. arousability	−	−	−	−
5. sociability	−	−	(−).05	−
6. calmness, relaxation	(+).05	(−).05	−	−
7. dominance	−	(−).05	−	−
8. social inhibition	(−).10	(−).10	(−).01	(−).05
9. openness	−	−	−	(+).10
E extraversion	−	(−).10	(−).01	−
N emotional lability	(−).05	−	−	(−).05
M masculinity	−	(−).05	−	−
EMI[b]	(N=45)	(N=36)	(N=48)	(N=33)
1. agitated expression of anxiety	−	(−).10	(−).05	(−).05
2. inhibition	(−).05	(−).001	(−).01	(−).10
3. vegetative expression of anxiety	−	−	(−).10	(−).01
4. exhaustion	−	(−).10	−	−
5. aggression	−	−	−	−
6. anxiety (about being threatened)	−	−	−	−
7. depression	−	−	(−).05	−
List of complaints[c]	(N=39)	(N=28)	(N=38)	(N=29)
Number of psychovegetative complaints in one week (Q1)	(−).05	−	(−).01	(−).05

[a] *The data refer to couples completing therapy who filled out the questionnaires at pretest 2 and follow-up 3. Statistical significance of mean differences P2 vs. F3 according to t-test. + = higher scores, − = lower scores for F3.*

[b] *A German mood list.*

[c] *From the diary Q1. The patients recorded for a week which of the eleven psychovegetative complaints (for example, headaches, tachocardia, loss of appetite, difficulty in sleeping, irascibility, faintness) they had on each day. The score is defined as the sum of the complaints marked down by patients during the seven days.*

TABLE 5.12

Changes in GT Scales (Self-Rating and Rating of Partner) One Year After Therapy[a]

	Patient		Partner	
	female dysfunctions	male dysfunctions	female dysfunctions	male dysfunctions
GT-S *(self-rating)*	(N=50)	(N=40)	(N=52)	(N=36)
1. social resonance (negative-positive socially resonant)	−	−	(+).05	−
2. dominance (dominant-accommodating)	−	−	−	−
3. control (undercontrolled-overcontrolled)	−	−	−	−
4. basic mood (hypomanic-depressive)	(−).01	−	(−).10	(−).05
5. permeability (open-retentive)	(−).01	−	−	−
6. social potency (socially potent-socially impotent)	−	−	−	−
GT-F *(partner rating)*				
1. social resonance	−	−	−	−
2. dominance	−	−	−	−
3. control	−	−	−	−
4. basic mood	(−).05	(−).10	−	−
5. permeability	(−).01	−	−	−
6. social potency	(−).10	−	−	−

[a] *The data refer only to couples completing therapy who filled out the questionnaire at pretest 2 and follow-up 3. Statistical significance of mean differences according to t-test, 2 vs. F3. + = higher, − = lower scores for F3.*

NOTES

1. About 5 percent of the couples could not be reached or were not informed due to organizational failures. The refusal rate was thus about 30 percent.

2. These tendencies are statistically significant for eleven (patient) and twelve (partner) of the fifteen items.

3. Twelve couples had bilateral dysfunctions so that there were 128 dysfunctions at follow-up.

4. Twelve of the couples had bilateral dysfunctions so that there were 111 dysfunctions at follow-up.

5. The figures cited here are based on the data for couples completing therapy (N = 99) and drop-out couples (N = 18) who were available for F4. They refer to therapist rating of overall outcome R2, item A (see p. 120).

Chapter 6

THERAPY SETTINGS

Ulrich Clement and Gunter Schmidt

Comparison of Therapy Settings

In our analyses so far we have simply compounded the data; we have as yet disregarded the problems involved in therapy settings and their varying effectiveness. We conducted therapy in three different settings: (1) two therapists, intensive therapy; (2) two therapists, long-term therapy; (3) one therapist, long-term therapy (see p. 86 for detailed definitions).

Whether therapy results are dependent on the setting is of particular practical relevance for us. Masters and Johnson emphatically propagate intensive (rapid) therapy with two therapists and reject both long-term treatment and treatment with only one therapist. Their setting involves great expense (two therapists and hotel accommodations for the couples); it sometimes also involved unreasonable and impracticable demands on the patients (dropping work and family commitments for three weeks, sometimes sacrificing their vacations for therapy).

Although couple therapy has long since been conducted in modified settings, there exist no controlled studies on the effect of these settings on therapy outcome. Having used three settings, we could answer two questions: First, are there differences in outcome between therapy with one therapist and therapy with a team? This will be answered by comparing settings 2 and 3. Second, does intensive therapy differ from long-term therapy? This will be answered by comparing settings 1 and 2.

For reasons discussed earlier (p. 86), the four diagnostic groups were spread very unevenly over the three settings (see table 4.8). It was thus necessary to constitute samples that differed only in terms of the settings we wanted to compare. For the two comparisons we composed subsamples that were matched according to diagnosis and patient education.[1] This matching involved considerable reduction in sample size (see table 6.1), to fifty-two couples (for one therapist versus two therapists) and to fifty-six couples (for intensive versus long-term). For the sake of simplicity we restricted the comparison to therapist ratings of overall outcomes (R2) and couple self-ratings (Q4). The date from other test instruments produced no findings that diverge from the trends we will discuss. Because there were relatively few cases, we also compounded the results for all diagnostic groups. Our statistical analysis included a breakdown of data by male and female dysfunctions; we can, however, neglect this differentiation because there is no indication that therapy settings had different effects on male and female dysfunctions.

ONE THERAPIST VERSUS TWO THERAPISTS

The matched samples of couples who were treated by one or two therapists are comparable both in terms of the two matched variables "diagnosis" and "school education" and all other important background characteristics, such as age and profession, marital status, duration of relationship and dysfunction (see table 6.1). Therapy with one therapist was divided equally between female and male therapists.

In therapist assessments therapy with one and with two therapists showed no sign whatsoever of differing in outcome (see table 6.2). This applies equally for follow-up on completion of therapy and follow-up one year later, for rating of sexual function, of relationships, of sexual experience, and, finally, for male as well as female dysfunctions. Neither did self-assessments of couples (patient and partner) differ in any items for the two settings, both at F1 and F3 (see table 6.3). In general a therapist team is no more effective than a single therapist, provided that the latter is experienced in couple therapy (as the therapists were in our investigation).

INTENSIVE VERSUS LONG-TERM THERAPY

The samples here matched for diagnosis and school education are also sufficiently comparable in terms of other background variables (see table 6.1). At the end of therapy the therapists' assessments of the overall outcome in the two settings varied significantly: treatment was, relatively often, broken off in long-term therapy, whereas intensive therapy was, comparatively often, completed with slight or moderate success. The number of "distinctly improved" or "cured" couples is roughly the same for both settings (see table 6.4). This outcome can be explained by formal peculiarities in the therapy format: patients participating in intensive three-week therapy had to make a number of arrangements (for example, providing for child care, arranging for a vacation or sickleave, finding hotel accommodations if they were not residents of Hamburg). Understandably, within three weeks they were less willing to break off therapy than were patients in long-term therapy for whom the stagnation and lack of prospects become all too clear after a few months. On average, long-term therapy was broken off prematurely after nineteen session—more sessions than were planned for the entire intensive therapy format. In other words, couples who dropped out of long-term therapy would presumably have completed intensive therapy without, or only with minimal, success. One year after completion of therapy there were no longer differences between intensive and long-term therapy; the initial differences had leveled out.

Changes in relationships induced by therapy did not vary in the different settings, both on completion of therapy and one year later (see table 6.4) This fairly general evaluation of therapy shows that long-term therapy did not manage to treat partner problems to an appreciable degree. Sexual satisfaction was assessed as being greater for couples completing long-term therapy, than it was for those completing intensive therapy. This difference also leveled out one year after therapy.

Assessment by couples themselves of subjectively experienced changes, both at F1 (see table 6.5) and F3, was the same for intensive and long-term therapy. Again, only the item "sexual problems" showed relatively frequent moderate success in intensive therapy (statistically significant only for the symptomatic partner); but this difference was also no longer evident one year after therapy.

In summary we can state the following: couples who complete long-term therapy tended to be slightly more successful than couples completing intensive therapy. These differences were, however, minimal and balanced out in the year following therapy, thus demonstrating that, in general, both therapy settings had the same effectiveness.

CONCLUSIONS

The therapy settings we investigated are for the most part comparable in their therapeutic effectiveness; apparently the formal setting was of relative unimportance. Neither diagnosis nor other variables relevant to dysfunctions permit a differential indication for the different settings. From the point of view of availability (treatment opportunities for as many patients as possible) and of economic concerns, long-term therapy with one therapist should, as a rule, be chosen if, as in our project, the therapist is experienced and has a permanent opportunity for supervision. However, the remaining therapy settings are preferable or inevitable under certain external conditions: 1) Team therapy is immediately preferable if one therapist is still inexperienced in treatment of sexual dysfunctions. This setting is particularly suitable for therapist training (see chapter 10). 2) Intensive therapy is suitable for couples who have no therapeutic opportunity near their homes or whose situation precludes long-term treatment for months (for example, if one partner is frequently away from home on a job).

We have focussed our attention here exclusively on the effectiveness of therapy settings. Equal effectiveness by no means implies that these settings are identical from a psychological point of view. Therapist experience with the therapy formats varied considerably.

The protection afforded by daily therapeutic contact, the compactness of therapeutic interventions, and the partners' confrontation with each other due to their quasi-isolation during therapy meant that patients in intensive therapy were more approachable and open. Resistance to therapy seemed to be less; the time between sessions was often too short to allow defenses to be rebuilt. As a result the willingness to expose themselves to new experiences and to accept new insights was greater. This may explain why the smaller number of therapy hours resulted in the same outcome as long-term therapy. The relationship between the therapy team and the couple was often far more intense in intensive treatment; because treatment was short the therapists could get far more involved without fearing patient dependency. Therapy was experienced as more "symbiotic"; it proceeded more dramatically because therapists and patients could not afford to let an hour pass without turning it to good use. Progress was very often far more impressive for therapists and patients because it took shape quickly. Progress of this kind also contributed to an intensification of the therapist-patient relationship, as did the awareness of having taken a great risk together. Failure in intensive therapy became evident within a mere three weeks and was thus a far more radical experience than it was in long-term therapy, where lack of success emerged gradually and therapists and patients found the time to prepare for and adapt to failure.

For the patients, intensive therapy was often a stronger mutual experience than was long-term therapy: most couples had never taken so much trouble to help each other or talked through their problems so intensely in their entire relationships. This mutuality probably activated the will to self-help after therapy far more than in long-term therapy, which may well be why a relatively large number of couples treated in intensive therapy, who had only moderately improved on completing therapy, made progress in the year after therapy. In intensive therapy priority was given to sexuality and the ad hoc relationship during therapy, that is, communication, feelings, and conflicts that arose there and then; the couple's real everyday situation was pushed aside in a bluntly artificial way. In long-term therapy the chronic partner problems and the daily burdens of work and family were experienced with far more intensity by the therapists and were discussed more thoroughly. The therapists gained a deeper knowledge of the patients' way of life. This advantage certainly improved the chances for patients in long-term therapy. The real concern of couple therapy is the relationship, and the relationship can provide an analogy that characterizes the psychological differences between the two therapy settings. The time limit, intensity, willingness to get involved, and commitment to instantaneous feelings typifying relations in intensive therapy are features comparable to the intense but transient state of being in love; long-term therapy which is spread over a longer period of time, moderate in emotional intensity and firmly rooted in everyday problems is comparable to married life—with the same risks and chances.

Compared with single-therapist treatment, team therapy involves special problems and complications arising from the relationship between the therapists. We shall discuss some of these problems later.

MALE VERSUS FEMALE THERAPIST

In the fifty nine single-therapist treatments we examined whether the gender of therapist and patient had any bearing on the outcome of therapy. Our analysis was restricted to a small number of cases: female patient and female therapist, N = 18; female patient and male therapist, N = 16; male patient and female therapist, N = 9; male patient and male therapist, N = 16.

Our criterion for changes induced by therapy is based on therapist ratings (overall outcome, R2) and couple self-assessments (Q4) from F1 and F3. There is no evidence that therapist gender had an effect on outcome of therapy for female dysfunctions; this applies for all assessed items and for both follow-ups. Therapeutically induced changes in male dysfunctions were rated more positively by male than by female therapists: ten of sixteen men with erectile dysfunction or premature ejaculation were classified as "cured" by their male therapists on completing therapy, but none of the nine patients was so classified by their female therapists (p = .01). The trend was the same one year after completion of therapy, although it remained statistically insignificant. Patient self-assessment did not corroborate the better results supposedly achieved by same-sex therapist treating male dysfunctions. None of the differences showed any insignificant tendency of being significant.

Figure 6.1 shows that there were distinct differences in therapy procedure with male and female therapists: male therapists needed the same amount of time to treat male and female disturbances (in terms of therapy duration and average length of therapy sessions); female therapists took much more time for female than for male dysfunctions. For therapy with a same-sex patient, female therapists needed on average fourteen sessions or twelve weeks more than did male therapists. By multiplying the average length of sessions by the number of sessions, we arrive at the following averages for therapy duration: twenty nine hours for female therapist, female dysfunction; seventeen hours for female therapist, male dysfunctions; seventeen hours for male therapist, female dysfunction; fifteen hours for male therapist, male dysfunction.

These data indicate that female therapists took great care with symptoms manifested in female patients. They apparently endeavored to develop a more differentiated and deeper understanding of the problems and of the relation between the female patient's symptom and her previous history They were more aware of a female patient's ambiguous motivation for therapy and thus responded more sensitively to her needs and perhaps, with more resistance to the latent demands made by the male partner. In any case, they protected women longer from sexual intercourse by prolonging therapy; for, concomitant with therapy duration, coitus prohibition was sustained for a particularly long time (see figure 6.1). Therapy was also sometimes prolonged by special problems the male patient had with the female therapist: many men found it hard to accept that they had to rely on the help of a woman in solving their sexual problems; this injured their pride because they were confronted by their own powerlessness to do something about the problem. (The resistance to accepting help from a fe-

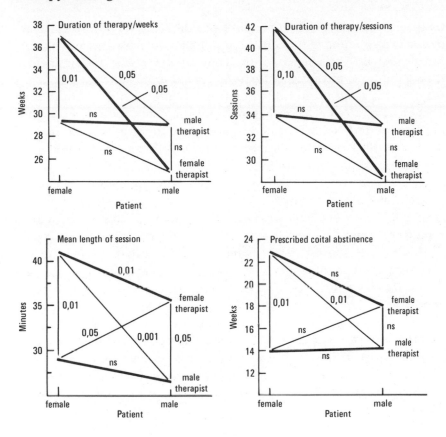

FIGURE 6.1

Characteristics of Therapy Procedure (Single-Therapist Treatment) in Relation to Sex of Patient and Sex of Therapist.

Note: Means. Significance of mean differences according to t-test. Only couples completing therapy were included: N=15 (female patient, female therapist.); N=11 (female patient, male therapist.); N=7 (male patient, female therapist.); N=16 (male patient, male therapist.).

male therapist was possibly another cause of the lower success rate of female therapists in treating male dysfunctions.)

It could be that in therapy by female therapists with female patients treatment had positive effects in areas we did not measure, for example, increased self-confidence, greater sensibility to sex-role conflicts, and strengthened female identity. This could explain why the prolonged therapy did not have any effect on therapy outcome. At this point we can do no more than make speculative suggestions.

In view of our findings on gender-dependent therapy results and procedure, we are inclined to recommend that in single-therapist

153

treatment the therapist and patient be of the same sex. Our recommendation is also founded on general arguments, such as: greater empathy for the sexuality of a person of the same gender; greater willingness to trust a therapist of the same sex with sexual problems; less risk of the patient acting out uncontrolled erotic desires with the therapist; a reduction of rivalry between therapist and the "nondysfunctional" partner. Inexperienced therapists, in particular, are often unable to cope with the difficult constellation of connections to a patient of the opposite sex in couple therapy. On the other hand, couple therapy with an experienced therapist of the opposite sex may under certain circumstances have a good chance of succeeding. For example, in transference to a male therapist a woman with sexual problems might start to experience herself more self-confidently as a female and feel accepted in this role, if she can accept him as a man and if he, despite the necessary therapeutic control of the complex relationship, also perceives her as a sexual being. Such transference processes may have an important therapeutic effect, but they are at the same time particularly difficult to handle in therapy. It is, of course, quite possible that similar interactions arise between a sexually dysfunctional man and a female therapist. However, in our team discussions we found again and again that female therapists were less apt to get involved in transference and countertransference of this kind or at least were less aware of the opportunity.

List of Abbreviations Used in the Tables

OD   orgasmic dysfunction
VA   vaginismus
ED   erectile dysfunction
PE   premature ejaculation
P1   pretest 1 (three to twelve months before therapy)
P2   pretest 2 (immediately before therapy)
F1   follow-up 1 (immediately after therapy)
F2   follow-up 2 (three months after therapy)
F3   follow-up 3 (one year after therapy)
F4   follow-up 4 (two and a half to four and a half years after therapy)
N   number of individual cases
Nc   number of couples
ns   statistically not significant
m   mean
s   standard deviation

TABLE 6.1
Therapy Settings: Comparison of Samples[a]

		1 Therapist (N=52)	2 Therapists (N=52)	Intensive (N=56)	Long-term (N=56)
Diagnosis	OD	31	31	25	25
	VA	3	3	10	10
	ED	12	12	15	15
	PE	6	6	6	6
Age (years)	means	31.0	29.7	29.1	29.6
			ns		ns
Age of partner (years)	means	31.8	30.5	30.0	30.4
			ns		ns
School education	9 years (Hauptschule)	22	24	23	24
	10 years (Mittlere Reife)	12	11	17	18
	13 years or more (Abitur)	18	17	16	13
			ns		ns
School education of partner	9 years (Hauptschule)	19	21	21	21
	10 years (Mittlere Reife)	15	14	18	19
	13 years or more (Abitur)	18	17	17	16
			ns		ns
Marital status	single	13	13	16	14
	married	39	39	40	42
			ns		ns
Duration of dysfunction	up to 2 years	5	7	7	7
	3–5 years	13	14	16	15
	6 years or more	34	31	33	34
			ns		ns
Employment	full-time	29	30	40	39
			ns		ns
Employment of partner	full-time	34	35	36	39
			ns		ns
Occupation	skilled or unskilled worker	9	5	11	6
	employee	18	18	19	26
	academic	16	16	18	13
			ns		ns
Occupation of partner	skilled or unskilled worker	11	9	11	9
	employee	18	13	21	14
	academic	13	20	14	19
			ns		ns
Duration of relationship (years)	mean	8.8	8.6	7.7	8.5
			ns		ns

[a] *Statistical significances according to chi-square, for age and duration of relationship according to t-test.*

TABLE 6.2

Therapy Settings, One Therapist versus Two Therapists: Overall Outcome; Ratings by Therapists

	F1		F3	
	1 Therapist (N=52)	2 Therapists (N=52)	1 Therapist (N=27)	2 Therapists (N=31)
Sexual functioning[a]				
(1) drop-out, separation of couples[b]	4	3	0	1
(2, 3) drop-out	6	12	—	—
(4, 5) therapy completed, not/slightly improved	4	2	4	2
(6) therapy completed, improved	16	11	8	9
(7) therapy completed, distinctly improved	8	9	5	10
(8) therapy completed, cured	14	15	10	9
		ns		ns
Relationship in general[a]				
(0) inapplicable	10	15	0	1
(1) disturbed as before	4	3	1	0
(2) disturbed as before, but more aware of problems	6	3	3	5
(3) positive state unchanged	3	3	2	2
(4) deteriorated	0	1	0	3
(5) improved	20	22	15	14
(6) distinctly improved	9	5	6	6
		ns		ns
Sexual satisfaction[a]				
(0) inapplicable	12	18	1	1
(1) less satisfying than before therapy	0	0	0	0
(2) just as unsatisfying	3	3	4	2
(3) somewhat more satisfying than before therapy	17	11	8	12
(4) satisfying	20	20	14	16
		ns		ns

[a] Ratings of overall outcome R2; for definition of categories see p. 120. Significances according to chi-square, for items 2 and 3 the category (0) was not included.
[b] For F3; couple separated in the year following therapy.

TABLE 6.3

Therapy Settings, One Therapist versus Two Therapists: Sexuality and Relationship Before and After Therapy; Couple Self-Rating[a][b]

	Patient (F1)		Partner (F1)	
	1 Therapist	2 Therapists	1 Therapist	2 Therapists
Our sexual problems are now . . . than before therapy				
worse/unchanged	1	1	0	2
slightly better	6	4	11	6
much better	22	27	19	21
fully removed	2	0	1	2
		ns		ns
Our relationship is now . . . than before therapy				
worse/unchanged	4	6	5	8
slightly better	10	12	8	8
much better	16	14	19	15
		ns		ns
Being affectionate to my partner is now . . . than before therapy				
more difficult/unchanged	7	7	6	10
easier	18	18	18	14
much easier	7	7	8	7
		ns		ns
We can now find solutions to nonsexual problems . . . than before therapy				
much more easily	6	5	5	6
more easily	13	14	14	12
as easily/less easily	13	13	13	13
		ns		ns
My sexual desire is now . . . than before therapy				
much stronger	0	4	2	6
stronger	16	16	13	11
as strong/weaker	15	11	17	14
		ns		ns
My sexual satisfaction after intercourse is now . . . than before therapy				
much greater	6	7	8	5
greater	18	17	13	12
unchanged/less	8	7	11	11
		ns		ns

[a] Questionnaire Q4, selected items. The data refer only to couples completing therapy. Statistical significance according to chi-square.
[b] Number of cases for all groups between N = 30 and N = 32.

TABLE 6.4

Therapy Settings, Intensive versus Long-Term: Overall Outcome; Ratings by Therapists

	F1		F3	
	Intensive (N=56)	Long-term (N=56)	Intensive (N=35)	Long-term (N=36)
Sexual functioning[a]				
(1) drop-out, separation of couple[b]	0	3	3	2
(2, 3) drop-out	6	11	—	—
(4, 5) therapy completed, not/ slightly improved	7	2	3	2
(6) therapy completed, improved	15	8	6	10
(7) therapy completed, distinctly improved	11	11	7	11
(8) therapy completed, cured	17	21	16	11
		.05		ns
Relationship in general[a]				
(0) inapplicable	6	15	4	2
(1) disturbed as before	2	4	0	0
(2) disturbed as before, but more aware of problems	9	2	4	5
(3) positive state unchanged	11	6	6	5
(4) deteriorated	0	1	2	4
(5) improved	21	24	14	12
(6) distinctly improved	7	4	5	8
		ns	⎪	ns
Sexual satisfaction[a]				
(0) inapplicable	7	16	5	3
(1) less satisfying than before therapy	1	0	0	1
(2) just as unsatisfying	2	2	2	1
(3) somewhat more satisfying than before therapy	21	10	9	10
(4) satisfying	25	28	19	21
		ns		ns

[a] *Ratings of overall outcome R2; for definition of categories see p. 120. Significances according to chi-square, for items 2 and 3 the category (0) was not included.*

[b] *For F3; couple separated in the year following therapy.*

TABLE 6.5

Therapy Settings, Intensive versus Long-Term: Sexuality and Relationship Before and After Therapy: Couple Self-Rating [a] [b]

	Patient (F1)		Partner (F1)	
	Intensive	Long-term	Intensive	Long-term
Our sexual problems are now ... than before therapy				
worse/unchanged	2	0	2	1
slightly better	13	4	11	7
much better	15	25	16	19
fully removed	3	5	6	5
	.01		ns	
Our relationship is now ... than before therapy				
worse/unchanged	7	7	5	6
slightly better	10	10	14	8
much better	16	17	14	18
	ns		ns	
Being affectionate to my partner is now ... than before therapy				
more difficult/unchanged	9	7	8	9
easier	16	18	17	14
much easier	9	9	10	9
	ns		ns	
We can now find solutions to nonsexual problems... than before therapy				
much more easily	6	4	5	6
more easily	15	16	18	12
as easily/less easily	12	14	11	14
	ns		ns	
My sexual desire is now ... than before therapy				
much stronger	3	5	3	5
stronger	15	16	13	14
as strong/weaker	16	12	19	13
	ns		ns	
My sexual satisfaction after intercourse is now ... than before therapy				
much greater	9	9	7	7
greater	15	16	17	13
unchanged/less	8	6	9	11
	ns		ns	

[a] Questionnaire Q4: selected items. The data refer only to couples completing therapy. Statistical significance according to chi-square.
[b] Number of cases for all groups between N = 31 and N = 35.

NOTE

1. We chose this variable because the school education of couples in the different settings varied slightly.

Chapter 7

DIFFICULT PATIENTS, UNDESIRED SIDE-EFFECTS

Friedemann Pfäfflin, Gerhard Thiessen-Liedtke,

and Roswitha Bulla-Küchler

In principle every kind of psychotherapy has to be modified according to the patient's specific situation and problems. No matter how refined the therapy program, it must still examine each patient's particular characteristics individually. This commonplace would not be worth mentioning were it not that the success of the Masters and Johnson couple therapy program has led sex counselors, psychologists, and physicians to ignore this basic and self-evident therapeutic rule and to conceive behavioral instructions as an easily prescribable and highly efficient therapeutic construct.

In this and the next chapter we shall supplement the foregoing discussion of therapy results by commenting on case histories, which should counteract such misunderstandings. We wish to outline the specific conditions that impede therapy, necessitate procedural modifications, undermine successful therapy outcome, or make it seem improbable from the very start. Complications in therapy do not always lead to a "negative" result; the outcome is open. Although our statistics mislead one generally to overestimate therapy results (see p. 88), they also underestimate results in individual cases, particularly for couples whose sexual functioning was only partly improved by therapy or who separated during or after therapy. There is more at stake in therapy than a sexual function in need of repair, which can be put straight with a few effortless twists and turns.

Difficult Patients

Selection criteria were more broadly defined in our project than in all other comparable studies (see p. 77) and, in contrast to Masters and Johnson, (1970), did not in principle explicitly exclude psychiatric patients. This meant that we saw many patients whose sexual dysfunction was just one symptom among other. Our selection criteria were defined so broadly for several reasons. First, we were not developing a completely new therapy program. Masters and Johnson had proved that their intensive couple therapy was a viable treatment concept for a carefully screened sample of couples. In modifying their concept we aimed at making therapy useful for a broader spectrum of patients. As experience with couple therapy grew, we had more confidence in our concept and ourselves. Second, except for acutely psychotic or addicted patients, there were no compelling reasons for excluding psychiatric patients. Mitigation of conflicts in sexuality and partner relations sometimes helped encourage a general stabilization in the patient and so contributed to relapse prophylaxis. Third, as a division of a psychiatric department, we felt responsible for these patients and their care. It was doubtless also much easier to accept more difficult patients because we knew we could fall back on inpatient treatment in our clinic when necessary; without this backing we probably would never have treated some patients. We emphasize this point to avoid giving the impression that we had simply experimented or that we would encourage experiments. Incidentally, the range of difficult patients was not limited to psychiatric patients.

We would not deny that therapists quite often symbolically threw up their hands in despair after their first meeting with the couple selected by the first consultant. At first sight there seemed to be too many factors impeding progress in therapy and jeopardizing a positive outcome. For example, when one of the partners was in considerable danger of becoming addicted to alcohol or suffered from pronounced compulsive symptoms; when we were faced by chronic psychosomatic disorders or elaborate sexually deviant fantasies and behavior; when the relationship seemed to be in a hopeless or desperate state; or when the patients' emotional reactions were in danger of being choked by the high doses of neuroleptic medication. Besides, even the formal requirements had not always been met in full: for example, contraceptives were not being used; covert sexual relations with other partners existed, or therapy sessions were disturbed by couples bringing their children with them.

Such difficulties frequently led to aggression and mutual accusations between the team members, thereby complicating the therapy process. Although the manual (see part 3) left room for therapists, after history-taking, to revise the evaluation made by the first consultant, fewer than ten couples were exempted from the project at this point. However, the word "exempted" is not quite right. To be precise, not one couple was exempted; rather, after history-taking about ten couples dropped out of the project because they had either been inadequately informed about therapy requirements by the first consultant or had not understood them properly and then found out too late, for example, that they were unable to keep appointments. In a very few cases patients said the whole therapy setting or parts of it—for example, prohibition of coitus—was sheer nonsense and chose not to participate. One can say that after history-taking therapists never doubted the recommendations for therapy so fundamentally that they were unable to commence therapy. We left the final decision to the patients because there were no reliable criteria for predicting therapeutic program and outcome. Furthermore, we did not want to send away patients who had been promised therapy and who had high hopes. Another factor may have been that some therapists felt it was a challenge to test whether the therapy concept was flexible enough to deal with such complicated cases.

We shall discuss in detail only those patients who, apart from their sexual dysfunctions, suffered from manifest psychiatric, neurological, or psychosomatic illnesses, neuroses, deviant sexual behavior, physical disabilities, or the consequences of disfiguring surgery. Such patients comprised about a quarter of all couples treated and their problems included disfigurement of a funnel chest and hunchback, blindness, recently cured alcohol addiction, encephalomyelitis disseminata, neurodermitis, ulcerous colitis, phasic depression, sadomasochistically structured partner relations, and sadomasochistic or fetischistic fantasies and behavior patterns.

In the following discussion, we attempt to show how flexible a therapeutic concept can be and must be to accommodate the broad spectrum of patients' problems and to enhance attentiveness to special features in individual cases. We also want to demonstrate that the couple therapy for sexual dysfunctions described here had a definite effect on symptoms that are or seem to be independent of sexuality. We shall not undertake a statistical breakdown for "additional diagnoses," which would be senseless in view of the wide spectrum of cases. Furthermore, we do not intend to encourage the trend to develop special forms of couple therapy for sexually dysfunctional psychotics, alcoholics, and so forth.

We consider extreme specialization, which is now coming into fashion, superfluous and misleading in its approach. In the following six case histories we shall illustrate special problems with difficult patients and then continue by discussing the consequences for therapy.

COUPLE 20: The partners have been married for ten years and are both in their late twenties. The husband is a glazier, and his wife is a part-time typist. They have a ten-year-old daughter. The wife has never had an orgasm during petting or sexual intercourse and has never masturbated. She says her body is completely devoid of sexual feeling. She merely feels burdened, harassed, or bored by sexual intercourse; she says she might just as well read a newspaper. She sometimes feels pain on intercourse. She never knew her mother because the latter had been permanently hospitalized owing to an endogenous psychosis. The patient had been raped when still a child; she has had sexual relations only with her husband, and she got involved with him sexually only because she was glad that someone, at least, wanted to stay with her—she offered compensation for his company, so to speak. She soon became pregnant and then depressive during pregnancy.

She has been in constant, partly inpatient, psychiatric treatment for almost ten years. Two and three years ago she experienced extremely severe depressive states with paranoiac episodes. For nine years now she has been treated with high doses of neuroleptics and antidepressants. At onset of therapy she had been taking the following medications for several months: three milliliters of fluphenazine once every two weeks; in addition, thirty drops of haloperidol three times a day; one milligram of lorazepam three times a day; one tablet of chloriazepoxide three times a day; one tablet of bipereden twice a day. At the onset of therapy, her other symptoms, apart from sexual problems, were: lack of incentive and apathy, sleep disturbance, severely depressive moods, tendency toward decompensation in weeping fits, pronounced extrapyramidal symptoms at least partly due to the side-effects of medication. In his previous history the husband tended to be distressed by retarded ejaculation or ejaculatory incompetence. The relationship is characterized by the wife's demanding, weak-willed attitude toward her husband, who mothers and pampers her.

COUPLE 21: The husband and wife are both in their mid-fifties; they have been married for twenty years. He is a roof tiler, and she used to work in a laundry but is now a part-time saleswoman. The wife was first taken to another hospital in a delirious state of withdrawal from alcohol and sleeping pills. She has been addicted for three years; in recent months she has been drinking at least half a quart of liquor a day, not to mention the numerous pills. In history-taking it was discovered that she had started drinking because of sexual problems, and her physician then referred her to us. She had not undergone proper withdrawal therapy. Ten years ago, while working in the laundry, she had an accident and contracted severe burns over her entire abdomen; the burns took years to heal and left extensive scars in the genital area. Since the accident, the scar tissue has prevented her from having sexual intercourse. She had been sexually exploited by her relatives and others in her youth, had a negative attitude toward sexuality for a long time, and worked for years as a prostitute. Her husband got her out of the brothel by marrying her "because she was nicer than other prostitutes." They have several children.

The marriage was experienced as a happy one until the accident; it was kept alive mainly by intercourse, which was performed several times a day without much tenderness. Both gave priority to the husband's satisfaction. At that time the wife already felt tenderness was missing, but this lack never became a problem. The accident changed the whole situation. She then felt pain during intercourse, and the scar tissue disgusted her husband, who frequently visited other women. Before the accident she was generally the active partner in the relationship; she was full of suggestions and talked a lot—so much, in fact, that his silence went completely unnoticed. When they argued she was the one who was quick to forgive, while he was moody for days on end. This, too, was quite different after the accident: they were both wearied by the prolonged complications; they hardly spoke to one another; and the marriage sank into silence. They now restrict their communication to talking to the children separately. Both are extremely afraid of a separation; they still like each other but cannot find a way of saying so because intercourse—once the important way of expressing affection—is no longer possible.

COUPLE 22: The wife is a secretary who was unfit for work at onset of therapy; her husband is an automobile mechanic. They are both in their mid-thirties, have been married for fifteen years, and have no children. They came with a burning desire for therapy because of her complete loss of sexual appetite, her arousal and orgasmic dysfunctions, and his premature ejaculation. After years of living together "like brother and sister," they now want to do something about the situation. For years they attempted intercourse only once or twice a year; they have no experience in masturbation, petting, or relations with other partners. Both come from extremely conservative families where sex is taboo, and they have faithfully adopted their families' values (the wife, for example, did not talk to her father for two years after finding condoms in his pajama top). They both have only a bare minimum of knowledge about sexual anatomy; she calls everything between navel and knee the "lap," and he believes that women urinate through the vagina. The wife has never been able to detach herself from her family, still lives with her husband in her parents' house, and is as dependent on her parents as on her husband. When times were particularly stressful, she suffered from long amenorrheal phases, heart and circulation complaints, obsessions and ruminations, and, finally, abdominal complaints which then led to oophorectomy and hysterectomy. Her basic anxious, hypochondriacal disposition turned into an agoraphobia. The husband has been suffering from recidivistic, periodic fevers for years, the cause of which is still unknown.

COUPLE 23:   The husband, a customs official, is 30; he has been suffering from occasional erectile disturbances, retarded ejaculation, and ejaculatory incompetence ever since his first coital experiences. The erectile dysfunction has become so intense in the last three years that sexual intercourse is now impossible despite regular attempts. He thinks his sexual disturbances, his lack of desire and appeal date back to his childhood. He has masturbated regularly since he was seven years old. His impression is that ejaculation is not retarded on masturbation. However, in order to masturbate he has to take the position of an "embryo curled up" on his left side in his bed, squeeze his penis down between his thighs, and imagine sadistic rape scenes. He is not aroused in any other position, by vigorous manual stimulation, or without these fantasies. His wife is the same age, does not work, has been married to him for four years and has no sexual dysfunctions. He got to know her through a computer dating agency; he was looking for a companion in life and did not find sex very important. After a time he came to like petting, but he is still reluctant to perform sexual intercourse and does so only for his wife's sake, if he can sustain an erection. However, he fails to ejaculate. The whole event is distressing for both of them and degenerates into sheer hard work. The only way he can be aroused during sexual intercourse is by imagining he is being brutal to his wife; he once bit and throttled her. At work he is submissive and is incapable of standing up for himself; when arguing with his superiors he loses his powers of concentration. He has been suffering for years from duodenal ulcers, which have been treated without surgery but still recur at regular intervals. When this malady recurs he avoids attempting intercourse. His comment on the relationship—which both, incidentally, agree is good—is that he should be happy his wife has not left him because of his sexual problems.

COUPLE 24:   Both partners are in their early forties. The husband is a tailor, and his wife is a dietician. They have been married for almost twenty years and have one child. They are distinctly motivated to enter therapy; he has been suffering form erectile dysfunctions and a tendency to ejaculate prematurely for the last three years. They have had intercourse or attempted intercourse two or three times a year at the most. For several years, the sexual difficulties are overshadowed by an overwhelming number of physical and psychological complaints and by the desperate state of the relationship. The husband has often been ill since his childhood and has spent several years in the hospital. He was injured in the war and still suffers from the effects. As a young man he was involved in a violent fist fight with drunkards and was kicked so hard in the testes that one of them had to be amputated and the other became atrophic. Furthermore, the patient suffers from hypertension, cardiac oppression, and convulsive pains in the stomach and intestines; a Billroth operation (resection of the stomach) is being considered. He has already been operated on once for renal cysts. In the last few years he has lost about twenty five pounds and has hardly slept at night.

His pronounced inferiority feelings can be traced back to his childhood and were exacerbated to the utmost after losing one of his testicles. This was such a shock to his identity that he became addicted to alcohol and indiscriminately consumed every kind of tranquilizer and analgesic he could lay his hands on. As a result he has often been under psychiatric inpatient care. His addiction to drugs led to violent marital arguments, after which he reacted with suicide threats and once with a dramatic suicide attempt. His wife, who on first appearance makes a far more robust impression, also has a history plagued by illness. She has pains in her joints which she had treated for years by several doctors simultaneously without any sign of improvement. Moreover, her back is badly disfigured by a large lipoma; she had been on sick-leave for fifteen months before therapy because of severe bronchitis.

They met each other at a resort and both wanted to put their unhappy past experiences behind them and marry quickly. The marriage has been marked from the start by crises and illnesses, reconciliations and breakdowns. Sexuality serves the sole purpose of reproduction. With the help of hormone substitution and artificial insemination this function at least has been fulfilled. However, the child alone is scarcely able to hold the marriage together. The problems persist in the typical form: she is the suffering and helpful mother and wife who sacrifices her health for husband and daughter. He is mortally ill, full of inferiority complexes, and convinced that he is of no use to a woman like her; he pumps himself full of medications and alcohol until he is delirious and in danger of being suffocated by his own vomit, but he is always saved just in time by his wife.

COUPLE 25: The partners are in their mid-forties and have just celebrated their silver anniversary. Their three adult children have already left home. Since then the relationship, which they felt was a happy and sexually satisfying one from the start, has become still more intimate and intense. The husband is an air traffic controller and a passionate model builder who spends a lot of time on his hobby.

He had a serious accident two years before therapy, and the consequences overshadow and threaten to tear apart their happy marriage. While working on an iron rod for a new model, he suddenly slipped and accidentally pushed the rod into his perineum between the scrotum and the anus. At first he felt strong pains and the wound turned blue, but he did not go to a physician. In the following two weeks his penis started to become erect more and more, but he was still able to have intercourse without pain. After four or five weeks when the the erection had become permanent, he finally ended up in an urological clinic with the diagnosis "priapism, cause unknown." The patient underwent a comprehensive check-up and was then heparinized (treated with an anticoagulant) and informed that an operation was necessary within the next few weeks. A little later the operation was postponed, and instead Marcumar (anticoagulant) treatment was begun, which was supposed to last a year. After four weeks in the hospital, the erection had been unilaterally reduced, and his penis was now bent to one side. The volume of the corpora cavernosa returned to normal only months later. In a post-operative urological check-up half a year later, he mentioned the erectile disturbances for the first time. The patient's wish for hormone treatment was not granted, and instead he was offered a penile prosthesis as an alternative, should the disturbances continue. About a year after the accident, Marcumar treatment was discontinued. In the proximal, dorsal area of the penile shaft there was still a bilateral, minor induration. Otherwise there were no findings apart from the erectile disturbances, which were as distressing as before. The patient was then sent to the Urological Clinic at the Hamburg University Hospital for preliminary consideration of implantation of a penile prosthesis. From there the couple was referred to our division for additional examination. The husband now feels frustrated by the delay in receiving the prosthesis and cannot understand "what it's all about." We tediously explain to the couple why they should undergo couple therapy as an alternative to surgery. Since the accident both have been so worn out and depressed that they eagerly hold to the prospect of a penile prosthesis, and are so insistent on this that they react with anger, aggression, and disappointment to our suggestion. They feel they have been made fun of and are at first extremely reluctant even to think about this alternative. Still skeptical, they finally let themselves be talked into therapy in the certainty that, should therapy fail, they can always fall back on prosthetic surgery.

These case histories demonstrate the wide range of complications at the onset of therapy and show how senseless it would be to examine the patient's sexuality in isolation and try to adjust it in therapy without taking the overall situation into consideration. It is far more appropriate to define objectives by reference to the patient's subjective needs; this premise applied to all patients in the project, not just the difficult cases. Therapy with couple 20 did not aim at attaining orgasm in coitus but at developing "pregenital" sexual activities, which enabled the wife to feel more warmth and security in the relationship with her husband; the ever present threat of an exacerbation of her psychosis was then mitigated and the partner problems relieved. For purely technical reasons the aim of therapy with couple 21 could not be to help the couple achieve satisfying sexual intercourse because the consequences of the burns made this impossible. Both partners had to be brought to accept other forms of sexual activity (for example, petting), which they considered a superficial and childish activity as a meaningful alternative for them. For couples whose deviant fantasies and activities played an important role (see couple 23), therapists attempted to create an awareness of the partner as a person, steering him or her out of the role of a mere object, and protecting him or her from the threat that the deviant desires represented. It proved necessary for therapists and patients to adjust, supplement, or limit therapeutic aims, which was something that did not automatically happen with the identification of the complicating problems.

In addition to altering the aims of therapy, it was necessary to determine which modifications to therapeutic procedure were necessary and adequate in individual cases. In the course of the project we discussed this question in many cases, not only when difficult patients were involved; opinions in the team were often contradictory. In retrospect, one can say that the strict demand for as much methodic consistency as possible proved its worth. Therapy with difficult patients never necessitated fundamental changes to therapeutic strategy, as described in part 3, with the two exceptions we shall discuss later. This was true even though certain exercises required more time or had to be split up into smaller and simpler steps, as is illustrated by the next two examples.

The therapists for couple 21 thought it was too demanding for the patients to start with caressing exercises immediately. The couple had avoided physical contact, even looking into each other's eyes for a long time, and verbal communication had practically sunk to nothing. At first it was agreed to plan therapy sessions at greater intervals, and the patients were asked to talk about daily events with each other, take walks together, hold hands, and so forth. Caressing exercises were suggested only after a basis for mutual communication had been established. One of the primary elements of therapeutic intervention for couple 23 was alteration of husband's compulsively restricted masturbatory habits, the shame they evoked in him, and his withdrawal from sexual activity with his wife. Exercises in masturbation were prescribed that broadened both his stimulation practice and the physical positions he found acceptable. Only then did we move on to exercises that involved his wife.

For couples 22 and 24 we decided on more fundamental modifications. Treatment of couple 22 was impeded by the pronounced agoraphobic symptomatology, which prevented the couple from coming to sessions more than once every few weeks. Their eighty-five therapeutic sessions were spread over three years. The problems worsened in the very first caressing exercises. Furthermore, her agoraphobia was accompanied by heart attacks and compulsive symptoms. In view of the severe agoraphobic symptoms, the therapists finally decided (between the eighth and the sixteenth session) to refer the patient to another unit in the clinic for behavior therapy parallel to couple therapy. After thus mitigating the external conditions, couple therapy continued, subordinating instructions in sexual behavior to the general partner relations. Once the psychiatric symptoms had started to diminish, the sexual symptoms started to improve; the wife was able to take pleasure in sexual intercourse and reach orgasm with additional manual stimulation. At the end of treatment the husband still showed a slight tendency to ejaculate prematurely.

While the procedural modifications proved helpful in this case and were, in retrospect, justified, they had a negative effect on the chaotic and desolate relationship of couple 24. The husband, who was always doubled up with abdominal pain in sessions, seemed to the therapists far too vulnerable. He often came to therapy sessions drunk; this behavior and the ensuing partner conflicts were then discussed. On one occasion he arrived tipsy with his pockets stuffed full of pills and threatened to take his own life. He did not want to stay in the clinic and finally had to be admitted to the hospital against his will. On another occasion therapy had to be temporarily discontinued because he suddenly felt prepared to undergo alcohol withdrawal treatment, but he relapsed afterward. Therapy failed to make progress for some time; the couple's chaotic relationship affected the therapists and induced them to think up new interventions again and again. An improvement first set in after the situation, which was just as distressing for the therapists, had been discussed in the supervision group and after the couple and therapists had then agreed on exclusive treatment of the specific sexual problem. After thirty-four sessions in one year, the couple was able to enjoy sexual intercourse to the satisfaction of both. This was an important stabilizing factor in the relationship, which was by no means rid of its problems.

How did the complicating symptoms develop further? No matter what causal connection may exist between sexual and general or partner problems, change in sexual behavior and experience almost always involved a change (as a rule, positive) in the partners' relationship and in psychological stability, as was apparent in the tests that showed a reduction in emotional lability and psychovegetative complaints. This holds true for couples with a psychiatric history who were referred to us in the hope that an improvement in sexual problems would relieve psychiatric symptoms. With couple 20 we made sure that one of the cotherapists was a psychiatrist who could control the reduction in medication. This reduction was necessary because the medication was, in addition to other causal factors, severely restricting the female patient's affective responsiveness. After completing therapy she was taking very low, almost "cosmetic" doses by comparison with the dosage of the preceding eight years (five drops of haloperidol daily; half a milligram of lorazepam and half a tablet chlordiazepoxide daily). The dosage did not have to be increased in the period up to three-year follow-up. The patient did not suffer once from depression during this period, was capable of making more and greater demands on herself, and was livelier. She had never before felt a stronger sense of inner harmony. In her husband's opinion, too, his wife and the relationship had made an "about-face." His wife mentioned only briefly that she regularly had an orgasm in coitus because orgasm was now less important to her than a general improvement in the relationship.

It should be said, however, that this positive development was not typical of all patients with psychiatric symptoms. There were other patients with whom we scarcely made any progress; others made impressively rapid steps forward only to relapse just as quickly and seriously in the follow-up period. Even if the long-term prospects of therapy success were less hopeful than for nonpsychiatric patients, the attempt at couple therapy helped many patients and was a rewarding experience for the therapists. Even if only every second or third patient in this group could be helped and a general stabilization could be established slowly through the improvement in sexual relations, this nonetheless represented a possible form of after-care. It hardly needs to be emphasized that we are not advocating single-handed therapy without supervision and without the backing of psychiatric facilities.

Although, as we noted, a modification of objectives for patients with deviant fantasies and behavior patterns was necessary, the technical realization was particularly difficult. We tried to incorporate deviant aspects of behavior into partner interaction without endangering the partner or reducing him or her to a pure object. Involuntary involvement in a deviant ritual is deeply offensive for a partner who wishes to embark on a relationship of mutual love. The patients were also aware of this, which is why they often hesitated in consenting to reveal their fantasies and wishes. A reduction in deviant tendencies was usually best achieved in men with primary erectile disturbances and general inhibition who, for example, used their sexual fantasies basically to disarm their female partners, who they imagined were dangerous, and so to master their own anxiety. The more they experienced reciprocity in the relationship and came to feel their own sexual competence, the sooner they were able to throw off their anxieties. The deviant activities consequently became less and less important.

Somatically and psychosomatically induced complications were the least troublesome in treatment. It was particularly important to stress to the patients that sexual experience and satisfaction could be developed anew even if somatic or psychosomatic factors were previously instrumental in evoking symptoms. This was, as a rule an immense relief for the patients. In view of the special problems of couple 25, who had placed all their hopes in a penile prosthesis implantation, it was extremely gratifying for the entire team and for the therapists in particular to have restored functions to full capacity within only sixteen sessions. Of course, the patients were also very pleased with the results. Three and a half years after therapy the couple was still able to have sexual intercourse as often and with as much satisfaction as they had before the husband's accident.

About every fourth couple had highly complicated symptoms at therapy onset; there was a statistically significant higher frequency for complicated erectile dysfunctions than for other diagnostic groups. A comparison of difficult patients with the remainder of the sample showed no statistically significant difference in terms of therapy outcome and stability of results.[1] However, this result conceals the real extent of problems.

Undesired Side-Effects

Difficult patients were recognized right from the start, so therapists could adjust to them and roughly plan how to handle them. The situation was different when in the course of therapy additional problems and conflicts crept in or suddenly appeared out of the blue, obviously sparked off by the therapeutic process. We have grouped these additional symptoms under the heading "undesired side-effects," assuming that there was a connection with treatment, although the causal relation was not always immediately evident and in many cases was hypothetical to the very end. The following discussion is based on the case histories; we will thus dispense with statistic evaluation. In general terms, about every fifth couple showed undesired side-effects. They can be classified in the following manner: shift of symptom from patient to partner; psychopathological symptoms; and somatic and psychosomatic complaints.

Shift of symptom from patient to partner. In the course of treatment, and usually when the dysfunction had improved or had been removed, the previously "nondysfunctional" partner sometimes developed a dysfunction that, in its turn, impeded sexual intercourse or made it impossible. This should be distinguished from the cases of so-called bilateral dysfunction in which both partners were sexually dysfunctional when therapy began (for example, they suffered from erectile and orgasmic dysfunctions). Such manifest bilateral dysfunctions were relatively rare. More often, the bilateral dysfunction appeared in disguised form and was first identified during treatment. For example, after curing a vaginistic woman we discovered that her partner regularly ejaculated immediately after inserting his penis, something that had never been noticed because of lack of previous coital experience. Bilateral dysfunctions were also concealed when one partner's dysfunction became the focal point in the relationship, absorbing all of the couple's attention and distracting them from the other partner's problem. By shift of symptom, however, we mean cases in which, first, the partner who was known to be nondysfunctional in previous relationships (or earlier in the present relationship) developed an acute dysfunction in response to the removal of his or her partner's dysfunction; and second, when the new dysfunction lasted quite some time so that it had to be worked through in therapy.

COUPLE 26:   The couple has been married for fifteen years. The husband, who is fifty, is an employee of an insurance company. His wife, who is ten years younger, was a saleswoman until she married and became a housewife. In the first three years of marriage, sexual contact occurs regularly; neither finds sex very exciting, but they do feel it is satisfying. The husband then develops a tendency to ejaculate prematurely and later a secondary erectile dysfunction. At the same time his wife's desire increases. Sexual activity soon becomes distressing for him, and he reacts with increasing aversion. Because of the erectile dysfunction, sexual intercourse has been impossible for the last ten years, and for three years no attempts have been made; neither do they caress each other. Otherwise both feel the relationship is very harmonious, loving, and amicable. While the first priority at the start of the marriage was to build up an economic existence together, both now wish to have a child "before it's too late." Artificial insemination proves unsuccessful twice. Apart from the wish for a child, both partners are highly motivated to improve the relationship. Neither has had previous sexual experience.

The wife grew up in a prudish family. When her husband-to-be kissed her for the first time, it was taken as a promise of marriage and was for her a commitment to marriage ("he was more in love with me than I with him"). After an engagement of three years they attempted intercourse for the first time on the wedding night but were unable to agree on the type of contraceptive so that "union was impossible." Until the wedding, the man slept in their marriage bed together with his widowed mother; she had set her mind on keeping her son at home and wanted nothing to do with her daughter-in-law.

From the very beginning, the couple has been extremely shy in sexual contact; they only touch each other above the waist ("his penis does the touching down below"). These inhibitions are quite easily broken through in therapy. Until the husband starts having erections again, his wife is active; all at once she is tight as a fist, finds her husband's whole body and particularly his penis much too hard and too big, is disgusted by his body, would rather caress a baby's delicate skin, and does not like to be touched any more. Lubrication ceases; when her husband tries to insert his penis, she feels pain and is finally no longer able to insert her own finger.

Nowhere is the potential for a dysfunction to maintain the equilibrium in a relationship so clearly demonstrated as in a shift of symptom. If the therapists fail to work through the specific function a symptom has in the relationship (see chapter 2, particularly p. 47), the old pathological equilibrium can swing into effect again in the reverse form. We found it remarkable that four of the men who originally had erectile dysfunctions and their partners, who reacted with dyspareunic or even vaginistic complaints in the course of treatment, had had an extremely close and latently incestuous relationship with their mothers or fathers, respectively. The dysfunction may well have served to ward off the incest anxieties which were transferred from the parents to the partners. Treatment in all four cases was formally completed with apparent success, but at the one-year follow-up three of the couples said that, apart from superficial caressing, they had practically given up any kind of sexual activity. The relationships had become stable and presented a picture of asexual, harmonious married life that children typically paint of their parents in their fantasies or sometimes actually experience.

As a rule, symptom shifts were so dramatic that the patients themselves started to ask what conflict they were avoiding with the symptom, and so made an important step forward in coping with their symptoms. The shift of a sexual symptom from one partner to the other was sometimes due to situational factors and was a signal used by the formerly nondysfunctional partner to express his or her insecurity in the new situation or to indicate a sense of being neglected. This sense of neglect was in response to the therapists' turning their attention away from treatment of the relationship problems and concentrating on special exercises for the symptomatic partner (for example, the use of dilators).

Psychopathological symptoms. Psychopathological symptoms occurred in both partners and patients in the course of treatment and repeatedly occurred in formerly "nondysfunctional" partners when signs of improvement in the symptomatic partner's dysfunction developed.

The degree of their intensity varied greatly and ranged from a few days of hypochondriacal testicular pain to severe states of depression.

COUPLE 27: The stocky man, a thirty-five-year-old architect, and his sturdy wife, a thirty-two-year-old housewife, have been married for ten years; they have a five-year-old son. Since the relationship began the husband has suffered from erectile dysfunctions. Sexual intercourse is only possible on the rare occasions when, still half asleep, he immediately makes use of his morning erections.

They met at a dance and fell in love at first sight. Neither had had previous sexual experience, and they both lived somewhat secluded lives; the wife was caught up in her parents' way of life, and her husband was fully absorbed by his education. It was weeks before they made the first physical contact and months before they attempted sexual intercourse, which was impossible because he failed to maintain an erection. The husband's reaction was depression; he wanted to end the relationship but could not bring himself to do it because he loved his fiancée and because he felt she was the only person who could accept him. They then started writing letters to each other in which they planned their future life style—the number of children, a new house, and so on—in minute detail, as if drawing up a contract. The wedding took place one day after his military service ended; two days later he accepted a short-term job in a distant city. Because it was not worth renting an apartment there together, his wife stayed with her parents, and the couple saw each other only on weekends.

The husband is an inexhaustible whiz kid and is always out to get recognition. At the same time he is mistrustful, never takes anything for granted, and has to control everything; he always "knows better" and is tight with money. His wife tends to subordinate herself to his wishes but does not feel she is accepted, let alone happy. However, she knew how to fend for herself: she retreated to her parents' home. The husband reacted with extreme jealousy to the close tie between his wife and his mother-in-law, as he did later to that between his wife and his son. Both would like to share tenderness and sex more often, but they never find the time because they are unable to agree on the right situation. When they do finally make love, the wife climaxes during petting, but her husband always has an erectile dysfunction. In his wife's presence he continually strives to achieve an erection. However, when he is alone—for example, sitting relaxed in a train on his way to work—he gets an erection automatically.

The couple undergoes intensive therapy with booster sessions. The initially tense and hostile atmosphere is soon relaxed by caressing exercises during which he regularly has an erection; by stimulating each other manually and orally he ejaculates and she reaches orgasm, although much earlier than intended at this stage of therapy. Both of them are astonished and happy, but at the same time somewhat irritated that the years-old bone of contention (sexuality) has suddenly lost all its virulence. The husband reluctantly backs down from his self-control and performance demands. However, he puts his wife under pressure by describing to her how he might be able to make good use of this newly acquired competence in other relationships. His wife's first reaction is one of tiredness, and later she reacts with headaches and backaches. While making more and more progress with their sexuality throughout the exercises and finally being able to have sexual intercourse, the wife increasingly shuts in her feelings, cries during therapy sessions, or just sits there, apathetic and absent-minded; she convinces her physician to prescribe her psychopharmaca, without telling the therapists at first, and then lapses into prolonged moods of severe depression. She is unmotivated, can no longer cope with the housekeeping, cannot get out of bed in the morning, wants to be alone, cannot put up with her son and husband any longer, and grudgingly sees the day through.

Symptoms developed in a similarly virulent manner in other women who initially had no psychopathological symptoms and whose husbands suffered from premature ejaculation or erectile dysfunctions. However an equally severe decompensation in the partners of female patients was not observed. The significance of such reactions has been discussed in chapter 2. No such clear-cut distinction could be made between the two sexes in terms of psychological complaints that arose in the patients themselves in the course of treatment. In general, they occurred in both male and female patients, although it seems that women were more often affected than men.

COUPLE 28: Both partners are in their mid-thirties and are clerks; they have known each other for fifteen years and married thirteen years ago. They have never been able to have sexual intercourse because of her vaginismus. Moreover, for the last three years the husband has had erectile difficulties when petting. For as long as his wife can remember, she has had a diffuse fear of sexual intercourse. When still a young woman she abruptly broke off several relations once she noticed that the men wanted more than a kiss. She also categorically refused to have premarital sex with her husband. After the wedding every attempt at performing intercourse failed. Now she is deeply afraid of pain and pregnancy and is almost incapable of allowing attempts at coitus, during which she presses her thighs together in panicky fear. Attempts are made less and less often as the months pass, and they cease completely after a few years. The couple resorts to petting once a week, during which she reaches orgasm. The couple enters long-term therapy for a total of thirty-one sessions. Both partners are highly cooperative from the start. When they caress each other she finds it hard at first to open her legs in his presence, but repeated exercises help her to lose her inhibition. She has the same difficulty in showing her genitals and is only able to surmount it step by step. Inserting dilators is then hardly a problem, and after nineteen sessions the couple is given the task of inserting his penis. At the first attempt he has erectile difficulties; at the second and third attempts insertion is possible. At this point two difficulties arise: first, she feels a strong irrational fear of pregnancy, although she takes the pill; second, she is irritated by the first successful coital attempts because she does not feel as happy as she expected. A few days later this leads to a pronounced depressive mood, which last fourteen days. The wife feels as if she is paralyzed, does not feel like going to work, weeps when she is alone, and feels "empty and at the end of my tether."

The most striking and serious undesired side-effect of treatment for couples in this project was severe depressive dysphoria. In our pilot study we observed one couple whose old agoraphobia revived. In none of the couples did we observe signs of psychotic decompensation as described by Kaplan and Kohl (1972).

Somatic and psychosomatic complaints. In therapy patients often complained of somatic disorders suddenly occurring: for example, headaches, gastric complaints, discharges, circulation disorders in the sense of a vegetative dystonia with inclination to collapse, stabs in the heart reaching down the arm. The appearance of such complaints, which may seem harmless in this incomplete list, usually indicated a dramatic turning-point in therapy and a radical change in interaction between the partners. The new illness absorbed all their attention, and the real reason for treatment (the sexual problem) receded into the background; exercises could no longer be done and, depending on how severe the illness was, treatment was interrupted several times, sometimes for long periods. Despite these reactions we did not once observe an unequivocally psychosomatic illness that could be said to have been acquired during treatment or to function as a substitute symptom in symptom shift. All we can say is that there were certain indefinite physical reactions.

In this section we have deliberately described case histories only up to the appearance of the side-effects. The aim in therapy was to understand the symptom's meaning and work it through with the couple. What sometimes actually happened was that therapists refused to deal with the side-effect further once it had clearly become the expression of blatant avoidance behavior and the connection had been explained to the couple.

Therapies in which undesired side-effects emerged can be divided into three roughly equal groups according to progress made. Couples in the first group succeeded in dealing so well with conflicts that the additional complaints had disappeared by the end of therapy and did not emerge again until F1 and F3 years later. In the second group the complaints receded later during the year after completing therapy. In the remaining cases the side-effects appeared partly after completion of therapy or were still evident at follow-ups. At this point it is worth mentioning some other observations. Side-effects were far more frequent in couples whose relationship was the first of any length and usually their first sexual relationship of any kind. If the change of symptomatic partner and depressive states lasted for a long time, a pronounced fear of separation became noticeable; these partners were unable to face up to separation, as if the mere thought of it was too much of a threat. Working through and removing the dysfunction mobilized the deep-rooted fear of being left alone; removal of the dysfunction was experienced as a danger and not as relief. The patients thus preferred to put up with any kind of symptoms that acted as a stabilizing adhesive.

To conclude, we wish to comment on the limits of the term "undesired side-effects" and on the role of side-effects in therapeutic change. One can classify such effects as "undesirable" if they persist and if the couple remains caught in an unsatisfying arrangement full of conflicts. However, it would be wrong to impute a damaging quality to undesirable side-effects. On the contrary, understanding and working through them is often an important contribution to successful therapy outcome; the aim of therapy can thus by no means be to avoid or forestall the occurrence of side-effects. Even if they cannot be treated successfully, they often bring patients to shake up their ideas about their problem and thus lead the way out of the stagnation that the intended solutions produced. Separation and discontinuance of therapy (see the following chapters) are also undesirable effects of treatment that could theoretically have overcome any of the couples entering therapy; however, for some couples they did in the long run open up new perspectives for alternative solutions. Therapists saw the appearance of side-effects as a sign that the conflicts were crystallizing and that a critical phase had been reached requiring special therapeutic care. Such crises cannot be as easily foreseen as the crises that are usually to be expected in couple therapy and that almost always emerge. This critical phase occurs when the newly acquired sexual competence (for example, erection) is put to the test for the first time and the old anxieties are mobilized with some force. We did not discover any signs that would have enabled us to predict the appearance of undesirable side-effects. Even if a prediction had been possible it would still not have enabled us to justify contraindication.

NOTE

1. Therapist rating of overall outcome R2, item A.

Chapter 8

DROPPING OUT
AND SEPARATIONS

Friedemann Pfäfflin, Gerhard Thiessen-Liedtke,
and Roswitha Bulla-Küchler

When a couple whose symptoms are unchanged drops out of therapy,
it is disturbing for both couple and therapist. The experience of failure
robs the couple of all hope of improvement in sexual difficulties. It
sparks off helplessness and perplexity in the therapist and can cause
the therapist to doubt his or her professional ability. However, the
relatively high success rate achieved with the couple therapy model is
sufficient acknowledgment of the therapist's ability, and so it seems
almost superfluous to consider therapy failures in any detail. Detailed
discussions of therapy drop-outs in treatment of sexual dysfunctions
are, therefore, almost completely missing from the literature. When
information is available, it is usually in the form of bare data; publications tend to stress the effectiveness of the author's therapy program
and thus banish drop-outs from the text to the tables. In this way the
therapist's narcissistic sense of offense, evoked by the failure, is cush-
ioned by percentages and so mitigated, but it essentially remains concealed. We believe this attitude is one of the primary reasons that systematic investigation of failure has always been the step-child of
therapy research. This situation is all the more regrettable because an
inquiry into the reasons for failure is likely to lead to an improvement
in the therapeutic concept as well as in the therapists' behavior. We,
too, were comparatively late in giving this enough thought. We were

at first impressed by our success and paid little attention to failures. For example, we dispensed with giving drop-out couples tests at follow-up appointments and confined ourselves to interviews that concentrated on the undesired therapy outcome. We did, however, have objective reasons: it would have been unreasonable to burden, and abuse, these patients with further testing.

In our program, 38 of the 202 couples broke off therapy prematurely; this amounts to 19 percent of the entire sample. A therapy drop-out is a couple who, first, had not been through all the steps described in the manual and, second, completed therapy without success, the criterion being "removal of dysfunction." Ten couples (26 percent of drop-outs) discontinued therapy because they separated; one year after therapy about 40 percent of all drop-outs had separated. The number of separating partners among the drop-outs is so large as to merit separate discussion (see p. 188). We shall now compare data for discontinuing couples who stayed together and for couples who completed therapy and then discuss further questions by citing case histories.

Dropping Out

STATISTICAL DATA

Among the drop-outs, orgasmic dysfunctions and premature ejaculation are overrepresented. There were otherwise no statistically significant differences between couples completing and couples dropping out of therapy in the evaluation of the following data at the start of therapy:[1] age, occupation, school education, professional training, duration of relationship, duration of symptom, characteristics of present sexual behavior, and attitude toward sexuality.

In the evaluation of pretest data from the GT, the FPI, the EMI, and the list of psychosomatic complaints (diary), there were significant differences at the 1 or 0.1 percent level in nine variables between drop-outs and couples completing therapy. This is interesting, first, because only two of the statistically significant differences were found for the symptomatic partner (patient), while the other seven applied to the partners; second, because there was an unequal distribution between male and female dysfunctions—eight of the differences were for male dysfunctions and only one for female dysfunctions.[2]

All differences show a tendency toward augmented psychoneuroticism. It seems that the prognosis of therapy for male dysfunctions were worse, especially if the female partner had psychoneurotic problems. This should not, however, lead one to making a prognosis in individual cases on the basis of test results.

THE PSYCHODYNAMICS OF DROPPING OUT

Motivation for therapy was a strikingly frequent problem for couples dropping out. If the female partner had an orgasmic dysfunction, it was frequently the man who decided the couple should enter therapy. The woman, on the other hand, said that she participated in therapy only "for my husband's sake"; she wanted to be "a good wife" to her husband and her opinion that "I cannot continually deny my husband something that every other man gets from his wife." Statements of this kind were combined with the wishful image of an "intact family," "happy parents," and so on, and if the couple still had no children, with the wish for a child. However, these women explicitly said that their lack of sexual desire and responsiveness did not present a problem for them personally. It was a source of dissatisfaction only in the couple's shared life, at first for the partner and, ultimately, for them as well. The reverse situation, that is, when the female partner of a dysfunctional male patient took the initiative for treatment and the man only went along "for my wife's sake," was far more rare. Secondary motivation of this kind could not always be identified when therapy began; the patients were often unable to express it with sufficient clarity, so that it became evident only later in therapy.

Some of the patients who later discontinued therapy had not provided for contraception before therapy, although this was a requirement of therapy stipulated in the introductory session. Intolerance of oral and mechanical contraceptives became the central topic of the first sessions in these cases. The "objective" side-effects of contraceptives were so distressing that it was extremely difficult for therapists to say to what extent these complaints could be attributed to the patient's resistance. During treatment with one couple it turned out that the wife (orgasmic dysfunction) had become pregnant despite taking oral contraceptives and was already in the fourth month of pregnancy. Both partners were pleased because they had wished for a child eventually. At first therapy was continued, but it soon stagnated because the couple was so caught up in their enthusiasm about becoming parents. The wife no longer had any desire for sexual contact and no longer wanted to do the exercises.

External interference was often a great hindrance: the patients, or their children, fell ill, made long-planned visits to a health resort, went on vacation and business travels. Interferences were characterized as "external" because that was how patients described them. How close the link between such factors and resistance can sometimes be was most clearly demonstrated by cases in which patients were forced to interrupt therapy several times and for long periods. Roughly every third drop-out couple interrupted therapy owing to illness, which aroused the firmly grounded suspicion that this reaction was psychosomatic in character. Although not always, it was mostly the symptomatic partner who fell ill. As a rule, complaints already recognized in his or her medical history were aggravated. If the patient then underwent treatment by the family doctor, the prescribed treatment with medication often did not induce any basic improvement.

Apart from the frequent psychosomatic reactions and pronounced avoidance behavior, it was noticeable that drop-outs very frequently acted out conflicts. Acting out is used in a wide sense here and means all actions enacted by the partners with each another, with the therapists, and with others in working against the declared aim of therapy. The technical meaning of acting out in the transference relation is only one aspect. Acting out is definitely a pronounced feature of discontinuing couple's behavior, as the following examples show. A husband, whose wife had an orgasmic dysfunction, spent the night with another woman after four sessions; because his wife did not react as jealously as he had expected, he refused to continue treatment. He was not prepared to discuss the event in further sessions. The wife (orgasmic dysfunction) of another man (premature ejaculator) frequently took tranquilizers or drank alcohol and then fell into a state of drowsiness. With the intention of provoking her husband, she became inebriated on the days both had agreed to do exercises; he reacted by beating her up several times. Consequently she no longer wished to be involved in sexual activities with him. Another man felt rejected by his wife because of her orgasmic dysfunction. He wanted to get the therapists to join his side of the argument, support him in the attempt to classify her as the patient, and assure him that it was not his fault. As soon as he had failed to do so and his part in the problems were discussed, he brought friends to the next therapy session to back up his point of view.

The question at this point is what meaning acting out, falling ill, and the other factors mentioned have, considering that they contribute to treatment failure. How do patients benefit from breaking off therapy prematurely? This question was answered in an earlier investigation of a subsample (couples with female orgasmic dysfunction), for which the results have been published elsewhere (Arentewicz, Schorsch, and Schorsch 1976; Arentewicz 1977). Three typical groups of drop-out couples separated out:

1. Couples for whom the sexual dysfunction acted as a stabilizing factor in a neurotic equilibrium between the partners. Therapy with such couples was characterized by patients' intense resistance to instructions, by pronounced avoidance behavior, and acting out by one or both partners.

2. Couples whose sexual disharmony was to a certain extent the most harmless and superficial symptom, one that concealed other, more explosive conflicts. Both partners concentrated their entire attention on the sexual dysfunction and deluded themselves in thinking that everything would be all right if only the sexual difficulties could be removed. The underlying problems of couples in this group were so immense that a removal of the sexual dysfunction would have amounted to burning the fuse to a gunpowder barrel right down to the end. To avoid this danger the couples ultimately stayed away from therapy.

3. Couples for whom the sexual dysfunction had become the only link in their relationship. In these cases therapy helped the couple to arrive at a mutual decision to separate. This was also true for couples who separated after dropping out of therapy.

The case histories of drop-outs can indeed be ordered more or less convincingly into these three groupings. We did, at least, find a few striking and conclusive cases in support of this classification. Moreover, drop-outs demonstrated more clearly than other couples how much the "nondysfunctional" partner is involved in sustaining the dysfunction: the "nondysfunctional" partner of about half the couples who broke off therapy had refused to cooperate further and had thus forced the premature termination of therapy.

Still, this threefold classification, based on what dropping out meant for the patients, is misleading. It relieves therapists of responsibility and, especially when based on convincing examples, suggests that "there's simply nothing to be done," that the patients need their symptom and so cling to it with all their strength. Furthermore it seems to encourage selective screening in that it describes those partner dynamics that apparently indicate reduced prospects for successful therapy. This kind of classification is probably best applied to couples who break off therapy in the first sessions and so refuse to take part in the process of change right from the start. However this is not true of the majority of drop-outs. Long-term treatment lasted on average fourteen weeks (nineteen sessions); it was sometimes broken off after only two sessions, and in other cases it lasted more than half a year. Most of the couples had invested a lot time and energy in therapy, which meant that dropping out, although actively provoked by the patients, was a disappointment; it also meant that, if separation did not follow, the status quo was stabilized.

The inevitable question is: To what extent could therapist intervention have encouraged drop-out or even have provoked it. This was not discussed in case histories, which created the impression that therapists hardly considered the question. What follows is a glaring example:

COUPLE 29: The man is in his mid-thirties, a clerk, and has been married for three years to a woman, a secretary, nine years younger than he. After six years of happy marriage, he left his first wife toward the end of her first pregnancy, when he fell head over heels in love with his present wife. Although she did not reach orgasm, sexuality was satisfying until they married, when she began to lose her desire for sexual activities; sexual intercourse was painful for her, and she only went along with it for her husband's sake.

The therapists describe development in therapy as follows:

Both partners are highly motivated for therapy. In history-taking one has the impression that they have a fairly mature way of communicating with one another. After being given the first instructions for caressing exercises, they come to the next session without having done them because the wife says she has fallen deeply in love with a friend at work. The husband is very taken aback; he is as surprised by the event as we are since there have been no signs of this happening. The wife seems somehow proud of the infatuation and expects understanding from her husband because his was a similar situation when they met. She actually concedes him no grief but merely expects understanding and support. Our impression is that she is neurotically acting out to avoid getting involved sexually with her husband. This seems all the more true because she finds the relationship with the other man hardly realistic and does not, for example say she intends to make love to him. We discontinue therapy with the remark that the couple can come again should the conflicts clear up or should they need help coping with the situation.

The only explanation we could find for the therapists' behavior is that they wanted to comply as strictly as possible with the formal prerequisite of therapy which stipulates that no extramarital relations are to be continued during treatment. By analogy with the pietistically internalized "sin in thought" the patient's short burst of amorousness was the grounds for discontinuing therapy. The couple did not come again and did not respond to the invitations to F3 and F4.

In the case histories of therapy drop-outs, it is striking how often therapists mentioned making use of special and supplementary interventions during therapy (for example, handing out tapes for relaxation exercises, frequent sessions with one partner instead of with the couple, therapeutic exercises for improving communication). Our impression is that such intervention was not systematically controlled but was rather a way in which the therapists gave in to the patients' acting out. Therapists' procedure occasionally seemed like an active way of dealing with their own helplessness and fear, like the behavior of busybodies lacking confidence in their own concept.

One final point: therapists sometimes overtly or covertly disagreed on procedure with couples who later dropped out, and their disagreement was probably not concealed from the patients. This was discussed in supervision but was given practically no mention in the case histories. We can only conclude that there is very little reliable, detailed information on the contribution of therapist variables to drop-out. The available material does, however, often show that these variables can definitely be said to have had some influence.

THE PROSPECTS FOR THERAPY DROP-OUTS

Dropping out of therapy meant discontinuing this particular therapy program for couples but did not necessarily signal the end of treatment altogether. About half the couples continued treatment, either individually or together in another therapeutic form. An analysis of the progress couples made up to F4 clearly shows that couples who separated after dropping out, shortly thereafter or later on formed the largest group. At F3 one year after dropping out, two fifths of the discontinuing couples had separated. Three years later we estimated that the figure was about two thirds. We have no precise data, but the case histories of drop-outs who did not refuse F4 enabled a rough estimation. We will discuss separating couples in more detail in the next section. The remaining drop-out couples can be divided into four groups in terms of their further development.

1. The dysfunction sometimes receded without any further therapeutic assistance, although this was very rarely the case. We saw this happen with the couple described on p. 180, who concentrated on their future roles as parents when the wife became pregnant. The situation was completely different at F3. After several months of continence before and after the delivery, both resumed the caressing exercises of their own accord and were able later on to have satisfying sexual intercourse with orgasm. Despite dropping out, therapy had

provided a sound basis for further progress, which was constant until F4.

2. The dysfunction continued but was no longer blamed as the cause of all other partner conflicts. The partners agreed to a compromise with the "appropriate resignation" (Giese 1962).

COUPLE 30:   The partners, both in their mid-thirties, have been married for nine years and have two children, aged seven and five. The husband has been distressed by premature ejaculation since his first sexual experiences. His wife's desire for sexuality is strong. She has frequently sought satisfaction from other men because, as she expresses it, this is something her husband cannot "offer" her or which he "withholds" from her. When her husband orally or manually stimulates her to orgasm, she feels her orgasm is something that happens "in spite of him" or even "to spite him." During intercourse he is so tense right from the start and so intent on controlling his ejaculation that he repeatedly ejaculates prematurely. They alternately threaten each other with separation which becomes an everyday topic. After twenty-four sessions they break off therapy.

About three years after dropping out, the couple appears for F4. The wife begins the session with the statement: "We're still together." They had celebrated their twelfth anniversary a week earlier. It now looked as if they were going to make it to their twenty-fifth. Life together is far better. They still have crises, but they do not take them so seriously any more; they talk them over, and, above all, no longer feel that each crisis is a fundamental threat to the marriage. "We enjoy each other's company again." The daughter recently remarked what a "happily married couple" they were. That had done them good. The wife says she finds more inner peace and is more content. She thought this was due to her working part-time and passing her driving test. She reports having had two operations because she had been menstruating for months. The husband still feels a little insecure with his wife. He sees that she is making a great effort and shows an interest in him, but still asks himself whether she is convinced of what she is doing or only does it for his sake. He often wonders if she will get involved with someone else again if the opportunity arises. He does not know whether he could rely on her in such a situation.

Both report that little has changed in their sexuality. Sometimes they do not sleep with each other for four weeks, but then continue to do so two or three times a week for several weeks. He can sometimes control his ejaculation a little better; ejaculation then occurs after about two minutes. Although the premature ejaculation is, in purely technical terms, now removed, the husband says that is still not enough; he feels like someone who used to earn four hundred dollars a month and now earns five hundred, which is still too little. Moreover, it still troubles him that his wife never actively takes the sexual initiative. He complains about her lack of willingness to experiment and her lack of sexual fantasies, but in general he now finds it easier to live with the situation. The sexual problem does not distress him so acutely. He feels like a patient who consults a psychiatrist for treatment of a tic; treatment does not help but the tic does not bother him any more.

3. Joint sexual activities were almost completely discontinued and were not missed by either partner. The sexual dysfunctions thus no longer played a role in their relationship. By dispensing with sexuality the relationship was stabilized.

COUPLE 31: The partners are not married, are both in their mid-thirties, and are employed in the same insurance company. They have known each other for eight years and have been living together for four years. Up to now the man has ejaculated prematurely in all sexual encounters, something that always distressed him greatly. In recent years this was compounded by a secondary erectile dysfunction. The woman has never had an orgasm in intercourse. Both have an extremely close and ambivalent relationship to their parents; the relationships to the parents of the opposite sex are incestuously tainted. Both find it difficult to get involved in a relationship. The man has had previous experience only in a brothel, which was unsatisfying. The woman allowed only petting fully clothed in the dark because she found her body unattractive. Their difficulties seem to complement each other exactly. It takes some time before she dares to enter into sexual relations. They interrupt their friendship several times by separating for long periods. The cause is usually an argument about sexuality or parental ties. Joint sexual activity has not taken place for a year.

Both partners have a well developed sexual fantasy world, which they conceal from each other. The woman imagines having sexual intercourse with partners who are the exact opposite of the type her partner represents. The man's masturbatory technique is strictly ritualized; the most important stimulus is a larger-than-life fantasy or drawing of a woman's buttocks. He can only ejaculate if he has drawn a picture or has sunk into his fantasy. One day his partner happens to witness this ritual, precipitating a severe crisis. She begins to abstain from eating and to neglect her body in order to avoid at all costs resembling his fantasied ideal. In therapy both try to keep their wishes and fantasies secret from each other. They form an alliance against the therapists by having sexual intercourse after the first session—for the first time in almost a year. Otherwise they hardly ever do the exercises. After several sessions they finally manage to talk to each other about some of their fantasies. This awakens a feeling of familiarity and being in love. The woman is highly aroused by caresses and has orgasms; her partner reacts with anxiety. He becomes jealous and reproaches her with her own fantasies. A power struggle develops, which both use to try and degrade each other and cope better with their feelings of inferiority. The couple nevertheless makes progress in the technical sense during therapy, which they then interrupt for a vacation. The couple returns happy and content from the vacation during which they had no kind of sex at all; they are astonished at not having regretted it. The man comes to the next session alone because his partner is not prepared to continue for reasons she cannot explain. After that neither of them come to further sessions.

At follow-up three years later the woman reports feeling practically no sexual desire any more and not regretting the lack of it. She only feels a longing for sexual intercourse sometimes when her partner is away from home. Intercourse has been attempted only twice in the past three years. They rarely talk about their fantasies because they are no longer important or a point of controversy. While she used to believe that infrequent sexuality was all his fault, she is now aware that she actually has no desire for sex. She is now able to accept her body and does not need to fast any more for fear of resembling her partner's fantasy. The man says the relationship is now excellent, far better than ever before. Since both agreed not to have sex any more, the never-ending squabbles have become redundant. He feels as if he has been given an injection that has put his sexuality into a deep sleep. He says he still follows his old way of masturbating, and he cannot remember having asked the therapists not to say anything about it to his partner at the start of therapy. His favorite fantasies are, however, no longer as arousing as before. He masturbates once or twice a year at the most, and less for pleasure than to test whether he still reacts. He no longer finds it satisfying.

4. The sexual dysfunction remains unchanged, as do the tense and distressing partner conflicts, which affect the whole relationship.

COUPLE 32:   The couple has been married for nearly three years and has a two-year-old child. The man is a baker, and she is a housewife; they are both in their late twenties. Since the marriage, the wife has completely refused any kind of physical tenderness. Although they have intercourse occasionally, it never arouses her; it sickens her, and she only goes through with it for his sake. Whenever he approaches her with sexual wishes, she becomes either angry or sad; he is then offended and withdraws. He very seldom resists being repulsed. Before the marriage things were different; they used to have sexual intercourse two or three times a week. She was not orgasmic then either, but she found sexuality "quite exciting because it was one of the few things he gave me." The relationship is characterized by the wife's outbursts of hate and anger. He reacts to them with helplessness or in a provokingly sober way. The power struggles have been going on for years. The wife felt financially exploited by her husband even before they married; on the other hand, she "forced" him to marry her by unexpectedly becoming pregnant. Later she fell victim to severe depressions, which then developed into an obsessive cleaning compulsion and so leads to a ritualization of the entire family life.

During caressing exercises the couple never gets beyond the first steps because after a few minutes an argument always breaks out; they collide head-on and then angrily avoid seeing each other for days. The wife locks her husband out of the apartment and does not open the door when he rings. They do not speak to each other for weeks. The therapists are confronted by a horror story they can do nothing about. Finally, the man wants to leave her, and when he mentions this in therapy for the first time she bursts into a fit of hate. Although they share a car and live a good way out of town, she sometimes refuses to take him home with her for even one night after the session. The husband is not prepared to continue treatment after twelve sessions. In the next few days she tries to persuade him to stay with her after all. He finally lets himself be persuaded to stay for at least a month longer until she has found work. Four weeks later the wife appears alone and says they understand each other much better now and they regularly have intercourse, which she quite enjoys.

At the follow-up one year after dropping out of therapy both describe their situation in the same way as they did at the beginning. They avoid and hatefully insult each other, and then withdraw resigned and depressed. The cleaning compulsion persists. The wife now wants to continue therapy alone. Until F4 three years after dropping out, the wife is given supportive psychotherapeutic counseling twice a month. At F4 she expresses the wish to make a new attempt at therapy together with her husband "to bring some life into the dead relationship." Four weeks later she says to the therapists on the telephone that since the last follow-up interview the situation at home has become more critical than ever before. Her husband had at first withdrawn completely and stopped talking to her. He had then written her to suggest separating, which startled her at first. She had stuffed herself full of psychopharmaca and was unable to sleep. Now, three days later, she is calmer again and looks forward to a carnival party. It remains unclear whether the couple will find the strength to separate or will continue their exasperating life of mutual ignorance and hostility.

Finally, it remained unclear what happened to the couples who refused to come to F4.

Separations

Ten couples separated during therapy, and thirteen in the year after therapy, for a total of twenty-three couples (11 percent). Since it was not possible to interview all couples one year after completing therapy (see table 4.7), this is a minimum estimate. By projecting the percentage for couples not followed up we can assume that 15 percent or every seventh couple separated during or within one year after therapy.[3]

The statistical analysis of the twenty-three separating couples shows that there were no differences between diagnostic groups in terms of the probability of separation. This surprised us because clinical evidence shows that orgasmic dysfunctions and premature ejaculation are often compounded with severe partner conflict. It was also surprising that the number of married couples who separated was disproportionately high (p = .01): every fifth married couple separated. As a rule, these couples were relatively young, had recently married, had no children, had little previous experience from other relationships, and in the therapists' judgment had married with undue haste and little reflection. The number of separating couples in which at least one partner was a university student was also significantly large (p = .001). They are part of a social group in which partners can change with relative ease, a mobility rarely sanctioned by moral attitudes. They were not interested in getting married, at this point in their lives, whereas marriage plans played an important part in motivating other young unmarried couples for therapy. That is, they were not as tied down to future plans as were younger, nonstudent couples.

As can be expected, the probability of therapy drop-outs separating in the year following therapy is higher (p = .05) than for couples completing therapy (see p. 179). Couples completing therapy who separated afterward were assessed as being "distinctly improved" or "cured" in sexual functioning; they thus separated despite removal or substantial improvement of the dysfunction.

Separation is a particularly serious consequence of therapy. It is just as short-sighted to consider separation generally a therapeutic success as it is to classify it generally as a failure. Only by analyzing cases individually can one show whether separation was a constructive solution to the partners' problems or an escape from arguing them out and changing the relationship. After analyzing the case histories written by therapists, three groups of separating couples can be distinguished.

1. The process of separation had sometimes developed to such a late stage that practically all therapy could do was to bring the relationship to an end. In such cases patients, or one of the partners, only began therapy to show they were right in their intention to separate, which they often still concealed from their partner. They wanted the official confirmation that there was no other solution in order to be relieved of the remnants of ambivalence or guilt feelings. Or the partner not wishing to separate insisted on making yet another, final effort to save the relationship. Although at first these couples often seemed highly motivated, they did not really participate fully in therapy. All treatment could do was round off the almost complete process of separation. Certainly, therapy can constructively help couples who separate, for example, by enabling the partners to come to an understanding about their separation or by helping partners unwilling to separate to see how senseless it would be to hold on to the relationship. Therapy is occasionally merely an alibi for the partner wishing to separate, and he or she goes through with it as if it were a last, troublesome duty.

COUPLE 33: Both partners are in their early twenties and are employed in the same company. They have known each other for a year and a quarter and have been living together for almost a year. The man has been suffering from premature ejaculation and erectile difficulties in the last few months. Life together has become increasingly difficult for both; they report repeated arguments about keeping the household in order. She feels she is bossed around, tied to the house, and under surveillance. She would like to pursue leisure activities on her own and feels attracted to other men. The crisis in the relationship is so severe that the therapists consider leaving off therapy, particularly because the woman says she only wants to help him overcome his sexual disturbances and then to separate from him. Therapy is nevertheless started so that the couple will not be left alone with their problems; at first therapy aims at clarifying the conflict over separation. After a few sessions the woman realizes she is participating in therapy only through pity for him and that this is not a sufficient reason for therapy. She separates from him. He is then depressed, sad, and helpless. Contrary to her fear, he accepts her decision and does not try to force her to stay. The man is offered a number of client-centered psychotherapy sessions to help him out of the crisis, but he does not take up the offer.

2. Other couples separated because a virulent partner conflict could not be handled in therapy, and probably because treatment aggravated it. In these cases the couples acted out their conflict by separating; it was an escape from tackling problems and a way out of therapy. This "solution" was often full of hate and fear; it involved the danger that both would fall back into similar mechanisms in later relationships and so come up against the same conflicts. The partners' resistance to working out their conflicts and therapists' helplessness or misjudgment of the seriousness of a conflict contributed to this effect to a greater or lesser degree. In four cases mistakes by therapists were clearly to blame, although they probably played an important role in other cases, too. This is naturally not documented in the case histories, where the tendency is rather to overemphasize the constructive aspects of separation.

COUPLE 34: Both partners are just over thirty and have been married for eight years; he is a policeman, and she is a secretary who has been a housewife since the birth of their child. He has had erectile problems for four years. When he is able to insert his penis, he can ejaculate only with difficulty or not at all. For two years he has felt practically no desire at all to make love to his wife and does not like her caresses any more either. His wife is very distressed by the sexual problem because she does not feel he accepts and desires her and she misses physical closeness and tenderness. Because her husband works shifts, they agree to intensive therapy. In history-taking the husband says he has been having a secret love affair with another woman for several months, which is free of sexual problems. He is unwilling to mention this problem to his wife or to discuss it in therapy. The therapists are in a dilemma: they are now in on his secret and, being bound by their pledge of secrecy, are unable to offer his wife a plausible explanation for the sudden postponement of the therapy that had been planned for so long and so carefully prepared for (taking sick leave, putting the child in care of relatives). The therapists decide to attempt therapy. The sexual dysfunction is for the greater part relieved by treatment.

On completing therapy both seem quite content; the husband does, however, complain that he is not as much in love as at the beginning of the marriage. A week after completing therapy the wife calls our division; she is clearly upset and explains that her husband has moved out. She feels deceived both by him and by the therapists, for good reason; the separation is a totally unexpected blow to her, and she despairs. Therapy has quite obviously activated the husband's fears of intimacy and closeness. The therapists failed to notice that he avoided these fears at the beginning of the marriage through his alcohol addiction and, later on, his erectile disturbance. Now that the disturbance has been removed and his wife's demands for tenderness have begun to grow again, he solves the conflict by separating from her. In the course of the following year he comes for individual counseling a few times, and it becomes clear that he is caught in the dilemma of choosing between living with his girlfriend and going back to his wife, which enables him to keep his distance from both.

3. Therapists assessed the majority of separations (fifteen) as constructive: separation put an end to a restrictive and empty relationship that no longer satisfied either partner's wishes or that was even an ordeal. Moreover, it opened up perspectives for a new, more satisfying, and less neurotic relationship. For the sake of clarity we shall order the dynamics of these separations according to three aspects, although a classification of this kind can, of course, only partially reflect the diversity of the problems.

In one group of sexually dysfunctional patients, the choice of partner was neurotic and symptom-related in that the partner chosen did not strongly activate fears because he or she was felt to be particularly unattractive sexually. If these patients' sexual anxieties are reduced in the course of a maturation process (for example, in therapy), the unconscious motives for the choice of partner become redundant, and their partner is then perceived as a nice, sympathetic friend who, however, does not exert the attraction of an intimate partner. It was striking how often patients began a new relationship, during therapy or immediately afterwards, in which the old dysfunction had absolutely no influence and had practically vanished into thin air. This readiness to turn to another partner cannot be seen as resistance to and escape from therapy but is rather an expression of liberation from the old, inhibitive anxieties. The patients are then aware of their sexual desires and accept them.

COUPLE 35: Both partners are in their early thirties and are employed in commerce; they have been married for two and a half years. The wife has never been able to have intercourse, either with her present partner or with other men before marrying, owing to her vaginismus. In therapy she gradually learns to perceive and express her physical aversion and disgust toward her husband. At the same time she finds it steadily easier to insert dilators and to accept that "something" is inside her vagina. About two months after the beginning of therapy, the patient starts to get interested in another man and then falls in love with him. She finds it more and more difficult to do the caressing exercises with her husband, and she finally refuses altogether. She becomes involved sexually with the other man and has no problems performing sexual intercourse. Very soon, and without much of any inner struggle, she moves into an apartment of her own and separates from her husband. The latter is extremely upset by her move and tries to make her change her mind, but for her the decision is clear-cut and final.

In other cases a neurotic dependency between two partners, which once stabilized the relationship, became psychologically anachronistic. This was usually because the woman had become more self-confident before or during therapy. She had realized how unnecessary dependence on her husband was, saw through his claims to dominance, articulated her sexual desires and other demands, and rebelled against him. Her protest, which had hitherto been silently and unconsciously expressed in her refusal of sex, took explicit form. The woman no longer accepted the power structures in the relationship. If the man was unable or unwilling to accept the woman's new consciousness, he tried to restore the old situation; or if the partners failed to establish a new equilibrium adapted to the woman's progress on their own or with therapeutic help, they separated.

COUPLE 36: Both partners are in their early twenties and are employed in commerce. They have been married for two years but have no children. The husband has an erectile dysfunction; his erection always subsides before ejaculation. Furthermore, he complains of a lack of sexual desire for his wife. She has never had an orgasm during petting or coitus. For six months now she has been masturbating to orgasm without difficulty. Both partners report an increasing tension between them in the last few months. He is so irritated by her contradicting manner that he hits her twice. She complains that everything has to be how he wants it, otherwise he starts shouting. She feels oppressed and robbed of her freedom. He even dictates the details of her daily life, for example, what clothes to buy. She often gives in merely because she is afraid.

Dropping Out and Separations

The couple is assigned to intensive therapy. During therapy the erectile difficulties are relieved and the wife is able to reach orgasm regularly during petting. In a follow-up interview two months after completion of therapy, the wife says she has become far more self-reliant and independent both of her husband and other people. She is now far more capable of asserting her point of view and insisting on her desires. This adds to tension in the relationship, but she defends herself more and consequently no longer swallows everything. However, she feels more and more trapped and sometimes wishes she could see what it would be like to be free again. The couple separates half a year later. The wife starts a new relationship. Her husband tries to remain "master" of the situation and immediately sends in his petition for divorce; he thus maintains the upper hand, and he continues to affect the pose of patronizing grandiosity in the divorce proceedings.

Finally, there were patients who saw little subjective danger of separation at the start of therapy. They denied there were any partner problems and believed that removal of the sexual dysfunction would rid them of all worries. In their view conflicts and tension in the relationship were exclusively the result of sexual difficulties. Although therapy often enabled rapid technical progress, the couple soon realized that once the sexual difficulties were alleviated, serious partner problems emerged that the sexual dysfunction had only kept hidden. They might also have become aware that despite intact sexual functioning they were unable to come up to their mutual expectations of the relationship, that their relationship would continue to be unsatisfying, and that their hopes of a change in the relationship through removal of the sexual dysfunction were unrealistic. A reversal of dysfunction opened their eyes to the real problems, and if they were unable or unmotivated to solve them, separation occurred.

COUPLE 37: Both partners are in their early thirties; they have been married for nine years and have an eight-year-old daughter. He is a self-employed businessman, and she has been a housewife since giving birth. In separate history-taking, both emphasize how harmonious their marriage is, how much they understand and like each other. This good relationship is impaired only by sexual problems: the man suffers from premature ejaculation; he always ejaculates on intromission. She is unsatisfied by intercourse because she never has an orgasm and has felt no arousal for years; she does not feel like coitus anymore. She is totally convinced that she would enjoy and be satisfied by intercourse if he had better control over his ejaculation.

Therapy proceeds without complications until it reaches the critical phase when he learns to control ejaculation during manual stimulation. His wife suddenly has no desire at all to do the exercises, is always unaroused and anorgasmic on stimulative caressing. Both partners then realize that their problems were concealed by the sexual disturbances and start to think them over. She becomes more critical, wants to be more independent, and insists on separate bedrooms and a temporary suspension of sexual contact. He is taken aback by her withdrawal, attempts to understand his and her reactions, and tries to stop denying them or sweeping them aside with his happy-go-lucky behavior. The partners decide to move apart and separate for the time being, but they want to go on working at a solution and feel they may live together again in the future. They do not request further therapeutic aid because they believe they can come to a clear understanding of their situation on their own.

"Constructive" separations, as we call them here, were often a relief to one partner only. If a partner's wife freed herself from the old power structures by moving apart from him, as a rule he had no opportunity to learn to cope with differently structured relationships and was, if anything, likely to get involved in the same kind of relationship with the same kind of problems. Only in three cases did both the partners want and accept the separation in "mutual agreement." In the other cases only one partner took the initiative, leaving the other partner considerably distressed; therapy seldom was able to alleviate his or her suffering, which very often had still not been overcome a year after completing therapy. This distress particularly affected men; in seventeen of twenty cases, that is, almost always, the female partner took the initiative for separation whether she or her partner had had the sexual dysfunction. This could well be because women are more often dissatisfied with their situation in the relationship than are men or because they are more willing to dispense with an unsatisfying relationship. Another reason might be that women are less willing or have fewer opportunities to compensate for frustration in the relationship in other areas.

Apart from the few cases in which both partners wanted to separate and both found the separation a relief, any separation was a depressing experience for the therapists, even if they did find constructive aspects. A separation will always mobilize therapists' fears of an uncontrolled, destructive influence, particularly when they realize their helplessness in the face of a partner unwilling to separate. However, relationships that therapy patches up sexually, but are as empty and monotonous as before therapy, are just as depressing for the therapist, even if the criterion of sexual functioning allows him to classify the couple as "cured."

Selection and Prognosis

In contrast to many somatic illnesses, the definition of the aim of therapy for psychological disturbances cannot be automatically deduced from the definition of the problem or symptom but has to be individually discussed and necessarily involves a process of step-by-step decisions. This is illustrated by the following example: a woman who felt desire for sex and got aroused, but had never had an orgasm in intercourse, began treatment with her husband. The husband was intent on being able to bring his wife to orgasm (preferably multiple) during intercourse. It did not interest him that she reached orgasm in petting. The couple had been fighting over this issue for the last five years, with the result that they hardly spoke to each other any more and had dispensed with sexuality for almost a whole year. One could envisage the following possible aims for counseling or therapy: (1) enhancing the woman's responsiveness so she can reach orgasm in intercourse; (2) correcting the man's and woman's attitudes so that they give her orgasm in petting full recognition; (3) "damping" the husband's sex drive (with antiandrogens or sedatives) to stop him harassing his wife so much; (4) developing alternative and more effective forms of communication between the partners so they can cope better with disappointment in sexuality; (5) separating so that they are free to start a sexually more rewarding relationship with another partner. This incomplete list shows clearly that defining the aims of therapy involves making value judgments. The above aims are not mutually exclusive. It should be said that damping sexual desire is clearly a grotesque method, even if it is still applied in everyday medicine. Consultants often force their own ideas about therapeutic objectives onto patients; this is easier the more uncertain and uninformed the couples are.

Once the aim has been provisionally defined, an appropriate therapeutic method must be selected. In our example, the appropriate method could be couple therapy for sexual dysfunctions as described in this book (objective 1), or couple counseling (objective 2), group therapy for so-called pre-orgasmic women (objective 1), or individual therapy for the woman (objective 1). In the last case just about any kind of psychotherapy, even treatment with psychopharmaca, could be chosen because all claim to be able to mitigate sexual dysfunctions. One could also consider general communication training or, for example, advising the couple to join a folk-dance group (objective 4). Finally, one could completely dispense with treatment and trust the female patient to find her own way somehow (objective 5). Of course separation can be adopted as an aim by varying therapeutic methods. Our list is merely an outline of the range of possible or actually implemented forms of treatment; however, it should hardly be necessary to emphasize that we consider some of them useless and abstruse. As a rule, the first consultant suggests the patients head in one or the other direction. The scope of his knowledge of the different methods and his ability to judge the effect they have are of vital importance. For the most part the process of deciding on selection, which we have described in rough outline here, proceeds by recourse to therapist "experience." In a survey on psychotherapy research, Grawe (1977) came to the conclusion that with a few exceptions all published information on selection and prognosis fails to stand up to methodological examination. It is consequently no great surprise that so many attempts at replicating prognostic studies misfired or led to divergent results. The most serious deficiencies in method are: first, the problem of differential selection for varying therapy concepts was often disregarded; second, the selection problem was as a result, reduced to the question of prognosis for a specific form of treatment; third, the therapeutic procedure is often only inadequately standardized or described, if at all; fourth, this also applies to patient samples; fifth, most of the studies measure only success but do not systematically investigate failure as well and so preclude a better understanding of individual prognoses. One of the most serious deficiencies in this connection is that studies are confined to comparing mean scores of relevant variables (before and after therapy) in measuring success and that they pay little attention to the distribution of these variables.

These shortcomings are also characteristic of the expanding literature on the treatment of sexual dysfunctions. Specific data on selection and prognosis that come up to methodological standards are nowhere to be found. The selection criteria for patients are based on the research group's preemptive decisions, which can only be termed arbitrary. To mention just one example: LoPiccolo and Lobitz (1973) excluded nearly every second couple from treatment and based their decision on a short interview, tests with the MMPI (Minnesota Multiphasic Personality Inventory, for excluding psychoses) and the Locke-Wallace Short Marital Inventory (for excluding severely distressed relationships).

In our research design we disregarded the problem of patient selection for different therapeutic methods from the start and confined ourselves to investigating the effectiveness of one therapeutic method.

Within this framework, setting variables were compared: intensive versus long-term treatment, one therapist versus therapist team, single-couple therapy versus group therapy. These different settings and the consequences for selection have already been discussed (see chapter 6).

The most important step in selection is to specify contraindications and protect patients from detrimental effects of therapy. In our opinion the risk of such effects in couple therapy is relatively low provided that the therapists are well trained and arrange for supervision.

The most important conclusion we reached on the question of prognosis in our investigation is that even severely neurotic or partner-dynamic conflicts are not compelling reasons for contraindication prior to therapy. Selection criteria tied almost exclusively to formal requirements proved the best alternative. Even if some formal conditions had not been fulfilled (for example, if one of the partners had concealed a love affair from the first consultant), treatment did not always end in failure. Even therapy with psychotic patients was not completely hopeless, provided treatment was not begun in the acute stage of the illness. We insist on this approach even though we are aware that it is in danger of being misunderstood as an appeal to experiment and to neglect diagnostic criteria. Our concern is to emphasize that strict selection criteria lead to the exclusion of certain patients who could find therapy helpful and would have good chances of success as long as success is not evaluated only in terms of length of ejaculation control in seconds, plethysmographically measured penile tumescence, depth of penetration in inches, or duration of plateau phase and breathing rate. One of our most telling experiences was that often couples who seemed to be quite uncomplicated cases showed no improvement, and couples who seemed to have no chance of success completed therapy with good results.

We consider it, moreover, illusory to believe that the success of individual cases in treating sexual dysfunctions can ever be predicted with a statistical accuracy that could morally justify excluding certain couples. In this respect Willi (1978) makes an important point when he says that strictly defined selection in psychotherapy is an essential factor in therapists' psycho-hygiene because it is a means of realistically assessing and respecting the limits of their own therapeutic abilities.

To conclude we shall touch on a few problems pertaining to selection and prognosis which presented themselves to us during our research work.

1. Therapists. Although it is a commonplace that, apart from the patient and therapeutic method, psychotherapy should give due consideration to therapist and therapist-patient interaction, we are far from being able to systematically analyze this interaction. But we do not intend to suppress this essential question even if we are lacking the relevant data. Team discussions, case evaluation, and supervision group-work did show us how much a therapist or interaction in a therapist team can influence the therapeutic process. To what extent does the therapist's own sexual behavior and value system determine what he or she encourages or avoids in a patient? How great a role does the therapist's own partner relationship play in the outcome of treatment? Do couples really separate more often if the therapist himself is fighting with the same problem? Does an initial prognosis act as a self-fulfilling prophecy or do highly unfavorable circumstances at the start of therapy mobilize extreme care and effort in dealing with difficulties? What role does the referring authority or institution and the atmosphere in the therapist's own institution play? To what extent does collaboration in an ambitious research project support or inhibit the therapeutic relationship? What reasons do some therapists have for withdrawing from couple therapy and turning to other fields of work after a certain amount of time? These are just some of the many questions that emerged in team discussion and supervision but not at the planning tables. It would probably be more profitable, or at least as profitable, to think over these questions than to attempt an increasingly more differentiated description of couples treated. Admittedly, such questions are, methodologically speaking, far more difficult to tackle because the researcher and the object of research merge into one another and the sacred cow of detached and alienating objectivity must be slaughtered.

2. *Patients without a partner.* By definition couple therapy excludes patients without a partner. Consequently, patients without a partner were not treated in our therapy project and are not discussed in this book. Formal exclusion of such patients does, however, conceal an important therapeutic problem for sexually dysfunctional patients.

In the United States a vehement controversy was fought out over the question of working with partner surrogates. Opinions ranged from strict rejection to the promotion of sexual relations between therapist and patient. In our view the only acceptable answer to such methods is that of strict rejection, not so much for legal or moral reasons but in view of the methodological objections that therapy itself dictates. Singles who suffer from a sexual dysfunction request treatment "because otherwise every relationship is bound to go wrong right at the start," as they say, and they consequently avoid every kind of contract. Our impression is that their dysfunctions are an absolutely peripheral problem by comparison with their social inhibitions and difficulties in starting relationships. Even if by doctoring the dysfunction in an unreal and "rented" relationship one could temporarily remove the dysfunction, afterward the patient would be catapulted back even deeper into his or her misery. Most of the singles who approach our department are men, with or without sexual dysfunctions, who have pronounced problems with relationships about which we can often do little.

The following is an example of a nondysfunctional patient:

A 26-year-old, chubby, and unkempt worker, who is under five feet tall and still lives with his mother, has been longing for sexual contact and a continuing relationship with a woman for some time. He considers himself unattractive, is often laughed at, is not taken seriously by his colleagues, and is completely isolated socially. Over the years he has slowly narrowed down his understanding of the problem to the lack of opportunity for sexual encounters; he dreams day and night of sexual intercourse and of becoming a pop star adored by women. He has practically no social acquaintances and feels permanently tormented by his sexual wishes. He cannot sleep at night and sometimes masturbates eight times in a row. Once in a while he goes to prostitutes who masturbate him; he has had sexual intercourse with a prostitute twice. These were the happiest moments of his life and yet are clouded by the thought that the "relationship" would only last a short while. He was exploited in his helplessness: none of the prostitutes wanted to take him upstairs for less than $45. In view of his low income he saw no alternative but to raise loans. After ten visits to prostitutes, he had debts amounting to more than $400. The repayments have cut his wage back to a subsistence minimum for years to come. He is tired of life, sees no light at the end of the tunnel, and is tormented by his strong sexual wishes and fantasies, but he would like to undergo the kind of "operation that sex offenders are subjected to" (castration) or at least be prescribed tablets "against my sex drive."

The patient's powers of speech are meager, and he describes his situation in stops and starts. The psychiatric consultant does not consider suicide to be so imminent that inpatient care is necessary. After referral, the behavior therapy group also rejects him for treatment (social training) because it is feared that the patient would merely be pushed further into his outsider position. He is treated with antiandrogens to cool his desire—a temporary and dubious emergency measure—but this only makes the patient more and more depressive and causes him to put on a great deal more weight.

In these and similar unhappy cases, one could perhaps consider making an exception to our earlier strict principle and proceed to treatment with a partner surrogate. That this thought even arises is clearly both an expression of helplessness and evidence of the narrow viewpoint that can result from years of couple therapy work. An institution that handles sexual problems all too easily becomes a regular port of call for patients who regard their problems as sexual difficulties; moreover it runs the danger of adopting this definition and of contemplating inadequate treatment.

3. *Alternative forms of treatment.* As pointed out above, alternative forms of treatment for patients without a partner need to be considered so that difficulties associated with the sexual problem can be worked through: social shyness, fear of making contact with the opposite sex, and anxieties over sexual relations. There are only a few methods of this kind for treating male disturbances.

In the wake of the women's liberation movement, however, a concept for treating female disturbances has emerged that diverges from the basic aim of couple therapy. This is evident in the way the problems are perceived; reference is no longer made to orgasmic dysfunctions but to women who, not having experienced an orgasm, are described as "pre-orgasmic." This makes allowance for the fact that lack of orgasm is no longer considered a functional disturbance or a defect in need of repair, but is felt to be an underdeveloped dimension of experience that is in principle accessible to every woman. In contrast to couple therapy, treatment is then open not only to women who have a steady partner but also to any woman who does not have a partner, does not want a partner, or wants to go her own way despite her partner, and to lesbians. (One might ask whether the word "treatment" is not as much out of place here as the word "therapy"; "participative experience" or "experience sharing" is perhaps better.) The emphasis is placed on experiencing one's physical senses and not on remedying sexual deficits.

In conclusion, the answer to the problem of selection and prognosis swings between two alternatives. One is the hope of some day waking up to a world where one no longer needs therapists; and the other is the opinion that there are no incurable patients but only incompetent therapists. While the hope of a world without therapists is a dream one can indulge in, the vision of the eternally competent therapist is a nightmare. It is all the more surprising how much is invested nowadays in efforts to perfect therapeutic programs and how little effort is made to alter social and working conditions that are, after all, etiological factors in the pathogenesis of sexual dysfunctions. It seems as if we are working more passionately at making the nightmare come true than the dream.

NOTES

1. Couples who dropped out of therapy without separating (rating 2 or 3 of item A, therapist rating of overall outcome, R 2) were compared with couples completing therapy who were at least distinctly improved (rating 7 or 8). The comparison was thus between extreme groups. Unless otherwise indicated female and male dysfunctions are compounded.

2. Male patients are more obstinate and impatient (GT 2, p = .01) and more easily exhausted (EMI 5, p = .01). Female "nondysfunctional" partners are more depressive (EMI 7, p = .001; FPI 3, p = .01), are more agitatively anxious (EMI 1, p = .01), are more nervous (FPI 1, p = .01), are more reactively aggressive (FPI 7, p = .01), and more retentive (GT 5, p = .01). Male "nondysfunctional" partners of female patients are more depressive (EMI 7, p = .01). Statistical significances according to t-test.

3. Twelve of ninety-nine couples separated between F3 and F4. Because there is no evidence of a connection between these separations and the original problems or the therapy procedure, we have disregarded them here.

Chapter 9

COUPLE THERAPY IN GROUPS

Ingelore Wickert and Gerhard Thiessen-Liedtke

Once we had established in an intermediate evaluation of the first ninety couples that the effectiveness of treatment was by and large independent of the formal setting, we asked ourselves whether couple therapy could be performed in groups. Our intention was to make use of the general advantages of group therapy in treating sexual dysfunctions: patients discovered they were not alone with their problems; they learned from others' problems and the solutions to other people's problems; they felt they were helping themselves and one another, were not so dependent on authorities, and so on. The economic advantages of group work meant that more couples could be treated and waiting-lists could be shortened. However, there were many doubts: can one expect patients to talk about sexuality in groups in the kind of detail required in discussing exercises? Is it at all desirable to "publicize" sexuality and intimacy to such an extent? Finally, might not intensive discussion of sexual experiences and problems encourage transference phenomena between group members in terms of sexual wishes and falling in love? These doubts were reflected in a fairly cautious therapy plan in which we "spared" the couples a discussion of sexuality in the first six to eight group sessions and instead tried jointly to identify relationship problems. After attempting this with eight groups we abandoned the idea and, as in couple therapy, began with the behavioral instructions immediately after discussing the outcome of history-taking. It became evident that the "mercy period" at the start of therapy had been more important for the therapists than for the patients.

To our knowledge only a few reports on couple therapy in groups have been published that applied behavioral instructions in the same way as Masters and Johnson did (Kaplan et al. 1974; Leiblum, Rosen, and Pierce 1976; McGovern, Kirkpatrick, and LoPiccolo 1976; Golden et al. 1978). Orgasmic dysfunctions and premature ejaculation were predominantly treated in groups that were homogeneous as regards symptoms; only Leiblum, Rosen, and Pierce treated various symptom categories, including erectile dysfunctions, in one group. In all these investigations the appropriateness of therapy was assessed strictly in terms of psychopathology and partner conflicts. The investigations mentioned report data for only five groups of couples, involving a total of twenty-five couples. They have come to the conclusion that the group version is an economical variation on couple therapy. Only Golden et al. made a controlled comparison of group and single-couple therapy, although with very small samples (eleven versus six couples); there were no significant differences in therapy outcome.

The Couples

Between 1976 and 1979 we treated nine groups with a total of thirty-seven couples; they were split into seven groups for female orgasmic dysfunctions and two for premature ejaculators. Our experiences with couple therapy in groups are thus quite limited.[1] The criteria for selecting patients were the same as for single-couple therapy: couples were not screened for neurotic or partner conflicts. The patients were aged between nineteen and thirty-nine years; at the start of therapy, relationships had lasted for between one and fifteen years, on the average for about eight years. Most of the couples (85 percent) said they had been suffering from their problems for more than three years. The data on school education and occupation showed the same middle-class bias as in the main investigation.

Although many of the patients at first felt uneasy about group therapy, they were quite prepared to consider seriously participation in a group. When asked to choose between group or single-couple therapy, most of the patients decided according to the "waiting-list" criterion, that is, which therapy they could enter sooner. All groups were homogeneous in terms of symptoms. We limited the groups to patients suffering from "premature ejaculation" or "orgasmic dysfunction" because in these cases partner conflicts are known to be very frequent and our group concept seemed particularly suitable because it focussed closely on partner conflicts.

The groups were assembled as the couples came up on the waiting-list and not with a view to age or social class. For example, one group included the following: a 38-year-old salesman and his wife of the same age (saleswoman), who had been married for fifteen years and had no children; an academic couple in their late twenties with two children; a male and female student both just over 20; the owner of a newspaper stand and a female clerk, both in their early twenties and unmarried. The variety here made for a wide range of experiences and a good many opportunities for mutual help: older couples could take a caring, parental attitude toward younger couples, for example, and perhaps show them how to be a little more patient and considerate with a partner. Younger couples could play the role of adult children toward the older couples, who could always benefit from a bit of advice on changed life styles, for example, a change of sex roles. Couples from lower social strata could see how middle-class couples accepted nongenital sexuality; middle-class couples could see that lower-class couples were less afraid of a direct and sometimes even physical approach to arguments.

Procedure

Therapy sessions took place once a week, lasted two hours, and were led by a female and a male therapist. The nine groups were treated by a total of five female therapists and three male therapists; all had conducted single-couple therapy several times before attempting group therapy. The groups comprised three to five couples; in our experience four is an ideal number. The group process takes some effort to start with three couples; with five couples, the dynamics are too complex and the therapists run out of time in discussing the exercises in detail. We shall only sketch our procedure in brief outline because we are still working out our concept for group therapy.

In the introductory session everyone gets to know one another and any reservations about therapy are discussed; furthermore, it has the same function as in single-couple therapy (see part 3). In the two to four weeks following this session each therapist interviews each patient on his or her history to gain a rough insight into the couples' problems. History-taking is shorter than for single-couple therapy because the couples talk about their previous history and problems in the course of the program, and so a kind of "group history-taking" takes place.

The first six to eight sessions with our first eight groups were reserved exclusively for discussing partner problems. In terms of formal procedure, this is where the single-couple and group settings differ most. Therapy started with practical tasks in the group (for example, writing down negative and positive traits for one's partner; reports on the last argument or disappointment). Although these tasks were taken from communication training programs, their purpose is not to teach effective communication techniques; they aim rather at working out and recognizing each couple's central partner conflict. Our experience with further groups proved that so long a warming-up phase is unnecessary. Because the couples were soon willing to discuss their sexual problems, we dispensed with this part of therapy.

In the next one to two sessions—or, following our revised procedure, in the first session—the couples talk about their sexual problems and their sexual development. At the end of this therapy phase, the group tries to arrive at an understanding of the way each couple's sexual dysfunctions developed, as in the "round-table discussions" in single-couple therapy.

The couples are then taken through the sequence of exercises from "caressing I" to "coitus in different positions" (see part 3). They are asked to do each exercise at least twice before the next session. Their experiences are discussed in the group: the therapists demonstrate how to ask direct and adequate questions, but encourage the group members to ask one another questions. The therapists concentrate their efforts more on initiation of a group discussion than on exhaustive discussion of each couple's experiences. At this stage of therapy, too, discussion of general partner problems takes up a large amount of time, in our experience far more than in single-couple therapy. The groups for orgasmic dysfunctions were sometimes supplemented by a women's group: the female therapist met with the women alone five to ten times for half an hour before group sessions to follow through the supplementary program on bodily self-awareness (see part 3).

Our initial fears that couples might feel so pressured by others' successes, that group competition might develop proved unfounded.

What was more likely was that a couple making rapid progress in one phase of therapy encouraged other couples to hope that they too could make some progress. We were thus able to proceed to new behavioral instructions with one or a few couples while others were still repeating the old exercises.

Results and Experiences

The only results we have as yet are those for the end of therapy (F1). We can say nothing about long-term effects. We considered the investigation of group therapy as a pilot study and restricted measurement of change to therapist ratings (R2).

In both the groups treated for orgasmic dysfunction and those treated for premature ejaculation about three fifths of the couples achieved improved sexual functioning, experienced fewer disturbances in the relationship in general, and found sexuality more satisfying (see table 9.1). Compared to single-couple therapy, group therapy succeeded less often in removing the sexual symptoms, achieved distinctly less often "satisfying" sexuality (p = .001) for the couples, and led more often to separation (p = .05). Changes in the relationship were evaluated as being the same for both forms of couple therapy.

In terms of sexual function and sexual experience, then, therapy in groups is less successful than is single-couple therapy; moreover, it more often leads to separation. One could interpret the data thus: groups may encourage tendencies to move away from the partner, that is, greater orientation on one's self or other people, greater independence, autonomy, and in extreme cases separation. Single-couple therapy, however, may give more support to tendencies to move toward the partner, that is, to more mutuality, more emotional involvement in sexuality, greater unity, and less detachment.

These assumptions should be examined more closely than is possible here in view of the limited measurement of changes in the groups. Observations in therapy did, however, confirm these assumptions, as will be seen.

In single-couple therapy the couple is a unit and is almost exclusively treated as such. A group of couples is not focused so strongly on this dyad: other couples are present and other problems, other ways of living together, of handling each other, or of dealing with conflicts

TABLE 9.1
Group versus Single-Couple Therapy;
Overall Outcome, Ratings by Therapists[a]

	Groups[b] (N=37)	Single couples[c] (N=139)
Sexual functioning		
(1) drop-out, separation of couple	19%	6%
(2, 3) drop-out	8%	16%
(4, 5) therapy completed, not/ slightly improved	16%	5%
(6) therapy completed, improved	19%	31%
(7, 8) therapy completed, distinctly improved/cured	38%	42%
		(.05)
Relationship in general		
(0) inapplicable, drop-out	(27%)	(22%)
(1) disturbed as before	3%	4%
(2) disturbed as before, but more aware of problems	11%	9%
(3) positive state unchanged	0%	5%
(4) deteriorated	0%	1%
(5, 6) improved, distinctly improved	59%	58%
		(ns)
Sexual satisfaction		
(0) inapplicable, drop-out	(27%)	(22%)
(1) less satisfying than before therapy	3%	0%
(2) just as unsatisfying as before therapy	3%	4%
(3) somewhat more satisfying than before therapy	59%	27%
(4) satisfying	8%	45%
		.001

[a] *Ratings of overall outcome R2; for definition of categories see p. 120; results at completion of therapy (F1).*
[b] *Orgasmic dysfunctions 29 couples (7 groups), premature ejaculators 8 couples (2 groups).*
[c] *Orgasmic dysfunctions 108 couples, premature ejaculators 31 couples.*

come to light. The therapeutic framework is not limited to two parties—patients and therapists—but is enlarged to involve a whole group. The dyad becomes more permeable in this group: each person experiences how he or she can find support from other people (even against his or her partner) and how helpful it is that mutual interests and alliances can develop other than those in the relationship, for example, between participants of the same sex, between the "weak" partners, and so on.

The conditions are thus created in which partners can discuss relationship problems and can name and admit what features of the relationship separate them. This is a process in which the couples can support each other mutually: in the role of observers, one couple can watch how another argues out a problem and so themselves become more sensitive to similar problems of their own; they dare to be more open and to expose their own problems. This process often assumed almost explosive dimensions when couples became willing to be open, to admit conflicts, to put an end to self-deceptive illusions of harmony. Group therapy is less indulgent to couples than is single-couple therapy. Encouraged by the model of other couples and strengthened by the solidarity of individual participants, partners in a group of couples are more likely to dare facing up to their own conflicts. This process was perhaps most pronounced in those groups in which partner problems alone were discussed in the first six to eight sessions and the couples were thus prevented from covering up conflicts by talking about sexual problems right away. Here therapy begins tackling the separating features sooner, for the first things discussed are: what one partner does not like about the other, what annoys one partner about the other, and what one partner would like to change in the other. In these groups of couples the patients become particularly aware that a sexual dysfunction is the symptom of conflicts in a relationship.

Finally, it was apparent that in single-couple therapy therapists could focus more attention on the couple's sexual problems. Generally speaking, discussion of sex exercises was less detailed and questions asked were less precise in groups of couples. This was in part the result of our decision that the therapists should not overly structure the group process and should not have too much influence on the discussions. However, therapists and patients probably also avoided discussing exercises in exact detail because they were unable to tolerate the voyeuristic and exhibitionistic character of such group discussions. From this point of view, the deliberate emphasis on partner problems was possibly a conspiratorial act between therapists and patients with the aim of avoiding the details of their sexuality. That the therapists were to a great extent responsible for this is demonstrated clearly by our initial decision not to start with sexuality right at the beginning.

The most striking evidence of the tendency of group therapy to move partners away from each other was the number of separations. They almost always occurred after several long disputes between two partners in the group sessions, disputes that affected all the participants. The process of separation always had a deep effect on all group members. It forced the other couples to acknowledge and deal with their own wishes for and fears of separation, to reconstruct the painful steps of separation, to take part in mourning, without having to take this step themselves. This was illustrated by the dramatic reaction of one female patient to the separation of a couple which took place after many hours of discussion: for the first time she was able to consider taking this step in her relationship and saw it as a possible solution for her and her husband; she was able to admit thoughts of separation to herself, to express them, and to talk them over with her husband. Other couples dealt defensively with anxieties that were triggered by the separation of another couple; they moved closer together and emphasized how stable and intact their relationships were. Anxiety in the group was sometimes so strong that the remaining couples joined forces against the "separaters," made them scapegoats for doubting the harmony of the group and the prospects for therapeutic success. Sometimes aggressive reactions were directed at the therapists for allowing the separation or—in the opinion of the participants—for not preventing it.

It is striking that in every group one couple separated. One cannot help asking whether group dynamics singled out a couple that drew the unconscious separation wishes and problems to itself and acted them out for others. We would not discount the possibility that some couples were, so to speak, pushed into separating, that the decision was not the consequence of problems in the relationship but of group dynamics. The first signs of separation problems should therefore be analyzed with great care by therapists to be sure the couple really is making its own decision.

Although group therapy proved less effective than single-couple therapy in terms of "sexual function" and "sexual satisfaction," our impression is that the participants were not less satisfied with therapy outcome than couples who were treated individually. Our comparison probably shows up the weaknesses of both settings: in groups the emphasis on dealing with general partner problems can lead patients and therapists to avoid working through the sexual symptom; in single-couple therapy the focus on the sexual dysfunction can tempt patients and therapists to avoid recognizing the relationship disturbances and problems. In any case, therapy in groups of couples is far more complicated than it is with single couples and should only be conducted by therapists who have conducted therapy with one couple a number of times and who have additional experience in group therapy.

NOTE

1. Since 1980 we have treated six more couple groups comprising almost forty patients; diagnoses in the groups were not always homogeneous (that is, the erectile patients within each group did not necessarily share the same dysfunction). The results correspond to those listed here.

Chapter 10

ADVANCED TRAINING

Friedemann Pfäfflin, Margret Hauch, and Ingelore Wickert

Although existing epidemiological data are incomplete nobody would doubt that dysfunctional sexuality is a widespread phenomenon and that there is thus a great need for qualified counselors and therapists. The fact that sexual dysfunctions occur with such a high incidence is not so much of a novelty as is the high value that people living in Western societies have set on sexuality in recent centuries. Everyday language was incapable of describing sexuality three hundred years ago (van Ussel 1970). Since then sexuality has become the topic of the day, a projection screen as much for the fear that it could ruin our civilization as for the hope that it could hold in store true happiness. Ignoring the question of reproduction for a moment, it seems that only when sexuality had assumed this dominant role in the conception of a fulfilled life could sexual dysfunctions be recognized as a source of problems. By claiming that psychosexual development is the key to maturation, Freud merely gave expression to a process that had long since begun and laid the foundations for the gradual development of therapeutic techniques. For about twenty years now sexual dysfunctions and their treatment have been the main concern of sex research. In the wake of overspecialization, sight was soon lost of the far more important question of whether the psychotherapeutic zeal of sex research had not contributed to the illusion that sexuality was the be-all and end-all of happiness, thus ultimately adding to the means of human manipulation (Foucault 1977).

Despite competition, the various therapeutic schools are all linked by the performance principle that they apply to sexuality with the aim of achieving greater efficiency and perfection in the private happiness of sexual relations. It may sound surprising to claim that this is just as true of Masters and Johnson's therapeutic concept, considering that they emphasize in nearly every therapy session that performance impedes sexual satisfaction. Nonetheless, the zeal with which the proponents of this school draw up their balance sheet and play off other techniques against their success statistics is proof enough of how firmly they are caught up in this general trend.

But then we are no exception. In our opinion it is important to ask why in our society more and more problems turn into symptoms requiring treatment and why medicine and clinical psychology turn to an ever larger number of new specialties.

We can only briefly hint here at the urgent need for skepticism in view of the profusion of new therapeutic specialties. These developments point to a disintegration of yet another sphere of life rather than to an improvement in social conditions or in care, contrary to the euphoria with which they are often welcomed. The distressed individual or couple may well be justified in giving in to this euphoria, but every new therapeutic specialty also strengthens the societal legitimation for precisely the misery it aims to eliminate. We have learned that this aspect is all too quickly ignored in daily therapeutic routine. We are also aware that we can only describe the dilemma; we cannot resolve it. These introductory comments are basically intended as self-admonition before going on to the practical question of therapeutic training.

For practical reasons our team was confronted with the problem of therapeutic training right from the start because the team members who had prepared the pilot study had to be introduced to the therapeutic concept. After a research grant had been allocated, the team was enlarged and new therapists had to be trained; the same situation arose again and again everytime a therapist left the team. The research project was begun with the aim of developing an easily practicable psychotherapeutic concept. Although we recognized that this would inevitably throw up the question of therapeutic training, it never became a part of the research project despite the fact that regular training in groups was introduced in 1975.

Aims and Target Groups of Advanced Training

Our opening remarks suggest a negatively defined objective: a new profession, the "sex therapist," should not be created. We conceive of therapy for sexual dysfunctions as a form of psychotherapy and not as a separate technique or school of thought among other psychotherapeutic concepts. Practically speaking this means that we require therapists to have completed or to have reached an advanced stage of training in one of the accepted forms of psychotherapy (psychoanalysis or psychoanalytic therapy; behavior, client-centered, or gestalt therapy). This is why we speak of "advanced therapeutic training" and not simply "training," as Kaplan (1977) does. The manual is not a recipe book for do-it-yourself enthusiasts; until publication of this book we were careful to give it only to those participating in advanced training so as not to encourage the trend for self-made therapy technicians. Our reason for making it available to the general public now is that we wish to depict the entire research project, including the therapeutic method. The manual is a useful instrument for training therapists, but is by no means a substitute for training.

The aim of advanced training is to remedy the disastrous lack of therapeutic care and to offer couples adequate treatment without their having to make a detour through unnecessary medical treatment and long waiting lists. This presupposes a widely woven network of qualified therapists who are also capable of coping adequately with sexual dysfunctions. Preparations for this therapeutic work have to be made by instructing family doctors, psychiatrists, gynecologists, psychologists, and counselors to enable them to indicate treatment and to refer couples to a competent authority. Our advanced training courses are intended principally for experienced therapists who wish to implement the therapeutic approach described in this book.

Didactic Concept

Our training courses have three main objectives:

1. *Communication of basic theoretical information on sexuality, sexual disturbances, and therapeutic help.* This is a kind of preparatory course intended to fill the gaps left by basic training. In addition to this book,

we make use of publications by Masters and Johnson (1970), Kaplan (1974a, 1979), and LoPiccolo and LoPiccolo (1978). Even at this stage of training correction of one's own reactions, prejudices, and attitudes is emphasized.

2. *Provision of practical experience with experienced cotherapists in team therapy.* Every trainee has to conduct at least one course of therapy as a cotherapist with an experienced therapist. This presents the opportunity for vicarious learning and immediate feedback and for understanding therapeutic procedure and theory. The therapy sessions are prepared together with the experienced cotherapist, and the recordings (audio or video) are then discussed. Situations for which the trainee anticipates difficulties can be rehearsed in role playing.

3. *Provision of regular group supervision (eight to ten trainees) led by two experienced therapists.* All therapy sessions are recorded, and the tapes are played back to the group. Although not every trainee can present all his or her sessions in group supervision, the trainee can learn from the abilities and mistakes of others. More important than communicating information is learning by modeling, particularly in terms of talking about sexual topics, feedback on therapists' behavior from the group, and recognizing and working through one's own emotional reactions to and experiences with various forms of intervention in difficult situations.

Once trainees have gained enough experience as cotherapists with an experienced therapist they can, and should, form therapist teams with each other and conduct therapy themselves with ongoing supervision.

Advanced Training Programs

About eighty therapists took part in advanced training from 1975 to 1981. Most of them were psychologists or physicians, some of them were psychotherapeutically trained nurses and social workers using psychotherapeutic techniques.

SETTINGS FOR ADVANCED TRAINING

Advanced training was conducted in two settings: long-term courses lasted between one and one and a half years. Each of the eight to ten group members started by conducting one long-term therapy with an experienced therapist from our team of a couple for whom treatment had been indicated by our division. They then conducted another long-term therapy with a fellow group member, for which they were asked to treat a couple from their own institution. Group supervision took place every two weeks and was led by two therapists from our team. In the intensive setting training consisted of three weeks of all-day courses; it was primarily offered to therapists not living in Hamburg. The groups were made up of ten trainees and six or seven therapists from our team. Each trainee conducted intensive therapy with one of our therapists and watched a second therapy through a one-way window. Three-hour group supervision took place every day (five trainees with three or four experienced therapists). In our experience intensive advanced training with three weeks of concentrated work and discussion is the more efficient and satisfying form of learning and teaching.

SELECTION OF TRAINEES

Participants in advanced training were selected with two aspects in mind: institutional and individual qualifications. In terms of *institutional qualification*, we gave preference to trainees working in institutions that functioned as community counseling centers for distressed couples; because they worked in teams they were able to pass on their experience by the snowball effect. Only noncommercial institutions were selected (that is, those supported by the government or a church). This was particularly important because we did not want to encourage privately financed and organized care for sexually distressed couples. Moreover, the research project had been financed by a public grant and the results were thus meant first and foremost to be made available to public and charity institutions. If there were still places free, therapists with private practices, preferably who worked in groups, were admitted. However, in view of the need for public health care we gave priority to institutional qualification.

In terms of *individual qualification*, we required that participants be trained in another recognized form of psychotherapy, but the scope of experience required was broadly defined. We found individual motivation was almost more important; indication of this included frequent confrontation with sexually dysfunctional couples in their jobs and willingness to deal with the couples' problems; the wish to provide more adequate help; the will and opportunity to participate in supervision regularly.

The advanced training programs confronted us with the various difficulties that resulted from transposing the therapeutic concept from the research environment to everyday life in counseling centers, clinics, and private practices. In general, psychologists trained in behavior therapy had the least difficulty with the therapeutic concept; for those trained in client-centered psychotherapy, history-taking and behavioral instructions presented problems to start with, whereas they readily adopted the concept of positive reinforcement. In the case of general practitioners, and particularly gynecologists, it was often not easy to persuade them that they were not treating a patient but a problem in a relationship; they had great difficulty in coping with transference and countertransference. Psychoanalytically or psychiatrically trained participants had to overcome considerable resistance before they could accept playing an active role in therapy by giving patients behavioral instructions. They often neglected to work on the sexual symptom and instead began interpreting the relationship; emerging partner problems all too easily tempted them into deviating from the concept. Trainees from other professions were less biased; social workers from family counseling centers coped particularly well. Length of professional experience was only decisive insofar as restricted experience, owing to years of work with the same concept, made progress more difficult. Therapists whose work brought them into frequent contact with sexual dysfunctions seemed to be more motivated and, furthermore, more capable of learning than others who were only interested in this area because they wanted to fill out their range of therapeutic qualifications.

THE THERAPY TEAM

Grouping the trainees and experienced therapists together in therapy teams was not based on consistent criteria. In most cases it depended on the availability of a place with an experienced therapist. Team therapy was a new working structure for almost all participants. Because until then they had been accustomed to facing a patient or couple alone, they were uncertain how to proceed with a therapy team of two people. The professional differences between psychologists, physicians, and other occupational groups were less relevant than the differences in therapeutic experience. The most friction arose from differences in style. It sometimes happened that cotherapists had so much difficulty with one another that cooperation became impossible, although the situation was discussed several times in supervision. The patients were as sensitive to such open conflicts as they were to any underlying tension between the therapists. The chances of therapy failing or even being broken off are considerable if therapists fail to resolve the tension.

SYSTEMATIC ERRORS

We shall now mention a few problems that required special attention in advanced training because they involved great difficulties for the trainees and repeatedly gave rise to misunderstandings, even though the subjects had been explained in detail in the introductory phase.

Special Problems. At first most of the trainees found it very difficult to compile a detailed sex history and to form an accurate picture of the patients' sexual difficulties at the beginning of therapy. They shied away from asking direct questions about sexual behavior and often were content with information such as "it doesn't work," "she doesn't like to be touched," and so forth. Some found they could not place enough distance between themselves and the patients in this procedure ("One cannot simply burst into someone's private life and start asking questions about such intimate things as sexual intercourse"); they did not want to be indiscreet, and, consequently, they preferred not to ask. Others did not know how to express themselves in sexual matters; their vocabularies were limited to Latin or slang, both of which made them feel uncomfortable. In this respect it is essential that therapists feel at home in their own language and norms and can at the same time understand and adopt the patients' language and norms. There is little use in handling such problems purely theoretically; a modification in behavior can only be achieved by rehearsing roles and listening to one's own voice on tape.

There was often great difficulty in the practical application of theoretical knowledge of the etiology of sexual dysfunctions to a couple's individual biography. This became clear in group discussions of the results of history-taking (for the round-table session) because then the causal relationship of a patient's history to his or her dysfunction had to be explained in plausible terms and the possibility that the dysfunction might even be a successful solution to a conflict be acknowledged. The therapeutic aim in explaining this connection between history and dysfunction to the patients is to relieve the pressure in the patients' relationship, to free it from the snares of mutual accusation, and to pave the way for a joint solution to the symptom. This can only happen if the explanation is convincingly given, a task that was apparently difficult for beginners. When preparing for the round-table session in supervision, great care has to be taken to find the key to the etiology of a problem.

Another fundamental requirement for successful therapeutic intervention is that the therapist be able to form an accurate picture of the patients' experiences with the exercises. In one case of vaginismus, the couple was asked to use the dilators. The patients said they had succeeded in inserting the dilators as deep as two to three inches, which meant that thicker dilators could be used. However, these fell out as soon as the female patient moved even slightly. The therapists did not become suspicious, asked no further questions, and began to have doubts only when therapy failed to make progress in eight further sessions. Only then did they have the patients explain in their own words exactly how they inserted the dilators; they were no longer content with the statement, "We did it just as you told us to." They then found out that the dilators had been squeezed into a fold of the skin between the major labia and upper thigh, without penetrating the vagina.

Many therapists find it hard to pass on detailed information, usually because they feel that instructions are unnatural and artificial. Of course, the patients sense their doubts about the effectiveness of instructions, and this gives rise to the notion, on the part of both patient and therapist, that joint sexual activity depends on the right kind of mood. Thus therapists merely give in to the patient's avoidance behavior and lose the concept in behavioral instructions.

Major difficulties with the therapeutic concept emerged in several areas. Many therapists were especially unaccustomed to concentrating attention on the disturbance in the relationship. For them the dysfunctional partner was the patient, and they then formed an alliance with the "nondysfunctional" partner, so driving the symptomatic partner even further into a corner.

One of the directives that both patients and therapists found difficult to accept was the instruction to open oneself to physical experiences without assessing them as successful or unproductive from the point of view of sexual arousal. Patients were often afraid that something was going to be taken away from them instead of trusting that they would make new discoveries. That trainees shared the same fear was evident in the way they assiduously questioned the patients about erection or lubrication during the therapy sequences caressing I and caressing II, or when the patients did not describe their sexual arousal spontaneously.

The therapeutic technique of reinforcing positive experiences is essential to the stabilization of positive patient developments. The repeated emphasis given to this point in the manual (see part 3) makes for tedious and boring reading. Many therapists felt ridiculous having to continually praise adults for the smallest success. On the assumption that patients were seeking therapeutic help for difficulties, therapists concentrated their attention on tracking down problems. For example, a couple might say that they had not had enough time to "practice" that week and, besides, that they had argued and so had not reached their "quota" but had only practiced once. Beginners in couple therapy often pounced on the "problematic content" of such a statement (the lack of time, the arguments, and skipping the exercises) and so put the patients in the position of having to justify themselves. Almost the entire therapy session would then be spent clearing up the misunderstandings and working through problems; any particularly satisfying experiences the couple might have had while doing the one exercise would be left unmentioned or not given the appropriate attention. The best way of explaining the concept of positive reinforcement to therapists and of encouraging them to adopt it is by handling their experiences and reports in exactly the same way, that is, by reinforcing whatever was good in their therapeutic behavior during supervision groups.

How to deal with patients' resistance is an important question for training groups. Although they had been explained the reasons in detail, some couples ignored the coitus prohibition required in the first therapy phase, confused the therapists, and occasionally provoked them to take restrictive measures. In this case the task for the supervising group is to understand the therapists' disappointment and to explain to them that the patients' aims and the therapists' aims do not always have to be identical and that the positive potential for resistance can be turned to good account in therapy. The resistance problem led to the critical question of how far one can accept patient autonomy in therapy.

Documentation. Although it was a matter of course that every therapy session was recorded on tape, some therapists found it hard to work with the tapes in supervision groups. They described in lengthy case reports how difficult patients' problems were to solve, and the group then had to rack their brains for a solution. Our experiences show that one can often achieve more clarity by analyzing short extracts from recorded sessions than by discussing reports for hours on end. We find it is important to insist on detailed documentation in advanced training groups; after all, the details of therapeutic interaction are the telling factor and show where correction is necessary. Cotherapists, for example, frequently fail to realize how unevenly they distribute their roles or that they have developed fixed language patterns over the year. A female therapist once pointed out to her cotherapist that when asking the patients to report, he frequently used such expressions as, "Did we sleep well?" or "How did we like caressing?" He then said that he definitely had not used such expressions; he considered them not only inappropriate, but stupid and embarrassing as well. That therapy session had not been taped, but the next was recorded. Although his attention had been drawn to the problem, these and similar expressions continually crept into his language. After hearing himself on tape he was gradually able to modify his habit.

Once the therapists had gained more control over detailed technical problems, reporting on case studies become increasingly important in the course of training. Other questions now had to be answered that went far beyond the technical scope of intervention strategies: therapists discussed therapies that stagnated, modification of procedure, transference and countertransference phenomena.

The problem of success criteria. Our aim in offering advanced training is to enable therapeutic practitioners, who are daily confronted by sexually dysfunctional couples, to establish criteria for choosing patients and to conduct therapy along the lines of our concept. We did not measure the success of trainees and neither did we stipulate any formal success criteria for completing the training program. This would have been of use only if training was intended as a legally recognized qualification. Basically that would amount to bestowing trainees with the title of "sex therapist"; we have already explained why there is little to be said for such a title. The only argument in favor of introducing this title is the protection of patients from charlatans; however, as experience has shown, this cannot be achieved merely by establishing formal accreditation criteria. Rather, we tend to rely on the therapists' own sense of responsibility, to leave it up to them to decide when their grasp of the therapeutic concept is sufficiently strong to be able to conduct therapy on their own. We have no doubt whatsoever that ongoing supervision is necessary, even for experienced therapists (see Mandel 1976). In the course of training and discussions in supervision groups, several participants came to the conclusion that they were unable to make anything of this form of therapy. We advised a few trainees not to continue conducting couple therapy.

Protection of patients. In the literature on training and advanced training of therapists for sexual dysfunctions, there is a distinct trend to require increasingly higher qualifications of therapists (Rosenzweig and Pearsall 1978; Kaplan 1977; Waggoner, Mudd, and Shearer 1973; LoPiccolo 1977b; Mandel 1976; WHO 1975; Sadock, Sadock, and Kaplan 1975). The plea for a tighter control on qualification requirements coincides with the observation that fewer and fewer so-called simple cases are seen in therapeutic centers. This corresponds to our experience, and we do tend to subject participants to stricter selection and more intensive and longer supervision. We still cannot be certain whether the clientele really has changed or whether the growth in therapeutic research has replaced the naïve therapeutic optimism of pioneer days with a greater skepticism about success.

In 1974 the World Health Organization (WHO) was still drawing a naïve distinction between sex educators, sex counselors, and sex therapists. Kaplan (see WHO reports 1975, 1977) had at the time spoken in favor of this triple division, only to revise her opinion later. This distinction is not without its problems, quite apart from the fact that an elaborated concept for sexual counseling has not yet been devised. It is presumably naïve to assume that there is any such thing as "plain and simple" sex counseling. And even if there were, short-term therapeutic intervention would probably require more skill than does psychotherapy and would only be possible with the backing of extensive therapeutic experience. Michael Balint, the pioneer of rapid treatment and so-called five-minute psychotherapy was, in our opinion, right in repeatedly insisting that short-term therapy is neither a simple form of therapy nor is it easily learned; quite the opposite, it represents the peak of therapeutic skill. No matter how elitist this may sound to some, we are inclined, in view of our experiences to date with advanced training groups, to raise our trainee requirements.

Therapist involvement. Our experiences with the participants in advanced training, whose behavior confronted us with many critical aspects of our own therapeutic work, inspired us to begin analyzing the therapists' situation more systematically. We noticed that the therapists' own steady relationships were seriously undermined and that many therapists separated from their partners. We believe this has something to do with the patients' particular symptomatology. Certainly one of the factors at play here is that sexual relationships develop between the cotherapists, in which they act out the kind of harmonious and exciting relationship that all their therapeutic skill fails to build up between the patients. At all events, the ongoing preoccupation with partner relationships and sexuality seems to incite much more identification or detachment than in any other field of psychotherapy. This preoccupation seems to act as a catalyst in that the relationship between cotherapists gradually assumes its own dynamics and in all probability influences the process of transference and countertransference in therapy. Whether the male and female therapists appear to be cooperating as colleagues, competitors, lovers, or a wise old married couple, their partner dynamics will always be influenced and modified by therapy.

If it is true that countertransference phenomena have a greater influence on scientific perception and the therapeutic process than do transference phenomena (Devereux 1967), one can expect success and failure in therapy to be essentially dependent on the structure of the relationship between the therapists. Unfortunately, we were blind to this extremely interesting aspect of methodology when planning and implementing our research project. In any case, we tried to avoid the problem through technical pragmatism and by requiring male and female therapists to conduct therapy with as many different cotherapists as possible, in the hope that this would statistically level out the differential factor of cotherapists' varying relationship dynamics. We believe that the analysis of these dynamics might be far more instructive than simple measurement of therapist values before and after therapy with the psychodiagnostic and behavior instruments designed for patients.

PART III

Manual of Couple Therapy for Sexual Dysfunctions

Margret Hauch, Gerd Arentewicz,
and Martina Gaschae

Contents

Overview   225

Outline of Therapy
   Therapists' Qualifications
   Indication for Therapy
   General Aims of Therapy

Therapeutic Procedure   231

Introductory Session
History-Taking
Discussion of Histories (Round-Table)
Caressing I
Caressing II
Explorative Genital Caressing
Stimulative Caressing and Playing with Arousal
Intromission
Coitus with Explorative and Stimulating Movements
Coitus in Other Positions
The Final Session

Additional Interventions   311

Bodily Self-Awareness: Women
Bodily Self-Awareness: Men
Additional Intervention for Vaginismus
Additional Intervention for Premature Ejaculation
Additional Intervention for Ejaculatory Incompetence

Overview

Our couple therapy manual can be used effectively only by helping professionals who are trained and experienced in psychotherapy and who have arranged for ongoing supervision by cotherapists, a supervisor, or supervision groups. This manual is not suitable for self-help. The behavioral instructions are only one part of the psychotherapeutic process and, if implemented without therapeutic support, can at best lead to disappointment or at worst to exacerbation of conflicts and symptoms.

Before using the manual read chapters 1 to 3, in which the basic theoretical principles of therapy are laid out. Also, work through the manual at least once before applying it in therapy. Every sequence (history-taking, behavioral instructions, discussion of experiences) should be rehearsed in role playing with a cotherapist or a member of the supervision group.

Outline of Therapy

Couple therapy for sexual dysfunctions can be used only with patients who have a steady relationship and a partner who is willing to participate in therapy. After the decision that the couple should undergo therapy, the therapists first decide which setting is appropriate for therapy. Therapy can be conducted long-term by a dual-sex therapist team or by one therapist only, who should if possible be the same sex as the symptomatic partner. In this setting the therapists take the partners' histories one to three weeks after the introductory session and discuss them in the next round-table session (in the sense of Masters and Johnson) with the couple. As a rule the couple then attends therapy sessions twice a week for six to eight months (thirty to forty sessions). Between each session the partners perform specific exercises twice at home as instructed by the therapists.

Therapy can be conducted in an intensive setting by a therapist team for three weeks with daily sessions (six a week). To allow enough time to do two exercises between the daily sessions, the couple should either take a vacation or go on sick-leave for the duration of treatment. Out-of-town patients should arrange for accommodations nearby. To avoid wasting time solving organizational problems, it is advisable to hold the introductory session for intensive therapy about two to three months before the start of therapy. Therapists take the patients' histories in the first two days of the three weeks; on the third day the histories are discussed in a round-table session. The remaining fifteen sessions are reserved for working through the therapeutic program.

The program for both settings[1] is the same and comprises the following sequences: caressing I, caressing II, explorative genital caressing, stimulative caressing—playing with arousal, intromission, coitus with explorative and stimulating movements, coitus in other positions, and the final session.

This basic program is to be used with all couples. Because sexual dysfunctions are the expression of sexual conflicts, anxieties, inhibitions, and learning deficits—whether they are manifested as erectile, ejaculatory, arousal or orgasmic disturbances, or vaginismus (see chapter 2)—we assume that all patients have to go through a similar process of learning and relearning in order to dissipate their difficulties.

The basic program is supplemented by additional therapeutic interventions for special problems. Exercises for bodily self-awareness are recommended for men and women who are not familiar with their own bodies, who have difficulty in accepting their bodies, or have no masturbation experience. These patients are introduced to the exercises for bodily self-awareness from the sequence caressing II, which they perform alone. The additional interventions for vaginismus, premature ejaculation, and ejaculatory incompetence are obligatory.

The time needed to work through each sequence should be assessed by the pertinent criteria indicated for each sequence. The therapists have to decide in each case when the aims of the sequence have been reached and the patients can proceed to the next. Table M.1 thus only offers a rough guide to the time needed.

In intensive therapy, therapists must set fairly tight overall time limits for working through each sequence. However, it is necessary to be flexible in allowing the couple enough time for the first sequences, regardless of diagnosis. In our experience a reasonable guideline is to aim for completion of explorative genital caressing by the middle of the second week. In exceptional cases the therapists can offer the couple two or three booster sessions after the three weeks to work through the final sequences.

Therapists' Qualifications

For responsible implementation of couple therapy, it is essential that the therapist has completed training in one of the recognized psychotherapeutic approaches, for example, behavior therapy, client-centered therapy, psychoanalysis, or psychoanalytically oriented therapy. Couple therapy is not primarily concerned with teaching sexual techniques but with working through attitudes, inhibitions, anxieties, and conflicts tied in with sexuality and with tackling relationship problems. The therapists should be able to establish a relationship of trust with the partners; therapists must be able to intervene appropriately in critical situations and to use material offered by the patients in a way conducive to therapeutic aims.

Our therapeutic concept is based on the principles of behavior therapy and uses behavioral instructions. If therapy is to be effective the therapist must understand the learning theory principles on which behavior modification is based. Ongoing supervision is essential in conducting couple therapy, particularly in view of the special problems that arise from the emotional and normative implications of sexuality. Inexperienced therapists should conduct at least their first couple therapy within a therapy team so that reciprocal supervision and discussion after each session is guaranteed and so that cotherapists can plan further procedures jointly. Reciprocal supervision by cotherapists is by no means a substitute for supervision by a group or other colleagues (see chapter 10 for a discussion of supervision). Therapists should, of course, be informed about current research and developments in psychotherapy and about the sociological aspects of marriage and relationships; an insight into the ideological implications of their work is also important.

Indication for Therapy

CRITERIA OF DYSFUNCTION

Therapy is indicated for couples with the following sexual dysfunctions:

Male	*Female*
Erectile dysfunctions	Lack of desire and arousal dysfunctions
Premature ejaculation	Orgasmic dysfunctions
Ejaculatory incompetence	Vaginismus

Of course, therapy is also applicable if both partners have a dysfunction, that is, for bilateral dysfunctions. It is of no importance to the indication for treatment whether the dysfunction is primary or secondary. Therapy is only indicated for chronic dysfunctions. As a rule, counseling is sufficient to deal with initial and temporary disturbances.

BASIC FORMAL REQUIREMENTS

Therapy is only feasible if the following requirements are fulfilled:

1. Because the program's premise is the treatment of both partners, patients must have a steady relationship. The relationship should be stable insofar as both partners wish to continue it and both are willing to try to improve it.
2. The possibility of an organic cause should be refuted by medical examination.
3. Couples should not be undergoing psychotherapeutic treatment elsewhere at the same time; they should concentrate fully on the new experiences involved in couple therapy.
4. Neither partner should be involved in another sexual relationship; this has been shown to impede or prevent full participation in therapy.
5. Contraceptives should be used because the fear of pregnancy impedes the performance of exercises and pregnancy itself can lead to therapy being discontinued.

Severe addiction to alcohol or drugs and acute psychoses are contraindications. After evaluating the results of our investigation, it has not proved necessary to take partner or neurotic conflicts as criteria for the appropriateness of therapy, nor is age a factor. We thus find it advisable to confine oneself at first to the basic formal requirements.

Overview

The choice of a therapy setting is based on practical criteria. We usually perform long-term therapy if the following requirements have been met: the partners have enough time to come to sessions twice a week and to do exercises twice between each session; they have a room or apartment where they can be undisturbed; no long or frequent interruptions (for example, vacations or business trips) will occur for the duration of therapy (about six to eight months). Whether therapy is performed by a therapy team or a single therapist depends on the number of staff members available.

In general we offer intensive treatment only to out-of-town couples, but in exceptional cases it is made available to couples who cannot take part in long-term therapy for other reasons (for example, shift work or regular absence from home on job assignments). It is essential that the partners drop all other commitments for the three weeks of intensive therapy. That is, in addition to taking a vacation or going on sick-leave, they should free themselves of family duties, such as child care. Intensive therapy is always performed by two therapists, not only because of the strain on the therapists (p. 150) but also for practical reasons: because the time allotted is short even the brief absence of one therapist (for example, due to illness) can lead to treatment failure; this is unacceptable for patients who have made extensive preparations for participation in therapy.

General Aims of Therapy

The primary aim of therapy is to improve or reconstitute sexual functioning and the sexual relationship with the help of corrective emotional experiences. A couple's relationship and previous history is expressed in their sexuality. In every session the therapists are confronted by a mass of psychodynamic and partner-dynamic material. The task of processing it all comprehensively and systematically falls outside the scope of our therapeutic concept. The therapists confine their work to identifying and working on the psychodynamic and partner-dynamic aspects that are directly responsible for the development and persistence of the sexual symptom and which could impede the progress of therapy or cause it to be discontinued. Therapists decide from case to case on the basis of their training when and how to supplement the basic program with further interventions. If this involved a radical departure from planned therapy procedure, one should examine whether the therapists have given in to patients' avoidance behavior.

The aim of improving sexual functioning and developing alternative forms of behavior is best achieved by resolving the self-reinforcement mechanism (see p. 57). The therapeutic concept provides specific guidelines for working toward various subsidiary aims:

1. Reduction of failure fears and avoidance behavior in sexual interaction by "prescribing" exercises that define a standardized anxiety-hierarchy and so enable a gradual desensitization of patients and, ultimately, sexual experiences free of anxiety.
2. Reversal of learning deficits by informing patients about the anatomy, physiology, and psychology of sexuality, by emphasizing nongenital sexuality, and by modifying inhibiting moral standards, where possible by reference to the patients' new experiences in the exercises.
3. Encouraging patients to be responsible for themselves in their sexual relationship by guiding them toward a more differentiated perception of their bodily sensations and their needs as felt in the exercises. The patients learn gradually to be responsible for the satisfaction of their needs and to rely more on their own experiences rather than on external norms or expectations, real or projected, of their partners.
4. Improving communication between the partners by establishing a model during sessions in which sexuality and emotional reactions to sexual experiences are discussed in detail; this is supplemented by specific instructions for exercises.

To achieve reconstitution of sexual functioning, it is often necessary to include the following aspects:

1. Disengaging psychodynamic conflicts and fears, which might possibly be etiological factors in sexual dysfunctions, from sexuality, that is, from the partners' actual sexual experiences (see p. 68). It is often impossible in couple therapy to go further than this disengagement when handling psychodynamic conflicts.
2. Working through partner conflicts insofar as they affect sexual interaction (see p. 68).
3. Modifying the social conditions that contribute to the development and persistence of the sexual dysfunction.

A particularly important factor here is the female partner's oppressed role as a housewife in the family (see p. 53); her situation is often so closely tied in with sexual problems that therapy success is sometimes impossible unless a change is made, for example, by her taking up part-time work.

Therapists work directly and systematically toward the above aims only insofar as sexual problems are involved. These aims are, however, equally relevant to other areas of a relationship. By transferring learning experiences, an overall improvement in the relationship can be achieved. The positive emotional experiences that partners share and the strengthened self-esteem that result from resolution of sexual symptoms can also clear the air in a relationship. These are additional positive effects that appear frequently in the course of therapy, but they can by no means always be expected.

It is important to keep in mind that even successful therapy usually achieves nothing more than restoration of the "everyday sexuality" of undisturbed couples. Since partners are often disappointed when they realize this, psychotherapy for sexual dysfunctions also involves helping patients to reassess the rewards they expect from sexuality.

Therapeutic Procedure

Our description of the therapeutic sequences is subdivided as follows: aims; procedure; discussion of experiences (when behavioral instructions are given); further procedure; special problems; timing. Our reasons for this subdivision are as follows: we consider it essential that therapists first understand the aims of each sequence. In the sections on procedure and discussion of experiences, we present the actual therapeutic techniques in detail. In some places, it seemed necessary to illustrate therapeutic procedure with therapy transcripts. The transcripts are meant to illustrate one possible way of proceeding. We have tried to highlight various therapeutic styles by selecting the transcripts of different therapists. In terms of special problems we can discuss only a few typical examples. Individual problems can be handled effectively only by the therapists and patients using their creativity.

Although this kind of subdivision means repeating certain instructions and information, this is precisely our intention. It is meant to help the therapists repeat themselves as is required by the principle that exercises and experiences should continually be repeated so as to attain the aim of "modified behavior."

INITIAL INTERVIEW (SCREENING BY THE FIRST CONSULTANT)

The initial patient evaluation and therapy are frequently conducted by different people and sometimes even in different institutions. This evaluation is a necessary part of preparation for therapy.

AIMS

The initial interview should establish whether the disturbance is a chronic sexual dysfunction for which couple therapy is appropriate or whether it is another kind of problem (information deficits, sexual deviations, partner conflicts without sexual dysfunctions) which requires different counseling or treatment. If a sexual dysfunction in need of therapy is diagnosed, there should be compliance with the basic formal requirements for couple therapy and certainty of the absence of any organic causes or contraindications.

PROCEDURE

Patients often only hint at sexual disturbances and try to conceal them behind other problems. Patients find it a relief if the first consultant asks the patients directly when he suspects there are sexual problems. Procedure basically resembles that for history-taking (see p. 235), except that diagnosis of the sexual problems and the present partner relationship is stressed.

An accurate assessment of the relationship necessarily involves talking to each partner separately; the one-to-one interview should establish his or her views on the problem and his or her motivation for treatment as a couple.

If the interviews show that one or both partners have a dysfunction and if both are motivated for couple therapy and meet the basic formal requirements, recommendation for therapy can be made and discussed jointly with the partners. The first consultant then discusses with both partners which setting suits the couple best. The recommendation for therapy should be reassessed by therapists after comprehensive history-taking.

Introductory Session

The introductory session is the first therapeutic session and is conducted by the therapists. In long-term therapy it takes place one to three weeks before history-taking, in intensive therapy one to two months.

AIMS

The introductory session helps the patients and therapists get to know one another. The practical and technical requirements of therapy are outlined in the session. Furthermore, the therapists explain the concept and outline of therapy and anything else the patients want to know.

PROCEDURE

The therapists introduce themselves and explain that both they and the first consultant (they mention his or her name) consider couple therapy capable of resolving the problems. The therapists then explain therapy procedure: sexual difficulties are not a "disturbance" of one or the other partner but a problem in the relationship. Even if only one of the partners has a dysfunction, both of them are, after all, involved or distressed. This is why their interaction is affected—as, for example, when they avoid sexual contact, which, in turn, reinforces the disturbance. This is why both partners are treated.

The therapists also explain that therapy is based on the insight that a person's sexual habits and difficulties are influenced by his previous experiences. Although every person is physically equipped for sex, sexual interaction is learned in the course of life just as, for example, one learns to talk. All sorts of things can go wrong during this process. It is therefore important first to find out as much as possible about the history of both partners and their relationship. This is the reason why the next two sessions are spent taking histories individually (approximately two hours); first the female therapist with the female patient and the male therapist with the male patient, and then vice versa; this second interview is as a rule somewhat shorter than the first.

In long-term therapy history-taking is followed by two sessions a week with all four participants[2] for a period of six to eight months. In intensive therapy history-taking is completed in the first two days and followed by daily sessions for the remaining three weeks (except Sundays). In the first joint session of both long-term and intensive therapy the results of history-taking are discussed (round-table session).

In the following sessions the partners are given behavioral instructions for exercises at home which will lead them to new experiences and enable them to restructure their sexual relationship. They must be prepared to dispense with intercourse for the initial period of therapy. Instead, they are shown new ways of experiencing sexuality together which will gradually mitigate the difficulties. Their experiences are then discussed in detail in sessions.

For long-term therapy the therapists should also ensure the following:

1. Provision should be made for contraception; the pill, minipill, or IUD are preferred because other contraceptives—for example, spermicidal foams and jellies—could severely inhibit partners' experiences and besides do not provide sufficient protection. The woman should ask her gynecologist about any problems the contraception might involve. Therapists can explain that pregnancy is known to lead patients to discontinue therapy and to nullify any progress made, and that even the awareness of the risk of conception considerably impedes the process of learning. This applies as well to couples whose motivation for therapy is based on the wish for a child.
2. The time commitment of partners should allow for two therapy sessions a week and for at least one hour between sessions to do the exercises twice. Moreover, no long or frequent interruptions (for example, business trips) should interfere for the entire duration of therapy. Vacation should not fall within the first eight weeks of therapy.
3. Couples should have the opportunity to withdraw to a quiet, undisturbed place for the performance of the exercises. Partners who live apart should, if possible, move in together for the duration of therapy.

In intensive therapy, requirements 1 and 3 are the same as in long-term therapy. The required time commitment, however, is more demanding. The couple should be asked to take a sick-leave or a vacation and to free themselves of remaining everyday duties (for example, household and children). The need to eliminate daily domestic demands should be made especially clear to couples who live nearby because they often do not really understand why this requirement is necessary. Out-of-town couples should be reminded that staying with relatives or friends often complicates the availability of both time and space. Out-of-town couples should also be reminded that because therapy takes up so much time any plans for sightseeing et cetera would be quite unrealistic. Menstruation ought not to coincide with therapy because this would, in effect, reduce the small amount of time available. Women should be reminded that menstruation can be delayed with hormonal contraceptives and asked to consult their gynecologists on this point. If this is not possible, therapy should be postponed to the time between two periods.

At the end of the introductory session therapists and partners agree on the schedule for the one-to-one history-taking interviews and also for the first joint session.

History-Taking

AIMS

The therapists should gain comprehensive insight into the couple's situation and difficulties so they can develop an understanding for their problems. It is important to elicit detailed information on the existing problem, the kind and extent of avoidance reactions, and the function symptoms have in the relationship; by doing so therapists can judge which conflict areas have to be examined with particular care in therapy. An overview of the partners' psychosexual history enables the therapists to formulate hypotheses on the development of the sexual dysfunctions, which are then discussed in the joint sessions. By encouraging open communication between therapists and patients on sexual problems the basis for a relationship of trust in therapy can be established.

PROCEDURE

In team therapy the female and male therapists at first take the history of the same-sex patient. In our experience these interviews last between one and a half and two and a half hours. The therapists then discuss the material from the first interview and jointly decide on the central topics for the next interview with the opposite-sex partner, which can be expected to last about one and a half hours. After history-taking therapists discuss patient material in detail. In treatment by one therapist, about two hours should be allowed for interviews with each partner.

The development of a trust relationship with the patient is enhanced if, at the beginning of history-taking, the therapist directly addresses the sexual problems that brought the couple to therapy. As a rule, patients are relieved when they find they can talk openly about their sexual problems. History-taking begins by simply asking the patient to describe the sexual problem. It is important here for the therapist to let the partners describe specific features of interaction, such as the last intercourse or attempt at it, and that he or she help them to describe their problem by asking, for example: "Did your wife touch your penis and rub your foreskin up and down?" or, "When your husband caresses you does he start with your face, your breasts, or between your legs?" The therapist can interpret answers to questions about emotional judgments and reactions accurately only if he is clear about the behavior patterns. The sexual problem is the first of three areas to be discussed in history-taking.

The second area concerns the partners' histories; this part of history-taking should help the patients understand the experiences that led to the development of the symptom. The present relationship, its development, and the current situation comprise the third area. Patients should also be asked about their motivation for therapy.

The catalogue of key topics below is ordered according to these three areas and covers all the topics that should be addressed; the sequence can, however, be reordered. The therapist should follow the patients' initiative in structuring the interview, without, however, forgetting to intervene if the partners avoid certain aspects of sexuality.

If one of the partners mentions something in history-taking that he or she has concealed in the relationship—for example, other sexual relationships or masturbation—and which have a bearing on the present situation and therapy, the therapist should ask what the reasons for secrecy are and conjecture what implications this could have for the relationship and therapy. He or she should encourage the patient to be more open and suggest that the therapy situation will present a good opportunity.

In team therapy not all questions should be repeated in the second interview; but neither should therapists be deterred from repeating important questions. Therapists should concentrate on the areas not fully covered in the first interview and mention topics that are particularly complex or unclear because, for example, the partners' statements are incongruent. The therapists should jointly discuss the procedure for the second interview in detail.

Discussion of sexual symptoms and history-taking generally requires that the therapists themselves are in a position to talk about sexuality openly and straightforwardly. One should always remember that there is no such thing as an ideal "sex therapist vocabulary," that patients use language quite differently, and that each therapist has to ask himself which kind of language he can and wants to speak.

236

Therapeutic Procedure

Present Sexuality and Sexual Disturbance(s)
  kind of disturbance
    duration, development, fluctuation of the dysfunction(s)
    desire
    sexual functions affected (for example, erection, ejaculation, lubrication, orgasm)
    satisfaction
    dependency of the dysfunction on partner, techniques, or situation
    own attitude toward the dysfunction and the presumed attitude of partner
  present sexual behavior
    coitus with partner (frequency, techniques, conflicts, sexual initiative, fantasies)
    body contact and tenderness (need, frequency, situation, sexual initiative)
    communication regarding sexuality (expression of desire and wishes, being able to say "no," erotic vocabulary)
    sexual preferences
    aversions (to, for example, techniques, odors, or secretions) and avoidance behavior
    contraception
    masturbation (frequency, techniques, conflicts, fantasies)
    homosexual encounters or wishes
    deviant behavior patterns and fantasies

Psychosexual Development
  parental home
    occupation of father/mother and financial status
    number of brothers and sisters, and birth order
    parents' relationship, sexual behavior, and standards
    relationship to father and mother, then and now
    opportunity for communication about sexual and personal problems in the family
    religious ties
    school and professional career
  sexual learning history—childhood
    sexual experiences in early childhood (playing doctor, watching parents, experiences with adults)

    parents' attitudes toward sexuality (nakedness taboo, tenderness, body contact, norms, punishments)

    masturbation experiences in childhood

    incestuous encounters

    sexually deviant encounters with adults

  sexual learning history—puberty to present relationship

    sex education

    menarche or first ejaculation (age, preparation, emotional response)

    masturbation (frequency, emotional response, techniques, fantasies)

    early dating and petting experiences

    first coitus (circumstances, contraception, emotional response, initial problems)

    number, duration, and development of sexual relationships (including prostitutes)

    sexual dysfunctions

    sexual satisfaction

    pregnancies and abortions

    children with other partners

    sexually deviant experiences

    homosexual encounters

Present Relationship

  general information

    marital status, marriage plans

    duration of the relationship

    children, wish for children, abortions

    financial status, occupation, work situation

    physical illnesses and psychological problems (including alcohol and drug abuse)

  development of relationship

    initial presexual period

    development of sexual relationship (problems, fears, sexual initiative, contraception)

    onset and development of sexual dysfunction(s)

    self-reinforcement mechanisms (avoidance, failure fears)

    masturbation (incidence and acceptance in the relationship)

    other sexual relationships (sexual functioning, secrecy, frequency and duration, kind of relationship and partner, responses of steady partner and effect on steady relationship)

relationship pattern
    distribution of roles and power structure
    attitude toward partner's positive and negative remarks (sexual and nonsexual)
    satisfaction in present situation (living and work conditions, behavior toward each other, distribution of roles, social contacts, joint interests)
    communication (form of discourse, arguments, expression of wishes and needs, expression of affection)
    children (education, relationship to children)
    effect and function of sexual disturbance in the relationship
    sexual ideology (love, faithfulness, jealousy, autonomy of partners)
motivation for therapy
    motivation for seeking therapy (one or both partners)
    immediate motive for therapy
    expectations, hopes, and fears of therapy (in terms of sexuality and relationship)
    previous therapeutic experiences (failures, partial success) and attempts at self-help

TRANSCRIPT[3]

COUPLE 38: The partners are both in their mid-thirties. He is an accountant and she is a social worker. They have been married for eight years and have never been able to have intercourse because of vaginismus and erectile dysfunctions. The couple was treated in intensive therapy.

The transcript contains excerpts from history-taking by the male therapist with both partners, first the husband and then the wife. We have selected only excerpts dealing with the sexual symptoms because we wish to illustrate specific aspects of history-taking in couple therapy for sexual dysfunctions. (In this transcript and all later ones *M.Th.* stands for "male therapist" and *F.Th.* stands for "female therapist.")

History-Taking with the Husband (excerpt)

M.Th.: Just describe what your difficulties are.
Man: Well, basically it's very simple; we haven't had intercourse since marrying. Basically speaking it probably all goes back to the fact that I hadn't had intercourse with any other girl before we married and my wife hadn't had intercourse with another man before, either. And, well, so it didn't work out on the first night after the wedding. And everytime we tried, the same thing happened; either I got an erection all right, but then when I

tried to slip it into my wife it was all over. Or perhaps my wife was a little cramped sometimes.

That went on for quite a long time. And then we went to a gynecologist about a half year after our wedding and she examined my wife. She gave her a medicine she was meant to take about half an hour before intercourse. I guess it was something to relieve the cramps but I can't remember exactly. But then it didn't work with the medicine either. Actually, what she said was that we should come again. Well, we didn't. That was probably our mistake.

M.Th.: So you didn't do anything else after the first visit to the gynecologist?

Man: No, nothing.

M.Th.: And did you give up trying to perform intercourse at some point or did . . .

Man: You can say so.

M.Th.: When was that, about?

Man: Maybe mid-1970. I can't really say . . .

M.Th.: So, and then you went on trying for two years, the first two years?

Man: Yes.

M.Th.: And then you stopped?

Man: Yes, I mean no—once after my wife's operation [incision of hymen, mechanical dilation of vagina under narcosis] again, that was three months ago. But she didn't really feel like it. And then we simply said, we had better wait until therapy before we start driving ourselves crazy again. Otherwise I feel, when we're lying next to each other and I touch my wife, basically there's nothing more natural.

M.Th.: Sure.

Man: Only, the real thing, that doesn't happen.

M.Th.: This attempt three months ago—I think it would be good if you described exactly what happened, how you felt.

Man: It was the same as in the early days, at first I reacted quite normally.

M.Th.: And your penis stiffened.

Man: Yes, yes. Then we probably waited a bit too long and it drooped again. And then my wife aroused it again with her hand, and then we tried, but then it was probably too late, or whatever. Anyhow, it didn't get stiff enough.

M.Th.: Didn't get as stiff as usual.

Man: No.

M.Th.: And then you tried to insert it. Or did you . . .

Man: I tried all right. Sure.

M.Th.: And what happened then?

Man: Just at the moment I wanted to insert it, we went at it a bit clumsily and it took a little too long, the erection had gone. You could say more or less completely gone.

M.Th.: Did the penis go in at all?

Man: Just a little. Certainly not the whole way.

M.Th.: I asked you before what your feelings were. Were you upset or . . .

Man: Yes, a bit, certainly.

M.Th.: Did you sweat, for example?

Man: Sweat, no, couldn't say so. Of course, it's difficult to remember after all this time.

M.Th.: What if you compare that situation with what you normally do with your wife sexually, I mean, the way you feel.

Man: It was really more unpleasant.

M.Th.: In what way?

Man: For me personally it feels like it's my debut. The gynecologist who operated on my wife told us, don't wait too long.

M.Th.: Debut means stage-fright?

Man: Yes, you could describe it that way.

M.Th.: And about how often did you try in the first year and a half?

Man: Twenty, thirty times. The time in between got longer and longer.

M.Th.: Were there times when your penis had stiffened fully, but when it still wouldn't go in when you tried?

Man: Yes, that happened too, at the beginning of the marriage. Both things. Sometimes my erection was quite alright in the beginning until I wanted to put it in and then it was all over; and the other times, in our early days, when I tried and my penis was stiff enough then my wife had pains and then just when . . .

M.Th.: And then your erection disappeared, or even earlier?

Man: Yes.

M.Th.: You said you had found other ways. Probably petting?

Man: Yes.

M.Th.: Thinking back to the last six months, how often did you do that?

Man: It varied; once a week.

M.Th.: Who was the more active?

Man: Both of us, in turns.

M.Th.: Hmm. Can you describe to me what you actually . . .

Man: Well, I caress my wife, thighs and neck, her breasts, she likes that. She caresses me and then stimulates my penis with her hand until I get an orgasm. With her it varies. Sometimes she has an orgasm, but not always.

M.Th.: What do you do to her?

Man: Well, often I just kiss her breasts intensely, occasionally I stimulate her clitoris, too.

M.Th.: But not so often.

Man: No, not so often.

M.Th.: Do you feel your wife's breasts are particularly sensitive?

Man: I would say so, yes.

M.Th.: Have you tried stimulating her genitals with your mouth as well?

Man: Sure, but she objects to it. Although she doesn't object because she doesn't like it; it probably has more to do with her education.

M.Th.: What's your impression. When you caress your wife's genitals, is it something she doesn't like or does she go all stiff and rigid?

Man: Sometimes, that's my impression.

M.Th.: Can you describe it?

Man: I just notice sometimes that she simply keeps her legs shut so I have to force my hand in a bit between them to get her to open her legs. But generally I think she has more pleasure and enjoys it more when I stroke

241

her breasts intensely with my hand or mouth than when I touch her genitals. It's not a total refusal, I wouldn't say that, but somehow it seems to me she reaches orgasm more often the other way than when I touch her genitals.

M.Th.: Are both of you naked?

Man: Yes.

M.Th.: Does your wife stimulate you to orgasm with her hand?

Man: Yes.

M.Th.: Have you noticed any reservations on your wife's part to touching your penis?

Man: No, I don't think so, definitely not.

M.Th.: And to your ejaculation . . .

Man: Not really, no.

M.Th.: How long does it last when you're petting?

Man: Between five and ten minutes.

M.Th.: So it's all over fairly quickly.

Man: Yes.

M.Th.: Do you sometimes insert a finger into your wife's vagina?

Man: Yes, but really only since three months ago.

M.Th.: You couldn't before?

Man: No, it was practically impossible before the operation.

M.Th.: And since the operation?

Man: Yeah, it works.

M.Th.: Do you only do that sometimes, or regularly?

Man: Only sometimes.

M.Th.: Does it go in fairly easily?

Man.: Quite easily.

M.Th.: Have you ever left your finger in there for a bit longer?

Man: Hmm.

M.Th.: That works too?

Man: Yes, that works, as well.

M.Th.: What are your feelings then?

Man: Unusual. Unusual really, at the time; or let's say at the beginning, after it happened, because I had never done it before.

M.Th.: Hmm.

Man: But otherwise strictly speaking without any particular feeling.

History-Taking with the Wife (excerpt)

M.Th.: Well, your husband told me that the main problem is that you have never been able to have intercourse.

Woman: Exactly, yes.

M.Th.: Have you any idea what the reason is?

Woman: I really can't explain it because there's nothing actually preventing it. I can imagine that since neither of us had had sexual intercourse before marrying, we both went about it a bit skeptically, on the whole.

M.Th.: Hmm.

Therapeutic Procedure

Woman: And then when difficulties developed we gave up pretty quickly, I must say.

M.Th.: Yes.

Woman: Probably another thing was that, I don't know, I've thought about it very often, but I almost think I even found it quite O.K., I guess. Considering I was afraid of it somehow. Though we never talked about it I sometimes think I really preferred it that way. At first.

M.Th.: In what way?

Woman: Well, somehow I was just a bit afraid of the whole thing because it was never mentioned in our family, no one explained sex to us.

M.Th.: Could you describe your fear a bit more specifically.

Woman: Yes, that's a bit too strong, fear, but somehow an uneasy feeling about the whole thing.

M.Th.: So that when it didn't work . . .

Woman: It was perhaps, hmm, pleasant for me, at that moment.

M.Th.: Which then protected you from . . .

Woman: . . . facing up to . . .

M.Th: . . . this uneasiness. What's the situation now?

Woman: Well, I would definitely like it to happen and to work out, quite definitely. Because I've gotten to know my husband much better over the years and didn't know him then as I do now, didn't know how he was going to be, sexually, whether he would be rough or demanding. I definitely want intercourse now. I mean, I have for years.

M.Th.: Supposing his erection is 100 percent O.K., what would happen then?

Woman: I'd really look forward to it, absolutely. Since it would be my first time. Even more because I really love my husband. That's why I think it would be lovely for both of us.

M.Th.: Yes. I can see that. But feelings are often ambiguous. They can be so mixed, I mean, somehow one looks forward to it and at the same time . . .

Woman: Actually I wouldn't say that I'm afraid of it, or anything. Especially because I know my husband is very careful, like if there were any difficulties, he definitely wouldn't try and force it or insist on going on. I know that for sure.

M.Th.: You feel quite certain that you can rely on him now.

Woman: Yes. Absolutely.

M.Th.: Then, could you tell me a little more precisely how things went, at the beginning as well. The first time you tried was on your wedding night?

Woman: Yes, I can still remember it quite well. First we got undressed, separately, put on our night things, and went to bed; then we started just cuddling with each other, caressing, and took off our things. And I caressed my husband; my husband caressed me, too, which I enjoyed a lot. And then I caressed his penis as well and it got pretty stiff. Then my husband tried to insert his penis, and we noticed how it started to droop.

M.Th.: Hmm.

Woman: And then he became extremely depressed and said, we should have tried it out once before; he had never had sexual intercourse with other

243

women. And it probably wasn't right not to try it out once before. And as I said, I didn't find it all that tragic. I tried to cheer him up and said, we would have to practice, perhaps, and that it can't work the first time. But he was terribly dejected right away. So we left off trying again right afterward.

M.Th.: What happened then?

Woman: Well, then the same thing happened again. But, I think first we put it off for weeks without doing anything . . .

M.Th.: At some point you gave up altogether, didn't you?

Woman: Yes.

M.Th.: When was that, roughly?

Woman: I'm not exactly sure. Besides, my husband wasn't working any more where we used to live, and then he was away altogether for half a year. We only met on the weekends. And I think it was then, I mean about half a year later or so. Afterward we only tried occasionally.

M.Th.: The last attempt was after the operation.

Woman: Yes, but it didn't work again.

M.Th.: Looking back over the years of your marriage, how often do you think you tried intercourse, at a rough guess?

Woman: Well, I think it was less than ten times, yes.

M.Th.: Did you sometimes try when his penis was stiff and still had no success?

Woman: No, it usually didn't get that far. When my husband tried to move on top of me then his erection gave way again.

M.Th.: So you went back to petting.

Woman: Yes.

M.Th.: Looking at the last half year, how often have you been doing it like that?

Woman: Difficult to say, it simply varies because sometimes I go to bed earlier than my husband in the evenings, and so we just don't get round to it. And there's often so much to do on the weekends. I would say two or three times a month. Perhaps more sometimes, it varies, you know.

M.Th.: Is that enough for you, or . . .

Woman: I could do with it more often. But then my husband is sometimes very tired.

M.Th.: Hmm.

Woman: Or as I said, there just isn't time for it.

M.Th.: Who takes the initiative?

Woman: Both of us, together.

M.Th.: Could you just describe what happens?

Woman: Usually we start caressing face and neck, my husband touches my breasts and goes on to my vagina, and I go down to his penis and usually give him an orgasm.

M.Th.: Manually?

Woman: Yes, manually.

M.Th.: Do you like touching his penis?

Woman: Yes, I find it's nice.

M.Th.: And when the semen comes out . . .

Woman: Sure, I feel it's really pleasant, for me too. Not unpleasant, not at all.

M.Th.: Does your husband bring you to orgasm then as well?

Woman: Far too seldom.

M.Th.: How many times in ten, roughly?

Woman: Maybe two.

M.Th.: Wouldn't you like it more often, or is that impossible?

Woman: Well, usually my husband gets there earlier and I just don't get as far because my husband somehow stops.

M.Th.: And if you do reach orgasm, how does it happen, what arouses you most?

Woman: Well, so far I would say when he caresses my breasts.

M.Th.: And you reach orgasm simply by him caressing your breasts?

Woman: Yes.

M.Th.: And when he touches your clitoris as well?

Woman: Yes.

M.Th.: But the breasts are better?

Woman: Yes.

M.Th.: Could you tell me something about the operation you had a few months ago?

Woman: What they did, you mean? Well, I spoke to the gynecologist, and she said she had done an incision of the hymen. Otherwise she said everything was O.K.

M.Th.: You were in the hospital for three days, weren't you?

Woman: Yes.

M.Th.: Did you have any kind of pain or complaints?

Woman: None at all. I bled a little, but not much. Otherwise there wasn't anything wrong with me.

M.Th.: And then afterward you tried intercourse again?

Woman: Hmm.

M.Th.: Could you tell me what it was like? That was about three months ago, wasn't it?

Woman: Yes, well actually I was pretty sure it would work really because there just wasn't any mechanical obstacle as such. So I caressed my husband again until his penis was fairly stiff, and my husband tried moving on top of me, and then the erection gave way again. And we tried it again in the reverse position, which my husband still didn't like at all, so that didn't work either. Although I was convinced there couldn't be any obstacle in the way.

EVALUATION OF HISTORIES

Discussing the results of history-taking (round-table) with the couple is one of the most difficult sequences in therapy. Therapists have to make careful preparations by closely examining history-taking findings, preferably in a team.

The therapists first reevaluate the initial recommendation for therapy using the criteria discussed earlier (p. 228). If they consider that therapy is not indicated because new aspects have been discovered in history-taking, they then confer with the patients: first, about whether there is some way they can fulfill the criteria and postpone therapy until then; second, about whether there are any therapeutic alternatives.

The therapists' task is to deduce from the patients' histories the conditions and causes that led up to the sexual dysfunction in the relationship by examining specific examples from the partner's experiences and those of the "nondysfunctional" partner as well. They should first analyze each individual's learning experiences prior to the relationship and then how the relationship developed up to the present time.

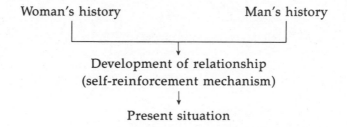

Woman's history   Man's history

Development of relationship
(self-reinforcement mechanism)

Present situation

When evaluating histories therapists should take account of sociocultural factors so they can demonstrate to the couple later that their difficulties and experiences are not merely subjective problems. Details of procedure are described in the next section. Comprehensive evaluation of history-taking findings is necessary so as to enable a clearer insight into the structure of the couple's relationship and a more extensive understanding of the presenting problems. Only then can therapists explain the full context of a disturbance to the couple.

Discussion of Histories (Round-Table)

AIMS

The therapists should acquaint the patients with the basic therapeutic concept: sexuality is to a great extent influenced by experience. The therapists then explain how the patients' sexual difficulties developed and the mechanisms sustaining them, in view of the patients' learning history, insofar as it could be elicited in history-taking. This helps relieve patients of their anxiety and enables them to see their problems in a new light; the therapeutic concept of learning and relearning helps patients to accept and reconstruct problems more easily. The discussion should establish what share the "nondysfunctional" partner has in the sexual problem in order to emphasize once again that the couple, and not the "dysfunctional" partner alone, is the "patient."

PROCEDURE

In this session therapists might easily be tempted to lecture to the couple and push the partners into a passive role. To prevent this happening they should try to involve the patients in the discussion by encouraging them to ask questions and expound on topics themselves.

The therapists explain the aim of the session: the first step is to discuss how the sexual difficulties came about by reference to material elicited in history-taking. Then the therapists ask the partners whether they have already talked to each other about history-taking and whether there is anything they would like to add. Any contradictions in what the partners have said are then discussed. The next step is to resummarize the therapeutic concept and to outline first therapeutic sequences.

In order to help the patients understand the bearing negative learning experiences have on their sexual difficulties and the concept of corrective emotional experiences, their histories are discussed with them with a view to the following aspects: (1) predisposing experiences in the "symptomatic" partner's life history until the couple met; (2) predisposing experiences in the "nondysfunctional" partner's life history until the couple met; (3) the combined effect of these experiences in the development of the couple's sexually disturbed relationship; (4) reinforcing and supportive mechanisms in the couple's sexually disturbed relationship.

In discussing these aspects therapists should try to elicit answers to the following questions: Do the partners have anxieties that make them sexually insecure or avoid intact functioning? (see p. 40); What kind of learning deficits favor or support the sexual dysfunction? (see p. 55); What kind of partner problems and conflicts caused, contribute to, or support the sexual dysfunction, and what significance does the sexual problem have in the relationship? (see p. 47); How does the couple's self-reinforcement mechanism work? (see p. 57).

The therapists should thus first identify negative experiences in both partners' learning history so they can reconstruct and understand the development of sexual problems. In this context it may help to begin with the "symptomatic partner's" learning history. It is in any case necessary to discuss the "nondysfunctional" partner's disadvantageous experiences and background too.

The therapists then shift attention to the development of the relationship and show how both partners' previous experiences impeded them in establishing satisfying sexuality in their relationship. The therapists also ask specifically about what kind of efforts the patients have made to overcome their sexual difficulties, and then therapists and patients discuss why they did not succeed. The therapists then describe how the self-reinforcement mechanism works in this situation: once sexual problems have arisen in a relationship—for whatever reasons, inexperience, fear, misinformation, and so on—the partners try to force sexual arousal or sexual functioning at any price. For example, the "nondysfunctional" partner fusses over the "dysfunctional" partner, thus naturally putting him or her under pressure. Performance demands and anticipation fears, however, reduce the likelihood of sexual arousal, just as the more one tries to fall asleep the more difficult it becomes; it cannot be willed. Both partners slip into a spectator role and an anticipatory fear that prevent any kind of playful approach to sexuality, any spontaneity and openness. Under such circumstances sexuality can neither "function" nor be pleasurable. The partners continually experience failure, which can lead to one or both of them ultimately resigning and giving up attempts altogether. From this point of view it becomes clear that the problem is not malevolence or hostility, but rather helplessness, anxiety, and disappointment. It then becomes obvious that the partners are overtaxed by the task of freeing themselves from this vicious circle of failure anticipation, performance demands, tension, and failure. The task of therapy is to make this clear. Because both partners are caught up in this problem and both assist in sustaining it, both must take an active part in therapy.

The therapists should also point out the positive aspects of the relationship, for example, that despite their sexual difficulties the partners are still affectionate with each other, that they can trust each other, or that they have interests in common. Besides, their decision to enter therapy together is a sign that both are willing to invest effort in the relationship. If previous therapy or attempts at self-help have had a certain amount of success, this should be used to illustrate the possibility of modifying relationships. The therapists reassure the patients further by pointing out that under the sociocultural conditions of our society a great many people are distressed by sexual difficulties and that this is not a purely personal failure.

The therapists then go on to explain the concept and aims of therapy: the partners have, as it were, learned their sexual difficulties, but that means they can also unlearn them again. This is why they should enter on new sexual experiences and repeat the sexual learning process, but this time under more favorable circumstances. The patients will first engage in experiences of tenderness, body touching, caressing, and closeness and learn to be confident, relaxed, and playful with one another in this important area of sexuality. This is instigated by the therapists suggesting that the patients do specific caressing exercises at home. Sexual arousal and coitus are at first prohibited and are reintroduced only when the patients have become more confident of themselves. The entire learning process is divided into small steps. This facilitates identifying and working through emerging difficulties, and it reduces the risk of failure and disappointment while it paves the way to positive experiences.

There is no one pattern of sexuality that works for all couples in terms of techniques or frequency and duration of sexual encounters. It is therefore important that both partners become more aware of their own wishes and desires in the course of therapy and learn to talk about them with each other. This is the only way they can build up a sexual relationship satisfying for both.

At this point therapists can mention the additional interventions described in the section on bodily self-awareness (see p. 311) if information has emerged in history-taking which indicates that it might be useful, for example, that one or both partners have no experience in masturbation. In cases of vaginismus the round-table session is also used to explain and illustrate the mechanism of this dysfunction. Therapists then also point out that there are corresponding additional exercises with dilators (p. 318).

Following the discussion of history-taking findings, instructions for caressing I are usually given (see p. 258).

TRANSCRIPT

COUPLE 39:   Both partners are in their mid-thirties and are office-workers. They have been married for nine years and have no children. Since first having intercourse the husband has had pronounced premature ejaculation and in the last few years increasing erectile difficulties as well. His wife has never had an orgasm in coitus but does reach orgasm during petting. She behaves with pronounced avoidance toward sexuality and reluctantly endures intercourse "if I really have to." The couple was assigned to long-term therapy with one male therapist.

M.Th.: Has anything new come up or is there anything to add to our last session?

Man: No, not really.

M.Th.: Well, what we want to do today is to look back over what you told me in the interviews so we can understand your problem better. We have a kind of basic belief here, which is that if a sexual problem arises in a relationship there is no such thing as a partner without difficulties, that sexual difficulties are something that involves two people and can only be solved by both of them. And I think you are actually a good example of this. You can see that in a number of ways. [To the man] Initially you said your problem was : "I ejaculate prematurely." And that certainly seems to be your problem since it happened with other women as well. But premature ejaculation is usually a sign of two things. First, fairly strong arousability; well, you could say, strong rather than weak sexual potency. And the second thing is uncertainty toward women. You even described this uncertainty yourself. You said that you had been shy of making contact with women. And the fantasies you described, which depicted a high degree of aggression toward women, at least until recently, are basically a sign of your uncertainty toward women.

I can't say exactly how the uncertainty came about; and it's not that important. But I do think that the abrupt break in the relationship to your father has something to do with it. I mean, in the middle of puberty, when your male identity and ideals about how to behave as a proper male were developing.

Man: Well, really it was just that I practically only lived with my father for five years because he was a prisoner of war until I was eight. When he died I was about thirteen.

M.Th.: As you said he was really a very important person for you. In any case you went through decisive years of your life without a key male person. Yes, I think this uncertainty was the reason why you found it more difficult than other men at the start of your sex life to learn what every man has to learn and what every man finds difficult at first—to control his ejaculation. To ration stimulation and so amplify your *and* your partner's pleasure. And once the problem is there it very quickly turns into a kind of vicious circle. Then comes the fear that it won't work again and that it might start too early. And added to that is the fear of failing. That's something that actually causes the failure, I mean the additional tension it produces. Of course this is all joined by your partner's disappointment and her sexual difficulties, which amplify this sense of failure. You had the feeling: if my wife doesn't want to make love to me then it's because I don't function properly.

And then recently you've been depressed by the erection problems. That too can at first be explained by your being constantly disappointed.

[To the woman] I think what plays an important part is your growing lack of desire, which is certainly due in part to the premature ejaculations but which, of course, also affects your husband as well. And it's obvious, if you don't feel like sex then you do it without enthusiasm. That's how you described it and, after all, it's no secret that you do it for your husband's sake. And I think you sometimes told yourself, Mr.————: "you can go ahead today, just get it over quickly, before she changes her mind." If you don't feel like it, it's bound be like that. You can't get a response from a partner who feels no desire. And that's an important part of sexual arousal.

[*To the woman*] So your lack of desire certainly has something to do with his premature ejaculation; which in turn has an effect on your husband. And then this erection problem came up and got distinctly worse in the last few years. That shows you how closely sexual reactions and counterreactions are linked, it's a reciprocal reaction. Does that make sense to you?

Woman: Yes, I already knew that really.

M.Th.: [*To the husband*] Up till now we've talked more about you and your problem.

[*To the woman*] But we briefly handled your problem, too. You also said you had never had an orgasm in intercourse yet. But I don't think that's your real problem because orgasm isn't a problem when you masturbate or when you two pet.

Woman: Hmm.

M.Th.: I think your problem is the fact that you don't feel any desire. And then that might have something to do with your simply finding it diffi-cult to accept or put up with closeness or intimacy, or tenderness, or affection.

Woman: Yes, that's one part of it and the other is that I find it hard to aban-don myself, let's say.

M.Th.: To let yourself go.

Woman: It's something I generally just don't do. I never let myself go, really. Always keep a stiff upper lip. And of course that has a strong effect.

M.Th.: Yes, that's true.

Woman: I think that's my main problem. Because if you can get it together and learn to find pleasure in it, then everything else probably falls into place.

M.Th.: Yes, that's true; an important point. But again, I think it proves that you influence each other. You probably had this problem before you got mar-ried. But your husband's premature ejaculation made it easier for you . . .

Woman: . . . to beat a retreat.

M.Th.: . . . to beat a retreat, which you were bound to do anyway in view of your difficulty in letting yourself go, of letting go control, of abandoning yourself, as you say.

Woman: Which always gets difficult in long relationships. In short relation-ships there's, you know, still that kind of curiosity and a feeling of discov-ery. I found that interesting and it was fun. But when it wears off . . . you already know how the other is going to react, what he likes and what he doesn't like. And then it all gradually faded away.

M.Th.: We ought to think about what made you react like that. I could imag-ine that your shifting relationships to key figures in your childhood played a part. You never had constant affection from somebody. In the first three years of your life, and later too, you were pretty much handed around. Your mother died early, your father a little later. And you never really experienced any relationship you could rely on. And if you were, so to speak, weened on this feeling early on, then it's likely that the deeper or more intimate a relationship threatens to become, the more you withdraw. Because somehow you've learned from experience that you can't really rely on relationships after all. Up till now it's always ended in disappointment; why shouldn't it again? I think it's more important to realize that this lack of desire definitely can't be attributed to your husband's premature ejaculations alone.

Well, that's the problem you came with. [*To the man*] The whole thing distresses you. You say you would like to have sex more often; above all that you'd like to have sex without any problems, that satisfies you more.

[*To the woman*] What you're really saying is: I've adapted myself well to the situation; I don't really need sexuality. On the contrary, the way we live together suits me; it exactly suits my wish for a little distance, my wish not to have to let myself go, for detachment as opposed to too much intimacy. And that means your motives and wishes to change something . . .

Woman: . . . are a bit thin.

M.Th.: . . . are thin. You definitely are motivated but only with a view to your husband. He should have it better. You don't say: *I* would like to be better off; but you say, it can't go on like this and we will have to make a change, for rational reasons. But in actual fact you could go on living like this. And that makes me skeptical about what we're doing now, although I'm perfectly aware of the dilemma. We can't simply say: have the wish to change yourself, because if it isn't there, then it just isn't. Besides, it's understandable that it isn't there seeing as you don't miss anything. But the problem now is that the sexual difficulties can only be alleviated if that is what both of you really want. Sexuality isn't only something where one . . .

Man: A reciprocal effect.

M.Th.: . . . where just one person gets involved, as the other's helper or, so so speak, as a dummy for the other. And I'm not sure how we should handle the problem.

Woman: Well, I haven't got much of an idea at all how you go about it in general. Besides, I'm skeptical whether one can learn to feel desire.

M.Th.: But I think the problem is somewhat different, that is, you don't have the *desire* to feel desire. Do you see what I mean?

Woman: Yes, but basically that's perfectly natural; if you've never experienced anything pleasant, how are you to know what's pleasant, just how?

M.Th.: I know exactly what you mean. Of course, I don't think it's something you can switch on like a light. And your husband and I won't be able to help you either. It's your responsibility. But then I'd like to put the problem in a different light. Well, personally, I feel rather unhappy.

Woman: Just a moment, there's something else I'd like to say about that.

M.Th.: Yes.

Woman: You said that's a problem you and my husband simply can't help me with, it's all up to me.

M.Th.: Yes.

Woman: I don't think I always lacked the will. So I ask myself, how I'm supposed to cope with it alone. If I could, then theoretically I would have done so already, wouldn't I?

M.Th.: I think you've understood me. I don't mean willing to make love to your husband. I mean the willingness that comes before that. Whether you're willing to change anything. Everything else that happens afterward, sexual desire or sexual demands, is something you'll just have to find out. But you know, I feel personally uneasy about it all: why should I try and palm something off onto you that you don't really want. You yourself feel quite content with things as they are.

Woman: Me personally. If I lived alone I would think, why change anything. There's nothing forcing me to change anything. Anyhow, my husband's someone I can live with quite well generally, and basically I want to go on living with him. But we can't go on forever with these difficulties, I guess; there must be some way we can find a compromise, come to an agreement. You might say, I would profit from it, too.

M.Th.: How?

Woman: How? Well, since we've found out that it can't go on like this, we'll have to think about what we're going to do. And no doubt what will happen is that we'll say, well, it's all very nice but this thing just won't work, so we'll have to separate somehow, and both of us will try it out with another partner; which means except me, probably, because that's just the way it's going to end up. My husband might try again with someone else. That would be the logical thing to do. But I don't want to at the moment because somehow I still believe that we could get a grip again. As far as I'm concerned there's nothing missing, but I do have very strong guilt feelings because I always feel the pressure, the demand that I really should feel something. That's not my own motivation, but I really feel the pressure.

M.Th.: I believe you. But the question nevertheless remains, why should you do something simply for guilt reasons.

Woman: Because the relationship to my husband matters to me. Not sexually at the moment, but on the friendship level.

M.Th.: Isn't is possible to keep the relationship going without sexuality? Does sexuality absolutely always have to play a part?

Woman: Well, I could keep it going, probably, but my husband couldn't.

M.Th.: You protest, Mr.———.

Man: Well, not really protesting. Sure one's old-fashioned, but somehow sex is a part of the whole thing. She's a person I like, I desire, or whatever. To whom I feel attached. Somehow I feel it leaves a large gap.

M.Th.: Hmm, yes, but how do you see the problem that your wife only wants to make a change for your sake?

Man: Well, you know, that's been my problem actually for a long time now, or our problem. Besides, my wife has told me so often enough, quite clear-

253

ly; she really only does it for my sake. And originally she felt she had been dragged here. And the whole time I just felt a bit stupid claiming the right to sort of force her into some happiness or other I had thought up.

M.Th.: Perhaps you're about to face up to the agonizing, painful fact that sex just can't work between the two of you. Or let's say, a sexual relationship which both find important and satisfying.

Woman: Well, up till now I just haven't accepted that it can't be managed. But I'm not convinced yet. And until I am, I would say we should somehow try and find a way.

Man: You know, what I really feel is that somewhere there's a Gordian knot that's ultimately the cause of my difficulties.

M.Th.: Hmm. Although I think your view is too one-sided. If there was a pill you could take immediately enabling you to control your ejaculation for as long as you want, it wouldn't change the sexual situation between you, I guess.

Woman: [To husband] Look, if it was that easy, you must have had the idea years ago of looking for a girl friend.

Man: Yes, sure, the *idea.*

Woman: I know, you tried it once, but it didn't work out. I just couldn't help feeling a certain malicious joy.

M.Th.: Hmm.

Woman: I hope you won't be angry at me, but basically you should have followed that up far more intensely. But you didn't. Which could be because you were never sure how it was going to turn out and whether you would have to face up to exactly the same experience of failure. If you just enjoyed yourself a bit now and then on the side, I'm quite certain it would change your feelings for me.

Man: I'm not so sure of that.

M.Th.: I don't quite understand; let me put it in the form of a question. Supposing you both signed an agreement to go on living together, but leaving sexuality out of it, and your husband could start a sexual relationship with a girl friend?

Woman: You know, in theory it's all well. But it does have consequences. And you can't put it into practice.

M.Th.: So you don't think that's a practical way out.

Woman: No, it's like blinders, or what should I call it; lying to your own face, or whatever.

M.Th.: No, but I thought you were suggesting the girl friend thing. Perhaps your sexual problem is a part, certainly not all, but a part of what holds your marriage together. Grotesque as it may sound, your sexual problems keep you together.

Woman: Yes, because they complement each other.

M.Th.: Exactly.

Man: But, I'd be afraid of starting a sexual relationship with a woman.

M.Th.: Besides, your wife is someone who accepts your sexual problem. She wants to live with you all the same. You don't need to explain to her that there are problems, with her you don't need to be ashamed of the problem. [To the woman] But then again, you feel the same way.

Therapeutic Procedure

Woman: Because it suits me fine. If you were a potent type I would be left high and dry.

Man: Because you always said you beat a retreat when you feel I am sexually demanding.

Woman: In my opinion you've mentioned something that's important for me, or important in my behavior. As long as I am the one who takes the initiative, things work out even better. As soon as I'm the more inferior of us two, let's say the one who is supposed to or who has to let herself be conquered, it's pretty awful. Generally I'm no good at submission. And I don't like being dependent on anybody or anything at all. In fact I don't usually make myself dependent on anything. That includes, of course, intense relationships to other people, which also create a certain dependency; so we're back to the point, aren't we, of this being a bit reserved and withdrawing a little.

M.Th.: You want to be responsible for yourself, independent, would rather be the conquering partner . . . than . . .

Woman: Yes, and you know our relationship, now that I think about it, was at least more or less O.K. I would say, as long as I had still not had this feeling.

Man: But then I play a part, too; when the first signs of retreat came, it was very disappointing because I didn't really realize that my wife was withdrawing more and more; so it gradually turned out that I was insisting. But then I couldn't understand the world any longer.

Woman: Well, the whole thing developed without our being aware of it. It gradually becomes routine and suddenly the situation is there.

M.Th.: Yes, but what if one reversed the process? [*To the woman*] I'm not sure whether there isn't something threatening about that for you. Or perhaps you both see things differently. What your husband sees is that he would be rid of a nuisance and be more self-confident and could at last have sex; while you probably feel you'll be more harassed, perhaps you'll have to do things again you don't want to, then he'll be permanently too close for you, perhaps you'll become more dependent on him. It could be that your ambivalent motivation has a lot to do with the fact that you do experience satisfying sexual relationships as threatening, at first.

Woman: Threatening insofar as it's all so uncertain for me. Rationally speaking, I do see that it's a two-way deal and that I could profit from it. The main thing is that something's left over for me. That's how I'd see it, and I don't see why I should mince words, that sounds egotistical . . .

M.Th.: No, that sounds great, I think it's the only way we'll get any further.

Woman: Well, there's no point in always beating about the bush, is there?

M.Th.: And sexuality *is* threatening. Let's just imagine for a moment you have a sexual relationship free of problems; the relationship would look quite different, wouldn't it?

Woman: Hmm, and then the positions have to be defined again first.

M.Th.: Or you feel strong enough to cope with your husband's strength. By strength I mean being free of sexual symptoms: that's a strong position, too. He's always the one who can't get it together, who thought the problem was mainly his, who says, I don't really function properly as a man: I always ejaculate prematurely, nothing works out, my penis goes limp when I want to make love to my wife. Being motivated to clear up the problem in your case *also* means: am I strong enough to accept such a strong partner at my side without being afraid.

Woman: Yes, I'm not as strong as that. Basically I'm not like how I'd like to be.

Man: And that's why I'm not allowed to be strong.

M.Th.:   . . . so you just say, I can allow him to be a little stronger and myself a little weaker.

Woman: I would say that's it. Because I'm perfectly aware that it's not something which only involves sex: it hinders me in other areas, too. Well, for example, what just comes to mind: I find it difficult to put up with criticism. And there are few people who can criticize me and get away with it.

Man: I can't, for one.

Woman: Yes, you can. If it's close acquaintances or people who I know are fond of me, I can put up with it far better. Other people criticize me too, of course, and I get over it. But I find it much more difficult.

M.Th.:   Hmm.

Woman: If you criticize me in some way or other . . .

Man: Then I have to be very careful when I do.

M.Th.:   And I think that in many respects you have an incredible respect for your wife.

Man: Absolutely.

M.Th.:   And tend sometimes to be shy.

Man: Yes, I don't want to hurt her consciously or intentionally, either.

M.Th.:   But it's not a question of hurting.

Man: But . . .

M.Th.:   But of looking after your own interests.

Man: Although my criticism wasn't meant to hurt, on the contrary, it was meant to help, but the reaction was always different.

Woman: Well, you're right in that respect. I must say, I really had got used to shutting off completely when something didn't suit me.

Man: Without me knowing why.

Woman: And that was a kind of mechanism that had somehow worked its way in and then went on working on its own. I literally closed up and then not a whisper.

Man: Sometimes for a whole week.

Woman: Then I tried to make my husband feel real bad and think: see, now you've annoyed her and it's your fault she's in such a bad mood now.

Man: Yes, it was a thing in between anger and "now what have you done." Then I tried to find out what it was. There was no way. I mean, no explanation to be found and then afterward I was angry: goddam it, you just can't get anywhere near her. It's like a glass cage all around her, and you bounce off; there was nothing I could do. And this feeling she wouldn't let me near her is there in our sexuality, too.

Woman: Perhaps this retreat is a kind of tendency to punish, you haven't behaved yourself . . .

M.Th.:   . . . so I'm not going to talk to you.

Man: My personal feeling about our marriage after all these ups and downs is, now the time has come when this risky business of sex can be tackled as well.

M.Th.:   Hmm.

Man: You know, that's simply a subjective feeling.

M.Th.:   Yes, well, I'm just as skeptical as before. But if you want, I can try and put you on the right track to rearrange your sexuality. Whether or how you'll manage or whether it . . .

Woman: Of course, we know there's no guarantee.

M.Th.:   For the most part it's up to you what you make of it. Therapy can only help you help yourself. But what you can do is to discuss the following question, because I'd like to come back to it again. You should both imagine how your relationship, your entire relationship would change or could change if the sexual symptoms were gone.

Woman: Were removed?

M.Th.:   Were removed. [*To the man*] So if you could control your ejaculation, the erection would come when you need it, [*To the woman*] and if you could feel the desire to make love to your husband. What would happen if you made love twice a week, if both of you found it satisfying and pleasant, and it became important to both of you to make love to each other. I would think about that and talk it over with each other. And we can talk about it next time. Do you understand what I mean?

Woman: Sure

Man: Yes.[4]

Caressing I

AIMS

This sequence is intended to provide partners with the opportunity to relinquish their one-sided orientation on sexual arousal and sexual "functioning," in coitus and orgasm as well. Experiences with body contact and nongenital caressing are emphasized, enabling partners to perceive and accept their own feelings and body reactions—pleasant or unpleasant—step by step. By concentrating on themselves the partners are meant to become more aware of their own needs and wishes. They can slowly learn to accept them, to talk to one another about them, and to come to terms with differing wishes and experiences. The standards they should apply are their own personal experiences, although there can be no "right" or "wrong." Each of the partners should slowly come to realize that he or she alone is responsible for the satisfaction of his or her needs and should come to believe the other feels the same way so they can develop a trustful and relaxed manner of handling each other.

PROCEDURE

After discussing histories, the therapists explain the behavioral instructions for caressing I. The instructions should include the following points:

Prohibition of coitus. The patients are asked not to attempt or perform coitus until further notice; the same applies at first for genital petting to induce sexual arousal. There are two reasons for this restriction, which the therapists explain: (1). Coitus and genital petting have been associated with disappointment and fear of failure for some time; renunciation of coitus and petting allows the partners to experience tenderness free of fear, without tension or self-consciousness. (2) The previous one-sided orientation on genital stimulation and coitus led to a decrease in the body's sensibility; by dispensing with coitus the partners can learn to enjoy nongenital caressing again.

The therapists try and make the reasons clear to the partners. If one or both of the partners raises some objection to coital prohibition, the therapists point out that it will be helpful to expose themselves first to the experiences before any difficulties can be properly discussed. (For the duration of coital prohibition, see table M.1.)

Exercises. The therapists then describe when and how the partners should begin engaging in these new experiences. The partners should allow thirty to sixty minutes for each other twice before the next ses-

TABLE M.1
Timing of Therapy Sequences

Therapy Sequence	Number of Sessions			
	Minimum		Maximum	
	Per Sequence	Total (Cumulative)	Per Sequence	Total (Cumulative)
Caressing I	2	2	8	8
Caressing II	1	3	4	12
Explorative genital caressing	3	6	5	17
Stimulative caressing and playing with arousal	3	9	9	26
Intromission	2	11	8	34
Coitus with explorative and stimulative movements	3	14	6	40
Coitus in other positions	1	15	5	45

sion. It is important that they are not under time pressure either immediately before or afterward from plans or appointments and that they have peace and quiet. They should get completely undressed and caress each other lying down. The room should be warm and not so dark as to prevent the partners from seeing each other's bodies.

When caressing the partners change roles every five minutes: the "active" (caressing) partner changing with the "passive" (receiving). The passive partner starts by lying face down. The active partner kneels or lies down at his or her side. He or she caresses the head, neck, shoulders, arms, hands, back, buttocks, legs, and feet, that is, the whole body. Different ways of caressing can be tried, for example, with the finger tips, the whole hand, the mouth, cheek, forearm, or hair, gently or vigorously, by massaging or kneading.

The passive partner tries to open up to and experience all the sensations and feelings while being caressed. It is not a question of passively "accepting" but of actively receiving any sensations, whether pleasant or unpleasant. What matters most is that the partners learn to relax and feel comfortable during caressing. At this stage arousal, erection, and orgasm should play no part at all. The reason given is that the partners can only break away from the spectator role and performance demands if they can forget about sexual functioning while caressing. It will help them if they ignore breasts and genitals for the time being.

The partners assume the passive role and the active role three times each. The second time the passive partner lies on his or her back and is caressed over the whole body from the front, except for the genitals and the woman's breasts. If the man's nipples are very sensitive they too should be avoided when caressing. The third time the passive partner lies on his or her back again. The therapists suggest who should be active first (usually the partner with the dysfunction); they can discuss their decision with the partners.

The partners should inform each other verbally and nonverbally what they find pleasant, what irritates them, and what should be done differently. The passive partner can do this by leading the active partner's hand to the parts of the body that he or she wants to be caressed, or away from those that spark off unpleasant sensations at the moment. He or she can then also show the pressure and rhythm desired. But the partners should also be encouraged to talk about their feelings and sensations.

Basic rules of partner interaction. The therapists explain the two basic rules of therapy:

1. At this stage of therapy (as in all others) the partner should caress

only for as long as they enjoy it or at least do not find it unpleasant, and no longer. If caressing becomes unpleasant they should tell their partner so, make him or her do it differently, change roles at the right moment, or, if it continues to be unpleasant, should discontinue and postpone caressing. There are two reasons for this rule: sticking through unpleasant experiences does not help the partners get any further but only consolidates the old experiences and disappointments. Second, the partners can learn to come to terms with differing sexual wishes by learning to express displeasure without the fear of hurting their partner and to put up with the disappointment that results from a "refusal."

2. While caressing the partners should at first follow their own feelings and not feel responsible for the other's reactions; they should be deliberately self-centered and "egoistic." As long as their partner does not say otherwise, they should assume that he or she finds the caressing pleasant. This self-centeredness amplifies perception of the partner's own sensations and relieves him or her of superfluous considerateness and responsibility.

General application of sexual restrictions. The partners should not do anything they are not supposed to do in exercises (for example, genital touching) at any other time. The reason given for this additional restriction is that the partners would be unable to get fully involved in exercises if they afterward exchanged caresses they find more stimulating at the moment but which are still cathected by anxiety. The restrictions do not apply, however, to kissing.

Discussion of experiences in the next session. The therapists tell the partners that their experiences with caressing at home will be discussed in the next session (round-table). The therapists do not expect "success statistics": all experiences, whether pleasant or unpleasant, are equally important; the partners should simply wait and see what happens. "Unpleasant" experiences are often the key to recognizing and working through problems and their causes. They are therefore an important component of the whole therapy program.

TRANSCRIPT

COUPLE 34:   The man is suffering from secondary erectile disturbances. The couple was described earlier (p. 190). The partners were assigned to intensive therapy.

M.Th.:   We'd like to suggest that you try experiencing something new together, without your going further than sharing a certain tenderness. Which means what we want you to achieve is to treat each other more tenderly

and less timidly in sex. To make that easier we want to exclude intercourse, orgasm, a stiff penis, and ejaculation for the moment. Which is
why you will have to stop having or attempting intercourse for the time
being.

Instead we would suggest something easier first. That is, we suggest you
take between a half and one hour twice before the next session, when
your daughter is in bed or at the kindergarten and you have peace and
quiet, and take off your clothes and lie down on the bed, a couch, or on
the carpet; wherever it feels nice and relatively warm, I mean, so you lie
naked without covering yourselves.

F.Th.:   ... nice for both of you. You'll have to talk about that; for example, if
one of you prefers a warm room and the other less heat, then you'll have
to try and find a place that suits you both.

Man: Yes, my wife likes more warmth than I do.

M.Th.:   Well, you'll have to chose a temperature in between. Then you, Mr.
————, simply lie down on your back and keep your eyes open or closed,
as you wish.[5] Stretch your legs and arms out. And you, Mrs.————, caress
your husband: his face, shoulders, arms, chest, stomach, legs, knees, feet,
anywhere—but not his penis or testicles, that comes later. You, Mr.————,
just wait and see what happens, try to relax, to feel at ease. But if any
negative feelings well up, just let them; it all has to come out, the things
that happen inside you, the reactions that come. And then after about five
minutes you change around. [To the woman] Then you lie down, and try to
relax. [To the man] And you caress your wife: her face, shoulders, arms and
legs, stomach, but not her breasts or genitals. After about five minutes,
without looking at your watch, you change around again. [To the man]
Then you're the passive one again. [To the woman] And you caress your
husband, with him lying on his stomach. [To the man] After that it's your
wife's turn to lie on her stomach. Then back to the beginning again until
both of you have been active and passive three times. The whole thing
lasts between half and three-quarters of an hour. It can last longer, that
doesn't matter. As I said, the point isn't so much getting sexually aroused,
having a stiff penis or an orgasm, but really to try and caress each other
freely again.

Man: Yes, that's clear.

M.Th.:   If it doesn't work right away, no matter; as long as you give it a try
and see how you feel, that's the important thing.

F.Th.:   And you can try all kinds of caressing. With your finger tips or hand,
the balls of your thumb very gently, by kneading or massaging, or with
your mouth. So you can try out all the different things and both of you
can see what you find more pleasant and what you don't like so much. It's
very important to be aware of your feelings because next time we want to
talk about it. Another important thing is to remember what you didn't like
so you can tell us your negative feelings and we can talk about them.

Man: Yes, O.K.

M.Th.:   We don't expect you to say it was a great success. Any negative experiences you may have or anything you find hard to do is just as important
in therapy as the positive aspects. And then there's a basic rule you should

know about that applies to everything we're going to do in the following sessions. If one of you feels anything is unpleasant, then it's not only your right . . .

F.Th.: . . . but your duty, too . . .

M.Th.: . . . to interrupt it. For example, if you feel uneasy or if it becomes too awful . . .

Man: . . . really repulsive . . .

M.Th.: . . . for example, or if you feel more inclined to jump out of bed, then you should say "no, look let's stop there and try it again tomorrow or later." Sticking through negative experiences to the end won't get you anywhere. And at the same time it's a good opportunity to learn to say "no," and for the other to learn to accept the "no."

F.Th.: Or then again, if you think of something else you would like to do instead, tell your partner.

M.Th.: That wouldn't be bad, either.

F.Th.: [*To the man*] You would probably find that more difficult than your wife. [*To the woman*] You already said you had once tried to talk about how you felt at the time and what you liked. And that you always waited a bit for your husband to say what he liked so you could be more certain of doing the right thing. [*To the man*] So don't expect to find it easy, it can be quite difficult, but try in any case.

Man: Yes, I'm aware of that.

M.Th.: Perhaps just one more thing: we would ask you not to do anything you are not supposed to do during exercises at any other time either. For example, you shouldn't say, "O.K., now we've done the exercise we can really get down to it," petting or whatever. The reason is to relieve you of the pressure of having to be aroused or get an erection; because then you can concentrate on this kind of caressing.

F.Th.: I'm not sure whether we already said it's important that you can see each other. That means you shouldn't lie under the sheets. And when you do it in the evening, turn the light on. How would you feel then?

Man: Well, we'll have to see. I'll just wait and see what happens.

Woman: Actually I feel quite confident. I think it could work like that.

Man: Sure, we don't expect miracles. . . . We'll just wait and see.

F.Th.: No, that would be dangerous if you expected miracles. Just see what comes of it. O.K., we meet again on the————.

DISCUSSION OF EXPERIENCES

The therapists discuss the partners' experiences with caressing. They first try to form an exact picture of how caressing went and the reactions to it. They leave the partners plenty of time to express themselves and so start the discussion with broadly formulated, unspecific questions (for example, "How was it?" or "Tell us simply what you did"). In the course of the discussion the therapists then focus on specific aspects of the exercise and the various experiences the partners have had (frequency of caressing; time of day; which partner initiates caressing; various reactions to passivity and activity, back and stomach position, different ways of caressing; preferences and dislikes; communication about feelings and wishes; signals used for ending or discontinuing caressing; feelings after caressing and so forth). The therapists help the partners to become aware of their reactions and move them beyond such statements as ("We did exactly what you told us to," or "It was very pleasant.")

By listening patiently and asking supportive questions, the therapists try to create an atmosphere that makes it easier for the partners to talk freely and openly about their sexuality. This is the first important step in developing differentiated and unreserved communication about sexuality between the partners. These discussions can also assist in releasing sexuality from the context of secrecy, shame, and anxiety and placing it in a new context of openness and affirmation. This can encourage patients to change their attitudes by achieving a greater acceptance of their sexuality.

The therapists give both partners equal opportunity to talk about their experiences. They should ensure that each speaks for himself and not for the other. This prevents one of the partners assuming a particular role (for example, "the dominant speaker," "the cotherapist," "the patient"). Each partner can thus recognize his or her share in the problem and accept that therapy aims at a change in both partners.

The partners often experience caressing as pleasant quite soon and feel comfortable and relaxed. The therapists should reinforce this response. They reemphasize how important it is to feel at ease and relaxed when sharing tenderness and sexuality. If the partners experience caressing as particularly pleasant, the therapists should point out that they cannot always expect their experiences to be as pleasant, that they will also have less satisfying experiences. It is important for them to learn to accept and tolerate these fluctuations and not to set up a new performance ideal. Most partners will at first report negative or ambivalent experiences. The therapists should not immediately begin analyzing these difficulties but should show understanding and emphasize that the partners need time and patience after all the years of disappointment and difficulties. The therapists try to explain that difficulties can also involve useful experiences: going through difficulties helps the partners to become more aware of their problems, anxieties, and conflicts; the partners can learn to handle their problems and solve them (for example, differing sexual wishes).

COUPLE 40: The man is thirty-six years old, a factory worker, and is now in his second marriage; the woman is thirty-eight years old, a saleswoman, and is now married for the third time. They have been married for two years. The man complains that he is only partially erect in intercourse and that he ejaculates immediately after intromission. This has always been the case and was the reason his first marriage failed. The woman has orgasmic difficulties but attributes them to her husband's premature ejaculation; in previous relationships she had experienced orgasms. The couple underwent intensive therapy.

M.Th.: Can you tell us what you did together? How often and what you did?

Man: Well, just as you told us; I started by caressing my wife for the first five minutes, you know, and then we went on in turns until the half hour was up. While we were caressing neither of us actually said it was unpleasant or "that irritates me." So generally it was very pleasant.

M.Th.: Is that your overall impression when you say it was very pleasant?

Man: Yes.

M.Th.: And it was like that both times?

Man: Yes.

M.Th.: You did the exercises yesterday afternoon and this morning?

Man: And this morning.

F.Th.: [To the woman] Was it the same for you?

Woman: Yes. I slept really well, and it was very pleasant, relaxing. As he said, he started with me for five minutes, then taking turns every five minutes; he did it very nicely. This morning too.

M.Th.: That's an extremely pleasing overall impression.

Woman: Yes, although I haven't slept at all well in the last two years, I fell asleep quite quickly.

M.Th.: When you say it was pleasant, it sounds to me as if you're surprised it was.

Woman: Yes, it was really good.

Man: And I tried touching my wife's skin with my mouth.

F.Th.: Caressing with your mouth, yes.

Man: And then she said she felt it getting moist down there, you know.

M.Th.: Hmm, that pleased you, didn't it?

Man: Yes.

M.Th.: Which isn't really important at the moment. That's just a reaction that happens quite incidentally, which you noticed perhaps because somehow you had been waiting for it. But that's unimportant now. You should just caress and forget you have genitals. Just look and see what your whole body experiences. But perhaps we could go through everything step by step. We might find some points you could improve on. When you started caressing your wife, what did you do?

Man: Well, I did circular movements with my fingers, from bottom to top and back again, over her arms and back again; and then I went on with

264

the same pattern. Part of the time I just used one hand, you know. Later both hands. Always these circular movements, from the sides inward and then upward.

F.Th.: Yes, [*To the woman*] and how did you like it?

Woman: Um, first it tickled, but then afterward I quickly got used to it. It only took seconds and then it was a nice, prickling sensation.

M.Th.: It prickled, which means it was pleasant?

Woman: Yes, um, yes. No, it wasn't an unpleasant tickling. I noticed that I had to start laughing.

F.Th.: A really pleasant excitement. What happened next?

Man: Well, then my wife did the same to me and then we did it on our backs.

F.Th.: What were your movements? Did you do it like your husband or differently?

Woman: I just caressed with one hand.

F.Th.: Yes, and you started on his neck?

Woman: Yes, shoulders, and arms and here at the sides. First I noticed he got goose pimples.

Man: But only a few seconds and then it was really pleasant.

Woman: And after that I went in circles and back again. I noticed it was sort of relaxing, too.

F.Th.: So you noticed he was getting softer and calmer, looser.

Woman: Uh, yes.

F.Th.: My feeling is that it did you good to feel how your husband reacted.

Woman: Yes, I was glad when I noticed that he let his hair down.

F.Th.: That you could help him relax.

Woman: Yeah.

Man: I liked it everywhere really. But I like it most up here round my head.

F.Th.: In the neck area?

Man: The neck area or here as well, on my shoulders and back, and then down my legs.

M.Th.: And you liked it least on your chest?

Man: I liked it all right, but not like the other places.

F.Th.: You feel you're more sensitive on other parts of your body, it's nicer there.

Man: Yes, nicer.

F.Th.: What was it like at your sides?

Man: Well, at the sides it was really nice, too. Under my feet it tickles me right away. But only if it's the fingers. When she rubs with the palm it's really pleasant.

M.Th.: It only tickles you if something surprising happens, or she does just a small movement. But if you do it with yourself then it's different. You can't really tickle yourself.

Man: No.

M.Th.: That means, one is only ticklish under certain circumstances.

Woman: Take my daughter, she does it the same way, holds her arm up and is surprised she doesn't have to laugh; and then she tries to laugh artificially. I noticed the other day.

M.Th.: Yes, if you know what's coming and realize that the other person doesn't want to annoy you somehow, then you're not ticklish at all.

F.Th.: [*To the woman*] And were there places where it was particularly nice for you?

Woman: Yes, here, my stomach, up here, that was very pleasant. Everything else was the same. Oh yes, here, this area, that was very nice too, I must say; that was more exciting than up here on my shoulder.

F.Th.: You suddenly noticed, oh, I'm really sensitive there, it's nice to be caressed there.

Woman: Yes, exactly.

M.Th.: What was it like on your buttocks?

Woman: That was fine, too.

M.Th.: You forgot to mention that in your description earlier, so I thought perhaps you had left them out altogether.

Woman: No, no, we caressed there as well and that was just as enjoyable.

Man: Yes, she did. I liked it, too. Great.

F.Th.: And your wife's face, did you caress her there?

Man: Only with the inside of my finger tips; sometimes I placed my whole hand like this on her cheek. And went round back here.

F.Th.: So you felt your way around the contours.

Man: Yes, and followed the lines with my finger.

F.Th.: [*To the woman*] And how did you find that?

Woman: Well, it was very pleasant. I also noticed I got tired, really relaxed; I really felt it.

M.Th.: Were there any differences in the way you caressed each other? You both described it the same way, both of you used circular movements on the back; you tended to use only one hand and you used both hands, moving in circles. Or did it vary, I mean, sometimes a little more firmly.

Woman: Yes, I did; you too.

Man: When I caressed, I did it more strongly as well and then she said, no, not too vigorously.

M.Th.: Yes, you prefer it more gentle.

Man: Like just putting my hand on her skin and then starting to caress.

Woman: Yeah.

M.Th.: Almost like gliding over the surface, that's what you like most. And what about you?

Man: Well, I prefer more pressure.

M.Th.: [*To the woman*] So did you use a little more pressure?

Man: Sometimes, yes.

F.Th.: But that's something you really will have to find out. [*To the man*] My feeling is that you would also really like to feel your muscles underneath it. [*To the woman*] Perhaps you could just dig in a little.

Man: Yes, sometimes, it could vary a bit. Sometimes gently and then a little harder again.

M.Th.: Was it a bit too unvaried, the way she did it?

Man: Yes, the pressure was a bit too repetitive.

F.Th.: [*To the woman*] Did you also feel you could have done with a little more movement, variety? Slower and faster?

Therapeutic Procedure

Woman: Not really. That was the nicest thing, the steady rhythm.

M.Th.: Perhaps your husband prefers something different from you. [*To the man*] What did you prefer, being caressed or caressing?

Man: I would almost say it was the same. I mean, if we were in each other's arms and caressed each other. That's something I would really enjoy.

M.Th.: That was something you missed a little, not going hand in hand.

Man: Yes. It's always only one who gives or takes and the other does the opposite.

F.Th.: Hmm.

M.Th.: You mean, when you were being caressed you couldn't really concentrate on yourself but thought you had to give something back in return or that you would like to give something in return.

Man: Not really, it didn't occur to me. I just let myself go.

F.Th.: Hmm. When you were caressing you found it pleasant.

Woman: Taking without giving anything back was really good.

M.Th.: You were happy you didn't have to react immediately, but could just take it in.

Woman: Yes. And that's why I'm a little astonished that my husband reacted like that; if he had said I should use a little more pressure then I would have done so right away, perhaps, but as it was I probably thought ...

F.Th.: That's what I thought before, that you felt a bit bad about it and thought, "it wasn't all that nice for him the way I did it." Perhaps a little disappointed.

M.Th.: Not that we're criticizing what you do, but just suggesting you try it like this or that; it might be a good experience. So it's just encouragement to try something else and [*To the man*] for you that certainly means forcing yourself to say so, because one easily thinks the other feels crititized or hurt if one expresses a wish.

F.Th.: Your husband did find it very, very pleasant.

Woman: Yes.

F.Th.: Just as you did. Only now you've seen, sometimes your wishes differ a little, but that you can cope with that.

M.Th.: [*To the woman*] I'm not yet altogether certain what you felt was best, being caressed or caressing.

Woman: Um, being caressed. I found that more enjoyable.

M.Th.: Hmm. Then you were able to ...

F.Th.: ... abandon yourself completely.

Woman: Yes. And this morning I noticed, well, normally everything's so incredibly hectic in the mornings and this morning it was all so slow; making the coffee I usually dash about the place. But not in the slightest this morning. Breakfast was so easy.

M.Th.: You felt balanced?

Woman: I was well-balanced, yes.

M.Th.: It seems it went very well the way you handled each other; but it's very important not to say next time, if we do it and it doesn't turn out the same as yesterday, then that's bad. It's not always the same. And you shouldn't start expecting that you'll have to produce the same result every time. But I'm glad you're so happy; that you say how pleased you were.

F.Th.: It must be really great for you to hear how much your wife liked what you did.

Man: Yes, I'm glad she did.

M.Th.: Was it difficult for you to keep to the limits? Especially when you were lying on your back?

Man: Yes, sometimes I had to take care not to let my hand touch her breasts. The thought was sometimes there, itching to do it.

M.Th.: [*To the woman*] How did you feel; did you regret your husband not touching you there?

Woman: No, I didn't regret it, but I noticed that he found it hard not to go any further.

M.Th.: But you didn't really miss anything?

Woman: No, not at all. I was looking forward to relaxing.

M.Th.: Was it hard for you not to touch your husband's penis?

Woman: No.

M.Th.: How did you feel when your wife made the detour?

Man: At the moment I didn't give it another thought. I was just completely relaxed.

M.Th.: I think it's great you could adjust to it.

F.Th.: And push the old habits aside.

Man: I didn't once imagine she was suddenly going to take my penis in her hand; the thought never occurred to me.

F.Th.: You practically always followed her hand wherever it was without thinking where it might otherwise have been.

Man: Yes, just exactly where it was.

Woman: Well, when he stroked over my skin from the top downward, then it struck me, "aha, that's taboo, he's not allowed to go there." But that was yesterday, not today. This morning it was wonderful. It worked. I didn't feel he was thinking, "I'd like to touch her there now," or anything like that.

F.Th.: And you weren't expecting him to touch you there?

Woman: No.

M.Th.: You didn't think, "I want more, do something different."

Woman: No, on the contrary. I woke up very early this morning and was happy I had this half hour again and didn't think, "now you've got to wake up half an hour earlier," or anything; in fact, I was up and lively.

Man: Yes, well, I just let things happen.

F.Th.: Simply trusting her to do it right.

Man: Yes. As I said, I should have told her to caress me a little harder, but it didn't occur to me to say anything.

M.Th.: While she was caressing it was quite good.

Man: Yes.

M.Th.: Who was it who said: "O.K., time's up, let's change?"

Man: Well, my wife, strictly speaking.

M.Th.: You always kept an eye on the clock?

Woman: That's the way I was lying; because I always do everything by the clock. It really makes me laugh.

Man: I paid less attention to the time. I even went on caressing longer than five minutes when it was my turn.

M.Th.:   Did it bother you when your wife said, "That's it, time's up?"

Man: No, not really. But it wasn't pleasant either, always having to check for the time.

M.Th.:   At the beginning it's difficult, but later on you'll do it without the egg timer, without watching the seconds. It's just a rule that each takes three turns with each role. And one minute one way or the other isn't so important. It would better if you just let things happen next time without checking whether the timing is right. Just try it out, don't worry about it at all; just put the clock where you can't see it. Who started caressing this morning?

Man: I did.

M.Th.:   You should vary that, too. I forgot to mention that. [*To the woman*] So next time you can start [*To the man*] and the time after you start again, so you're always taking turns.

Man: Yes, we already thought of that yesterday when I started, and this morning we said it should start the other way around; so I should start being caressed first. But then somehow it turned out the other way and my wife lay on her back and I started again.

M.Th.:   But you really should alternate.

F.Th.:   And that's not another criticism. I think you're getting along fine.

M.Th.:   Yes, I think it's going just fine.

Woman: I told my husband yesterday evening before falling asleep, little things like that really make me satisfied. In the evenings I always used to be a bundle of nerves.

Man: Yes, really.

Woman: And then I couldn't go to sleep. But these little things are exactly what make me feel peaceful. Which is why I was real pleased, this morning too.

M.Th.:   Well, that means we can actually think about what you should do before the next session. This experience is so new to you so we don't want to start you on anything bigger, so the new experiences can settle in a bit. The best thing would be to repeat the exercise and pay a bit more attention to the different kinds of caressing; and have a bit more trust in each other so you can state your wishes and discover what you like more. By the way, your preferences will vary from exercise to exercise. It might be that your neck isn't the nicest place next time, but your chest, instead. It's not always the same place. And then try a few experiments and touch the places that weren't given priority yesterday and today; don't just stick to what you already know. The exercises are deliberately meant to start slowly at first. That way you can feel quite sure that it can be just as good and satisfying when you ignore the genitals. You've already experienced how pleasant it is. And you should have the courage to tell each other to do something else. You needn't be afraid of the other wanting to criticize you. That's one of the most important things: being able to say that without being afraid of the other feeling hurt.

Man: Exactly.

M.Th.: One is often far too considerate toward the other, and one thinks, "I shouldn't say things like that, because he'll think he's not doing it well enough." And then one prefers to say nothing at all and somehow one is a little unsatisfied after all.

F.Th.: And you should let each other know where it feels particularly nice or where you like it most. Not simply, "now I want something else," but really make it clear that this is where you feel it's really very pleasant.

Man: Yes, I understand.

M.Th.: O.K., we've already agreed on the next appointment.

PROCEDURE IN FURTHER SESSIONS

In the subsequent sessions of caressing I the therapists take up the following points:

Additional behavioral instructions. The partners can take a bath or a shower together before caressing and rub cream or oil on each other's bodies, except breasts and genitals. This helps them to relax and increases familiarity with the other's body. Before caressing the partners can also lie down and create as much body contact as possible. They should however avoid pressing their genitals together. In this way they can learn to tolerate and enjoy physical closeness. This is also a way the partners can conclude the exercise. This is an important way of supplementing the exercise if the partners miss close body contact when caressing.

Sexual tension and masturbation. Restriction of sexual behavior does not apply to masturbation. Sexual tensions and dissatisfaction of one or both partners may impair the general sense of pleasure when caressing. It is perfectly natural if masturbation is then desired, but it should not happen in the partner's presence. The partners should talk with each other about it and discuss with the therapists any problems that arise (aversion or disgust, jealousy or envy, which may be particularly strong if one of the partners has never masturbated). Partners do, however, often notice that sexual tensions do not arise to the extent they had expected. The therapists can use this to show that sexuality is not merely a matter of coitus and orgasm but that, on the contrary, sexual satisfaction and relaxation can also be achieved by caressing and tenderness not intended to elicit sexual arousal.

SPECIAL PROBLEMS

A whole series of problems can be expected in this therapy sequence; we can only mention the most frequent here.

Lighting and nudity: The partners are often so shy with each other that they are unable to tolerate bright lighting or dislike getting fully undressed. They give various reasons for this, for example, "We always used to do it in the dark," "It was so cold in the room," "I found it so embarrassing to lie there fully naked beside him," "If we're not supposed to caress the genitals then I can keep my underpants on."

"French" kisses and saliva: Reactions of disgust can arise when kissing or caressing with the mouth or tongue. These reactions, for example, wiping the wet spot dry, can hurt a partner's feelings.

Fears of being touched: While caressing involuntary reactions can occur, such as tickling sensations, jerking away, or persistent goose pimples. This is a sign that the partner is not relaxed or that the body is not used to being touched.

Performance demands and fears of failure: "Other people probably enjoy that far more"; "One should really get an erection from it"; "I was always expecting to get aroused"; "My partner could relax immediately, he never has problems"; "I simply can't manage to make my partner feel it's good"; "It was so nice yesterday, we'll never get that far again," and so forth.

Communication problems: "Neither of us really likes starting"; "She always says, we'll have to do our homework, and then I don't feel like it anymore"; "If she doesn't want to, I feel rejected"; "When he gets an erection I feel guilty and think, I really must do something for him now," and so forth.

Breaking rules: Partners do sometimes have sexual intercourse despite the coital prohibition. This may be an expression of relief from performance demands or alternatively, if it happens more frequently, it can imply a refusal to get involved in therapy. How this experience develops should be discussed in detail. The therapists use the generally negative or ambivalent experiences during intercourse to demonstrate once again the relevance and purpose of coital prohibition. It is advisable to tell the partners in plain terms that the prohibition is not a "trick" rule the therapists secretly expect to be broken.

Avoidance behavior: Almost all of the difficulties mentioned above may be rationalizations of overt or covert avoidance behavior. Other, more direct forms of avoidance behavior are: "We didn't have any time for the exercises," "Neither of us was in the right mood for exercises," "We only did it once," "We've been so tired the last few days," "It was all so terribly technical," and so forth.

These problems can often be solved by discussing them in detail in sessions, by repeating the exercises, by recapitulating the rules and the purpose of caressing, or, where necessary, by adding behavioral instructions, for example, for desensitization of specific reactions of aversion and unpleasant physical sensations. If avoidance behavior persists the therapists should insist on compliance with the rules and confront the partners with their avoidance behavior and the underlying problems. Most difficulties can be solved by these methods. However, there are couples who put up a strong resistance; the basic problems then have to be discussed and worked through as best the therapist can with his specific training and therapeutic orientation.

The therapists should not start questioning the partners about sexual arousal and functions in the first sessions of caressing I. As a rule, the partners do not react to caressing with sexual arousal. If this makes them unsure of themselves, the therapists explain that these reactions are not at all important at the moment. What really matters is that they feel good when caressing, that they relax and gradually start to enjoy it no matter whether they become aroused or not. If the "symptomatic partner" reports sexual arousal, then the therapists again explain the connection between relaxation and sexual functioning; they also emphasize that arousal is unimportant at the moment and that the partners should not expect to become aroused every time. If the "nondysfunctional" partner reports sexual arousal, the therapists should point out that this puts the partner under pressure. He or she should also be encouraged to open himself or herself to the experience of caressing for once without sexual arousal or to calmly accept arousal.

TIMING

Caressing I should be terminated when the partners are able to experience caressing as pleasant and relaxing and have started to communicate their feelings and wishes to each other. This sequence requires at least two sessions (see table M.1).

Caressing II

AIMS

In this sequence the same basic aims apply as in caressing I, that is, the partners should learn to experience and enjoy caressing and body contact with relaxation and without performance pressure. The exercises are supplemented by allowing the partners the opportunity to include breasts and genitals in relaxed, tender caressing of the whole body. They should understand that touching these parts of the body is not necessarily a signal to "go further," for example, as far as coitus.

Therapeutic Procedure

Unpleasant sensations and fears of being touched that frequently arise in this situation should be gradually reduced, and partners should also have the opportunity to perceive and accept their feelings and sensations from breasts and genitals without performance pressure. In so doing they can develop a broader basis for a concept of sexuality not centered alone on genital arousal.

PROCEDURE

After discussing their experiences with the last exercises the therapists suggest that the partners go a small step further. Before the next session the partners should take time twice for caressing and again alternate in active and passive roles three times. The first time, the partners caress each other just as they have done until now. The new step is made by including the woman's breasts, and the man's if they had been excluded previously, and including the man's and the woman's genitals the second and third times. These areas should be caressed exactly as have the others: they are no longer ignored, but they are not given preference. Breasts and genitals are caressed only briefly and superficially: the man only brushes over the woman's breasts and should not yet touch the woman between the labia; the woman should not yet massage his penis and should not move his foreskin back and forth over his glans. Breasts and genitals should not be directly stimulated.

The therapists emphasize that the main thing is still to relax and enjoy caressing, just as when breasts and genitals were not touched. Arousal, erection, and orgasm continue to be unimportant. This means that the genitals and breasts lose their signaling function (for example, "Now I've got to get aroused" or "I should get an erection now"), and the partners can gradually learn to accept and enjoy genital sensations openly again.

The therapists point out again that both fundamental rules of therapy still apply: do only what is enjoyable and for as long as it is enjoyable; concentrate self-centeredly on your own feelings. All other instructions and rules from caressing I continue to apply as well: coitus and petting are prohibited; communication of sensations and wishes is stressed. Additional exercises, such as showering or bathing together, can be continued.

TRANSCRIPT

COUPLE 41: The woman is twenty-four years old, and the man is twenty-six. Both are students. The woman has never had an orgasm during petting or coitus with her present partner, nor when masturbating. The man, for whom the relationship is the first of any length, tends to ejaculate prematurely and feels sexually incompetent and inexperienced. The couple was assigned to long-term therapy with one male therapist.

M.Th.: So now we can safely go one step further. You go on changing roles and lie down again together; cuddle with each other first, and then one of you caresses the other.

Woman: I see, yes.

M.Th.: And then in the second round you can caress the breasts and genitals as well, but without giving them any special attention. So nothing else besides adding the places we had left out; and it's important not to concentrate more on the genital area and breasts than on other parts of your body. You no longer ignore them but they aren't anything special, either, just another part of your body like your stomach or thighs. What's important is [To the woman] not to rub your partner's penis or pull back his foreskin as if you wanted to get him aroused. Just stroke over the surface of his penis and testicles. No matter whether it's stiff or not. [To the man] And you only caress her genitals on the surface, and, for example, don't caress between her labia or in her vaginal opening with your fingers or hand, just over the surface.

Man: O.K.

M.Th.: And getting sexually aroused isn't important at all; all that matters is that you relax and feel good. The reason we want you to include your breasts and genitals is that they are meant to lose their signaling character. What happened before was probably that one of you began touching the other's breasts or genitals and that meant, "This is the run up to intercourse," which immediately brought back the fears again: "Will it or won't it work"; "I'd prefer not to, really, because it won't work or won't be as good as we imagine." The point is gradually to unlearn this alarm function when you touch those parts of the body, that's important. And then you can begin to feel: "I can relax and it still feels pleasant."

Man: Aha.

M.Th.: That's the real point of the next step. It would be best to do that twice, or even three or four times, but at least twice.

Man: No upper limits.

M.Th.: No upper limits.

Man: O.K.

DISCUSSION OF EXPERIENCES

The same applies here as for caressing I. Just as the instructions require that there is no special emphasis on the genitals and breasts but that they should be caressed casually and superficially, the therapists do not immediately ask what sensations they felt there but wait for the partners to describe their experiences with the entire exercise in detail.

274

Therapeutic Procedure

Additional interventions. At this stage in therapy the therapists should consider whether there is any sense in offering one or both of the partners the exercises for bodily self-awareness (see p. 311) in addition to caressing II. This is often the best procedure in preparing the partners for the exercises in the next section, explorative caressing.

In therapy for vaginismus the woman should in any case be acquainted with the instructions for body self-awareness at this stage in preparation for the exercises with dilators.

SPECIAL PROBLEMS

As a rule, the following difficulties arise at this phase in therapy: unpleasant sensations when breasts or genitals are being touched; aversion to touching the other's breasts or genitals; disappointment about the lack of sexual arousal; strong arousal of one partner, which puts the other under pressure. The therapists discuss these difficulties and ask for details of experiences; they should analyze the causes and the underlying anxieties and, if necessary, give the partners special behavioral instructions to densensitize particular fears. They encourage the partners to repeat the exercises and to be open to the whole body being caressed. It is also important to deal with the often varying way in which the man and woman experience touch in the genital area.

Partners sometimes describe how sexual tensions built up during caressing, which then led to an uneasiness and lack of satisfaction. This can be reduced by the partners concluding caressing not after touching breasts and genitals but after caressing some other more "neutral" parts of the body so arousal can die down; or they can lie next to each other afterward to let any arousal that may have arisen subside again. Masturbation is also allowed in this sequence but, as before, not in the partner's presence.

TIMING

Caressing II is completed when the partners can experience a pleasant feeling when their whole bodies, including breasts and genitals, are touched without the expectation of sexual arousal; when they can exchange experiences without anxiety; and when unpleasant sensations and tension generally no longer arise when caressing or being caressed. This sequence requires at least one to two sessions (see table M.1).

Explorative Genital Caressing

AIMS

The aim of this sequence is for the partners to become more acquainted with and acceptant of their genital areas by learning explorative caressing. The partners should learn to look at each other's and their own genitals without reacting negatively. They are meant to become acquainted with the various possible ways of caressing the genitals and to explore their preferences and dislikes in terms of these possibilities. They should get to know and experience the manifold and, above all, constantly varying reactions to genital stimulation (arousal, relaxation, comfort, irritation, and so forth) and understand how important it is to talk about this to each other.

In this way information deficits, shame and anxiety barriers, difficulties in expressing oneself and taboos can be slowly reduced, and relaxed caressing can be extended to the genital area.

PROCEDURE

The therapists suggest that the partners go one step further. Before the next session the partners then take time twice again for caressing and, as before, each assumes the passive and active role three times in turn.

In the first phase the partners lie on their stomachs again and let their entire backs be caressed. This encourages relaxation and creates the right atmosphere. In the second phase, lying on their backs, they first caress the whole body again, also brushing over the genitals and breasts, and then go on to the next part of the exercise.

In the next phase the couple engages in explorative genital caressing not intended to elicit arousal or orgasm. The woman gently caresses the man's penile shaft, glans, and testicles. If he is not circumcised, she then moves his foreskin back and forth. She massages his penis with her fingers or her whole hand. She tries to find out which movements, pressure, and rhythm her partner particularly likes. The man should tell his partner in words or show her with her hand where and how he likes his penis to be touched or stimulated. What matters is not whether erection occurs during caressing but rather that the man can enjoy this caressing and can feel the pleasure of his limp penis being stroked without having to feel fear.

The man then also experiments with the various possible forms of genital caressing, for example, playing with his partner's pubic hair, indirectly stimulating her clitoris by rhythmically pressing on her labia and pubic bone, stroking between her vaginal orifice and clitoris, gently rubbing around her clitoris with circular movements. Again, the point here is not to induce arousal or orgasm but to relax and feel comfortable. While being caressed the woman tries to concentrate on her feelings in order to find out when, where, and with which pressure and rhythm she likes to be caressed in the genital area. She should tell her partner this or show him by leading his hand and she should tell him when she wants something else.

The therapists explain that the aim of exploring the genitals is not to discover a technique for effective stimulation that will be valid for all occasions. There is no one particular way a person always likes to be caressed; it depends on moods and the feelings one has at the moment for one's partner. What is important is to develop the ability to say or show what one wants at that moment.

The therapists explain that the man's glans and the area between the woman's major labia—that is, the vaginal orifice, the minor labia, and clitoris—are formed by sensitive skin. Unpleasant sensations can easily ensue if they are handled too roughly. If the skin is dry even a light touch can often be unpleasant. It is therefore advisable to moisten the genital area with saliva or a lubricant.

The partners can also explore each other's genitals with their mouths. As with all "more unusual" sexual techniques (for example, masturbating in front of each other, petting or intercourse during menstruation, unusual coital positions), the therapists point out the possibilities and encourage the partners to try them out so they can experience what they feel like. But they should also mention that couples have varying opinions on these techniques: some find them arousing and consider them an important element in their sexuality; others use them occasionally as supplementary techniques; and yet others do not like them or reject them. The point is that the couples form their own opinions. When asked the therapists emphasize that there are no objective reasons, for example, hygiene, for not having oral intercourse or sex during menstruation. If one form of caressing evokes arousal the partners can interrupt caressing in the genital area briefly and let the arousal subside again before they continue with explorative caressing.

Anatomical knowledge and reduction of shame and fear of looking at each other's genitals are of great help in explorative caressing. The partners are therefore asked to show each other their genitals and examine them. The man should show the woman his penile shaft, glans, foreskin, frenulum, and testicles and she should look at them closely.

Then the woman shows the man her major and minor labia, clitoris, vaginal orifice, and urethral opening. Many patients find this difficult at first because they had always learned to keep these areas concealed. As a rule these exercises are facilitated if the partners examine their own bodies and genitals alone beforehand.

By displaying and looking at their genitals the partners should come to understand how they are constructed and function. In doing so they should be aware of their feelings, including negative ones of rejection or disgust. They do not need to look at their genitals in every exercise in this sequence, but should do so until they have gotten to know the other's genitals visually as well. If there are gaps in partners' knowledge of genital anatomy the therapists illustrate male and female genitals with diagrams.

It helps communication if each partner shows the other how he or she touches and stimulates himself or herself when masturbating. The partners should not masturbate in each other's presence but should show the technique they use. The other partner can then try to imitate that way of caressing until he or she knows the optimal kinds of stimulation for the partner. This instruction need not necessarily be given in the first session of explorative caressing. This is, of course, impossible if the partners have no experience of masturbation.

After the third phase of explorative caressing the partners move to the fourth phase in which they again alternately lie on their stomachs and caress each other's backs. Afterward they can continue lying close to each other for a while. The therapists point out again that both fundamental rules of therapy still apply: only do what is enjoyable and for as long as it is enjoyable; concentrate self-centeredly on your own feelings. All other instructions and rules continue to apply as well: no coitus or petting to orgasm, communication of sensations and wishes, coping with sexual tensions and urges. Additional exercises, such as showers and baths together, can be continued.

TRANSCRIPT

COUPLE 36:   The man has secondary erectile difficulties; the woman has orgasmic problems. This couple has been discussed earlier (p. 192). The couple was assigned to intensive therapy with two therapists.

M.Th.:   The important thing now is to get to know each other's genitals a bit better. So we would like to suggest the following: get undressed again and caress each other for the first five minutes as before, to get the feel of it and to relax.

Therapeutic Procedure

Woman: Yes.

M.Th.: And then the second time, when you caress your husband, take a look together at his penis.

Man: Hmm.

M.Th.: No matter whether it's stiff or limp, that's irrelevant. Just take a look at the testicles and touch them and then pull back the foreskin. [*To the man*] Then you show your wife, where the glans, the foreskin, and the frenulum are; do a bit of real anatomy. And when you've seen everything properly just experiment to see what you can do with it all, the penis and the testicles.

Woman: Hmm.

M.Th.: Find out how to handle the testicles, how to caress or press so it feels pleasant. Then take his penis either in three fingers or your whole hand; just see how far you can pull back the foreskin, how much pressure you can use. And [*To the man*] you tell your wife what you like: "Do it a bit harder" or "Don't do it quite so strongly."

Woman: Well, I think you've already taught me to do that, my dear.

M.Th.: And then try again. [*To the man*] And you just put your own hand there and say, "I usually do it like this." So you take hold of your penis but don't masturbate in front of your wife, just show her the movement. Just the grip, so to speak. [*To the woman*] And then you try to imitate him.

Woman: Hmm.

M.Th.: What matters is not getting a hard-on or being aroused, but, as it were, to explore the genitals, with your eyes and hands.

Woman: Yes.

F.Th.: I'm sure you've done it before, so you can just as easily do it again. Ask all the questions that might otherwise have been swallowed. Find out whether you can do it a bit stronger or more gently, or whether it's at all nice to be touched here. So you both find out what he likes most. In between you can go over the whole body again and when you notice it's getting difficult, it's too arousing, then simply take a break or go back to caressing the face, arms, or whatever.

Woman: Hmm.

F.Th.: Well, and then you change around, and look at your wife, that is, you both look together. [*To the woman*] You sit up and spread apart your labia a bit, and show your husband what you explored yourself yesterday. Show him where the clitoris, the vaginal opening, and the minor labia are. And you both take a close look together. If you want you can use a mirror.

Woman: Yes, I think I'd prefer it that way.

Man: Well, for me that's kind of funny insofar as, how should I say, yes, well, I just have to describe what my impression is: I find it funny insofar as I know it definitely won't please my wife. She doesn't like that sort of thing. I already did it once, just for fun—"Come on, let me have a look"—she goes crazy and all nervous, don't you?

Woman: True, I didn't like that. Perhaps if we try it now it won't be so disagreeable.

M.Th.: Besides you've seen that when you look at yourself you don't suddenly . . .

Woman: Yes, but perhaps if someone is watching me I won't find it so pleasant; yes, there I would agree.

M.Th.: [*To the man*] But it could be it's more difficult for you than for her.

Man: I would like to try.

M.Th.: And if it's difficult for her then I think it would help if you simply tried to understand her a little and not to laugh at her for it.

Man: No, I don't laugh at her at all, only she always thinks I do. I just smile at her. Just having fun.

F.Th.: Perhaps it would be best in that situation if you didn't make fun of her, but instead understood that it's difficult for your wife and that she gets insecure very easily. [*To the woman*] And then lie down, and [*To the man*] you caress your wife in the genital area. But not with the aim of arousing her, just to find out how to touch her down there. For example, you can try vigorous movements up and down between vaginal opening and clitoris; or you can caress around her clitoris; or you can press the palm of your hand on the clitoris area without drawing the labia apart. Try to find out what feels good. [*To the woman*] You can tell him: "That's nice now, you just have to do it more gently" or "You'll have to press a little harder." Don't aim at finding the button to press, as it were, which would give her an orgasm; instead you should find it quite natural to talk about it. Because what you like can change from one day to the next.

Woman: Yes, I've noticed that, too.

F.Th.: What matters more to us is that you just learn to make yourselves understood. You should always talk it over and watch how it works out that day. [*To the woman*] And then perhaps you could simply demonstrate what you do when you masturbate.

Woman: I can't!

M.Th.: No, you're not supposed to masturbate in front of him.

Woman: No, I couldn't even try doing it. I can't touch myself in front of my husband. Not now, but maybe it'll be easier in two or three days.

F.Th.: I'm only trying to explain to you what's important. If you still find it too difficult today or tomorrow, then wait till the day after. In principle it would be good if you said: "Look, this is how I do it—I put my hand here." And then show him how you touch yourself. And [*To the man*] you just try it exactly the same way, imitating her, so to speak.

Man: Hmm.

M.Th.: And you go on giving him hints: "Harder, not too much, here more, there more," and so forth. I'm sure that's very difficult, but you've seen so often now that if you trust each other it's not as difficult as you think.

Woman: That's true.

M.Th.: And you should decide yourself when you're ready or when you can get it together for the first time.

F.Th.: Perhaps you would find it easier to start with if you led his hand.

Woman: Yes, I think so too. Perhaps if I lead his hand.

F.Th.: Yes, that's a good way to start. Although it's not as easy as showing him the right way with your own hand. But perhaps you'll find it easier for the first time. One more thing: [*To the woman*] you told us that you were often moist; but getting aroused isn't what matters. So we're going to give you a lubricant to take with you. Please use it when you're not moist and moisten your genitals a little, when it scratches; the skin is sensitive there. If you don't like using a lubricant, saliva is just as good—and natural besides.

DISCUSSION OF EXPERIENCES

Although the partners often immediately start reporting on their new experiences in this sequence, the therapists should take care to collect information on how the entire exercise progressed before going on to new exercises. The principles valid for caressing I and II continue to apply. As in all other stages of therapy, it is important that the therapists do not hesitate to repeat themselves, for example, for fear of boring the patients; their emphasis on the earlier phases of the exercise will help the couple to realize that those phases will continue to facilitate important experiences.

Only then are the new experiences discussed: first what the partners actually did, and then what they had already done earlier and whether they noticed anything new or have any questions that can then be discussed, in turn. When discussing emotional reactions the therapists first take up and reinforce the positive experiences before they examine rejection reactions more closely to find an approach to working out the problem. To conclude, the positive experiences are reviewed once again.

TRANSCRIPT

COUPLE 40:   This couple has already been discussed (p. 264). The couple was assigned to intensive therapy for the man's erectile dysfunction.

Man: Well, yesterday evening we started doing what you told us to, taking an exploration trip and so on. It was interesting. I thought it was pleasant, anyway. Yes, and the usual caressing again.

M.Th.:   Yes.

Man: Well, I enjoyed it, my wife too, when we talked about it.

M.Th.:   So, your experience yesterday was just as we described it.

Woman: Yes. It all seemed quite normal. We didn't give it a thought.

F.Th.:   How did you do the first part, as always?

Woman: Yes, starting with the back.

F.Th.:   Who's turn was it first yesterday?

Man: Hers yesterday evening, and I was the first to caress this morning. Yes, well, we first looked at our genitals the second time around.

Woman: Exactly.

Man: Then she lay on her back. She was lying on her stomach before.

F.Th.:   It was important for you to start by caressing the whole body and to wait until the second time around before doing the new exercise.

281

Man: Exactly. So I held the major and minor labia apart with two fingers. That went quite well.

M.Th.:   Did you discover anything new, now that you've looked closely at her genitals?

Man: No, I was never really shy of looking at her. Because I'd already done it once. Not as deliberately as now, but I did take a close look at everything. I didn't really feel any change.

M.Th.:   Then more the sense of letting yourselves get involved, without getting sexually aroused?

Man: Yes.

F.Th.:   And were able just to let things happen as they did?

Woman: Yes, well I didn't think anything sexual.

M.Th.:   Without thinking about what will happen next?

Woman: No, I didn't think about that at all.

F.Th.:   What happened there and then was the right thing, and good.

Woman: Yes, well, as I said yesterday, I was quite relaxed. I hadn't given it any thought at all, I felt quite free. And this morning as well, that's how it is now, it's all part of it and quite normal.

M.Th.:   You're nodding all the time in agreement as if you felt the same.

Man: Yes, I do. We're not distracted by any other kinds of thoughts; not that I had any other thoughts, not at all. Just calmly stroking everything and looking at it without giving it any particular thought.

M.Th.:   Perhaps we should discuss your experiences in detail. You've already begun to tell us what you did. You went along the labia, major and minor.

Man: Yes.

M.Th.:   Up around the clitoris as well?

Man: Yes.

M.Th.:   And down toward the buttocks as well?

Man: No, not there.

M.Th.:   Can you describe what your husband did, what you felt was most pleasant, assuming you could tell the difference?

Woman: Well, in general it was all pleasant. I watched in the mirror. We went slowly over my clitoris, that was very pleasant as well, and then he sort of investigated it a bit. I can't say what I found most pleasant. Everything was.

M.Th.:   Some women, for example, don't much like their clitoris being touched directly. Or some don't like their labia being touched directly. You were able to enjoy it?

Woman: Yes, I was able to enjoy it.

M.Th.:   Was it gentle the way your husband . . .

Woman: Yes, very gentle.

M.Th.:   Firmly, or with real pressure?

Woman: No, it was really nice, just the way I like it.

F.Th.:   Were all places the same, vagina, labia, clitoris, or were there places where he could have been more gentle . . .

Woman: It was perfect, just the way I like it. But there was one thing; when he moved downward it hurt. But that was just for a second.

M.Th.:   Did you say so and did you [to the man] do it differently?

Therapeutic Procedure

Man: Yes, yes. I used my whole hand then, the palm; before I'd used my finger tips. And then I put my whole hand there and then went on caressing.

M.Th.: Fine.

Woman: Yes, exactly; I noticed a twitch and then I put the flat of his hand there and then it immediately went away again.

F.Th.: It went away quite quickly.

Man: Yes.

M.Th.: What did you do then to your husband's genitals?

Woman: Well, I pulled back his foreskin and took a close look at everything, and stroked his glans, too.

M.Th.: O.K.

Woman: That was really pleasant as well, and the scrotum, I took a close look first. And then I went on caressing and then looked at it again.

F.Th.: Did you also try and find out how you could caress everything?

Woman: Yes. And then I went on caressing, and I think my husband found it very pleasant.

Man: It was; although I would have soon ejaculated. But I quickly rejected the thought, lay back again, and relaxed and stayed that way. So the feeling died down again.

M.Th.: Did you feel that moving it up and down three or four times would have been enough to . . .

Man: Yes.

M.Th.: Although it never went that quickly before; you always used to say it never happened that quickly.

Man: Well, it did really, it often happened fairly quickly.

M.Th.: And where did you like your wife to touch you most?

Man: Well, when she had my scrotum in her hand and pushed the foreskin back and forth a little.

M.Th.: Did you like her touching you right on your glans?

Man: Yes, that too.

M.Th.: That turned you on as well?

Man: Yes, that turns me on as well.

M.Th.: You know, that irritates a lot of men; they don't really like being touched there. But you do?

Man: Yes, I do.

M.Th.: And the pressure your wife used on your testicles?

Man: It could have been a tiny bit stronger.

M.Th.: Sure.

F.Th.: Your testicles, you mean?

Woman: I'm afraid of hurting him, or something.

F.Th.: You could do with a bit more pressure on your testicles?

Man: No, on my penis.

M.Th.: Ah, yes. [*To the woman*] You don't need to be all that cautious. The penis is fairly insensitive when it gets stiffer because it's more or less filled with blood, like a water bag. So one can press quite tightly. The stiffer it is, the harder you can press, and even when it's quite limp you can press fairly hard. If not, your husband will tell you when it's enough.

But do just try it out. Being a woman you probably go at it carefully because you can't really know how hard a man actually likes it. Doesn't look all that robust either, a penis. And it's important you make each other understood. We've quite forgotten to ask about the other "sensitive parts," your breasts.

Man: Yes, well, the nipples were already a bit stiff, but then I stroked around the edges of her breasts. But it was only pleasant for my wife when I touched her nipples.

Woman: It hurt; you misunderstood me. You pressed down a little and that hurt. It wasn't arousing; I felt it really hurt.

M.Th.: On your nipples, or when he . . .

Woman: Yes, he put his whole hand there. And the pressure was a bit too strong.

M.Th.: Ah, yes. What I didn't understand was whether you liked your breasts being caressed gently . . .

Woman: Yes.

M.Th.: . . . or whether your nipples aren't a bit oversensitive.

Woman: No, gently and softly is O.K. But it doesn't always hurt. Perhaps he did it a bit harder without noticing, I don't know.

F.Th.: Or perhaps you were a bit more sensitive yesterday. That's also possible.

Woman: Everything was fine again this morning.

F.Th.: But you didn't caress her with your mouth or tongue?

Man: Sure. I went over her pubic hair with my nose once. But only briefly. But nothing with my mouth apart from that.

F.Th.: What was it like when your husband's face was close to your pubic hair?

Woman: Well, I was a little startled because I'd closed my eyes. I was really surprised. But I just put up with it. I told him so, and then he didn't do it again. I might have gotten used to it, maybe if he had stayed there a bit longer.

M.Th.: I think it's great you were able to experience how nice it can be when he touches your genitals and that you're not at all disappointed afterward if it doesn't go any further.

Man: No.

M.Th.: But as it is, you feel it's satisfying all around. Yesterday we asked you what words you use when you describe things to each other.

Woman: Well, I say "penis," and my husband says "vagina."

Man: Yes, "large labia," "small labia," "the clitoris," and I say, here's "the opening to the urethra."

M.Th.: Yes.

Man: Um, that's how I said it. She called them my "testicles," "penis," "glans," "foreskin."

M.Th.: Was it a little embarrassing to talk about them?

Woman: No, not at all.

M.Th.: And then we said that apart from the exercises you could give yourself an orgasm by masturbating, if you felt like it.

Man: Not really; we talked about that yesterday afternoon. I don't feel any desire to, I prefer not to at all; maybe it'll happen again some time or other, but I don't feel any desire to masturbate at the moment.

M.Th.: At the moment you're fairly satisfied. You're active twice a day and are happy, so that's understandable. On the other hand, masturbation can still be pleasant; it's an opportunity to be sexually active, which you can still make use of if the relationship is working out mutually. Perhaps you don't feel like it as frequently as before, but you shouldn't merely think of it as a substitute but as an alternative open to you. And if you're under pressure or feel you'd like to, then there's no harm in doing it.

Woman: I used to masturbate before.

Man: I was quite surprised when I heard her say here that she masturbated. Wasn't really expecting it. I mean, I've masturbated as well. I should have known that a woman needs that as well, if she isn't satisfied after having intercourse.

F.Th.: You needn't think that your wife only masturbates when she isn't satisfied. Women do it even though they are satisfied.

Man: They do it all the same.

M.Th.: And men as well, when they're together with a woman. It isn't a way of hurting your partner.

F.Th.: It's another part of sexuality you can enjoy all on your own.

M.Th.: I think it's great you talked about it, that you could mention the subject. It's lost its character of secrecy. You've gotten to know each other a little better; you're aware something's happening that isn't directed against you.

F.Th.: So, tomorrow you should develop the explorative caressing a little further; take more time for it so you can slowly try and find out the pressure your husband wants on his penis, for example, from very gently to real hard. Pull back the foreskin again and don't be afraid to explore the area a bit. And you [*To the man*] take your turn at doing that as well. You should take more time than before, without trying to get the other into "fourth gear" or to arouse each other; just so that your genitals become a part of the body you can caress quite freely without feeling inhibited.

Man: Yes, sure.

M.Th.: And then it would be good if you tried stroking with your lips. Since you seem to like that you might as well do it.

Man: Yes.

M.Th.: Over the labia or between the legs with your lips or tongue, and then the other way around, over his penis.

F.Th.: Try and find out what it feels like with your lips and tongue.

Man: Yes.

M.Th.: And don't forget: the point is not to get aroused. Just let it happen the way it comes.

SPECIAL PROBLEMS

Lack of anatomical knowledge.   Female partners especially become insecure when confronted with their own bodies, particularly with their genitals. Inhibited by their lack of knowledge, they at first hesitate to ask questions. This is often true of men as well. Consequently, it sometimes takes several sessions to find out, for example, that one of the partners thinks the vaginal orifice is the urethral opening or can't find the clitoris. The therapists should not hesitate to supply the relevant information by using illustrations. They explain that just as the length, circumference and so forth of the penis or testicles differ among men, there are considerable differences among women as well (for example, the position and length of the clitoris, the length of the outer and inner labia, color, and so on).

Fear of injury to genitals while caressing. If the woman is not confident enough to press the man's penis as tightly as he would like her to, the matter should first be discussed in greater detail. It can help if the partners can agree to the woman trying, for example, to hold the penile shaft as tightly as she can, if her partner is not circumcised) or to pull back the foreskin as far as possible. She should rely on her partner to tell her when it becomes unpleasant for him; in this way she can discover his pain threshold.

If the man avoids touching the woman's inner genital area, that is, between the major labia, or if she is afraid of being hurt by his fingers, for example, these fears will have to be discussed. It can help if the therapists again point out that the skin there is definitely sensitive to touch when in a dry state, but that by applying saliva or a lubricant the skin can be made to feel smoother and touching becomes pleasant. It is, moreover, important to remind partners repeatedly of this auxiliary aid so that the woman is not put under pressure in terms of lubrication.

Shyness and disgust. On close inspection of the genitals the partner may respond with shyness and disgust; these reactions are evoked largely by the sight of something unknown, by color, skin texture, shape, creases or folds, and so forth. Partners often react with disgust and aversion to body secretions and odors. After the therapists have discussed the details of the particular situation evoking these emotional responses, they encourage the partners to go through the experience once again for familiarity's sake and also remind them to interrupt the exercise should it again become unpleasant. These problems often solve themselves after a few sessions as the couple becomes more self-confident. If necessary the therapists and partners discuss the possibility of intermediate steps that could enable them to do the exercise more easily.

At this stage in therapy it often becomes evident that many couples refuse sexual interaction during menstruation. The therapists explain that there are no objective reasons for such restraint, that couples react differently to the problem, and that each couple has to find its own way. The therapists encourage the couple to try the experience of caressing during menstruation.

Response to signs of arousal. Partners are often irritated if one or both of them become aroused during the exercise. They are sometimes embarrassed by their own arousal because they think they have done something wrong; or they try to persuade their partners to go beyond the rules and make the best of the arousal by petting to orgasm or having intercourse. Their partners' arousal can put them under the kind of pressure that they feel guilty when they break off genital caressing as instructed. If this happens the therapists explain that arousal is "allowed" and can be enjoyed if it arises. They should also make it clear that at the moment the primary aim is explorative caressing and that it is useful to experience how arousal can subside again. They should point out that if the partners react by letting themselves be pressured by arousal or by wanting to profit from the opportunity it means that they have relapsed into the old, problematic behavior patterns.

TIMING

The aim of explorative genital caressing has been reached when the partners have experienced intense, explorative caressing of breasts, genitals, and other parts of the body as relaxing and pleasant on several occasions. They need not feel they have to become sexually aroused, become erect, or lubricate at this stage. At least three sessions are required for this sequence (see table M.1).

Stimulative Caressing and Playing With Arousal

AIMS

The aim of this sequence is to develop caressing experiences further so that partners can react playfully and without anxiety to pleasant genital sensations and sexual arousal. The partners should become acquainted with the various ways of stimulating each other by caressing. They should be open to and enjoy stimulative genital caressing without anticipatory fears. By playing with sexual sensations—deliberately letting them die out and then working them up again—they can become more confident of their sexual reactions. Moreover, they should learn to accept any lack of sexual arousal.

After several experiences with stimulative caressing, the partners are given the option of bringing each other to orgasm. This helps them to become more familiar with the reactions and anxieties they experience through orgasm. They can discover that petting alone, with or without orgasm, can be satisfying and does not always have to lead up to sexual intercourse.

PROCEDURE

The therapists ask the partners first to caress each other's bodies all over without taking particular notice of the genitals. This is an opportunity for them to relax and to feel their way into the new caressing experiences. Two positions are then suggested to the couple which have proved to be particularly suitable for the new exercise. The therapists use illutrations to explain the positions.

In the first position, the man caresses the woman while they both are sitting. The man props himself up (against the wall or headboard) at the head of the bed and opens his legs. He cushions his back so he can sit up comfortably. The woman places herself between the man's legs with her back to him and puts her legs over the man's so he can caress her genitals and she can lean her head on his shoulder. The advantage of this position is that many women feel a sense of protection and don't feel so closely watched. The man begins caressing the woman, at first in a kind of "X pattern," the woman's genitals being the point of intersection: he strokes her breasts, then her genitals, and then her thighs; and he repeats the caresses in the same way moving upward. After doing this for a while he focuses more on the genitals, caressing her pubic hair, the inner labia, the clitoris, and the vaginal opening. He should always determine the pressure, rhythm, and so forth, according to his previous experiences with "explorative caressing." The woman concentrates on her sensations and tells the man when what she feels is pleasant or arousing, leads his hand when necessary, or shows him how she touches herself when masturbating. The couple should ensure that the woman's genitals are moist by applying saliva or a lubricant.

If the woman becomes aroused, she should not be stimulated to climax. Instead she should ask her partner to interrupt stimulation briefly so the arousal can die down again. If the woman so wishes, the man can go on caressing her elsewhere during the pause. Once the arousal has died down, the man can go on with his stimulative caressing, until she is aroused again. She then lets the arousal subside again, and they then repeat this game with arousal three or four times. If there is no sexual arousal, then the couple can continue playing with pleasant genital sensations.

It is important for the woman to tell the man immediately when the caressing becomes unpleasant so he can change the way he does it. This applies particularly to caressing in the genital area; some women, for example, find that direct stimulation of the clitoris is pleasant at first, but then soon feel irritated by it.

In the second position, the woman caresses the man while he is lying on his back. It it essential that the man relaxes when lying on his back; he draws up his knees and spreads his legs wide enough so the woman can sit comfortably between them, her own legs extending along the sides of his body. She then caresses the man with both hands in an "X pattern" from his upper body down over his stomach to his thighs and then back again; again, the genital area is the point of intersection. She then starts intense stimulation of his penis. The man tells her what he does or does not find pleasant and also leads her hand to show her the right pressure and rhythm for stimulating his penis and the way he likes to do it when masturbating. Stimulation stops before he ejaculates. If the man is aroused and gets an erection, he gives her a sign to break off stimulation.

After general, introductory caressing the partners should take turns and go through the exercise as described. The therapists point out that arousal often does not occur despite intense stimulation of the genitals. What matters first is that the partners get used to the new assignments, find out which kind of stimulation they enjoy and for how long, and how well they adapt to alternating genital and nongenital stimulation. They should therefore under no circumstances try to force arousal. Caressing in each position should not last longer than five to ten minutes. Afterward the partners should caress each other's entire body again without taking special notice of the genitals.

The therapists explain that the purpose of playing with arousal is that the partners should be able to let arousal die down without feeling anxiety and to enjoy the pleasure of arousal without orgasm.

TRANSCRIPT

COUPLE 42: The man is a mechanic, and the woman is a salesperson. They are both in their late thirties. They have been married for eleven years and have no children. The man has been suffering from premature ejaculation and erectile problems for eight years; the woman complains of a lack of sexual desire. The couple has not had any kind of sex for over a year. They were assigned to long-term therapy with one therapist.

M.Th.: The instructions are basically the same. First of all, caressing as before. The new part starts the second time around. [*To the man*] You sit down somewhere where you can lean back, perhaps putting a pillow behind your back. Then you spread your legs out. [*To the woman*] You sit down between your husband's legs so he can still put his arms right around you. Just as in the diagram here. It's important you let your arms hang down by your sides so your husband can reach under them; men sometimes reach around them and then the woman is sort of trapped, which shouldn't happen. [*To the man*] Then you caress your wife. You should be able to reach everywhere with your arms. Around her breasts and down her sides, the inner thighs, and then the genitals, the way you found it worked best last time. [*To the woman*] And you lean back against your husband, close your eyes and just wait and see if it's pleasant or not. You might lead his hand, perhaps. Just wait and see what stimulates you and what doesn't. And if you get a pleasant feeling or aroused then tell him to caress you somewhere else so the pleasant feeling in your genitals or the arousal can recede. Then your husband can caress your genitals again and you watch for any feelings or arousal. If possible, go through this three or four times. When you caress your husband do it in this position: he lies down on his back, legs spread out wide, and you sit down between his legs so you can see your husband, as in this picture.

Woman: Yes.

M.Th.: And then you caress him, too. You only need to lean forward a little bit. Start with his chest and legs. And then you play with his penis, watching the way he shows you to touch it: on the shaft, further up, or down around his testicles. [*To the man*] And you say what's pleasant and what isn't. And if you notice you're going to ejaculate, you know the feeling when it's about to come, well, then give your wife the sign to stop.

Man: O.K.

M.Th.: When your husband gives you the signal then caress him somewhere else. You can go back to his penis when the feeling that he's about to come and his erection have gone again. And then concentrate on caressing his penis until he's aroused again and let the feeling die down. Repeat this three or four times. [*To the man*] You shouldn't get as far as ejaculating. [*To the woman*] And you shouldn't let yourself be caressed to the point of orgasm. But finish the exercise by caressing each other over the entire body again, without especially stimulating the genitals, and let the whole thing fade out. Is that all clear so far?

Man: So far, yes.

M.Th.: Well, begin the way you used to and then go on to the new exercise.

Woman: O.K.

M.Th.: Fine; unless there are any more questions?

Woman: No, not from me.

Therapeutic Procedure

The therapists first let the partners give their descriptions. If they start describing their own experiences right away, the therapists should interrupt and ask them about nongenital caressing and so show them that it is not only the new assignment that is important but their experiences with the entire exercise as well. The therapists should also reinforce the partners' positive experiences with these familiar parts of the exercises; for example, if both were able to relax fully and enjoy caressing although they were about to face a new exercise. When discussing the new exercise the therapists should ask them to describe exactly what happened in both positions: how the couple coped with the two positions; how they started caressing; how they stimulated each other; how they experienced their genitals being stimulated; which kind of stimulation was particularly pleasant; whether it aroused them or not; and what they felt about the alternation between genital and nongenital caressing, about playing with sexual arousal, or about the lack of arousal. Their experiences with "fade-out" caressing and their mood afterward should also be discussed.

FURTHER PROCEDURE

At this point a start should be made on the special therapeutic interventions for the different dysfunctions as described later in this manual (see p. 311).

Before going any further with this sequence, the couple should have done the exercises several times as instructed, and both partners should have had the experience of being aroused by stimulation, allowing arousal to die down when genital caressing is interrupted, and being aroused again by renewed stimulation. Once the partners feel more confident of themselves in these "games with arousal," they no longer feel under pressure to "exploit" arousal everytime it arises by going as far as orgasm or coitus. The therapists then suggest the following: once they have let the arousal subside at least twice, they stimulate each other for as long as they want, that is, until they no longer feel like it, until they climax or ejaculate, or until the arousal subsides again before orgasm despite continual stimulation.

SPECIAL PROBLEMS

The couple fails to get involved in the new experiences. The new behavioral instructions may cause partners so much anxiety that the old avoidance behavior reemerges; the partners shy away from genital stimulation because it reminds them too vividly of their difficulties with petting and coitus. When this happens they lose their sense of fun and desire, feel tired, do not find the time for exercises, or complain of psychosomatic disorders which they then blame for their inhibition. The therapists then explain how these exercises are different from the partners' sexual relations before therapy for example, that the partners should interrupt caressing as soon as they feel unpleasant sensations and that, furthermore, the coital prohibition makes quite a difference. They encourage the couple to feel their way into the new exercises because this is the only way anxieties and difficulties can be identified and worked on.

The couple fails to adapt to the positions. It can sometimes happen that a couple finds the positions so uncomfortable or unusual that they are unable to relax while caressing. In that case the couple should first experiment with the positions again, without immediately starting to caress. The therapists explain the advantages of the positions again and do not immediately suggest alternatives. If the couple or one of the partners is still unable to accept the positions after a few attempts, the therapists suggest the couple go through stimulative caressing in the position they are used to when caressing.

The couple concentrates exclusively on genital stimulation. Sometimes the preliminary and final caressing are left out by the couple. Therapists will often be able to use the partners' earlier unsatisfying experiences to show how important nongenital caressing and tenderness are for satisfying sexual encounters. They explain that if the partners ignore this a quasi-relapse into old "in-and-out techniques" already known to be unsatisfying will result. The therapists then elucidate any underlying performance pressures and fixations on genital stimulation and carefully outline the aims of the sequence once again in the light of these problems.

The couple has difficulty in coping with growing arousal. The partners may have difficulty in letting the evoked arousal die down again. They stimulate each other too much, are startled by their own reactions, break off caressing or stimulation, and are left in an unpleasant state of arousal. A state of tension results, mingled with feelings of frustration and disappointment. The therapists explain how important it is to interrupt genital stimulation soon enough and to caress other parts of the body in order to let the arousal subside. Masturbation can again be pointed out as one possibility.

The couple rejects petting as far as orgasm. One or both of the partners may feel petting is an unsatisfying, childish substitute technique, is improper, disgusting, humiliating, and so forth. In this case the therapists will have to go into the underlying fears in close detail to find some kind of solution. This kind of attitude is, as a rule, closely associated with the tendency to uphold the prevailing symptom. It is therefore difficult to respect it as a personal value judgment and leave it unanalyzed. An effective approach to the problem can often be found by examining informational deficits, rigid norms, insecurity, feelings of disgust, and so forth. The therapists can point out that it is important to confront this experience at least for a while so as not to endanger progress in therapy. The couple can, after all, dispense with it later on.

Aversion to body secretions. Lubrication, preseminal emission, and ejaculation often occur at this stage as well, sometimes irritating or even nauseating the partners. It is essential to analyze both partners' attitudes and reactions carefully. If necessary, the therapists can suggest desensitization techniques.

Lack of lubrication. Women often believe they are not aroused simply because they notice little or no lubrication. Or, alternatively, their partners do not believe them when they say they are aroused. In this case it should be carefully explained that for women lubrication is no proof of arousal. Lubrication in many women is only minimal even at advanced stages of arousal; others may fail to lubricate under particular circumstances, for example, tiredness. In such cases repeated reference should be made to auxiliary aids, such as lubricants or saliva. Once given the option of orgasm, some patients inquire about the woman's "ejaculation"; this should be explained.

Only one partner reaches orgasm. In such cases it is explained that mutual orgasm is not a way to "even the score" and that the orgasmic partner is not the better, healthier, or more normal of the two. This situation is an opportunity for the partners to learn to cope when one of the partners does not reach orgasm or has no desire to be stimulated the same way. It may be necessary to discuss any competition problems that ensue.

Avoidance of orgasm for fear of losing control. Many women with orgasmic difficulties have this problem if they have never climaxed in their partner's presence. After careful analysis it can help if therapists suggest that the woman imitate a "wild" orgasm in her partner's presence and with his knowledge in order to scale down her anxieties. If the woman has no difficulties with orgasm when masturbating, the therapists suggest that it might be a relief if the partners first masturbate in front of each other until orgasm in order to reduce their fears.

The couple disregards coital prohibition. If, after genital caressing, the couple has sexual intercourse, the therapists remind them emphatically, without dramatizing, of the negative implications this could have: it might put them under pressure again to exploit sexual arousal for intercourse every time, and this could give rise to the old performance demands and the anxious anticipation of sexual arousal.

TIMING

The sequence has been completed when the couple has repeated the exercise several times and has managed to evoke sexual arousal playfully in a situation free of fear, letting it die down by interrupting stimulation and then stimulating it again.

The therapists can consider giving instructions for the next step (intromission) even if the partners still have problems reaching orgasm regularly or at all. In this way a new performance demand can be avoided, provided that the partners' experiences have been carefully discussed after giving them the "option" of orgasm and that their sensations are for the greater part pleasant. At least three sessions are needed to work through this sequence (see table M.1).

Intromission

AIMS

This sequence aims at getting the partners to feel that insertion of the penis is not the start of "real" sexuality but a continuation of caressing. They learn to experience insertion of the penis without feeling performance demands and failure fears. At this stage it is particularly important to reduce these anxieties because insertion of the penis is more closely associated with previous coital experiences than are all preceding sequences. In this way the partners experience the relief of realizing that insertion is not necessarily the signal to "go further," but that insertion by itself without further movement can create a pleasant physical sensation and inner closeness to one's partner which both can enjoy without the "compulsion to perform" coitus.

PROCEDURE

The therapists explain the next step to the couple. The partners should again take the time to do the familiar exercises twice before the next session, the only change being insertion of the penis. The therapists point out that this is a supplement to the exercises, that is, that the other assignments should be repeated. The couple thus begins the exercise by caressing each other all over their bodies, taking turns in the active and passive roles.

The therapists suggest beginning the second phase in the squatting position. They ask the couple about their previous experiences with this position and explain the technical details using a diagram. The partners first caress each other over their entire bodies, in turn, and then go on to stimulative caressing. When the man is passive the woman stimulates him for a while and then kneels over him at hip height. The woman then takes her partner's erect penis in her hand, opens her major and minor labia with the other hand so the vaginal opening is more approachable, and slowly inserts his penis. To facilitate insertion the therapists again recommend the use of a lubricant. Once the penis is inserted neither of the partners moves. Both keep still in this position and concentrate on their own feelings, such as impatience, the wish for coital movements, enjoyment of physical closeness and warmth, and so forth. If after a few moments of not moving one of the partners feels the wish for additional caressing, he or she should tell the other where and how it is wanted. In addition, if the woman feels the need for more body contact after insertion or finds the upright position uncomfortable, the woman can lean forward and lie relaxed with her chest on her partner's. After a short time the penis is retracted if it has not already slid out through lack of stimulation. It is important to remind the man that his penis can be expected to go limp at this stage.

The partners then go on caressing and the woman inserts the penis again once or twice, in the same manner as before. They then come to some agreement about whether they want to stimulate each other manually or orally to orgasm, to masturbate together, or simply to let the arousal die down again.

If the woman is stimulated and caressed first, then she can even let herself reach orgasm before insertion because this does not make insertion impossible. The basic rules of therapy continue to apply in this sequence.

TRANSCRIPT

COUPLE 36.   This couple has already been described (p. 192). They were assigned to intensive therapy for erectile dynsfunction.

M.Th.:   What we want to do next is to lift the prohibition on sexual intercourse and, as it were, allow "a little" intercourse. This is how it works:

first you caress each other all over again; lie next to each other for a while and caress each other. [*To the woman*] And then you stimulate your husband intensely.

Woman: Hmm.

M.Th.: And if you then feel comfortable and the penis is stiff, you can insert it. But take your time about it. Don't hurry, it doesn't have to happen within two minutes; allow yourself a lot of time when you try it. As I said, you make his penis stiff with your hand and then insert it in the squatting position, as in this picture. So your husband simply lies there on his back, you play with his penis, and then you sit down on him in the squatting position so you're facing each other. Take his penis in your right hand and draw your labia apart a little with your left hand . . .

Woman: O.K.

M.Th.: . . . and then insert the penis yourself. It's very important that you put your vagina round his penis, so to speak.

Woman: Uhuh.

M.Th.: But you should take care not to sit straight down on him but from an angle.

F.Th.: That's a little clearer in the illustration. [*To the man*] And what's important is that you have no part in the matter, your wife is in control. You simply put yourself at her disposal, so to speak. That's probably a little strange to you.

Man: But she leans forward.

F.Th.: No, she sits upright first; she will have to move about a bit to get it in right.

Man: Well, normally she doesn't need to.

M.Th.: She should anyway.

Man: Hmm.

F.Th.: It's best that way because your wife can participate more in the whole thing.

M.Th.: And the penis doesn't have to be all that stiff, but just as it is; and if it doesn't work the first time, then the next. You can give it a try without feeling it has to work out immediately. [*To the woman*] And once his penis is in, then sit quite still or perhaps lean forward just a little, as you saw in the picture, or even a little further forward.

F.Th.: If you want to, you can lie right down on your husband's chest.

Woman: O.K.

F.Th.: And don't do anything. Don't move. Neither of you. The penis will then go limp, which it should. Once it's limp or has even slipped out by itself, then take it in your hand again and stroke it until the erection slowly comes back. Then you insert the penis again, but again without moving.

Man: Stroke or rub?

M.Th.: Both. Then stay still as before until the erection dies down again. [*To the woman*] After a few moments take the penis out again. Once you've inserted the penis just concentrate on it being in your vagina. And try to relax in this position. The feeling you usually had in this position was: will it remain stiff and what will the ejaculation be like. But now you will be able to relax in this situation with the penis in your vagina and enjoy it as one kind of tenderness, no matter what happens.

F.Th.: When the penis goes limp again, you know it's bound to because you don't move. And you'll notice there's no big disappointment; it's on purpose, so to speak.

M.Th.: Yes, and when you've done that twice you can do anything you want to: petting until both of you or one of you reaches orgasm. Or you can simply say, let's cuddle together a bit. Whatever you want. So what you do afterward is up to you.

Man: But no intercourse?

M.Th.: No, not intercourse.

Woman: One question: when I insert my husband's penis, do I pull the foreskin back or can it stay as it normally is?

Man: It's pulled back automatically.

F.Th.: Yes, as your husband says, it slides back on its own when it enters the vagina. Although it's better to use a little lubricant beforehand. Just rub a little foam over the penis and spread a little on yourself so it slips in nice and easy.

Man: And no kind of movements.

F.Th.: Even if you're aroused and think it's going to work real fine, you just say to yourself, "We'll wait and see what it's like and won't move."

DISCUSSION OF EXPERIENCES

When discussing the exercises the therapists again demonstrate that new kinds of experience can still occur during the "familiar" assignments by letting the partners report first on how they felt while caressing each other's bodies. They try to discover whether the prospect of insertion inhibited relaxed enjoyment or prevented the erection. The therapists then go on to discuss the new assignment.

After the couple's report the therapists ask them about any technical difficulties, for example, did they have any problems with the position? Did she know how to kneel over her husband? Did she find the vaginal opening immediately? Did she wish she had a "third hand"? Was the position comfortable or strenuous? These questions make the couple aware that the expected disappointment or difficulties when first attempting insertion have nothing to do with failure but are quite natural at this point.

In this sequence the man frequently fails to achieve erection, even if erection occurred with regularity in previous exercises. This is also true of couples being treated for a female sexual dysfunction even though the man had never complained previously of erectile prob-

lems. The failure is due to the performance pressure the man is subjected to: because insertion of the penis is the next step in the therapeutic program, it seems as if he carries the entire responsibility for
what is going to happen since insertion is impossible without erection.
The therapists explain this point to the couple and emphasize that
insertion is "allowed" as of now, but it is not necessary. If the penis
does not stiffen, the woman can still place it in the vaginal opening or
can stroke her genitals with it. In this way the partners can get used to
doing the exercise without his having an erection.

SPECIAL PROBLEMS

Anticipatory fears and performance pressure reappear. The partners often experience more tension at first in this exercise than in previous
exercises because insertion of the penis evokes stronger associations
with negative experiences in coitus or attempts at it. They may feel
that anxieties and performance pressure being reawakened is a relapse, thinking they had already overcome them ("We're back at the
beginning again; there's just no sense in it; caressing just isn't sexuality," and so forth). A man with erectile dysfunctions is gripped by
panic if his erection is insufficient or subsides after insertion; a woman
with orgasmic dysfunction despairs because insertion does not amplify
her arousal.

The therapists should not pay too much attention to these feelings
of disappointment and resignation by questioning the partners. On
the contrary, they concentrate on any progress the couple mentions in
passing, for example, that preliminary caressing was pleasant despite
the prospect of a new assignment, that they felt relaxed at first in the
situation, that the partners were able to talk to each other about their
disappointment, and so forth.

It is essential that the therapists do not let themselves be influenced
by the couple's panic. For example, if the man's erection fails for several exercises they should consult with the couple about intermediate
steps the couple can take to relieve the tension. The couple is asked to
give priority to playing with arousal and to deliberately let the erection pass without exploiting it for an attempt at coitus. Or they insert
the penis as far as the partial erection will allow.

TIMING

The therapists can proceed to the next sequence if insertion of the
penis has been possible several times, and both partners were relaxed

and experienced it as pleasant. The aim of this sequence can be achieved at the earliest after two sessions (see table M.1).

Coitus with Explorative and Stimulating Movements

AIMS

The partners should aim at gathering experience with various kinds of pelvic movement during coitus. They should become aware of their preferences and dislikes and gradually gain confidence, both emotionally and technically. They should learn to feel that the pelvic movements are a continuation of caressing or a special kind of caressing and to use them with the according relaxation and lack of performance pressure.

PROCEDURE

The patients are instructed to go through all previous exercises as before. The therapists then explain the next step: once the woman has taken up the squatting position and the penis has been inserted she should, after a short pause, move her pelvis up and down slowly and carefully three to five times. She can prop herself on her hands. The man remains lying still and concentrates on the sensations he feels. The woman then pauses briefly and repeats the movements in a similar way. This should be repeated several times. She should try to find out how far she can lift her pelvis without the penis slipping out of her vagina. The penis is then retracted, and the partners lie next to each other or caress each other. After a short break, the penis is inserted again, and the exercise is repeated in the same way. The therapists explain that the movements are meant to increase the couple's confidence. They should learn to relax and enjoy the movements as a part of caressing, and they should get used to the unaccustomed distribution of roles during coitus—the man in the passive, the woman in the active role. The squatting position has the advantage of enabling the woman a considerable degree of freedom of movement. Again, the aim in question is not to achieve optimal stimulation or orgasm; on the contrary, if one partner notices he or she is becoming highly aroused, he or she should interrupt the movements until the arousal has died down again. However, the penis should remain inside the vagina. The movements can then be resumed. Once this assignment has been com-

pleted and the penis has been retracted, the partners can decide
whether to stimulate each other to orgasm, masturbate in front of each
other, or let the sense of mutual tenderness wear off by going back to
nongenital caressing or lying close to each other. It is important that
the sequence does not end with the new assignment but is concluded
by the partners caressing in this way.

DISCUSSION OF EXPERIENCES

First, the repeated exercises are discussed: the situations caressing
took place in, the atmosphere, and so forth. The therapists then ask if
the patients could cope with the instructions, whether they were able
to move easily, whether the penis slipped out at all, and so forth. The
man is asked how he felt in the passive role assigned to him. Both are
asked how they felt, how they experienced the movements (warm,
painful, pleasant, soft, or disappointing) and whether there were any
differences between long and short movements. If necessary the partners' reactions to the penis slipping out by mistake are discussed, and
the therapists point out that this frequently happens during this exercise. If the partners express disappointment by saying, for example,
that the movements "didn't really work," the insertion was difficult
again, arousal was not amplified or decreased by comparison with
manual stimulation, the therapists should reassure the partners. They
point out that the partners will first have to go through more experiences to be more confident and that intense genital stimulation is not
what matters at the moment, which fully explains why arousal diminishes. They again demonstrate to the partners that positive experiences
were nonetheless possible.

FURTHER PROCEDURE

In the following sessions the woman should experiment with the
various ways she can move, for example, circular pelvic movements,
up and down, fast, slow, short, long, or rhythmical movements; however, there should always be short breaks in between and neither of
the partners should reach orgasm. If the partners then feel fairly confident, they should begin moving alternately: first the woman a few
times, then after a short pause she raises her pelvis slightly and the
man does a few movements, and so forth. The partners can also try
imitating each other's movements or "mirroring" each other.

If they feel confident doing this they can go on to move simultaneously. The therapists point out that simultaneous movement is by

no means always the "best" way, but that the partners will have to discover their preferences and dislikes during the exercise and agree later on the preferred technique. If the patients feel confident doing this exercise they can continue the movements until climax or ejaculation, after pausing once or twice. The therapists should have explained by now that, as a rule, movements after insertion are more stimulating for men than for women, that men consequently usually ejaculate before the woman reaches climax or that many women do not reach orgasm at all through coitus alone. Orgasm is therefore not a measure of success in the exercise. The woman is then encouraged to allow the man to stimulate her manually or orally to orgasm before or afterward, to have her partner stimulate her with his hand while his penis is inserted, or to stimulate herself.

SPECIAL PROBLEMS

Insertion is no longer possible. If the partners report that in contrast to previous exercises insertion failed completely, the therapists should inquire what exactly happened. They will usually discover that the patients, being overenthusiastic or anxious about the new assignment, abandoned the other assignments, that is, both nongenital caressing and genital stimulation, or they felt under pressure to perform again. The therapists make this clear to the partners and encourage them to repeat the exercise with these points in mind.

Ejaculation on first movements. Even men who were not previously distressed by premature ejaculation sometimes report that ejaculation occurred after only the first movements. The therapists take a reassuring approach and explain that after prolonged coital abstinence the movements are bound to be particularly stimulating. If this happens again the couple should take a short break after ejaculation, stimulate and then insert the penis again. The problem will solve itself the more confident they become.

Disappointment about lack of arousal. Sometimes the partners, usually the woman, express disappointment at arousal failing to increase or even dwindling despite the movements during coitus. The therapists point out that particularly in the first phase of this sequence the emphasis is on playful experimenting and not on optimal stimulation. They ask the patients to concentrate on pleasant feelings such as warmth, closeness, and so forth, and not to wait for arousal. They can also mention that the man can stimulate his partner manually as well or that she can stimulate herself during coitus.

301

This sequence has been completed once the partners are able to perform coitus without technical difficulties and feel it is pleasant. It is not essential that they reach orgasm. They should, however, be in a position to tell each other their wishes, preferences, and dislikes in regard to the various ways of moving and stimulating during coitus. At least three sessions are needed to achieve these aims (see table M.1).

In long-term therapy the therapists then go on to the next and final sequence. In intensive therapy the next step is discussed with the couple only in the final session (see p. 305) in view of the limited number of sessions.

Coitus in Other Positions

AIMS

The partners should learn to transfer the positive experiences they have had so far in sexual interaction to other coital positions and gradually develop more confidence in their abilities. They will be able to clarify preferences and dislikes in terms of varying coital positions, to reduce anxieties associated with previous failures and avoidance behavior, and to extend the range of possibilities for sexuality and playing with each other. The partners may well argue about the point that women are often not stimulated optimally by the movements during coitus, even though they do experience it as pleasant. The couple can then experiment with various coital positions in which it is easy to give the woman additional manual stimulation.

PROCEDURE

At this point the partners often feel the need to try out other positions as well. The therapists encourage them to do so but point out how important it is not to neglect caressing. If it does not occur to the partners to try other positions, the therapists make their own suggestions and discuss them with the couple. The therapists make it clear that the point is not to practice a whole variety of different positions when making love but to discover that there are several positions more conducive to satisfying certain needs, such as close body contact or optimal freedom of movement. If they wish to the partners can go as far as orgasm, although this is only an option and not a requirement. Partners should decide on the basis of their personal experiences. It is also important to emphasize repeatedly that the partners, as in all new assignments, should communicate their intentions and feelings. The therapists warn the partners not to expect the first attempt to succeed immediately. They point out the positive experiences the partners have had so far in coping with difficulties in new assignments.

If the woman does not reach orgasm during coitus, the therapists can suggest that she lie on her back with her knees bent and one leg thrown over the hips of her partner, who lies on his side beside her. In this position the man can insert his penis from the side, and she can quite easily be stimulated manually during coitus, either by herself or by her partner. The couple is encouraged to try out this position. The therapists can also mention that the choice of position can influence the degree of indirect clitoral stimulation. Many women thus find that different positions vary considerably in degree of stimulation. It may be useful for partners to widen their experience in this respect; some women do, however, prefer an orgasm by caressing without intromission.

DISCUSSION OF EXPERIENCES

As before, the therapists inquire about frequency of sexual interaction and about experiences during caressing and stimulation before asking about experiences with other positions. If the couple was able to perform sexual intercourse in new positions without difficulty, the therapists point out that this is a sign of growing confidence and relaxation in sexual encounters. If a couple commits itself to a preferred position after one or two attempts and the therapists find no signs of anxieties and inhibitions indicating avoidance behavior, the therapists should respect the couple's choice.

The therapists also inquire about the couple's experience with additional manual stimulation for the woman and whether it was performed by her or her partner; they reinforce positive experiences and encourage patience and further practice.

SPECIAL PROBLEMS

Earlier symptoms reappear. If the partners report that on attempting coitus in a new position the penis failed to stiffen at all or that insertion was hindered by a constriction of the vaginal muscles, the therapists first inquire whether the partners caressed or stimulated each other properly before they tried the new position. They also remind the partners how they managed to solve similar problems in previous sequences. They repeatedly urge the couple to be patient and encourage them to go on with the exercises.

Avoidance of additional manual stimulation for the woman. If the woman would actually like to climax during coitus but the partners report again and again that they did not use additional manual stimulation, the therapists will have to analyze the reservations had by both. For example, it could be that the man feels piqued by having to put in a little more "manual labor" to bring his wife to climax. On the other hand, they may be inhibited by moral reservations on the woman's part or a deep-rooted misconception of "mature vaginal" orgasm. In such cases the therapists carefully explain how essential clitoral stimulation is for female arousal and orgasm. If a woman is able to enjoy the pelvic thrusts during coitus in the absence of arousal or orgasm and the couple refuses additional manual stimulation, the therapists should accept the situation.

TIMING

The aim of this sequence has been achieved when the partners have experienced coitus in a few positions as satisfying and when they are able to cope calmly with occasional feelings of displeasure, lack of arousal or erection, and so forth. The therapists then indicate that the final session will soon take place and that the last phase of therapy has thus been reached. They do so even if a few details have yet to be worked through or the original aims of therapy, especially in terms of sexual functioning, have not quite been achieved. This is often the case with orgasmic dysfunctions, when the couple is capable of finding pleasure in caressing and coitus, but the woman has not yet reached orgasm.

The therapists can now mention that in their experience the positive changes induced continue to have an effect and develop after completion of therapy. It may make it easier for the couple if therapy is slowly faded out: the therapists suggest scheduling the last two or three sessions before the final session at intervals of two weeks. The couple's anxieties about completing therapy, about relapses, and so forth, should also be dealt with in these last sessions. The therapists inform the patients in advance that they will be available for counseling after therapy should the need arise.

In our experience therapists tend to have exaggerated expectations of therapy outcome, especially if a good relationship with the couple has developed in the course of therapy. It is therefore advisable to discuss the timing of therapy completion in the supervision group.

The Final Session

AIMS

The partners should comment on therapy outcome and address any unanswered questions or anxieties and fears about the period after completion of therapy. The therapists should summarize therapy outcome from their point of view and point out which behavior modifications are particularly important to the couple's changed sexual relationship. The therapists remind the partners that counseling after completion of therapy is possible if any serious problems arise. Therapists should also discuss with the partners how they are going to integrate their experiences into everyday life in the first few weeks after therapy.

PROCEDURE

As before the therapists first ask the partners about their experiences since the last session. Subsequently they inquire about the partners' feelings about the pending completion of therapy. The following questions should be considered: how satisfied the partners are with therapy outcome; which of the original aims have been achieved; whether there are any problems still to be resolved; what the patients' expectations, fears, or plans concerning the period immediately after completion of therapy are.

The therapists explain again that the positive changes often develop further after completion of therapy, as long as partners go on complying with the basic rules they learned in therapy (for example, talking openly about feelings toward each other and about their needs; not doing anything merely for the partner's sake; not trying to force certain sexual reactions, and so forth). The therapists point out that even after completing therapy successfully problems will always arise, even with sexual functioning. But this will not present any particular difficulties if the partners handle the problems in the way they learned to during therapy.

The partners have usually set aside other interests for a while in favor of therapy; once therapy is completed they will obviously devote more time again to them. However, the partners should not allow this to impede sexual activity for any length of time because they still need to gain more confidence. The couple is encouraged to continue joint sexual activities regularly after therapy and to feel that sexual activity does not necessarily have to lead to orgasm or coitus: they should in any case caress regularly and then wait and see how far they wish to go and what they feel like doing. This will help them to accept caressing, petting, and coitus as equally valid alternatives.

If their wish is for children—particularly if it was one of the main motives for therapy—the couple is informed that pregnancy coming immediately after therapy could endanger previous achievements because the positive experiences still have to take hold. It is therefore advisable to wait at least a half year before discontinuing the use of contraceptives.

In conclusion, the therapists remind the patients again of their offer for counseling whenever the patients have the feeling they cannot cope alone with a problem. In our experience extremely few couples take up this offer.

TRANSCRIPT

COUPLE 24: We have already discussed this couple (see p. 165). The man suffers from erectile dysfunctions. The couple was assigned to long-term therapy with two therapists.

Man: We went on doing what we've done so far, twice. Caressing with all the trimmings.
F.Th.: And insertion in the sideways position?
Man: Yes, sure.
F.Th.: Last time you mentioned other positions briefly. You said you had already had some experience with another position, didn't you?
Man: Yes.
F.Th.: Did you feel like trying it out again?
Man: No, that's not the real thing, you know.
Woman: No, we didn't . . .
Man: . . . really get it together.
F.Th.: So you did try something out?
Man: No, we didn't try it this time.
F.Th.: I see.
Man: There are probably still some dislikes or inhibitions there preventing one or both of us from experimenting, as you so nicely put it.
M.Th.: When you think about it the old disappointments come back?
Man: Exactly.
F.Th.: Something you probably want to avoid.
M.Th.: I still don't quite understand. When does your wish emerge to try another position?
Man: Well, you know, we talked about it, but . . .
F.Th.: After the exercise?
Man: Yes. But we couldn't agree.
Woman: Besides we don't know whether we really ought to, whether it's really the right thing.
M.Th.: Yes, that's what I wanted to know; whether you ask yourselves, perhaps our therapists expect us to try out another position.

Therapeutic Procedure

Man: Yes.

Woman: I don't know either how and what and whether we really ought to. I mean, as far as I'm concerned.

F.Th.: So you don't really feel the desire yourself?

Woman: Not really.

F.Th.: I think it's very important that there are no rules saying what you should or shouldn't do.

Man: Right.

F.Th.: And it just isn't absolutely necessary to have intercourse; you can use your hand to reach climax.

Man: Sure.

F.Th.: Each person has to find out his or her own preferences. At the moment it seems you don't feel like any other position at all, or . . .

Woman: Well, maybe, we just don't know whether it's really the right thing to do.

M.Th.: I think that's the decisive point. The moment you ask yourself whether it's the right thing, should we or shouldn't we, it's no longer a playful decision but something like having to do the rest of the homework on top of it all.

Man: Yes, I guess you could . . .

Woman: Yeah, something like that.

M.Th.: In that moment you're not really relaxed any longer; you start watching yourself, how you have to lie down, what you're supposed to do, and then it doesn't work any more.

Woman: Or whether we would feel better staying on the old track.

Man: On the same old, oh so familiar track.

M.Th.: Then you feel under pressure to try something else because we two said "experiment."

Man: Right. Honestly, it's like a psychological block.

M.Th.: You want to comply but notice that you don't really feel the need at the moment.

Man: Exactly.

M.Th.: Well, I think we'd better tell you quite clearly that you don't have to. That applies for later, too. Let's get that straight once and for all. It could be you'll really feel the wish yourself sometime, and then you can go ahead.

Woman: But, at the moment we lack the fantasy; I do in any case. And we didn't let it bother us, at least I didn't. We talked about it.

F.Th.: It's good you talk to each other about it.

Woman: As I said, we just lack the fantasy.

Man: We talked about it and decided not to.

F.Th.: Perhaps I should mention another important point; a lot of couples try out different positions and have no problems with them; a lot of them do, in effect, have a kind of standard position. Which one is another matter. They vary a great deal in their choices of the most pleasant one.

Man: Yes, sure.

F.Th.: But the times you were together, did you enjoy it?

Man: Yes.

F.Th.: No problems?

Man: No.

M.Th.:   You had sexual intercourse?

Man: Sure, yes.

M.Th.:   And you ejaculated?

Man: Yes.

M.Th.:   [*To the woman*] Did you have an orgasm during sexual intercourse or while caressing afterward?

Woman: No, during intercourse.

M.Th.:   I see. Are there any differences in the way you experience or assess orgasm during intercourse and orgasm during caressing?

Woman: Not really, not that I know.

M.Th.:   You like both equally.

Woman: Yes.

M.Th.:   I think it's very important to be able to accept both as pleasant and not to think one is inferior.

Woman: Oh no.

Man: No, we couldn't say that one way is first on the list and the other is only second best, I wouldn't say that. At least as far as I'm concerned.

F.Th.:   So you can decide quite freely when and how you want to be together.

Man: Yes.

F.Th.:   And talk about who wants what and how.

Man: Right. It's something we hardly ever talked about before, you know, and as I said last time, the whole spectrum of our life together has opened out; problems we used to think of as unimportant are now talked over in detail. We quarrel far less often than before therapy.

M.Th.:   Hmm.

Man: Yes, I would say so.

M.Th.:   Yes. There's something else I'd like to know: when exactly do you ejaculate?

Man: It varies a lot.

M.Th.:   Can you tell us what you think your ejaculation depends on? For example, whether there are situations in which you feel highly aroused and can't control yourself any longer?

Man: No, no, not any more. It used to be like that. But nowadays, there's quite a difference, I would say.

M.Th.:   In the sense that it goes on longer.

Man: Yes.

M.Th.:   And both of you benefit more from intercourse?

Man: Yes, sure. I would say so; I don't know if my wife feels the same way.

Woman: Yes, I do.

Man: For my part . . . what happened before was that the ejaculation came practically within seconds. Now I can delay it for quite some time mostly, but not always yet.

M.Th.:   And how do you do that?

Man: Well, more or less by putting up a block and saying, not yet.

M.Th.:   You give yourself a kind of instruction?

Man: Yes.

M.Th.:   And the instruction helps you cool down a little.

Therapeutic Procedure

Man: Right.

M.Th.: And then you don't feel so aroused.

Man: Exactly.

M.Th.: Do you stop moving then?

Man: No. I can control it much more consciously than I ever thought possible before.

F.Th.: So you feel more confident during intercourse?

Man: Yes. And you know, above all, to put it blandly, I wasn't really ashamed before but it was often terribly embarrassing when the ejaculation came so incredibly quickly. And then somehow I knew my wife wasn't satisfied. It was probably a kind of guilt complex and that certainly had a strong effect.

M.Th.: By making it happen again and again?

Man: Yes.

M.Th.: Because you were afraid from the start it would happen.

Man: Yes.

Woman: And then you got angry.

Man: Yes, then I was angry.

F.Th.: [To the woman] You were as well, if I remember correctly?

Woman: Not as much as my husband.

F.Th.: I see.

Woman: He was insulted and piqued.

F.Th.: So you really got each other worked up?

Woman: Right.

F.Th.: You were afraid of it happening, so it promptly happened. And then you were both angry.

Man: Yes.

F.Th.: And then there's no way it can work.

Man: Exactly. It's a joke even thinking about it now.

Woman: Sure, now. But you used to go purple with anger.

Man: Yes, more or less.

F.Th.: So you both take a different approach altogether and feel safer.

Woman: Yes, definitely.

Man: I would say the difference is like between day and night.

F.Th.: Hmm.

Man: I mean not only in sexuality, but generally as well. Our relationship as a whole has changed completely, isn't so embittered as before. This bitterness has backed down a good way. And if it does come up again, when there are somehow disagreements, then we talk about them and discuss them until we find a compromise. So we don't just march past each other any more.

F.Th.: You're no longer irritated when a problem arises; you've noticed that you *are* capable of solving problems jointly.

Man: Yes. We had an experience recently that used to send us reeling, as they say. Then our son had an accident and broke his leg. O.K., so my wife cried, of course she did.

Woman: But I really must say my husband always, always used to shift the responsibility onto me. Even for small things. This time he took care of everything himself. Of course I was real glad, you know. I didn't have to do anything at all, hardly. He picked him up from school, brought him here to the hospital. I used to have to do all that. Without a word being said, it was just a matter of course. He used to say, "Why don't you, I don't feel like it." Now it's the other way round; we take turns anyway.

Man: Well, yes let's say, as you already described it, I more or less left the leading role up to you, played it into your hands.

F.Th.: You mean pushed it into her hands.

Woman: Yes. Because you never did anything. Someone has to get the things done, you can't always put everything off.

F.Th.: So now you really share the responsibility for things like that. What I find important is that on the one hand you feel much more confident and treat each other more affectionately; and on the other hand, you have learned to cope with problems which will crop up again and again.

Man: Yes.

Woman: The sun doesn't shine every day, does it? But then it's not the same as before when we used to drive each other crazy and stayed out of each other's way. If one of us doesn't want to, O.K., he's in a bad mood, so there's nothing you can do.

F.Th.: Right.

Man: Yes, well, and one might just as well talk about the reason for the bad mood.

Woman: After all, there usually is a reason.

Man: Which one can talk about.

F.Th.: Without always sweeping it under the carpet.

Man: Sure. Not if we can help it.

Woman: Or if he's got trouble at work, so we talk about it. Of if I'm in trouble, we talk about that too. Was it the right thing or the wrong thing to do, or should you have done this, that, or the other.

M.Th.: But it's important not to count on things being as they are at the moment; sometimes you'll be more annoyed or will be more likely to get depressed about a problem.

Man: Oh no, I'd contradict you there, definitely.

M.Th.: Hmm.

Man: Of course there'll be problems which we won't be able to avoid, but one can try and make the best of it.

M.Th.: Well, you seem realistic so we won't have to warn you of any setbacks.

Woman: They'll always happen.

Man: They'll always happen, I'm perfectly aware of that.

M.Th.: You aren't afraid it could knock you right off course?

Man: No.

M.Th.: So you calmly try to identify the problem and work it out together, and that makes you quite optimistic about finding a way out.

F.Th.: All the same, if any problems do crop up which seem too difficult for you, you can always give us a call.

Woman: Yes.

Man: That's a kind offer.

M.Th.: Because the period after therapy especially is a time when the couple has, so to speak, got to adapt to the situation without a therapist, has to be its own therapist.

Man: Exactly, and find its way alone, if I understand you right.

M.Th.: Precisely. And sometimes that can lead to a kind of insecurity at first. But if you do feel you're getting bogged down in something then just give us a call and we can talk on the phone or you can drop in for a talk.

Woman: Fine.

F.Th.: My impression is that the thought that the regular sessions have come to an end and that this is the final one doesn't bother you and you seem quite optimistic about the future.

Woman: Yes, I must say I haven't given it any thought, not once.

Man: Well, I wouldn't say I haven't thought about it. But, as you said last time, if any apparently unsolvable problems do arise—note I said "apparently," because there's no such thing as an unsolvable problem—then we'll call you.

M.Th.: I just think you shouldn't start being quite as ambitious as wanting to cope with everything, but . . .

Woman: Of course not.

Man: No.

F.Th.: If there are any questions . . .

Woman: . . . we'll call you. That's a reassuring feeling. We might need that to start with.

Man: So we practically have a safety valve, yes, that's really quite reassuring, I must say.

Additional Interventions

In the following we shall describe some supplementary interventions that have proved useful in dealing with particular problems. As the title implies, these are not alternatives to the basic therapy format but additional interventions that the therapists integrate into the basic format as required.

Bodily Self-Awareness: Women

CRITERIA

Exercises for bodily self-awareness are an important supplement to the basic program for patients who are not familiar with their own bodies and their reactions, do not accept their bodies or have no experience with masturbation. How intensely and how far one should proceed with "bodily self-awareness" has to be decided in each individual case. The first steps (inspecting the body and genitals, explorative genital caressing) can adjust informational deficits and inhibitions, and so be a great help to partners of dysfunctional males who themselves have no sexual dysfunctions. The same applies to women with vaginismus, even if they are able to reach orgasm with petting or masturbation. In their case exact knowledge of their own bodies is required before going on to the special exercises with dilators (p. 317). We generally assign all women with primary arousal or orgasmic disturbances to exercises for bodily self-awareness as a supplement to the basic program, although not necessarily to all parts of the exercises. The exercises for bodily self-awareness can also help women who reach orgasm only by using special masturbation techniques (for example, thigh pressure, pressing their genital area against objects, and so forth). In any case, the first steps in this sequence are an important diagnostic instrument and often show up many previously inaccessible anxieties and inhibitions.

AIMS

Women should generally get to know and learn to accept their bodies and their reactions more, including the genitals. In the absence of performance pressure, a woman can experience step by step how she reacts to various kinds of touch and stimulation and thus develop greater familiarity with her body. Any obvious problems with self-esteem or any doubt about her own "femininity" should be worked through. The opportunity for new experiences without her partner can convey a new feeling of autonomy in sexuality and make it easier for her to deal with her sexual anxieties, particularly the fear of losing control.

PROCEDURE

This part of the program is implemented in conjunction with therapy sessions of the female patient alone with the female therapist, which last about twenty minutes each prior to the couple therapy sessions. The exercises should not begin before caressing II so that the couple can first engage in more joint experiences. Procedure is based on the work of LoPiccolo and Lobitz (1972).[6]

By taking examples from her own history, the woman is shown that her present situation is the result of specific conditions of socialization, which in our society are predominantly hostile to the body and to sexuality, and particularly to female sexuality. Consequently her problem is not an individual failure "as a woman." Many women's knowledge of their own bodies and especially their genitals is impaired by the anatomical fact that, in contrast to men, they are not automatically confronted by the sight of their own genitals.

The female therapist questions the patient about her attitudes in this respect and explains that experience with and confidence in her own body are an essential premise for satisfying sexual relations. The patient is then asked to take time to do the exercises once or twice before the next session. If she is alone, she should (after bathing or showering, if she wishes) examine her naked body in a large mirror from all sides and pick out the places she likes and those she does not. She should then lie down in a comfortable place, bend her legs up slightly, open them, and look at her own genitals closely with the help of a small mirror; she should try to identify the various parts of her genitals, such as the clitoris, major and minor labia, vaginal opening, perineum, and urethra. The therapist shows the woman an illustration of the female genitals and explains the position and function of each part. It often helps to give the woman an illustration to take home with her.

DISCUSSION OF EXPERIENCES

When discussing the patient's experiences, the therapist first inquires how the woman felt, whether she found it difficult to do the exercise, how often she took time for it, and so forth. She next questions her as to her specific reactions both at the sight of her entire body and at the examination of her genitals and particularly reinforces any tendency for the woman to view herself in a positive light. If the woman was unable to identify all parts of her genitals, the illustration is again explained in detail and individual differences in size, color, and so forth, are pointed out.

FURTHER PROCEDURE

If the patient is now well acquainted with her own body and her genitals, she is asked to touch herself the next time as well and feel her labia, clitoris, and so forth, with her fingers. She should not hesitate to use a mirror and the illustration as aids again. To avoid unpleasant sensations when doing these exercises, the therapist recommends the use of a lubricant. Furthermore the patient should occasionally tense and relax the pubococcygeus muscle voluntarily

(Kegel's technique) and at the same time watch for any changes in the genital area in the mirror.

The next step is for the women to continue manual and visual exploration of her genitals and then to watch for any differences in her sensations when touching clitoris, labia, vaginal opening, and perineal area with varying pressure and rhythms and to be aware of what she finds pleasant or unpleasant. The therapist encourages the patient to take a playful, experimental approach and points out how important it is to inspect the entire area around the labia and perineum and not to close out certain areas so that she can become more familiar with all possible reactions and experiences and reduce any fears she may have.

Once the woman has been sensitized to the different kinds of sensation in the genital area, she is asked to make use of these experiences the next time and to caress herself the way she enjoys most. If she becomes aroused she should not stimulate herself to orgasm at first but should let the arousal fade out again and then revive it through stimulative caressing just as in the "playing with arousal" exercises. She can then continue until "something happens," that is, until orgasm or until she no longer feels like it.

If necessary, previous assignments can then be intensified and modified further. After discussing her sexual fantasies the therapist can, for example, encourage the patient to use arousing fantasies or even pictures and texts when stimulating herself. By showing and jointly discussing a film on masturbation or teaching her how to act out a "wild orgasm," the woman can be helped to reduce her fear of losing control. Although they have learned in the exercises to accept their bodies including their genitals, and are able to enjoy and be aroused by stimulating themselves, some women have never had an orgasm either before therapy or during the exercises for bodily self-awareness. For them an orgasm brought about by highly intense stimulation, for example, by using a hand-spray or a vibrator, can mean breaking through their emotional barriers. This technique is useful only if any reservations either the patient or the therapist may have about such mechanical stimulation (on the ground of "artificiality" or "expediency," for example) can be dispelled and if no new performance pressure ensues.

The first orgasmic experience can relieve a woman of the anxiety of not being able to function fully. This relief often results in the woman being able to relax far more when stimulating herself or when petting with her partner, and she thus experiences high levels of arousal or orgasm. However, it is often necessary for the therapist to guide the woman step by step in transferring these experiences to other forms of stimulation.

SPECIAL PROBLEMS

Intense avoidance behavior. In the first phase particularly, it often happens that women cannot find the time for the exercises, do not like them, or quite simply refuse to do them because they think they are "plain stupid." The female therapist should react exactly as in couple therapy. Besides, the first assignment can be divided into two steps, the first being for the woman just to look at her naked body.

Disgust at one's own genitals. Many women experience the sight or touch of their own genitals as unpleasant or disgusting, as a kind of wound that mobilizes fears of injury and so forth. They often cannot manage to integrate this area into their body image. This problem often solves itself when the woman becomes more familiar with her body after a few sessions. Many women can be helped in this situation by the therapist explaining the functional reason for certain genital features: the reddish color of the labia is caused by increased blood supply; the skin is creased because only then is there sufficient elasticity for giving birth. If despite using a lubricant women still say they experience even a light touch as unpleasant, then they are frequently misinterpreting familiar sensations. The problem can be solved by the therapist suggesting another interpretation or name for the sensations.

What does arousal or orgasm mean? Many women have completely unrealistic ideas about the way their bodies express arousal and orgasm. The existence of this problem usually becomes clear when they are asked to focus caressing on the genitals and exaggerated expectations lead to intense disappointment. In this case the female therapist closely questions the patient's sensations during the exercise, for example, whether the patient experienced a feeling of warmth or a pleasant tickling in her abdomen or whether she noticed any changes during the exercise (darker color or swelling of clitoris and labia). The therapist explains that this is a sign of arousal. She outlines the wide range of variations in arousal and orgasm between individuals and within one individual's experience. In this context the therapist can make the point that it is wiser to measure one's experiences against subjective feelings and not against objective physical functioning.

Arousal "breaks off" just before climax. Some women report being highly aroused when stimulating themselves, but that arousal then suddenly breaks off without their changing stimulation or climaxing. The therapist again carefully explains that the point is to achieve a general sense of pleasure. She asks the woman to play the game with arousal. Only then can she go on stimulating herself for as long as she likes; but she should not count on an orgasm. The therapists must also clarify whether the break in arousal is due to fear-inciting fantasies or fear of losing control.

INTEGRATION IN COUPLE THERAPY

Both in individual and in couple sessions therapists and the couple discuss how the woman is to introduce her experiences with herself into the joint exercises. She can do this by explaining the position and function of the clitoris, vaginal opening, and so forth, to her partner during explorative caressing and by expressing her wishes during stimulative caressing as to how she likes to be caressed most and by leading his hand. Acting an orgasm in her partner's presence and the experience of stimulating herself to climax in front of him are both sometimes important intermediate steps in the basic program for women with orgasmic disturbances. Moreover, in the basic program sequences following insertion of the penis, the woman can always refer to her experience with bodily self-awareness, and, for example, express her wishes for specific stimulation.

Bodily Self-Awareness: Men

We did not include bodily self-awareness for men as a systematic supplement to couple therapy for the reason that we had mistaken the advanced masturbation experience of almost all the men for bodily self-awareness and consequently did not realize the necessity for an appropriate program.

However, we did assign some men with specific problems to self-awareness exercises. Because of fantasied or real physical conditions (for example, phimosis), some men are afraid of pain when their genitals are touched or stimulated. As a result they do not like to touch themselves and cannot let their partners do so either. Explorative caressing mobilizes intense fears of injury which, if they fail to be noticed or worked out, can result in therapy stagnating. Self-awareness exercises (inspection of genitals, touching the penis and glans) enable these fears to be gradually reduced.

Many men masturbate mechanically and without recourse to fantasies. When masturbating these men never imagine inserting the penis into a vagina or ejaculating there. It can be of help to men with erectile disturbances and premature ejaculation if they "practice" erection and ejaculation control in their fantasies while masturbating.

A good many other men have been masturbating secretly and rapidly for years, attempting to reach orgasm in the shortest possible time. This often conceals an insecure attitude toward sexuality. By masturbating in this way they learn a hasty sexuality that results in both partners being frustrated during intercourse. These men can be helped in therapy by learning to play with arousal when masturbating.

In view of the experiences described, it is important to analyze carefully the male partner's masturbation fantasies and techniques, no matter whether they are the symptomatic partner or not, to discuss them, and if necessary to give behavioral instructions for modification.

Additional Intervention for Vaginismus

Couples being treated for the woman's vaginismus will already have prepared for this additional sequence in the discussion of histories when the therapists explain how vaginismus functions. The program is integrated in the basic program during the sequence of explorative caressing. By this time the female patient should have acquainted herself with her own body, especially the genitals, in the exercises for bodily self-awareness.

AIMS

The aim is to help the woman to be able to relax and accept insertion of the penis without fear of pain by gradually reducing reflexlike vaginal constriction at imagined or real vaginal intromission.

PROCEDURE

The therapists lead on from the discussion of histories to explaining how to use dilators.[7] They emphatically stress that the function of dilators is not to widen the vagina but to familiarize the vagina with something being inserted and being left there. To explain the point the therapists once again refer to an illustration that shows that the vagina is not "too narrow" but that constriction of the vaginal muscles creates a bottleneck, which can, however, be removed by relaxing.

The female therapist then gives the female patient the thinnest of the five dilators and questions her about her feelings on seeing and touching it. The therapist then asks the patient whether she would prefer to insert the dilator in her partner's presence or alone at first. Most women find it less inhibiting to try insertion alone; a few do, however, feel that the presence of their partners as passive spectators is a support.

The woman should practice using the dilator twice before the next session. For insertion the female therapist recommends that she lie on her back, spread and bend up her legs slightly, and (as in bodily self-awareness) hold the inner and outer labia apart with one hand so the vaginal opening is exposed. Then, either alone or in her partner's presence, she should insert the dilator, which she has moistened with lubricant and warmed with her hand. Before insertion she also spreads lubricant around the vaginal opening. The therapist shows the woman how to hold the dilator (curve facing upward) and the correct angle of entry into the vagina.

While slowly inserting the dilator, the patient concentrates her attention on the sensations in her vagina; if an unpleasant sensation or pain occurs she should not insert the dilator any further, but should not pull it out again, either. She tries to relax and after a while inserts the dilator further.

Once the dilator has been inserted as far as it can go, that is, about four inches, it should be left in the vagina for ten to fifteen minutes. In the meantime the woman concentrates intensely on herself, on her feelings: whether she is relaxed or relieved that it does not hurt, whether she feels pain or any pressure, or whether the sensations change as time passes, and so on.

If the first attempts at insertion are made in the partner's presence, the partners inform each other when one or the other feels the need to caress or to be caressed. The couple may caress each other both when the dilator is inserted and afterward.

TRANSCRIPT

COUPLE 43: The woman, a waitress, is almost thirty; the man, an office clerk, is in his late thirties. They have been married for eight years and because of vaginismus have never been able to have sexual intercourse. Neither has had any sexual experience with other partners. The couple was assigned to intensive therapy with two therapists.

F.Th.: We've already talked about it once, this fear that it might hurt, that nothing can be inserted, which reinforces pain and tension. And the feeling that absolutely nothing will go in. Which isn't true, of course; the vagina can adapt.

Woman: Yes, of course, otherwise sexual intercourse would be impossible.

F.Th.:   Where the vagina opens there's a muscle that relaxes and contracts. You can contract it voluntarily and learn to relax it. And we want to give you the opportunity to try that now, I mean inserting something into your vagina without it hurting or you getting cramped; so you can have the experience of having something inside your vagina without it hurting or you getting cramped.

Woman: Hmm.

F.Th.:   And to do that we've got these dilators that you might have seen at your doctor's; I'll show you one. It looks like this. Would you mind holding it? This one's relatively small, thinner than a tampon, for example. It's very smooth so it slips in very easily. And I'd like to ask you to try to insert the dilator.

Woman: What?

M.Th.:   Warm it a little with your hand before . . .

Woman: What, this thing?

F.Th.:   I'll explain everything exactly once again: what you do is warm the dilator with your hand, that just makes it more comfortable. Have you still got some lubricant?

Woman: Yes, I do.

F.Th.:   Then spread some over the dilator, real thick. Then it'll be nice and smooth. The next question is, how do you want to do it: preferably on your own, when your husband's not there, or whether you want your husband to be there or you want him to do it.

Woman: Oh no!

F.Th.:   O.K., the first time you try it alone.

Woman: When do I have to be finished?

F.Th.:   What do you mean, "finished"?

Woman: I mean, how much time have I got, if it doesn't work?

F.Th.:   All the time in the world; you're only meant to try it out. You don't need to get in a panic if it doesn't work right away. So, you hold it just as you're doing now, that's important. You lie down on your back and try to spread your legs and then draw your labia apart a little with one hand, O.K.? And at the same time feel where the vagina goes in. You've already looked at it and touched it. And then you just try to insert the dilator.

Woman: Couldn't I damage something?

F.Th.:   No, you needn't be afraid of that.

Woman: I won't dig into anything?

F.Th.:   No, you can't.

Woman: I mean, I might go straight through my stomach.

M.Th.:   Through your stomach?

Woman: Well, O.K., I mean through my bladder or something.

F.Th.:   Your vagina is so long that you really can insert the dilator two thirds of the way. So anything you feel when you insert it is muscle tension, but nothing that could cause damage.

Woman: Not that something . . .

M.Th.: No, you needn't worry at all.

Woman: Is it hard? I mean the vaginal opening, where it goes in down there.

F.Th.: Actually, it's completely soft.

Woman: Yes, I mean, can't it get damaged by tearing or . . .

M.Th.: No, nothing can be damaged, really. You just have to try.

Woman: Yes, and if the man is so big, I mean his penis? What is the vagina? A narrow pipe like an air pipe, or what?

F.Th.: A tube that can stretch.

Woman: Like rubber; so you can go through it.

F.Th.: Do it quite slowly. Insert the dilator just a little way. It could be you'll notice you're getting very tense because you're afraid; or if you notice it hurts a little or there's pressure or resistance, then stop. But don't pull the dilator out again; leave it in there and try to relax a little. Then try to insert the dilator a little further. If you notice there's some resistance again, then stop again and relax, and so on. When you've inserted it half way you'll have done well.

Woman: Yet bet! But not the whole thing right away?

F.Th.: No. Try and go as far as you can. And when you've gotten that far, leave it in for about twenty minutes.

Woman: That long?

F.Th.: Yes.

Woman: I won't be able to get it out again!

F.Th.: That's no problem. You only have to insert it about this far.

Woman: I mean, I might get a fright and it'll vanish.

F.Th.: That can't happen either. Could you repeat what you're supposed to do, step by step.

Woman: Well, first I'm supposed to caress. And when I'm moist . . .

F.Th.: Even if you aren't, try it all the same; that's why you're meant to lubricate the dilator.

Woman: Yes, then it just slips in on its own. And when I'm really relaxed, I should simply try it. [*To the man*] You can hold my hand or just watch, and I'll do it on my own. And then should I lie down like this, or like this?

F.Th.: Just try it out.

Woman: If it hurts and gets cramped, then I should relax. And then I'm supposed to insert it half way and lie still for fifteen minutes.

F.Th.: The most important point is: the dilator is not meant to widen or expand your vagina.

Woman: No, no, it widens on its own.

F.Th.: All that matters is that you experience what it's like to insert something into your vagina without it hurting.

Woman: I really must say, I think it's incredible anything like this is possible. It's perfectly normal, I guess. I mean it doesn't have to hurt, I believe you there.

F.Th.: You can be quite certain that nothing will be damaged. But what might happen is that it pinches a little or you'll notice resistance. And the reason is that you're tensing yourself. So I can't say it's going to be easy.

Woman: No, sure.

F.Th.: But you'll be surprised to find it's possible. If you notice anything, then it's just muscle tension.

Woman: Like at the dentist when I tense myself because I'm waiting for the pain.

F.Th.: Exactly.

Woman: [*To the man*] You're going to be there.

Man: You bet I am.

F.Th.: If you would, try it twice, but don't forget to caress. If caressing irritates you when you're doing the exercise then leave it out, especially if you can't relax when caressing because you're thinking about the dilator.

Woman: What I'm really curious about—I do have a certain curiosity—is what it's like when my husband has an orgasm and he's there inside me. I mean, does it come out again, or what happens?

F.Th.: Part of it runs out again.

Woman: What happens to the rest?

F.Th.: It's absorbed by the vaginal walls.

M.Th.: Once you've inserted the dilator part of the way, you'll find that the rest of the dilator goes in much easier.

Woman: If you say so, I'll believe you. I trust you. [*laughs*] That's a great help, anyway.

DISCUSSION OF EXPERIENCES

The therapists first let the partners report on the caressing exercise. Whether the couple mentions negative changes or not, the therapists should ask them whether the new assignment had an effect on them while caressing.

The therapists should not accept general descriptions, such as "and then it simply slipped in" or "and then it simply wouldn't go in any further," when discussing the new exercise. They inquire about the woman's feelings by saying, for example, "That sounds as if you were very astonished it was so easy" or "Try and describe more exactly why it wouldn't go in any further; was there some pressure in the vagina or a burning sensation? Were you afraid it would hurt?" They try to find out to what extent difficulties were due to technical mistakes, discuss them, and reinforce the woman's positive experiences.

The man's feelings should also be analyzed: whether he felt left out, what he thinks of the dilator, whether he watched or felt insecure, and so forth. The questions asked depend on whether the man was present on insertion or not. During the entire additional program, care should be taken not to center too much on the woman.

SPECIAL PROBLEMS

Many therapists have objections to using dilators when conducting the supplementary program for vaginismus for the first time. It is important that the therapists are aware of these reservations. In our experience, these objections are for the most part dispelled in the course of therapy once the therapists see that the dilators enable the female patient to attain a certain amount of autonomy with her own body and that the dilators are not an instrument for dilation.

The woman is often gripped by a slight panic when hearing the assignment explained or just before the first attempt at insertion, but she is usually soon surprised by how easy it is to insert the first thin dilator. If the dilator can be inserted only with difficulty, or not at all, the therapists have to find out whether the woman is holding the dilator incorrectly (with the curve facing downward or at a steep angle from below or above), whether she is unable to find the vaginal opening, or whether the dilator has been lubricated enough. If necessary, all this should be explained once again. Insertion can also be facilitated by tensing the stomach muscles (diaphragmatic breathing) because this relaxes the vaginal musculature.

Once the dilator has been inserted for the first time the women often still feels too insecure to make any movements or let herself be caressed. She is encouraged to draw up her legs a little the next time or to lie on her side once the dilator has been inserted. Many women also report being alarmed at the dilator revolving slightly when they let go of it. This is an opportunity for the therapists to point out how wide the inner part of the vagina is.

FURTHER PROCEDURE

Once insertion of the thinnest dilator is possible, the woman is given the next thickest. She starts by inserting the thinnest dilator for three or four minutes, takes it out, and then inserts the larger one, leaving it in for at least ten minutes. Depending on how secure the women feels and on her initiative, the man sooner or later takes an active part in inserting the dilator. The therapists outline each step (for example, the man watches; then he places his hand on the woman's while she inserts the dilator; the woman places the dilator in the vaginal opening, and the man inserts it). At all events the woman holds her labia apart and corrects the angle and speed of insertion.

The couple proceeds slowly from one dilator to the next and is given the next thickest only when the previous dilator can be inserted without difficulty. In each exercise the woman uses two dilators: the one she can insert and the next thickest, inserting the former only briefly and the latter for about ten to fifteen minutes, so she can relax and feel more secure. If the woman is able to insert the first two or three dilators, the therapists suggest that she try inserting one of her fingers into her vagina. If this causes no problems the man should try inserting his finger. Any reservations or fears he may have with regard to female genitals will have to be discussed and dealt with.

If the woman has no difficulty in inserting the fourth dilator, the therapists suggest that the woman attempt inserting the dilators in the squatting position. They inform her that initially it could be more difficult in this new position because the leg and pelvic musculature is more tensed.

The therapists encourage the woman to attempt the so-called Kegel exercises in this squatting position, that it, she should tense her pubo-coccygeus muscle. By first feeling with a finger in the vaginal opening, she will find out that she can voluntarily cause contractions in the vaginal opening and need not feel helplessly exposed to the reflexes of her vagina.

If the woman is able to insert the thickest dilator without difficulty the therapists instruct the couple to insert the penis. Immediately before inserting the penis, the woman should once again insert the thickest dilator. Women are often uneasy about the penis being larger than the dilators. The therapists then remind them of previous experiences with the dilators (flexibility of the vagina) and point out that a penis is softer and more flexible than a dilator.

Many couples still have difficulty in inserting the penis after several exercises. The partners are not always immediately able to transfer their experiences with the dilators to insertion of the penis. Such technical problems should always be discussed patiently with the partners. If the woman continues to feel pain on insertion of the penis over a number of exercises or if the penis cannot be inserted the therapists should analyze the underlying anxieties (for example, have the partners sorted out the question of children? Is the woman afraid of pregnancy? Is the man distressed by castration fears—"a biting vagina"? Does the woman want sexual intercourse with her partner at all?).

TIMING

Use of dilators can be terminated once the penis can be inserted into the vagina without causing unpleasant sensations, but at the earliest after eight sessions. The therapists then continue with the basic program (movements with penis inserted).

Additional Intervention for Premature Ejaculation

The additional interventions for men distressed by premature ejaculation belong to the sequences stimulative caressing and coitus with explorative and stimulative movements. They are merely modifications of these sequences.

AIMS

A more exact knowledge and differentiated perception of his body's reactions helps the man to learn to control the moment of ejaculation and to enjoy caressing and genital stimulation without fear of failing. As the man's sense of security grows the woman will be relieved of "prophylactic" tasks and can react just as she feels without controlling herself.

PROCEDURE

The therapists suggest that the man pay close attention to "how far away" or how "near" ejaculation is when passive during stimulative caressing. Did he take the precaution of signaling his partner to stop stimulation when he was still some way off from ejaculating or was he just in time? The therapists advise him to give the woman a signal very early on so he can gradually move closer and closer to ejaculation by delaying the signal for longer. The more the patient can discriminate between lower and higher levels of arousal, the more secure he will feel. By playing with arousal during stimulative caressing he can carefully "feel his way" forward to the point just before ejaculation.

DISCUSSION OF EXPERIENCES

The discussion should be structured as for stimulative caressing. The therapists try to find out whether one of the partners felt insecure when the man was being stimulated; for example, whether the woman broke off stimulation "just in case," without waiting for her partner's signal. They emphasize that the man should decide when stimulation is to stop so he can learn to distinguish the various phases of arousal.

The therapists dispel the couple's fear of an involuntary ejaculation by pointing out that it might be vital for the man consciously to experience that it is too late to stop. The therapists take care not to center the discussion too much on the topic of ejaculation and arousal and to go through the caressing experiences and the woman's feelings in detail.

Additional Interventions

Many couples have difficulty in breaking the chain of preventive techniques they have used for so long with each other. The woman, for example, may be overly considerate and might interrupt stimulation of her own accord, or the man will only allow very cautious stimulation. Despite the therapists' suggestions, they stick to their cautious behavior in order to spare themselves the experience of failure. The therapists explain that this cautiousness prevents the man from improving his perception and gaining confidence.

In this phase the woman often has the feeling she is being used as a "masturbation machine" because she follows her partner's wishes all the time when stimulating him. It is therefore essential to ask the woman what she felt while caressing him; for example, whether she found it difficult to stop stimulation at his command; whether she was able to accept stimulating the man for so long; whether she managed to get "her part of the deal" in the remaining time.

Some therapists recommend using the "squeeze" technique for premature ejaculation (Masters and Johnson 1970). We consider this technique necessary only in very few cases because stimulative caressing improves ejaculatory control just as efficiently, is not nearly so mechanical, and is more pleasant for the couple.

FURTHER PROCEDURE

If the man feels he can control the timing of ejaculation and if he is satisfied with the time he can delay ejaculation, he can ask the woman to conclude stimulative caressing by stimulating him until he ejaculates. At least four sessions are needed for this phase. If this causes no problems the couple proceeds to intromission. Prior to insertion the woman stimulated the man manually twice until he almost ejaculates.

Once the couple is able to experience relaxation on insertion and the man does not immediately ejaculate, the partners go on to the sequence coitus with explorative and stimulative movements. In following this general procedure the partners should adhere to the principles outlined earlier. In this sequence, too, the woman stimulates the man prior to insertion one or two times with her hand until just before ejaculation.

Additional Intervention for Ejaculatory Incompetence

The additional interventions for ejaculatory incompetence are modifications of the therapeutic sequences stimulative caressing and coitus with explorative and stimulative movements. Masturbation assignments may also be helpful.

AIMS

The man is meant to gain experience with his body and its reactions while his genitals are being stimulated manually. He is supposed to learn how to react to various kinds of stimulation both alone and together with his partner; he will find out under what circumstances tension and performance pressure arise and when relaxation and a feeling of pleasure allow him to renounce fears and control. The couple thus learns to determine the time taken to reach ejaculation on petting and intercourse by using the optimal stimulation. To do so the man must be able to demonstrate his masturbation techniques to his partner so she can find out more about him and can change her own behavior in such a way that inhibitive anxieties no longer arise.

PROCEDURE

The procedure depends on the severity of the disturbance. If the man's ejaculatory incompetence is total (he is unable to reach orgasm during masturbation, petting, or coitus) and if a physical examination has precluded any organic causes, the man is encouraged to masturbate alone after caressing II. The therapists instruct him how to explore the possibilities for intense sexual stimulation. He can use sexually arousing pictures and texts and indulge in any sexual fantasies. It sometimes helps to show and discuss a film of a man masturbating. Use of a lubricant is recommended. Because completion of this phase is necessary for proceeding further with the additional program, the therapists should be sure that the patient has reached ejaculation several times on his own.

If the man is able to ejaculate when masturbating, he is asked to masturbate until ejaculation in the presence of his partner, first without her watching but afterward so she can see. It is important that the therapists respond to the patients' feelings when they introduce this possibility. The man may, above all, have fears of losing control; the woman is often disappointed at not being able to give her partner an orgasm, has fears of being rejected, or is disgusted by his semen. Once the man is able to ejaculate in his partner's presence, he shows her during explorative caressing how to hold his penis and leads her hand when she caresses him so she can feel what he finds particularly arousing and pleasant.

The main point of stimulative caressing for ejaculatory incompetence is again to play with arousal without aiming at orgasm. The woman should stimulate the man to orgasm only if he has experienced several times that he can enjoy the game with arousal without performance pressure. This is easier if the man stimulates himself beforehand to an advanced stage of arousal and the woman then stimulates him further until ejaculation.

DISCUSSION OF EXPERIENCES

The therapists elicit the partners' preferences and dislikes during stimulation. They should create an atmosphere in which the man can report without fear on fantasies, techniques, and aids (for example, pictures or texts) that stimulate him. Control anxieties, the fear of letting oneself go, and characteristics of the failure to ejaculate are discussed. As for the woman, special care should be taken to note with what feeling and attitudes she reacts to her partner. It is essential that the therapists stress how important the preceeding caressing exercises are and that they reinforce the couple's general sense of pleasure and relaxation and help them not to wait impatiently for ejaculation.

FURTHER PROCEDURE

Once the partners feel comfortable and secure during stimulative caressing and ejaculation has occurred several times, the partners proceed to intromission. The basic procedure is not modified for this sequence.

During coitus with explorative and stimulative movements, the partners first experiment with highly stimulating kinds of movements. When they are able to understand each other's wishes (at the earliest after three sessions), the woman stimulates the man (or he stimulates himself) manually until just before ejaculation. The woman then inserts his penis in the squatting position, and the couple moves the way they prefer. If after several attempts ejaculation has not occurred, it may help to suggest that the man give the signal to insert his penis only when ejaculation can no longer be voluntarily controlled. This can help reduce the fear of ejaculating in the vagina. It is essential that the female partner complies with the basic rule not to do anything she finds unpleasant, for example, moving until she is exhausted when it has become strenuous for her. If this is so the couple should find alternatives. She should also remain aware of what she particularly likes so that the couple does not focus its sexuality exclusively on ejaculation.

When the exercise has been completed satisfactorily several times, the couple can then insert the penis when the man's level of arousal is still relatively low.

SPECIAL PROBLEMS

Aside from the difficulties mentioned above, erectile disturbance may arise in this sequence. Because this sequence of treatment can only be "finished off" if the man has an erection every time, some men become victims of an extreme performance pressure. Moreover, it can happen that ejaculation fails to occur or occurs only after a long, exhausting effort. In such cases it is essential for the therapists to inquire carefully about anxieties and difficulties and if necessary to agree with the couple on further intermediate steps.

TIMING

The additional program can be terminated when the man is able to ejaculate during petting and intercourse within a period acceptable to both partners.

NOTES

1. Behavioral instructions in the basic program apply in principle for group therapy as well. Procedure is modified accordingly as described in chapter 9.

2. If one of the cotherapists is unable to participate the session may take place with only three participants. If one of the partners is unable to attend the session should be canceled.

3. The abbreviations used in the transcripts are as follows: "M.Th." = male therapist; "F.Th." = female therapist; "Man" and "Woman" refer to the partners (the authors chose not to discriminate between married and unmarried couples).

4. Because the therapist was not satisfied that the couple was motivated enough for therapy, he arranged a second discussion of history-taking findings. A supplementary session of this kind will sometimes prove to be necessary in exceptional cases. As a rule, behavioral instructions for caressing I are given after the first discussion.

5. Contrary to the basic rules the therapist first instructed the partners to lie on their backs instead of face down.

6. Some women may find it helpful to read the book For Yourself: The Fulfillment of Female Sexuality by L. Garfield-Barbach (Doubleday: New York, 1975) when doing exercises for bodily self-awareness.

7. We used a set of five Hegar dilators. These dilators are made of steel, are hollow and matched to the shape of a vagina; they are easy to disinfect and warm. The diameters are as follows: 1.0, 1.3, 1.8, 2.1 and 2.6 centimeters.

Bibliography

Abraham, K. 1917. Über Ejaculatio praecox. *Int Z Psychoanal* 4: 171–86. In: Abraham, K. 1969. *Psychoanalytische Studien zur Charakterbildung und andere Schriften;* S 43–60. Frankfurt: Fischer.

Alexander, F, French, T. 1946. *Psychoanalytic therapy: principles and applications.* New York: Ronald Press.

Arentewicz, G. 1977. Verhaltens- und Kommunikationstherapie bei Orgasmusstörungen: Erfahrungen mit 73 Paaren. Dissertation, Universität Hamburg.

Arentewicz, G., et al. 1975. Verhaltentherapie sexueller Funktionsstörungen. Erfahrungen mit 23 Paaren. In: Schorsch, E., Schmidt, G., eds. *Ergebnisse zur Sexualforschung,* S 154–223. Köln: Kiepenheuer and Witsch.

Arentewicz, G., Höflich, B., Eck, D. 1978. Therapie soziosexueller Ängste von Männern. Erste Erfahrungen mit einer verhaltenstherapeutisch orientierten Gruppentherapie. *Sexualmed* 7: 639–44.

Arentewicz, G., Schorsch, E., Schorsch, E.-M. 1976. Therapieabbrüche bei der Behandlung von Orgasmusstörungen der Frau. *Sexualmed* 5: 38–42.

Auerbach, R., Kilmann, P.R. 1977. The effects of group systematic desensitization on secondary erectile failure. *Behav Ther* 8 (3): 330–39.

Bancroft, J. 1970. Disorders of sexual potency. In: Hill, O. W., ed. *Modern trends in psychosomatic medicine.* Bristol: Butterworth, pp. 246–61.

Bancroft, J. 1983. *Human sexuality.* London: Churchill, Livingston.

Barbach, L. G. 1974. Group treatment of preorgasmic women. *J Sex Marital Ther* 1: 139–45.

Barbach, L. G., Flaherty, M. 1980. Group treatment of situationally orgasmic women. *J Sex Marital Ther* 6: 19–29.

Becker, N. 1975. Psychoanalytische Ansätze bei der Therapie sexueller

Funktionsstörungen. In: Sigusch, V. ed. *Therapie sexueller Störungen*, S 1–12. Stuttgart: Thieme.

Beckmann, D., Richter, H. E. 1972. *Giessen-Test Handbuch*. Bern: Huber.

Benedek, T. 1974. Sexual functions in women and their disturbances. In: Arieti, S., ed. *American handbook of psychiatry*, vol. 1. New York: Basic Books, pp. 569–91.

Bergler, E. 1937. *Die psychische Impotenz des Mannes*. Bern: Huber.

———. 1944. The problem of frigidity. *Psychiat Quart* 18: 374–90.

Bieber, I. 1974. The psychoanalytic treatment of sexual disorders. *J Sex Marital Ther* 1 (1): 5–15.

Blakeney, P. et al. 1976. A short-term intensive workshop approach for the treatment of human sexual inadequacy. *J Sex Marital Ther* 2 (2): 124–29.

Brady, J. P. 1966. Brevital-relaxation treatment of frigidity. *Behav Res Ther* 4: 171–77.

Brand, T. 1979. Sexologische Poliklinik: Dokumentation. Med. Dissertation, Universität Hamburg.

Burt, J. C. 1977. Preliminary report of an innovative surgical procedure for treatment of coital anorgasmia. Paper read at the Congress of the International Academy of Sex Research, 3rd Annual Meeting, Bloomington, Indiana.

Caird, W., Wincze, J. P. 1977. *Sex therapy. A behavioral approach*. New York: Harper and Row.

Clement, U. 1980. Sexual unresponsiveness and orgasmic dysfunctions: an empirical comparison. *J Sex Marital Ther* 6: 274–81.

Clement, U., Pfäfflin, F. 1980. Changes in personality scores among couples subsequent to sex therapy. *Arch Sex Behav* 9: 235–44.

Cole, T. M. 1975. Spinal cord injury patients and sexual dysfunctions. *Arch Phys Med Rehabil* 56: 11–12.

Cooper, A. J. 1963. A case of fetishism and impotence treated by behavior therapy. *Br J Psychiatry* 109: 649–52.

———. 1968. A factual study of male potency disorders. *Br J Psychiatry* 114: 719–31.

———. 1969a. An innovation in the "behavioral" treatment of a case of non-consummation due to vaginism. *Br J Psychiatry* 115: 721–22.

———. 1969b. Outpatient treatment of impotence. *J Nerv Ment Dis* 149: 360–71.

———. 1969c. Disorders of sexual potency in the male: a clinical and statistical study of some factors related to short-term prognosis. *Br J Psychiatry* 115: 709–19.

Bibliography

Deutsch, H. 1965. Frigidity in women. In: *Neuroses and character types: clinical psychoanalytic studies.* New York: International University Press. pp. 358–62.

Devereux, G. 1967. *Angst und Methode in den Verhaltenswissenschaften.* München: Hanser.

Dicks, H. V. 1967. *Marital tensions.* London: Routledge and Kegan.

Eicher, W. 1975. *Die sexuelle Erlebnisfähigkeit und die Sexualstörungen der Frau.* Stuttgart: Fischer.

Ellison, C. 1968. Psychosomatic factors in the unconsummated marriage. *J Psychosom Res* 12: 61–65.

———. 1972. Vaginism. *Med Aspects Hum Sex* 6 (8): 34–54.

Erikson, E. H. 1957. *Kindheit und Gesellschaft.* Stuttgart: Klett.

Everaerd, W. 1977. Comparative studies of short-term treatment methods for sexual inadequacies. In: Green, R., ed. *Progress in sexology.* New York: Plenum.

Fahrenberg, J., Selg, H., Hampel, R. 1973. *Das Freiburger Persönlichkeitsinventar. FPI Handbuch.* Göttingen: Hogrefe.

Faulk, M. 1971. Factors in the treatment of frigidity. *Br J Psychiatry* 119: 53–56.

Fenichel, O. 1945. *The psychoanalytic theory of neurosis.* New York: Norton.

Fisher, S. 1973. *The female orgasm.* New York: Basic Books.

Fleck, L. 1969. Die Beurteilung der orgastischen Kapazität der Frau und ihrer Störungen aus psychoanalytischer Sicht. *Psyche* 23: 58–74.

Flowers, J. V., Booraem, C. D. 1975. Imagination training in the treatment of sexual dysfunction. *Couns Psychol* 5: 50–51.

Fordney-Settlage, D. S. 1975. Heterosexual dysfunction: evaluation and treatment procedures. *Arch Sex Behav* 4: 367–87.

Foucault, M. 1977. *Sexualität und Wahrheit: Bd 1, Der Wille zum Wissen.* Frankfurt/Main: Suhrkamp.

Frank, R. T. 1948. Dyspareunia: a problem for the general practitioner. *JAMA* 136: 361–65.

Frankl, V. E. 1975. *Theorie und Therapie der Neurosen.* München: Reinhardt.

Freud, S. 1905. Drei Abhandlungen zur Sexualtheorie. Leipzig Wien: Deuticke. Ges. Werke, Bd V, S 27–145 (1949).

Freud, S. 1908. Die "kulturelle" Sexualmoral und die moderne Nervosität. Sexual-Probleme. *Mutterschutz* 4: 107–129. Ges. Werke, Bd VII, S 141–67 (1941).

Freud, S. 1916. Vorlesungen zur Einführung in die Psychoanalyse. Leipzig Wein: Heller. Ges. Werke, Bd XI (1940).

Freud, S. 1926. Hemmung, Symptom und Angst. Intern. Psychoanal. Leipzig Wien: Deuticke. Ges. Werke, Bd XIV, S 111–205 (1948).

Frick, V. 1973. Frigidität und Anorgasmie. *Sexualmed* 2: 58–61.

Friedman, L. J. 1962. *Virgin wives: a study of unconsummated marriages.* London: Tavistock.

Friedmann, D. E. 1968. The treatment of impotence by brietal-relaxation therapy. *Behav Res Ther* 6: 257–61.

Gagnon, J. H. 1974. Scripts and the coordination of sexual conduct. In: Cole, J. K., Dienstbier, R., eds. *Nebraska Symposium on motivation,* pp. 27–59. Lincoln: University of Nebraska Press.

———. 1975. Sex research and social change. *Arch Sex Behav* 4: 111–41.

Gagnon, J. H., Simon, W. 1973. *Sexual conduct.* Chicago: Aldine.

Garfield, A. H., McBreaty, J. F., Dichter, M. 1968. A case of impotence successfully treated by desensitization combined with in vivo operant training and thought substitution. In: Rubin, R., Franks, C. M., eds. *Advances in behavior therapy,* pp. 97–103. New York: Academic Press.

Gebhard, P. H. 1966. Factors in marital orgasm. *J Soc Iss* 22 (2): 88–95.

Geboes, K., Steeno, O., DeMoor, P. 1975. Sexual impotence in men. *Andrologia* 7: 217–27.

Giese, H. 1962. Die angemessene Resignation. In: Giese, H., ed. *Psychopathologie der Sexualität,* S 592–98. Stuttgart: Enke.

Giese, H., Schmidt, G. 1968. *Studenten-Sexualität. Verhalten und Einstellung.* Reinbek: Rowohlt.

Golden, J. S., et al. 1978. Group vs. couple treatment of sexual dysfunctions. *Arch Sex Behav* 7: 593–602.

Grawe, K. 1977. Indikation in der Psychotherapie. In: Pongratz, L. J., ed. *Klinische Psychologie. Handbuch der Psychologie,* Bd 8 (2), S 1849-1883. Göttingen: Hogrefe.

Gutheil, E. A. 1959. Sexual dysfunctions in men. In: Arieti, S. ed., *American handbook of psychiatry,* vol. 1. New York: Basic Books.

Haslam, M. T. 1965. The treatment of psychogenic dyspareunia by reciprocal inhibition. *Br J Psychiatry* 111: 280–82.

Hastings, D. W. 1971. Common sexual dysfunctions: I. impotence, II. ejaculatio praecox, III. lack of female response. *Psychiatr Ann* I (4): 10–31.

Hitschmann, E., Bergler, E. 1936. *Frigidity in women: its characteristics and treatment.* New York: Nervous Mental Disorders Publishing.

Bibliography

Hogan, D. R. 1978. The effectiveness of sex therapy: a review of the literature. In: LoPiccolo, J., LoPiccolo, L., eds. *Handbook of sex therapy*. New York: Plenum.

Hunt, M. 1974. *Sexual behavior in the 1970s*. Chicago: Playboy Press.

Husted, J. R. 1975. Desensitization procedures in dealing with female sexual dysfunctions. *Couns Psychol* 5: 30–37.

Johnson, J. 1965. Prognosis of disorder of sexual potency in the male. *J. Psychosom Res* 9: 195–200.

Johnstone, R. W. 1944. Dyspareunia. *Practitioner* 152: 142.

Kaplan, H. S. 1974a. *The new sex therapy*. New York: Brunner/Mazel.

———. 1974b. The classification of the female sexual dysfunctions. *J Marital Ther* 1 (1): 124–38.

———. 1977. Training of sex therapists. In: Master, W. H., Johnson, V. E., Kolodny, R. C., eds. *Ethical issues in sex therapy and research*, p. 182. Boston: Little, Brown.

———. 1979. *Disorders of sexual desire*. New York: Brunner/Mazel.

Kaplan, H. S., Kohl, R. N. 1972. Adverse reactions to the treatment of sexual problems. *Psychosomatics* 13: 185–90.

Kaplan, H. S., et al. 1974. Group treatment of premature ejaculation. *Arch Sex Behav* 3: 443–52.

Kaufman, G., Krupka, J. 1975. A sexual enrichment program for couples. *Psychother Theory Res Pract* 12 (3): 317–19.

Kieseritzky, I. V. 1978. *Trägheit oder Szenen aus der vita activa*. Stuttgart: Klett-Cotta.

Kilmann, P. R. 1978. The treatment of primary and secondary orgasmic dysfunction: a methodological review of the literature since 1970. *J Sex Marital Ther* 4: 155–78.

Kilmann, P. R., Auerbach, R. 1979. Treatments of premature ejaculation and psychogenic impotence: a critical review of the literature. *Arch Marital Ther* 8: 81–100.

Kilmann, P. R., Julian A., Moreault, D. 1978. The impact of marriage enrichment program on relationship factors. *J Sex Marital Ther* 4: 298–303.

Kinsey, A. C., Pomeroy, W. B., Martin, C. E. 1948. *Sexual behavior in the human male*. Philadelphia and London: Saunders.

Kinsey, A. C., et al. 1953. *Sexual behavior in the human female*. Philadelphia and London: Saunders.

Kockott, G., Dittmar, F., Nusselt, L. 1973. Systematische Desensibilisierung, eine kontrollierte Studie. *Schweiz Arch Neurol Neurochir Psychiatr* 113: 313–24.

———. 1975a. Ergebnisse einer Untersuchung zur systematischen De-sensibilisierung von Erektionsstörungen. In: Sigusch, V., ed. Therapie sexueller Störungen, S 41–53. Stuttgart: Thieme.

———. 1975b. Systematic desensitization of erectile impotence: a con-trolled study. *Arch Sex Behav* 4: 495–500.

Kohlenberg, R. J. 1974. Directed masturbation and the treatment of primary orgasmic dysfunction. *Arch Sex Behav* 3: 349–56.

Kolodny, R. C. 1972. Sexual dysfunctions in the diabetic female. *Med Asp Hum Sex* 6: 98–106.

Kolodny, R. C. 1981. Evaluating sex therapy: process and outcome at the Masters and Johnson Institute. *J Sex Res* 17: 301–18.

Kolodny, R. C. et al. 1974. Sexual dysfunctions in the diabetic man. *Diabetes* 23: 306–9.

Kraft, T., Al-Issa, I. 1967. Behavior therapy and the treatment of frigid-ity. *Am J Psychother* 21: 116–20.

———. 1968. The use of methohexitone sodium in the systematic de-sensitization of premature ejaculation. *Br J Psychiatry* 114: 351–52.

Lauritzen, C., Müller, P. 1977. Pathology and involution of the geni-tals in the aging female. In: Money, J., Musaph, H., eds. *Hand-book of sexology*, pp. 847–57. Amsterdam, London, New York: North Holland Biomedical Press.

Lazarus, A. A. 1963. The treatment of chronic frigidity by systematic desensitization. *J Nerv Ment Dis* 136: 71–79.

———. 1965. The treatment of a sexually inadequate man. In: Ullmann, L. P., Krasner, L., eds. *Case studies in behavior modification*, pp. 243–45. New York: Holt, Rinehart and Winston.

Leiblum, S. R., Ersner-Hershfield, R. 1977. Sexual enhancement groups for dysfunctional women: an evaluation. *J Sex Marital Ther* 3 (2): 139–52.

Leiblum, S. R., Rosen, R. C., Pierce, D. 1976. Group treatment format: mixed sexual dysfunctions. *Arch Sex Behav* 5: 313–22.

Lidberg, L. 1970. Somatische Krankheiten bei Patienten, die an Impo-tenz und Ejaculatio praecox leiden. *Nord Psychiatr Tidsskr* 24: 293–98.

Lobitz, W. C., Baker, E. L. 1979. Group treatment of single males with erectile dysfunctions. *Arch Sex Behav* 8: 127–38.

Lobitz, W. C., LoPiccolo, J. 1972. New methods in the behavioral treat-ment of sexual dysfunction. *J Behav Ther Exp Psychiatr* 3: 265–71.

Lobitz, W. C. et al. 1974. A closer look at the simplistic behavior thera-py for sexual dysfunction: two case studies. In: Eysenck, H. J., ed. *Case studies in behavior therapy*. London: Routledge and Kegan.

LoPiccolo, J. 1977a. Direct treatment of sexual dysfunction. In: Money, J., Musaph, H., eds. *Handbook of sexology*, pp. 1227–44. Amsterdam, London, New York: North Holland Biomedical Press.

——. 1977b. The professionalization of sex therapy: issues and problems. *Society* 14 (5): 60–68.

LoPiccolo, J., Lobitz, W. C. 1972. The role of masturbation in the treatment of orgasmic dysfunction. *Arch Sex Behav* 2: 163–71.

——. 1973. Behavior therapy of sexual dysfunction. In: Hammerlynch, L. A., Handy, L. C., Mash, L. J., eds. *Behavioral change: methodology, concepts, and practice*, pp. 343–58. Champaign, Ill.: Research Press.

LoPiccolo, J., LoPiccolo, L., eds. 1978. *Handbook of sex therapy*. New York and London: Plenum Press.

LoPiccolo, J., Miller, V. H. 1975a. A program for enhancing the sexual relationship of normal couples. *Couns Psychol* 5: 41–45.

——. 1975b. Procedural outline sexual enrichment groups. *Couns Psychol* 5: 46–49.

LoPiccolo, J., Steger, J. C. 1974. The sexual interaction inventory: a new instrument for assessment of sexual dysfunction. *Arch Sex Behav* 3: 585–95.

Lorand, S. 1939. Contribution to the problem of vaginal orgasm. *Int J Psychoanal* 20. Reprinted in: Ruitenbeek, H. M., ed. 1966. *Psychoanalysis and female sexuality*, pp. 238–45. New Haven: College and University Press.

Madsen, C. H., Ullmann, L. P. 1967. Innovations in the desensitization of frigidity. *Behav Res Ther* 5: 67–68.

Malleson, J. 1942. Vaginismus: its management and psychogenesis. *Br Med J* 2: 213–16.

Mandel, K.-H. 1976. Psychotherapeuten und Berater für Partnerkonflikte. Lehrpläne des Instituts für Forschung und Ausbildung in Kommunikationstherapie E. V. München. *Partnerberatung* 13: 80–90.

Marks, I. M. 1981. Review of behavioral psychotherapy, II: Sexual disorders. *Am J Psychiat* 138: 750–56.

Marquis, J. 1970. Orgasmic reconditioning: changing sexual object choice through controlling masturbation phantasies. *J Behav Ther Exp Psychiatr* 1: 262–71.

Masters, W. H., Johnson, V. E. 1966. *Human sexual response*. Boston: Little, Brown.

———. 1970. *Human sexual inadequacy.* Boston: Little, Brown.

———. 1979. *Homosexuality in perspective.* Boston: Little, Brown.

Mathews, A. et al. 1975. Behavioral treatment of sexual inadequacy. (mimeograph) Oxford University.

Matussek, P. 1971. Funktionelle Sexualstörungen. In: Giese, H., *Die Sexualität des Menschen. Handbuch der medizinischen Sexualforschung,* S 786–828. Stuttgart: Enke.

Mayer, M. D. 1932. Classification and treatment of dyspareunia. *Am J Obstet Gynecol* 24: 751–55.

McCarthy, B. W. 1973. A modification of Masters and Johnson sex therapy model in a clinical setting. *Psychother Theory Res Pract* 10: 290–93.

McGovern, K. B., McMullen, R. S., LoPiccolo, J. 1975. Secondary orgasmic dysfunction. I. Analysis and strategies for treatment. *Arch Sex Behav* 4 (3): 265–75.

McGovern, K. B., Kirkpatrick, C. C., LoPiccolo, J. 1976. A behavioral group treatment program for sexually dysfunctional couples. *J Marr Fam Couns* 2: 397–404.

McWhirter, D. P., Mattison, A. M. 1978. The treatment of sexual dysfunction in gay male couples. *J Sex Marital Ther* 4: 213–18.

Mears, E. 1958. Dyspareunia. *Br Med J* 16: 443–45.

Menninger, K. A. 1935. Impotence and frigidity from the standpoint of psychoanalysis. *J Urol* 34: 166–83.

Meyer, A-E. 1971. Psychoanalytische Aspekte. In: Giese, H. *Die Sexualität des Menschen. Handbuch der medizinischen Sexualforschung,* S 981–96. Stuttgart: Enke.

Meyer, J. K. et al. 1975. Short-term treatment of sexual problems: interim report. *Am J Psychiatry* 132: 172–76.

Minsel, W.-R. 1974. *Praxis der Gesprächstherapie.* Wien Köln Graz: Böhlaus.

Mirowitz, J. 1966. The utilization of hypnosis in psychic impotence. *Br J Med Hypn* 17: 25–32.

Money, J., Ehrhardt, A. A. 1972. Man and woman, boy and girl. Baltimore: Johns Hopkins Press.

Moore, B. E. 1961. Frigidity in women. *J Am Psychoanal Assoc* 9: 571–84.

Obler, M. 1973. Systematic desensitization in sexual disorders. *J Behav Ther Exp Psychiatr* 4: 93–101.

———. 1975. Multivariate approaches to psychotherapy with sexual dysfunctions. *Couns Psychol* 5: 55–56.

O'Connor, J. F. 1976. Sexual problems, therapy, and prognostic factors.

In: Meyer, J. K., ed. *Clinical management of sexual disorders*. Baltimore: Williams, Wilkins.

O'Connor, J. F., Stern, L. O. 1972. Developmental factors in functional sexual disorders. *NY State J Med* 72 (14): 1838–43.

Pocs, O., Godow, A. G. 1976. The shock of recognizing parents as sexual beings. (mimeograph)

Price, S. et al. 1981. Group treatment of erectile dysfunctions for men without partners: a controlled evaluation. *Arch Sex Behav* 10: 253–68.

Raboch, J. 1970. Two studies of male sexual impotence. *J Sex Res* 6: 181–87.

Raboch, J., Mellan, J., Kohlicek, J. 1976. Prostatitis und Potenz. *Sexualmed* 5: 33–36.

Raddatz, F. J. 1978. Kontakt-Sperre. *Zeit* 43: 33–36.

Rainwater, L. 1965. *Family design*. Chicago: Aldine.

––––––. 1966. Some aspects of lower class sexual behavior. *J Soc Iss* 22 (2): 96–108.

Reding, G., Ennis, B. 1964. Treatment of a couple by a couple. *Br J Med Psychol* 37: 325–30.

Reich, W. 1927. *Die Funktion des Orgasmus*. Wien: Deuticke.

Renshaw, D. C. 1975. Impotence in diabetics. *Dis Nerv Syst* 36: 369–71.

Reynolds, B. S. 1977. Psychological treatment models and outcome results for erectile dysfunction: a critical review. *Psychol Bull* 84 (6): 1218–38.

Rieber, I. 1979. Die chirurgische Implantation von Penisprothesen bei Männern mit Erektionsstörungen. Eine kritische Bestandsaufnahme. In: Sigusch, V., ed. *Sexualität und Medizin*, S 177–203. Köln: Kiepenheuer and Witsch.

Rosenzweig, N., Pearsall, F. P. 1978. *Sex education for the health professional: a curriculum guide*. Seminars in psychiatry. New York, San Francisco, London: Grune and Stratton.

Sadock, V. A., Sadock, B. J., Kaplan, H. S. 1975. Comprehensive sex therapy training: a new approach. *Am J Psychiatry* 132: 858–60.

Salzman, L. 1954. Premature ejaculation. *Int J Sex* 8: 69–76. Reprinted in: Martino, M. F. de, ed. 1963. *Sexual behavior and personality characteristics*, pp. 302–20. New York: Citadel Press.

––––––. 1968. Systematic desensitization of a patient with chronic total impotence. In: Rubin, R., Franks, C. M., eds. *Advances in behavior therapy*, pp. 131–37. New York: Academic Press.

Sandler, M., Gessa, G. L. 1975. *Sexual behavior: pharmacology and biochemistry.* New York: Raven Press.

Sarrel, P. M., Sarrel, L. J. 1978. The significance of medical conditions among patients presenting for sex therapy. Paper read at the Congress of the International Academy of Sex Research. 4th Annual Meeting, Toronto.

Schmale, H., Schmidtke, H. 1966/67. *Manuale zum Berufs-Eignungstest BET.* Bern and Stuttgart: Huber.

Schmidt, G. 1975. Sexuelle Motivation und Kontrolle. In: Schorsch, E., Schmidt, G., eds. *Ergebnisse zur Sexualforschung*, S 30–47. Köln: Kiepenheuer and Witsch.

Schmidt, G., Arentewicz, G. 1977. Sexuelle Funktionsstörungen. In: Pongratz, L. J., ed. *Klinische Psychologie. Handbuch der Psychologie*, Bd 8/2, S 2269–2312. Göttingen: Hogrefe.

Schmidt, G., Sigusch, V. 1971. *Arbeiter-Sexualität.* Neuwied: Luchterhand.

Schnabl, S. 1972. Funktionelle Sexualstörungen. In: Hesse, P. G., Tembrock, G., eds. *Sexuologie*, Bd 1, S 368–414. Leipzig: Hirzel.

———. 1974. *Intimverhalten—Sexualstörungen—Persönlichkeit.* Berlin: VEB Deutscher Verlag der Wissenschaften.

Schneidman, B., McGuire, L. 1976. Group therapy for nonorgasmic women: two age levels. *Arch Sex Behav* 5: 239–47.

Schoof, W. 1975. Ein Jahr sexologische Poliklinik. In: Schorsch, E., Schmidt, G. eds. *Ergebnisse zur Sexualforschung*, S. 123–53. Köln: Kiepenheuer and Witsch.

Schoof-Tams, K., Schlaegel, J., Walczak, L. 1976. Differentiation of sexual morality between 11 and 16 years. *Arch Sex Behav* 5: 353–70.

Schorsch, E. et al. 1977. Zur Versorgung von Patienten mit sexuellen Störungen. *Sexualmed* 6: 585–90.

Segraves, R. T. 1977. Pharmacological agents causing sexual dysfunction. *J Sex Marital Ther* 3 (3): 157–76.

Semans, J. H. 1956. Premature ejaculation: a new approach. *South Med J* 49: 353–57.

Shainess, N. 1968. The therapy of frigidity. In: Masserman, J., ed. *Current pyschiatric therapies*, pp. 70–79. New York: Grune and Stratton.

———.1975. Authentic feminine orgastic response. In: Adelson, E. T., ed. *Sexuality and psychoanalysis*, pp. 145–60. New York: Brunner/Mazel.

Shapiro, B. 1943. Premature ejaculation; a review of 1130 cases. *J Urol* 50: 374–79.

Bibliography

Sharpe, R., Meyer, V. 1973. Modification of "cognitive sexual pain" by the spouse under supervision. *Behav Res Ther* 9: 285–87.

Sherfey, M. J. 1966. The nature and evolution of female sexuality. *J Am Psychoanal Assoc* 14: 28–128.

Shusterman, L. R. 1973. The treatment of impotence by behavior modification techniques. *J Sex Res* 9: 226–40.

Sigusch, V. 1970. *Exzitation und Orgasmus bei der Frau*. Stuttgart: Enke.

———. 1973. "Diagnose" Orgasmus. *Sexualmed* 2: 10–17.

———. ed., 1980. *Therapie sexueller Störungen*. Stuttgart: Thieme.

———. 1980a. Sexuelle Funktionsstörungen: somatischer Anteil und somatische Behandlungsversuche. In: Sigusch, V., ed., 1975. *Therapie sexueller Störungen*. Stuttgart: Thieme.

Sigusch, V., Maack, T. 1976. Ejakulationsstörungen. Ein Überblick. *Sexualmed* 5: 23–32.

Sigusch, V., Schmidt, G. 1973. *Jugendsexualität. Dokumentation einer Untersuchung*. Stuttgart: Enke.

Snyder, A., LoPiccolo, L., LoPiccolo, J. 1975. Secondary orgasmic dysfunction. II. Case study. *Arch Sex Behav* 4: 277–83.

Sotile, W. M., Kilmann, P. R. 1977. Treatments of psychogenic female sexual dysfunctions. *Psychol Bull* 84 (4): 619–33.

———. 1978. Effects of group systematic desensitization on female orgasmic dysfunction. *Arch Sex Behav* 7 (5): 477–91.

Stekel, W. 1920. *Die Impotenz des Mannes*. Berlin: Urban and Schwarzenberg.

———. 1921. *Die Geschlechtskälte der Frau*. Berlin: Urban and Schwarzenberg.

Stoller, J. R. 1975. *Perversion: the erotic form of hatred*. New York: Pantheon Books.

Story, N. L. 1974. Sexual dysfunction resulting from drug side effects. *J Sex Res* 10: 132–49.

Ullrich de Muynck, R., Ullrich, R. 1977. *Das Assertiveness-Training-Programm ATP. Einübung von Selbstvertrauen und sozialer Kompetenz. Teil IV: Das Emotionalitätsinventar*. München: Pfeiffer.

Ussel, J. van. 1970. *Sexualunterdrückung. Geschichte der Sexualfeindschaft*. Reinbek: Rowohlt.

Vogt, H. J. 1974. Anorgasmie des Mannes. *Sexualmed* 3: 116–18.

Waggoner, R. W., Mudd, E. H., Shearer, M. L. 1973. Training dual sex teams for rapid treatment of sexual dysfunction: a pilot program. *Psychiatr Ann* 3 (5): 61–76.

Wallace, D. H., Barbach, L. G. 1974. Preorgasmic group treatment. *J Sex Marital Ther* 1: 146–54.

Walthard, M. 1909. Die psychogene Ätiologie und die Psychotherapie des Vaginismus. *Münch Med Wochenschr* 56: 1998–2000.

Watzlawick, P., Weakland, J. H., Fisch, R. 1974. *Change.* New York: Norton.

WHO-Report. 1975. Education and treatment in human sexuality: the training of health professionals. Geneva: WHO.

Willi, J. 1975. *Die Zweierbeziehung.* Reinbek: Rowohlt.

———. 1978. *Therapie der Zweierbeziehung.* Reinbek: Rowohlt.

Wish, P. A. 1975. The use of imagery-based techniques in the treatment of sexual dysfunction. *Couns Psychol* 5: 52–55.

Wolpe, J. 1958. *Psychotherapy by reciprocal inhibition.* Stanford: Stanford University Press.

Zeiss, R. A., Christensen, A., Levine, A. G. 1978. Treatment of premature ejaculation through male-only groups. *J Sex Marital Ther* 4: 139–48.

Zilbergeld, B. 1975. Group treatment of sexual dysfunction in men without partners. *J Sex Marital Ther* 1: 204–14.

Zilbergeld, B., Evans, M. 1980. The inadequacies of Masters and Johnson. *Psychology Today,* August, pp. 29–43.

Name Index

Abraham, K., 38, 47
Alexander, F., 71
Al-Issa, I., 62
Arentewicz, G., *xi*, *xiii*, 50, 65, 66, 84, 182
Auerbach, R., 65, 66

Baker, E. L., 65
Balint, M., 221
Bancroft, J., 33*n*2, 36
Barbach, L. G., 65
Becker, N., 38, 40–42
Benedek, T., 25, 41, 57
Bergler, E., 25, 42, 47
Blakeney, P., 64
Booraem, C. D., 63
Brady, J. P., 62
Brand, T., 31, 32
Burt, J. C., 59

Carid, W., 61
Christensen, A., 65
Clement, U., 80, 122*n*15, 130
Cole, T. M., 34
Comfort, A., 5
Cooper, A. J., 62, 63

DeMoor, P., 34
Deutsch, H., 25, 26, 57, 67
Devereux, G., 222
Dichter, M., 62
Dicks, H. V., 63
Dittmar, F., 65, 66, 74*n*6

Eck, D., 65

Ehrhardt, A. A., 42
Eicher, W., 17, 19, 20, 23, 34, 35
Ellison, C., 34, 50, 63
Ennis, B., 63
Ersner-Hershfield, R., 65
Everaerd, W., 74*n*6
Evans, M., 73*n*5

Faulk, N., 99
Fenichel, O., 25, 40, 42, 44, 47, 70
Fisch, R., 57
Fisher, S., 24, 26, 42
Flaherty, M., 65
Fleck, L., 25, 41, 69
Flowers, J. V., 63
Fordney-Settlage, D. S., 15, 33
Foucault, M., 211
Frank, R. T., 63
Frankl, V. E., 57
French, T., 71
Freud, S., 25, 40, 42, 44, 211
Frick, V., 19, 23
Friedman, L. J., 50, 62, 65, 70
Friedmann, D. E., 62

Gagnon, J. H., 55, 63
Garfield, A. H., 62
Garfield-Barbach, L., 328*n*6
Gebhard, P. H., 24, 30
Geboes, K., 34
Gessa, G. L., 34
Giese, H., *vii*, 24, 79, 185
Godow, A. G., 55
Golden, J. S., 64, 203
Grawe, K., 196
Gutheil, E. A., 63

Haslam, M. T., 62, 63
Hastings, D. W., 21, 33*n*2
Hitschmann, E., 25
Höflich, B., 65
Hogan, D. R., 64, 66
Hunt, M., 81
Husted, J. R., 65, 74*n*6

Johnson, J., 62
Johnson, V. E., *vii*, *viii*, *xi*, 18, 20, 21, 23, 30, 32, 33*n*2, *n*4, *n*5, 34, 35, 39, 44, 49, 57, 58, 60–66, 68, 73*n*4, *n*5, 78, 85, 98–99, 160, 161, 212, 214, 226, 325
Johnstone, R. W., 63
Julian, A., 73*n*3

Kaplan, H. S., 17–19, 23, 25, 26, 30, 32, 33*n*5, 34, 47, 49, 50, 61, 63, 64, 68–70, 122*n*15, 176, 203, 213, 214, 221
Kaufman, G., 73*n*3
Kieseritzky, I. von, 7
Kilmann, P. R., 65, 66, 73*n*2, *n*3
Kinsey, A. C., 21, 23–25, 29, 30, 32, 73*n*4, 79
Kirkpatrick, C. C., 64, 203
Kockott, G., 65, 66, 74*n*6
Kohl, R. N., 50, 176
Kohlenberg, R. J., 63
Kohlicek, J., 34
Kolodny, R. C., 34, 74*n*5, 78
Kraft, T., 62
Krupka, J., 73*n*3

Name Index

Lasch, C., 8n1
Lauritzen, C., 36
Lazarus, A. A., 40, 62
Leiblum, S. R., 64, 65, 203
Levine, A. G., 65
Lidberg, L., 35
Lobitz, W. C., 38, 58, 61–65, 78, 99, 196, 312
LoPiccolo, J., 38, 39, 61, 63–66, 73n3, 74n6, 78, 87, 99, 196, 203, 214, 221, 312
LoPiccolo, L., 39, 64, 87, 99, 214
Lorand, S., 67

Maack, T., 22, 34, 35
Madsen, C. H., 63
Malleson, J., 63
Mandel, K.-H., 220, 221
Marks, I. M., 66
Marquis, J., 63
Masters, W. H., vii, viii, xi, 18, 20, 21, 23, 30, 32, 33n2, 33n4, 33n5, 34, 35, 39, 44, 49, 57, 58, 60–66, 68, 73n4, 73n5, 78, 85, 98–99, 160, 161, 212, 214, 225, 325
Mathews, A., 66, 74n6, 99
Mattison, A. M., 64
Matussek, P., 17, 25, 27, 33n2
Mayer, M. D., 50, 63
McBreaty, J. F., 62
McCarthy, B. W., 64
McGovern, K. B., 64, 74n6, 99, 203
McGuire, L., 65
McMullen, R. S., 74n6, 99
McWhirter, D. P., 64
Mears, E., 50, 63
Mellan, J., 34
Meyer, A.-E., 41, 44
Meyer, J. K., 99
Meyer, V., 20
Miller, V. H., 73n3
Mirowitz, J., 34, 62
Money, J., 42
Moore, B. E., 25, 40–42
Moreault, D., 73n3

Mudd, E. H., 221
Muller, P., 36

Nusselt, L., 65, 66, 74n6

Obler, M., 65, 74n6
O'Connor, J. F., 42, 60

Pearsall, F. P., 221
Pfafflin, F., 80, 130
Pierce, P., 64, 203
Pocs, O., 55
Price, S., 65

Raboch, J., 31, 32, 34
Raddatz, F. J., 7
Rainwater, L., 32
Reding, G., 63
Reich, W., 23, 29
Renshaw, D. C., 36
Reynolds, B. S., 66, 73n2
Rieber, I., 59
Rosen, R. C., 64, 203
Rosenzweig, N., 221

Sadock, B. J., 221
Sadock, V. A., 221
Salzman, L., 47, 53, 62
Sandler, M., 34
Sarrel, L. J., 42
Sarrel, P. M., 42
Schlaegel, J., 44
Schmale, H., 96
Schmidt, G., vii, xiii, 24, 55, 79
Schmidtke, H., 96
Schnabl, S., 19, 23, 24, 26, 30, 32, 33n2
Schneidman, B., 65
Schoof, W., 31
Schoof-Tams, K., 44
Schorsch, E., 31, 36, 50, 79, 182

Schorsch, E.-M., 50, 182
Segraves, R. T., 34
Semans, J. H., 63
Shainess, N., 25, 29, 56
Shapiro, B., 22
Sharpe, R., 20
Shearer, M. L., 221
Sherfey, M. J., 25
Shusterman, L. R., 34
Sigusch, V., vii, 22–24, 34, 35, 55, 60, 79
Simon, W., 55
Snyder, A., 99
Sotile, W. M., 65, 66, 73n2
Steeno, O., 34
Steger, J. C., 66
Stekel, W., 46, 52, 57, 70
Stern, L. O., 42
Stoller, R. J., 5, 44
Story, N. L., 34

Ullman, L. P., 63
Ullrich, R., 83
Ullrich de Muynck, R., 83
Ussel, J. van, 211

Vogt, H. J., 63

Waggoner, R. W., 221
Walczak, L., 44
Wallace, D. H., 65
Walthard, M., 63
Watzlawick, P., 57
Weakland, J. H., 57
Willi, J., 53, 197
Wincze, J. P., 61
Wish, P. A., 63
Wolpe, J., 62
World Health Organization (WHO), 221

Zeiss, R. A., 65
Zilbergeld, B., 65, 73n5

342

Subject Index

Abandonment, fear of, 41, 42
Accreditation criteria, 220
Acting out, 181; giving in to, by therapists, 183–84; separation as, 190
Adrenalectomy, 35
Advanced training, *see* Training, therapeutic
Adverse reactions of "functional partner," 50
Age: of study couples, 78; of group therapy participants, 203–4
Aggressive fantasy, 41
Aggressive impulses, 47; delegation of, 48; dysfunction as expression of, 53
Agoraphobia, 165, 168, 176
Alcohol addiction, 161, 162; case examples of, 163–64, 166, 169; as contraindication, 228
Algopareunia, 20
Ambivalence management, 53–55; case example of, 54–55
Amenorrhea, 165
Anal stage, frustration during, 41
Anatomical knowledge, 277–78; lack of, 285–86
Androgen therapy, 37
Anorgasmia, 23
Antiandrogen therapy, 37
Anticipatory fear, 39, 57–58, 248; in intromission sequence, 298
Antidepressants, 163
Anxiety: anticipation, *see* Anticipatory fear; attachment, 40–42; bypassing, 69–70; castration, 36; defense against, 39–47; discussions of, 247; over gender identity, 40, 42–44; in group therapy, 209; incest, 173; instinct, 40–41; lack of desire and aversion arising from, 17; moral, 40, 44–45; separation following reduction of, 191–92; treatment techniques for, 62–63; warded-off, 45–47; working through, 66, 68
Approach phase of sexual interaction, 15; dysfunctions of, 16–18

Arousal: during explorative genital caressing, 287; playing with, *see* Stimulative caressing and playing with arousal sequence
Arousal dysfunction, 16, 18–19, 228; case examples of, 11–13; dyspareunia and, 20; hypochondria and, 164–65; incidence of, 31, 32; motivation for therapy for, 101; organic factors in, 35; orgasmic dysfunction and, 23, 100; outcome of therapy for, 89; partner-related, 28; percentage of cases in study, 78; in psychiatric patient, 163; severity of, 81–82; therapeutic improvement rate for, 66
Arousal reconditioning, 63
Arrangement, dysfunction as, 50–51
Assertive training, 65
Assessment procedures, 82–84; design of, 108; validity of, 97–98
Attachment anxiety, 40–42; delegation and, 48
Attitudes, sexual: changes in, during therapy, 93, 115; long-term changes in, 127
Autoeroticism, 7
Aversion, sexual, 16–18; arousal dysfunction and, 18; case examples of, 11–14; dyspareunia and, 20; incidence of, 32; orgasmic dysfunction and, 81, 100; outcome of therapy for, 89
Avoidance behavior, 17, 82; in caressing I sequence, 271–72; reduction of, 230; therapeutic approach for, 71

Balint group, 88
Basic rules of therapy, 259–60
Behavior therapy, 71, 227; advanced training and, 213, 216
"Berufseignungstest," 96
Bilateral dysfunctions, 172
Bisexuality, 73n4
Bladder disease, 35
Blindness, 162

Subject Index

Blood-supply disorders, 34
Bodily self-awareness, 63, 93, 226; aims of, 312; caressing II sequence and, 275; criteria for assigning intervention, 311–12; discussion of, 248; discussion of experiences with, 313; exercises for, 72; in group therapy, 205; integration into couple therapy of, 316; for men, 316–17; orgasmic dysfunction and, 101; procedures for, 312–15; special problems in, 315–16
Body contact experiences, *see* Caressing I exercise sequence
Body secretions, aversion to, 293
Bypass mechanisms, 69–70

Caressing I exercise sequence, 226, 257–72; aims of, 257; discussion of experiences in, 260–70; procedure for, 258–60; procedure in further sessions, 270; special problems in, 270–72; timing of, 272
Caressing II exercise sequence, 226, 272–76; aims of, 272–73; discussion of experiences in, 274–75; procedure in, 273; special problems in, 275; timing of, 275
Castration, 37
Castration anxiety, 36, 41, 43, 73
Childbearing, 95
Childbirth, vaginismus following, 20
Client-centered psychotherapy, 71, 227; advanced training and, 213, 215
Clitoral displacement operations, 59
Clitoral orgasms, 25–27
Closeness-distance ambivalence, 53–55; bypassing, 70
Cognitive sexual pains, 20
Coital prohibition, 72, 258; breaking rule of, 271, 294; resistance to, 219
Coitus, 16; with explorative and stimulating movements, 61, 298–301, 327–328; frequency of, in study couples, 80; frequency of female orgasm during, 24; and long-term results of therapy, 127; in other positions, 302–5; pain during, *see* Dyspareunia; Vaginismus; prolonged, 21; therapy outcomes and, 90–92, 100
Colpitis, 35
Communication: in caressing I, 271; as end in itself, 6; improvement in, 72, 230
Compulsive symptoms, 161
Concrescence of labia minor, 35
Conflicts: acting out, 181; lack of desire and aversion arising from, 17; working through, 66, 68; *see also* Partner conflicts; Psychodynamic conflicts
"Conspiracy of silence," 44
Contraception, 180, 234; required for therapy, 228

Contraindications to couple therapy, 77
Corrective emotional experiences, 71, 229, 247
Cotherapists, dynamics of, 221–22
Countertransference, 61, 154, 220, 222
Couple therapy: discussion of histories in, 246–57; general aims of, 229–31; history-taking for, 235–46; indications for, 228–29; initial interview in, 232; introductory session in, 233–35; outline of, 225–27
Cysts, genital tract, 35

Defense against anxiety, 39–47
Deformities, genital, 34
Delegation of dysfunction, 48–50; case example of, 48–49
Dependency, fear of, 41, 42
Depression, 132; case example of, 163, 170; of drop-outs, 187–88; phasic, 162; as side-effect of treatment, 175–76
Design of study, 82–85
Desire, lack of, 16–18, 82, 228; case example of, 12
Deviant sexual behavior, 162, 170
Diabetes mellitus, 35, 36
Difficult patients, 161–71; case examples of, 163–67
Dilator exercises, 62, 63, 65, 73, 248, 317–23; bodily self-awareness and, 275
Dirt, fear of, 41, 72
Disgust, sexual, 41
Documentation, problems with, 219–20
Dropping out of therapy, 179–88; prospects for couples after, 184–88; psychodynamics of, 180–84; separation rates after, 189
Drug addiction, 228
Dual-sex therapist team, 61, 147, 225, 226; for intensive therapy, 86; for long-term therapy, 86; single therapist compared with, 148, 151, 155, 157
Duration of dysfunction, 29
Dyspareunia, 16, 20; incidence of, 33; organic factors in, 35; as undesired side-effect of therapy, 173
Dysphoria, *see* Postorgasmic dysphoria

Educational aspect of therapy, 71–72
Educational background of study couples, 78, 104; therapy outcomes and, 96
Ego ideal, sexually affirmative, 45
Ego regression in orgasm, 42
Ejaculation without satisfaction, 16, 23

Ejaculatory incompetence, 16, 20, 22–23, 228; additional intervention for, 226, 326–28; anal pleasure in, 47; anxiety over gender identity and, 43; incidence of, 30, 32; mechanical stimulation for, 63; organic factors in, 35

EMI scales, 130, 145, 170

Emotional Inventory, 84

Emotional satisfaction, 4; blocking of, 17–18

Encephalomyelitis disseminata, 162

Endometriosis, 20, 35

Erectile dysfunctions, 16, 18, 228; age when treated for, 79, 103; bypass technique for, 69; caressing I sequence for, 260–62; caressing II sequence for, 273–74; case examples of, 14; delegation and, 50; deviant fantasies and, 165; explorative genital caressing sequence for, 278–85; gender of therapist and, 152; genital trauma and, 166–67; group therapy for, 203; incidence of, 29–32; initial, 28; intromission sequence for, 295–97; limitations on success of treatment for, 134; long-term results of therapy for, 127; organic factors in, 34–36; outcomes of therapy for, 89, 91, 94, 98–99, 113, 114; percentage of cases in study, 78; physical disorders and, 165–66; separation and, 190–93; severity of, 28, 82; situational, 28; successful treatment of, 132–33; therapy settings for, 86; transcript of history-taking for, 239–45; undesired side-effects of treatment of, 172–75; warded-off anxiety in, 45, 46

Estrogen therapy, 36

Exercises: sequence of, 226; therapeutic training and, 218; timing of (table), 258; see also specific sequences

Experience, deficiencies in, 39, 55–57

Explorative genital caressing sequence, 61, 226, 227, 276–87; aims of, 276; discussion of experiences in, 281–85; special problems in, 285–87

Extramarital relationships, 5

Extrapyramidal symptoms, 163

Failure, fear of, 17, 57–58; in caressing I sequence, 271; decrease in, 94, 230; organic factors and, 36; orgasmic dysfunction and, 101; sexual aversion and, 17; therapeutic approach for, 71

Failure rates, 98–99

Fantasy: aggressive, 41; as bypass mechanism, 69; deviant, 161, 165, 167, 170; fetishistic, 162; masturbation, 316–17; orgasmic dysfunction and, 24; partner conflicts and, 186–87; sadomasochistic, 162; therapeutic use of, 63; warded-off anxiety in, 45

Father-child relationships, 41, 42

Fear: of being touched, 271; of failure, see Failure, fear of; of injury to genitals, 286; organic factors and, 36; of orgasm, 27; of pain, 20; see also Anxiety

Female therapists, 151–54; see also Dual-sex therapy team

Feminine identification, 43

Fetishism, 162

Final session of therapy, 305–11; aims of, 305; procedure for, 305–6; transcript of, 306–11

Five-minute psychotherapy, 221

Follow-up program, 83–85; long-term, 123–30, 136–44; sample size in, 108

Freiburg Personality Inventory (FPI), 80, 83, 106, 121n3, 130, 145, 179

"French" kisses, 271

Frigidity, 19, 24, 33n2; and absence of vaginal orgasm, 25

Funnel chest, 162

Gender identity, anxiety about, 40, 42–44, 46; therapeutic approach to, 72

"General Aptitude Test Battery," 96

General psychological status, assessment of, 83

General sexual unresponsiveness, 19, 24, 32

Genital hyperemia, 18

Genital trauma: erectile dysfunction and, 166–67; vaginismus and, 20

Gestalt therapy, 71; advanced training and, 213

Giessen Test (GT), 80–81, 83, 107, 121n3, 130, 146, 179

Gonadal dysfunctions, 34–35

Gonorrhea, 35

Group therapy, 202–9; female, 102; patient selection for, 203–4; procedure for, 204–6; results of, 206–9; for sexual enhancement, 73n3; for single people, 66

Gynecologists, advanced training of, 214

Hegar dilators, 328n7

History-taking, 225, 235–46; aims of, 235; discussion of histories, see Round table; evaluation of findings, 245–46; for group therapy, 205; key topics in, 237–39; procedure for, 235–36; revision of evaluation after, 162; symptoms and, 11, 15; training in, 217; transcript of, 239–45

Homosexual male couples, 64
Homosexuality, prejudice against, 73n4
Hormonal contraceptives, sexual dysfunctions caused by, 35
Hormone medication, 36
Housewives, oppressed role of, 230–31
Hymen, resistant, 35
Hyperemia, genital, 18
Hypnosis, 62
Hypogonadism, 37
Hypogonadotropism, 37
Hysterectomy, 165

Ill temper, postorgasmic, 27
Imagination training, 65
Impotence, 33n2; fear of, 72; see also Erectile dysfunction
Incest anxieties, 173
Incidence of dysfunction, 29–33
Individual therapy for single people, 66
Individual qualification of trainees, 215
Inflammatory diseases, erectile dysfunction caused by, 34
Inhibited sexual desire, 17
Inhibitory attitudes, modification of, 71–72
Initial interview, 232
Initial dysfunctions, 28; counseling for, 60
Instinct anxieties, 40–41
Institutional qualification of trainees, 215
Intelligence, therapy outcomes and, 96
Intensity of orgasm, dissatisfaction with, 23
Intensive therapy, 61, 86, 147, 226; caressing I sequence in, 260–62, 264–70; criteria for choice of, 229; explorative genital caressing sequence in, 278–85; introductory session in, 233–35; intromission sequence in, 295–97; long-term therapy versus, 148–51; transcript of history-taking for, 239–45
Intestinal disease, 35
Intravaginal contraceptives, allergic reactions to, 35
Intromission sequence, 294–99; discussion of experiences, 297–98; procedure for, 294–95; timing of, 298–99
Irritation, postorgasmic, 27

Kegel exercises, 232
Kissing, "French," 271

Language patterns of therapists, 220

Learning deficits, 55–57; compensation for, 66; discussion of, 247; reversal of, 230; therapeutic approach to, 71–72
Learning theory, 38; principles of, 227
Lesbians, 64; frequency of orgasm of, 24
Libido, loss of, 17
Lighting, 270–71
"Limerence," 6
Locke-Wallace Short Marital Inventory, 196
Long-term therapy, 64, 66, 86–87, 109, 147, 225; caressing II sequence in, 274; criteria for choice of, 229; intensive therapy versus, 148–51; introductory session in, 233–34; stimulative caressing sequence in, 290
Lubrication, lack of, 293
Lubrication-swelling reaction, impairment of, 18

Male therapists, 151–54; see also Dual-sex therapy team
Manual stimulation, negative attitudes toward, 71–72
Marital enrichment, 73n3
Masculine identification, 43
Masochistic impulses, 47
Masturbation, 55–56; caressing I and, 270; control of ejaculation during, 22; with deviant fantasies, 165, 168; ejaculatory incompetence and, 22; erectile dysfunction and, 18; explorative genital caressing and, 278; fantasies and, 316–17; frequency of female orgasm during, 24; incidence of, in study couples compared to general population, 79–80; intercourse as, 7; lack of desire and, 17; negative attitudes toward, 71–72; orgasmic disturbances and, 24, 25; systematic learning of, 63; therapy outcomes and, 92–93, 100; in therapy for single people, 65; in treatment of ejaculatory incompetence, 326; warded-off anxiety in, 45
Mechanical stimulation, 63
Medication: relaxation-inducing, 62; side-effects of, 35
Menopause: atrophy of vaginal mucous membrane after, 35; reduction of hormone levels during, 36
Menstruation, 234–35; caressing during, 286–87; sex during, 277
Methodological problems, 97–98
Middle class, see Social class
Minnesota Multiphasic Personality Inventory (MMPI), 196
Moral anxiety, 40, 44–45
Mother-child relationships, 41, 42

Motivation for therapy, 101–2; dropping out and, 180
Mysophobia, 41

Nakedness taboos, 71
Narcissistic deprivation, 4–6
Neurodermitis, 162
Neuroleptic drugs, 35, 162, 163
Neurological disorders, 162
Neuroses, 162; dropping out of therapy and, 179–80, 812; expressed in choice of partner, 191, 192; prognosis and, 197
Nocturnal emission, 22
Nondemanding touching, 72
Nongenital caressing, see Caressing I exercise sequence
Nudity, 270–71

Object-loss, 42
Occupation of study couples, 104
Oedipal situation, ineffective resolution of, 42
Oophorectomy, 35, 36, 165
Operant conditioning, 72
Oral intercourse, 277
Oral needs of infant, frustration of, 40
Oral stimulation, negative attitudes toward, 71–72
Organic factors, 34–37; in dyspareunia, 20; in ejaculatory incompetence, 22; medical examination to rule out, 228; in retrograde ejaculation, 23
Orgasm: in bodily self-awareness sequence, 314; in coitus with explorative and stimulating movements, 299–302; despite lack of desire and aversion, 17–18; in stimulative caressing sequence, 288, 291–93
Orgasm phase of sexual interaction, 16
Orgasmic dysfunction, 16, 20, 23–27, 228; arousal dysfunction and, 19; caressing II sequence for, 273–74; case examples of, 11–13; difficulties in treating, 99–102; dropping out of therapy for, 179–81, 186; dyspareunia and, 20; explorative genital caressing sequence for, 278–81; fear of losing control in, 293; group therapy for, 203; incidence of, 31–33; influence of women's movement on perception of, 200; long-term results of therapy, 127, 129; mechanical stimulation for, 63; organic factors in, 35; outcomes of therapy for, 89–90, 94, 95, 99, 110, 111; percentage of cases in study, 78; personality traits and, 81–82; separa-

tion after treatment of, 192–93; severity of, 82; successful treatment of, 131–32; therapeutic improvement rate for, 66; waiting list drop-outs with, 121n2
Outcomes of therapy: case examples of, 131–35; evaluation of, 97–102; group therapy, 206–9; influence of social class on, 95–97, 119; limitations of, 135–39; in sexual behavior and attitudes, 91–95; in sexual experience and relationships, 94–95, 116, 117; stability of, 123–30, 136–44
Ovaries, injury to or deformation of, 35
Overall therapy outcome, 88–90, 110
Oviducts, injury to or deformation of, 35

Partner conflicts, 39, 47–55; ambivalence management in, 53–55; arrangement in, 50–51; bypass techniques for, 70; delegation in, 48–50; of difficult patients, 169; discussion of, 247; of drop-outs, 182, 185, 187, 188; group therapy and, 203–5, 208; orgasmic dysfunction and, 101; prognosis and, 197; resolution of, 66; selection process and, 77–78; separation due to, 190–91; use of symptom against partner in, 51–53; therapeutic approach and, 68, 72–73; working through, 230
Partner-related dysfunctions, 28; defense against anxiety in, 46
Painful intercourse, see Dyspareunia
Patient selection process, 77–78; failure rates and, 99; for group therapy, 203–4
Penile intromission, see Intromission
Penile prostheses, 59, 167, 171
Penis envy, 43
Performance demands, 248; in caressing I sequence, 271; in intromission sequence, 297–98; orgasmic dysfunction and, 100, 101; in treatment of ejaculatory incompetence, 328
Perineal rupture, 35
Personality traits of study couples, 80–81, 106, 107
Perversions, 5
Phallic stage, 41
Phasic depression, 162
Phimosis, 35–36, 134, 316
Phobias, coital, 19, 20
Physical disabilities, 162, 170–71; case examples of, 165–66
Pituitary dysfunctions, 34
Playful arousal, see Stimulative caressing and playful arousal sequence
Positive reinforcement, 219
Postorgasmic dysphoria, 16, 27
Postorgasmic phase of sexual interaction, 16

Potency disturbance, 33n2
Power conflicts, 51–53; therapeutic approach to, 72
Predisposing experiences, 247
Pregenital sexuality, regression to, 72
Premature ejaculation, 16, 20–22, 228; additional interventions for, 226; additional sequences for, 324–25; aggressive impulses in, 47; anxiety over gender identity and, 43; caressing I sequence for, 264–70; case examples of, 13–14; delegation and, 48, 50; dropping out of therapy for, 179, 181, 185; gender of therapist and, 152; group therapy for, 203, 204, 206; hypochondria and, 164–65; incidence of, 30–32; long-term results of therapy, 127; organic factors in, 35; outcomes of therapy for, 89, 91, 94, 99, 113, 114; percentage of cases in study, 78; psychosocial factors in, 37–38; round table for, 248–57; separation and, 190; separation after treatment of, 193–94; severity of, 28, 82; shift of symptom to partner after treatment of, 172–73; "squeeze technique" for treatment of, 62, 63; stimulative caressing sequence for, 289–90; therapeutic improvement rate for, 66; therapy settings for, 86; as undesired side-effect of therapy, 172, 175
Pre-oedipal mother-child relationship, 41
"Pre-orgasmic" women, 200
Primary dysfunctions, 28
Progesterone, 36
Prognosis, 195–200
Progressive muscle relaxation, 62
Prostatitis, 34
Prostheses, penile, 59, 167, 171
Protection of patients, 220–21
Psychiatric patients, 161, 162, 169–70; case examples of, 163, 166
Psychoanalysis, 71, 227; advanced training and, 213, 216; "clitoral" versus "vaginal" orgasm debate in, 25; on defense against anxiety, 40–43; on premature ejaculation, 38; self-reinforcement mechanism and, 67
Psychoanalytically oriented therapy, 227
Psychodynamic conflicts: disengagement from sexuality of, 230; orgasmic dysfunction and, 101; therapeutic approach and, 68, 70–73; working through, 66
Psychological stability, 130, 145, 146; and improvement in sexual disorders, 169
Psychopathological symptoms: as undesired side-effect of therapy, 171, 173–75; see also Psychiatric patients; Psychosis
Psychosexual development, history of, 237–38

Psychosexual therapy, 17, 71
Psychosis: acute, as contraindication, 228; case example of, 163, 167; prognosis and, 197
Psychosocial factors, 37–58
Psychosomatic disturbances, 132–33, 161, 162, 170–71; of drop-outs, 181; as undesired side-effect of therapy, 171, 176–77

Qualifications: of therapists, 227; of trainees, 215–16, 221

Rapid ejaculation, 21, 22
Rapid treatment, 221
Relationships: assessment of, 83; conflict in, see Partner conflict; of difficult patients, 169; function of sexual disturbance in, 47–55; history of, 238–39; impact of societal changes on, 3; improvement in, as outcome of therapy, 89, 94–95, 100, 116–18; multiplicity of, 6–7; narcissistic gratification in, 4–5; replenishment mechanisms in, 6; stable, as requirement for therapy, 228
Relaxation techniques, 62; in resolution of self-reinforcement mechanism, 71
Repressed impulses, release of, 47
Reproduction, 95
Resistance: dropping out and, 180–81; training in dealing with, 219
Responsibility, encouraging patient's, 230
Retarded ejaculation, 22
Retrograde ejaculation, 22
Role games, disinhibiting, 62–63
Romantic ideal, 5
Round table, 246–57; aims of, 246–47; procedure for, 247–49; transcript of, 249–57

Sadomasochism, 162
Saliva, reactions of disgust to, 271
Secondary dysfunctions, 28
Selection of treatment mode, 195–200
Self-disintegration, fear of, 41
Self-reinforcement mechanisms, 57–58; discussion of, 247, 248; resolution of, 66, 67, 71
Sensate focus, 61
Separations, 179, 182–84, 186, 188–94; as aim of therapy, 195, 196; constructive, 191–94; fear of, 177; after group therapy, 206, 208–9
Setting, see Therapy settings
Severity of dysfunction, 28–29

Sex-role clichés, 72
Sexual enhancement, 73n3
Shift of symptom from patient to partner, 171–73; case example of, 172–73
Side-effects: of couple therapy, undesired, 171–77; of medication, 163
Single people: sexually dysfunctional, 198–200; therapeutic approaches for, 64–65
Singles movement, 7
Situational dysfunctions, 28; warded-off anxiety in, 46
Social class: of group therapy participants, 203–4; incidence of sexual dysfunction and, 32–33; influence on outcomes of therapy of, 95–97, 119; of study couples, 78
Social conditions, modification of, 230
Social inhibitions, 199
Social workers, 214, 216
Socialization, sexual, 44, 55, 56
Somatic complaints, 170–171; as undesired side-effect of therapy, 171, 176–77
Spinal cord lesions, 34, 35
"Squeeze technique," 62, 63
Stability: psychological, 130, 145, 146; of therapy outcomes, 123–30, 136–44
Stimulation phase of sexual interaction, 15–16
Stimulative caressing and playing with arousal sequence, 61, 226, 287–92; aims of, 287–88; discussion of experiences, 291; for ejaculatory incompetence, 326–27; for premature ejaculation, 324–25; procedure for, 288–89; special problems in, 291–93; timing of, 294
Success criteria in training, 220
Superego: modification of, 73; sexually negating, 45, 46
Supervision of therapists, 88; ongoing, 227; training and, 214, 220
Surgery: disfiguring, 162; sexual dysfunction after, 34, 35
Surrogate partners, 64, 199
Symbiosis: mother-child, 41; sexual, 5
Symptom use against partner, 51–53; case example of, 51–52
Systematic desensitization, 62, 63, 73n2; of fear of pain, 20; for self-reinforcement mechanism, 71; in therapy for single people, 65

Taboos, 44; nakedness, 71
Team therapy, see Dual-sex therapy team
Technique-related dysfunctions, 28
Tenting effect, 18
Therapeutic concept, 246–47

Therapists, 87–88; assessment and follow-up by, 83; comparison of treatment with single versus team of, 148, 151, 155, 157; male versus female, 151–54; overall outcome ratings by, 110, 120–21; prognosis and, 197–98; qualifications of, 227; therapeutic experience of, 109; training of, see Training, therapeutic
Therapy settings, 85–87, 109; choice of, 229; comparison of, 147–59; failure rates and, 99; sample size and, 109; training in, 214, 216–17
Time commitment to therapy, 234
Traditional sex roles, 43
Training, therapeutic, 211–22; aims and target groups of, 213; didactic concept of, 213–14; selection of trainees, 215–16; settings for, 214–15; systematic errors in, 217–22; teams for, 216–17
Transference, 61, 154, 220, 222; acting out in, 181
Trauma: childhood, 42; dysfunctions caused by, 68; genital, 34, 164–66
Tumors, genital tract, 35

Ulcerous colitis, 162
Urethral strictures, 35
Urethritis, 34
Uterine support ligaments, injury to or deformation of, 35

Vaginal orgasm, 25–26
Vaginismus, 16, 19–20, 218, 228; additional interventions for, 226; age when treated for, 78–79, 103; aggressive impulses in, 47; bodily self-awareness exercises for, 312; bypass technique for, 69–70; caressing II sequence for, 275; case examples of, 13; depression as side-effect of treatment of, 175–76; dilator sequence for, 317–23; incidence of, 31, 32; individual therapy for, 65; limitations on success of treatment for, 134; long-term results of therapy for, 127; organic factors and, 35; outcomes of therapy for, 89–91, 94, 99, 112; percentage of cases in study, 78; personality traits and, 82; round-table discussion for, 248; separation after therapy for, 192; severity of, 29, 82; shift of symptoms to partner after treatment of, 172; surgical treatment of, 59; therapeutic improvement rate for, 66; therapy settings for, 86; transcript of history taking on, 239–43; as unconscious arrangement between partners, 50; as un-

Vaginismus *(continued)*
  desired side-effect of therapy, 173; waiting list drop-outs with, 120*n*2; warded-off anxiety in, 45
Vaginitis, 35
Validity of problem, 97–98

Violence, fear of, 41

Women's groups, supplementary, 205
Working class, *see* Social class